ACCEL WORLD 04

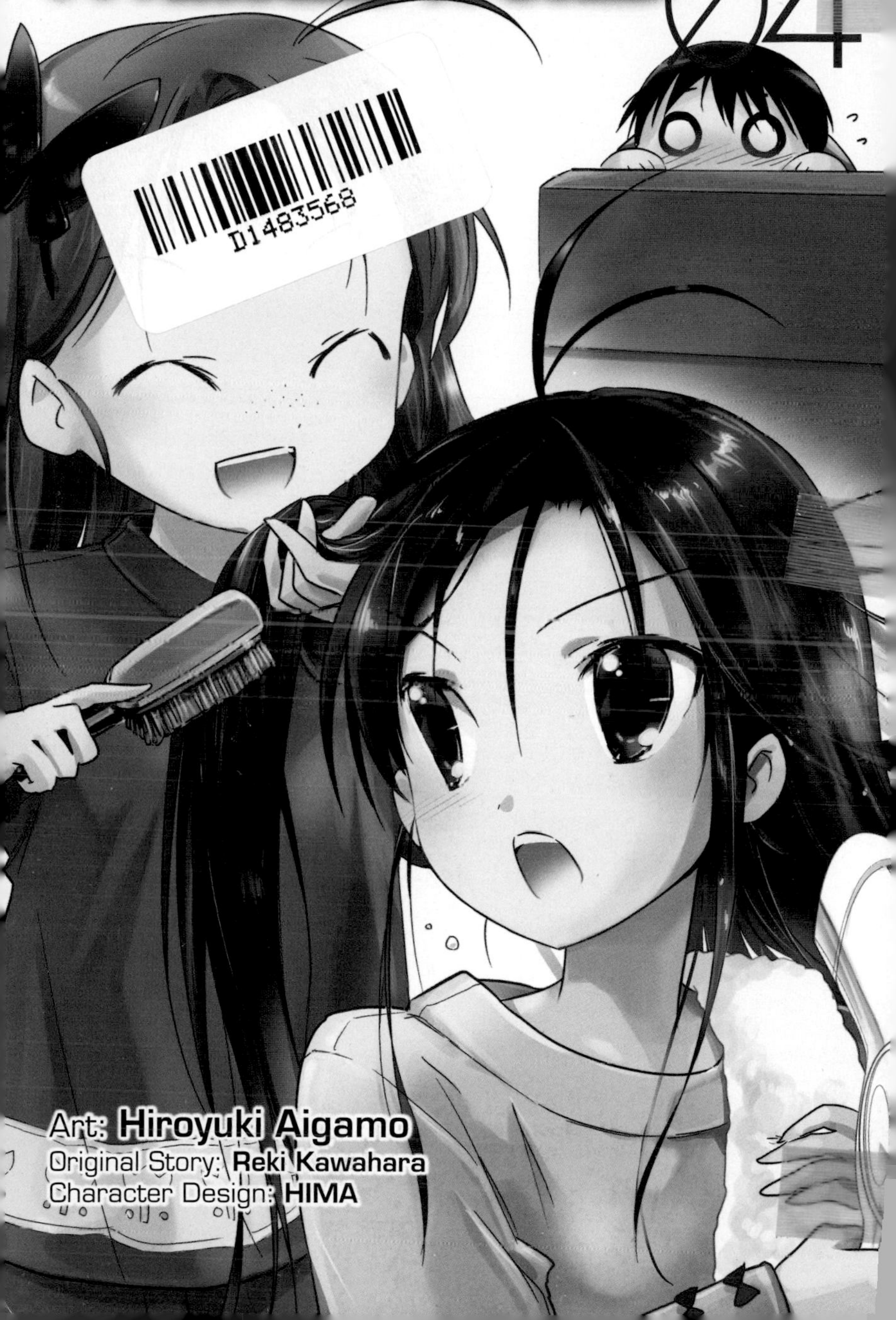

Art: **Hiroyuki Aigamo**
Original Story: **Reki Kawahara**
Character Design: **HIMA**

■ Neurolinker = A portable terminal that connects with the brain via a wireless quantum connection, and which supports all five senses with enhanced images, sounds, and other stimulus.

■ Brain Burst = Neurolinker application sent to Haruyuki by Kuroyukihime.

■ Duel avatar = Player's virtual self, operated when fighting in Brain Burst.

■ Burst points = Points required to use the power of acceleration. To obtain them, players must win duels against other duel avatars. If a player loses all their points, Brain Burst is forceably uninstalled.

■ Legion = Groups, composed of many duel avatars, with the objective of expanding occupied areas and securing rights. The Seven Kings of Pure Color act as the Legion Masters.

■ In-school local net = Local area network established within Umesato Junior High School. Used during classes and to check attendance. Umesato students are required to always be connected to it.

■ Global connection = Connection with the worldwide net. Global connections are forbidden on Umesato Junior High School grounds, where the in-school local net is provided instead.

■ Enhanced Armament = Items such as weapons or personal armor owned by duel avatars.

■ Normal Duel Field = The field where normal Brain Burst battles (one-on-one or tag matches) are carried out.

■ Unlimited Neutral Field = Field for high-level players where only duel avatars at level four and up are allowed. The game system is of a wholly different order than that of the Normal Duel Field. ::

accel world

art:
hiroyuki aigamo
original story:
reki kawahara
accel world 02: the red storm princess
character design:
hima

contents

characters

■ Kuroyukihime = Umesato Junior High School student council vice president. Trim and clever girl who has it all. Her background is shrouded in mystery. Her in-school avatar is a spangled butterfly she programmed herself. Her duel avatar is the Black King, "Black Lotus."

■ Haruyuki = Haruyuki Arita. Grade Seven at Umesato Junior High School. Bullied, on the pudgy side. He's good at games but is shy. His in-school avatar is a pink pig. His duel avatar is Silver Crow.

■ Chiyuri = Chiyuri Kurashima. Haruyuki's childhood friend. A meddling, energetic girl. Her in-school avatar is a silver cat.

■ Takumu = Takumu Mayuzumi. A boy Haruyuki and Chiyuri have known since childhood. Good at kendo. His duel avatar is Cyan Pile.

■ Niko = Yuniko Kozuki. Grade Five girl who pretended to be Haruyuki's cousin to get in direct contact with him. Her real identity is the Red King, ruler of the Red Legion. Her duel avatar is Scarlet Rain. ::

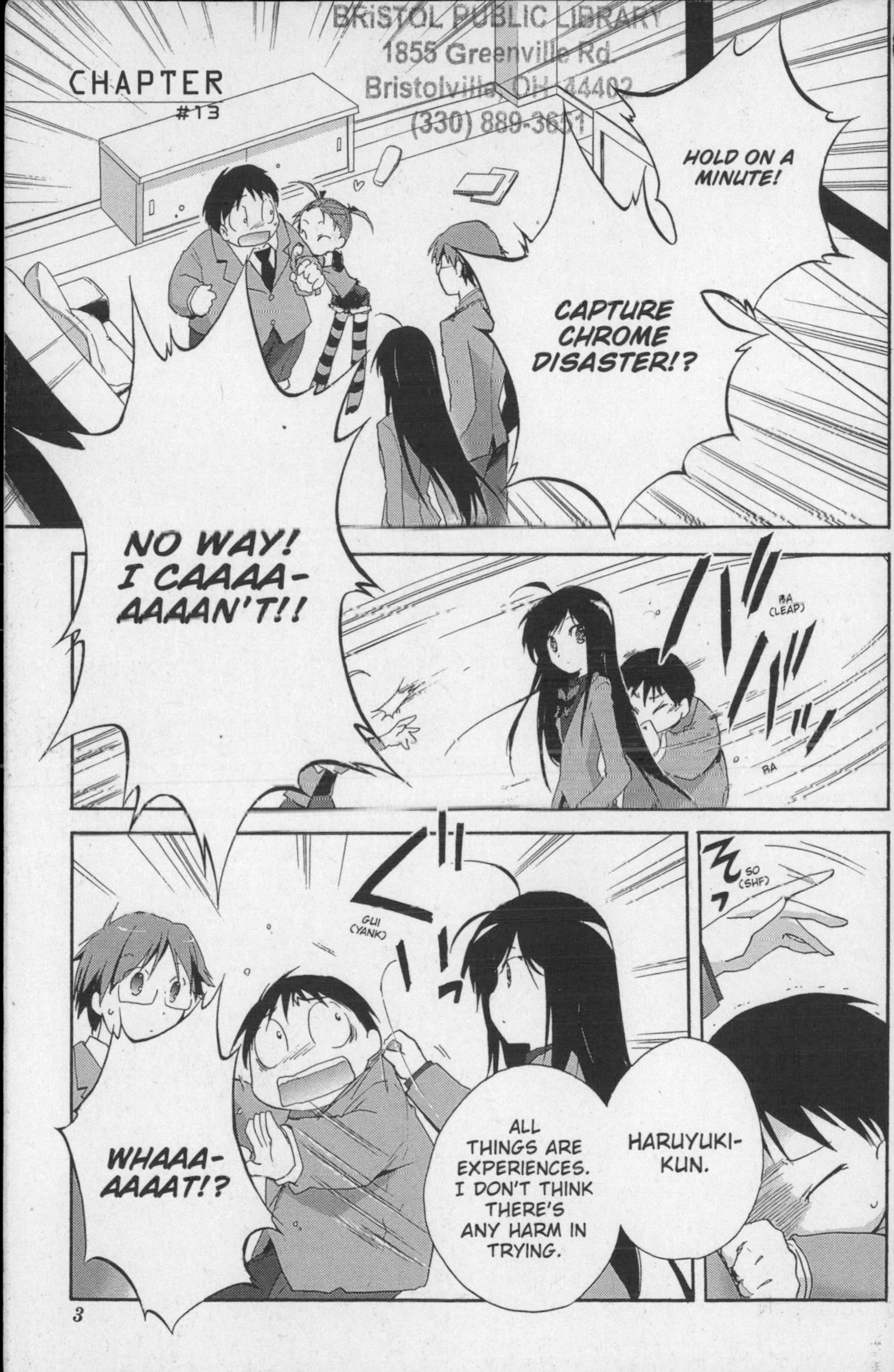
CHAPTER #13
HOLD ON A MINUTE!
CAPTURE CHROME DISASTER!?
NO WAY! I CAAAA-AAAAN'T!!
BA (LEAP)
BA
SO (SHF)
HARUYUKI-KUN.
ALL THINGS ARE EXPERIENCES. I DON'T THINK THERE'S ANY HARM IN TRYING.
GUI (YANK)
WHAAAA-AAAAT!?

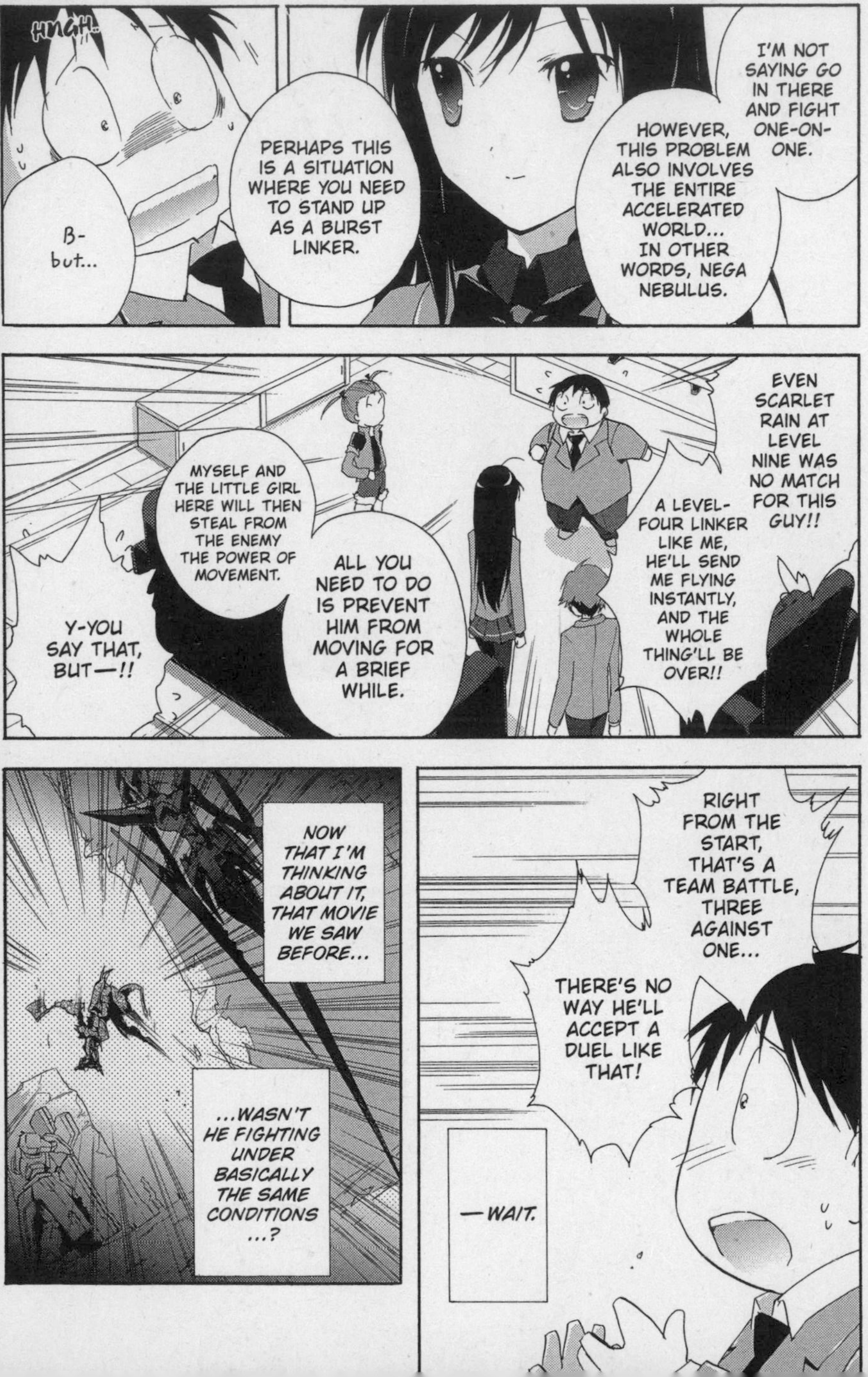
I'M NOT SAYING GO IN THERE AND FIGHT ONE-ON-ONE.
HOWEVER, THIS PROBLEM ALSO INVOLVES THE ENTIRE ACCELERATED WORLD... IN OTHER WORDS, NEGA NEBULUS.
PERHAPS THIS IS A SITUATION WHERE YOU NEED TO STAND UP AS A BURST LINKER.
HNGH..
B-but...
EVEN SCARLET RAIN AT LEVEL NINE WAS NO MATCH FOR THIS GUY!!
A LEVEL-FOUR LINKER LIKE ME, HE'LL SEND ME FLYING INSTANTLY, AND THE WHOLE THING'LL BE OVER!!
ALL YOU NEED TO DO IS PREVENT HIM FROM MOVING FOR A BRIEF WHILE.
MYSELF AND THE LITTLE GIRL HERE WILL THEN STEAL FROM THE ENEMY THE POWER OF MOVEMENT.
Y-YOU SAY THAT, BUT—!!
RIGHT FROM THE START, THAT'S A TEAM BATTLE, THREE AGAINST ONE...
THERE'S NO WAY HE'LL ACCEPT A DUEL LIKE THAT!
—WAIT.
NOW THAT I'M THINKING ABOUT IT, THAT MOVIE WE SAW BEFORE...
...WASN'T HE FIGHTING UNDER BASICALLY THE SAME CONDITIONS ...?

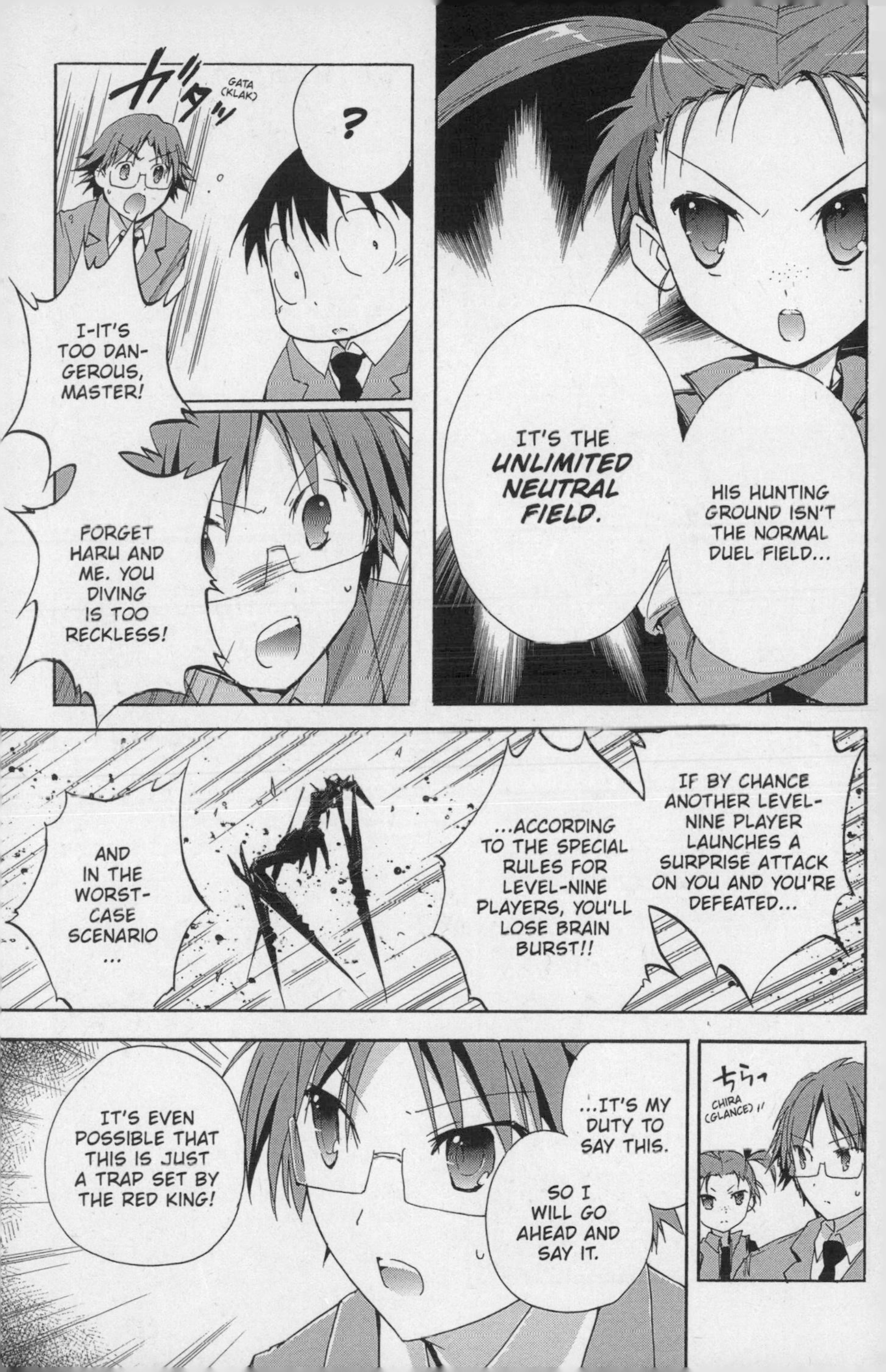

HIS HUNTING GROUND ISN'T THE NORMAL DUEL FIELD...
IT'S THE *UNLIMITED NEUTRAL FIELD.*
ガタッ
GATA (KLAK)
?
I-IT'S TOO DANGEROUS, MASTER!
FORGET HARU AND ME. YOU DIVING IS TOO RECKLESS!
IF BY CHANCE ANOTHER LEVEL-NINE PLAYER LAUNCHES A SURPRISE ATTACK ON YOU AND YOU'RE DEFEATED...
...ACCORDING TO THE SPECIAL RULES FOR LEVEL-NINE PLAYERS, YOU'LL LOSE BRAIN BURST!!
AND IN THE WORST-CASE SCENARIO...
ちらっ
CHIRA (GLANCE)
...IT'S MY DUTY TO SAY THIS.
SO I WILL GO AHEAD AND SAY IT.
IT'S EVEN POSSIBLE THAT THIS IS JUST A TRAP SET BY THE RED KING!

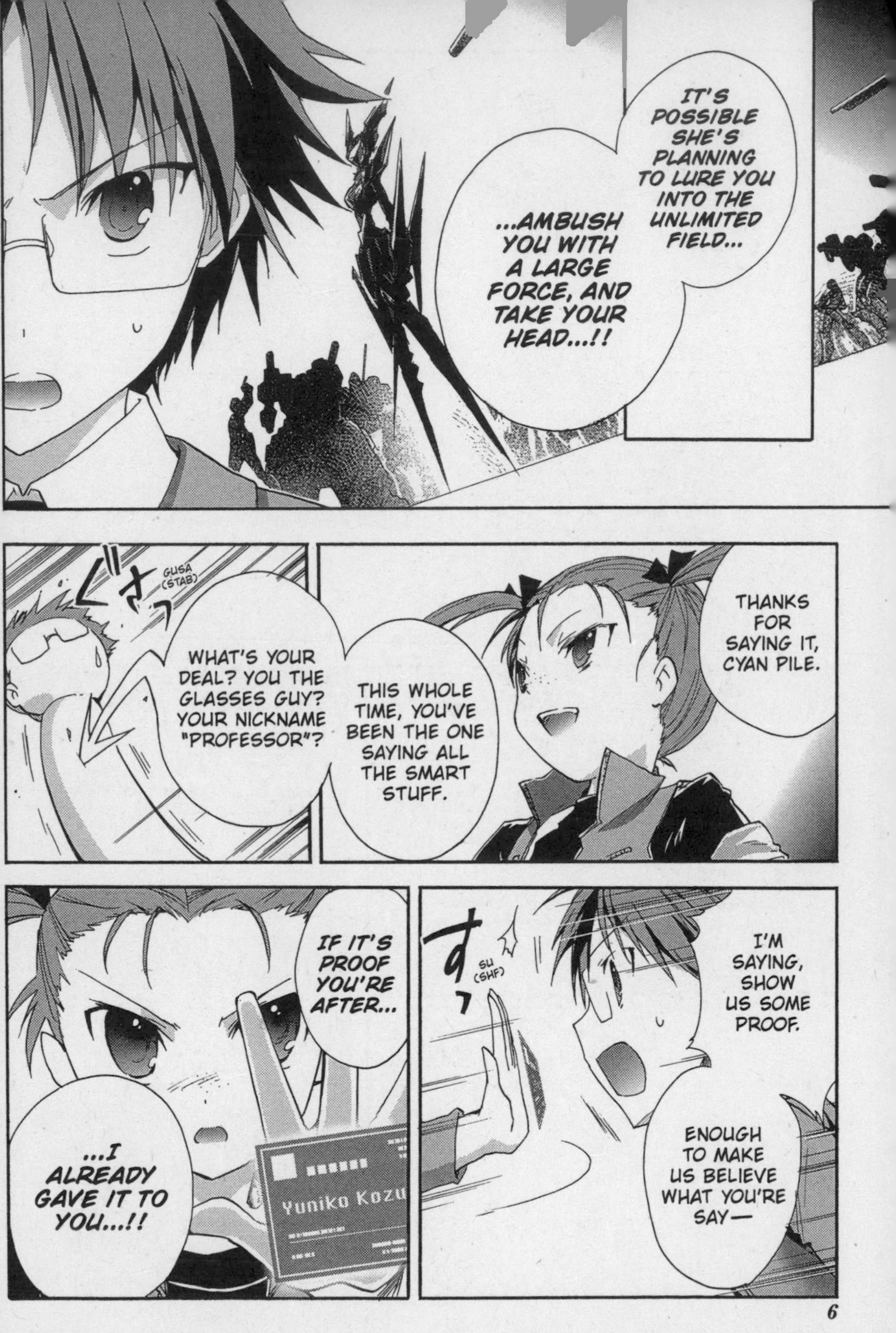
IT'S POSSIBLE SHE'S PLANNING TO LURE YOU INTO THE UNLIMITED FIELD...
...AMBUSH YOU WITH A LARGE FORCE, AND TAKE YOUR HEAD...!!
THANKS FOR SAYING IT, CYAN PILE.
THIS WHOLE TIME, YOU'VE BEEN THE ONE SAYING ALL THE SMART STUFF.
ぐさっ
GUSA (STAB)
WHAT'S YOUR DEAL? YOU THE GLASSES GUY? YOUR NICKNAME "PROFESSOR"?
I'M SAYING, SHOW US SOME PROOF.
すっ
SU (SHF)
ENOUGH TO MAKE US BELIEVE WHAT YOU'RE SAY—
IF IT'S PROOF YOU'RE AFTER...
...I ALREADY GAVE IT TO YOU...!!

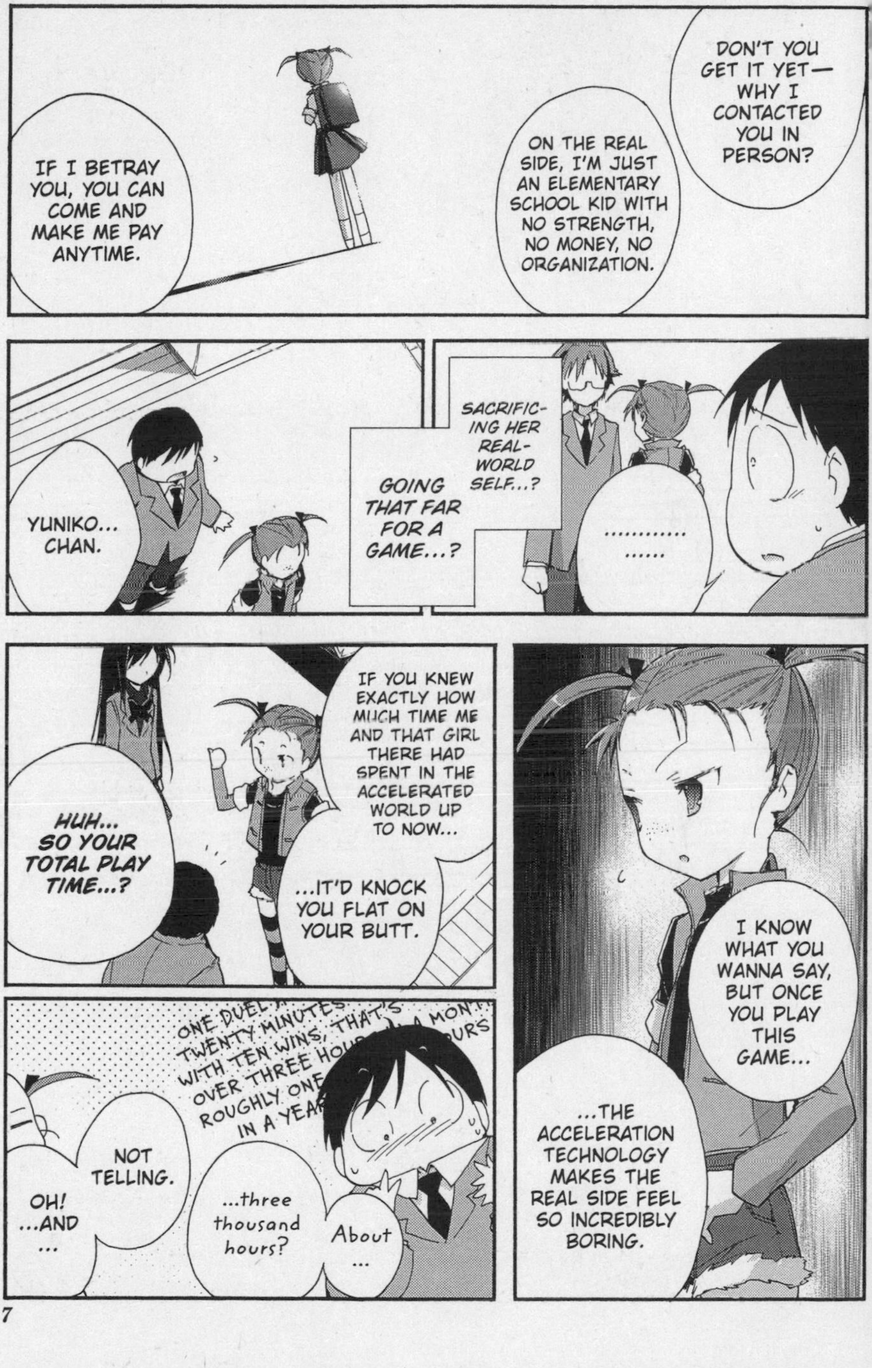
DON'T YOU GET IT YET— WHY I CONTACTED YOU IN PERSON?
ON THE REAL SIDE, I'M JUST AN ELEMENTARY SCHOOL KID WITH NO STRENGTH, NO MONEY, NO ORGANIZATION.
IF I BETRAY YOU, YOU CAN COME AND MAKE ME PAY ANYTIME.
....
SACRIFICING HER REAL-WORLD SELF...?
GOING THAT FAR FOR A GAME...?
YUNIKO... CHAN.
I KNOW WHAT YOU WANNA SAY, BUT ONCE YOU PLAY THIS GAME...
...THE ACCELERATION TECHNOLOGY MAKES THE REAL SIDE FEEL SO INCREDIBLY BORING.
IF YOU KNEW EXACTLY HOW MUCH TIME ME AND THAT GIRL THERE HAD SPENT IN THE ACCELERATED WORLD UP TO NOW...
...IT'D KNOCK YOU FLAT ON YOUR BUTT.
HUH... SO YOUR TOTAL PLAY TIME...?
ONE DUEL
TWENTY MINUTES
WITH TEN WINS, THAT'S
OVER THREE
ROUGHLY ONE
IN A
About ...
...three thousand hours?
NOT TELLING.
OH! ...AND ...

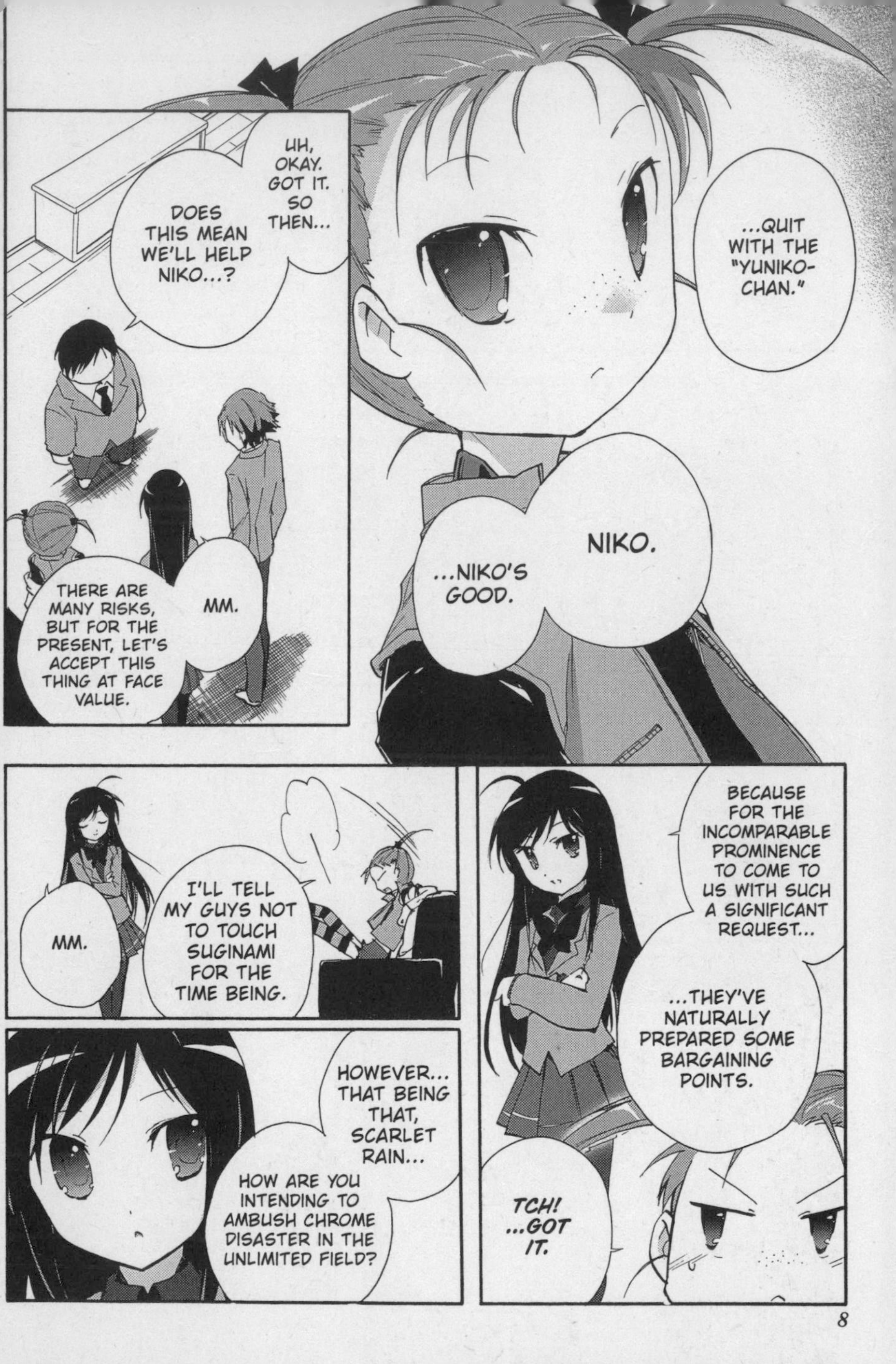
...QUIT WITH THE "YUNIKO-CHAN."
NIKO.
...NIKO'S GOOD.
UH, OKAY. GOT IT. SO THEN...
DOES THIS MEAN WE'LL HELP NIKO...?
MM.
THERE ARE MANY RISKS, BUT FOR THE PRESENT, LET'S ACCEPT THIS THING AT FACE VALUE.
BECAUSE FOR THE INCOMPARABLE PROMINENCE TO COME TO US WITH SUCH A SIGNIFICANT REQUEST...
...THEY'VE NATURALLY PREPARED SOME BARGAINING POINTS.
TCH! ...GOT IT.
I'LL TELL MY GUYS NOT TO TOUCH SUGINAMI FOR THE TIME BEING.
MM.
HOWEVER... THAT BEING THAT, SCARLET RAIN...
HOW ARE YOU INTENDING TO AMBUSH CHROME DISASTER IN THE UNLIMITED FIELD?

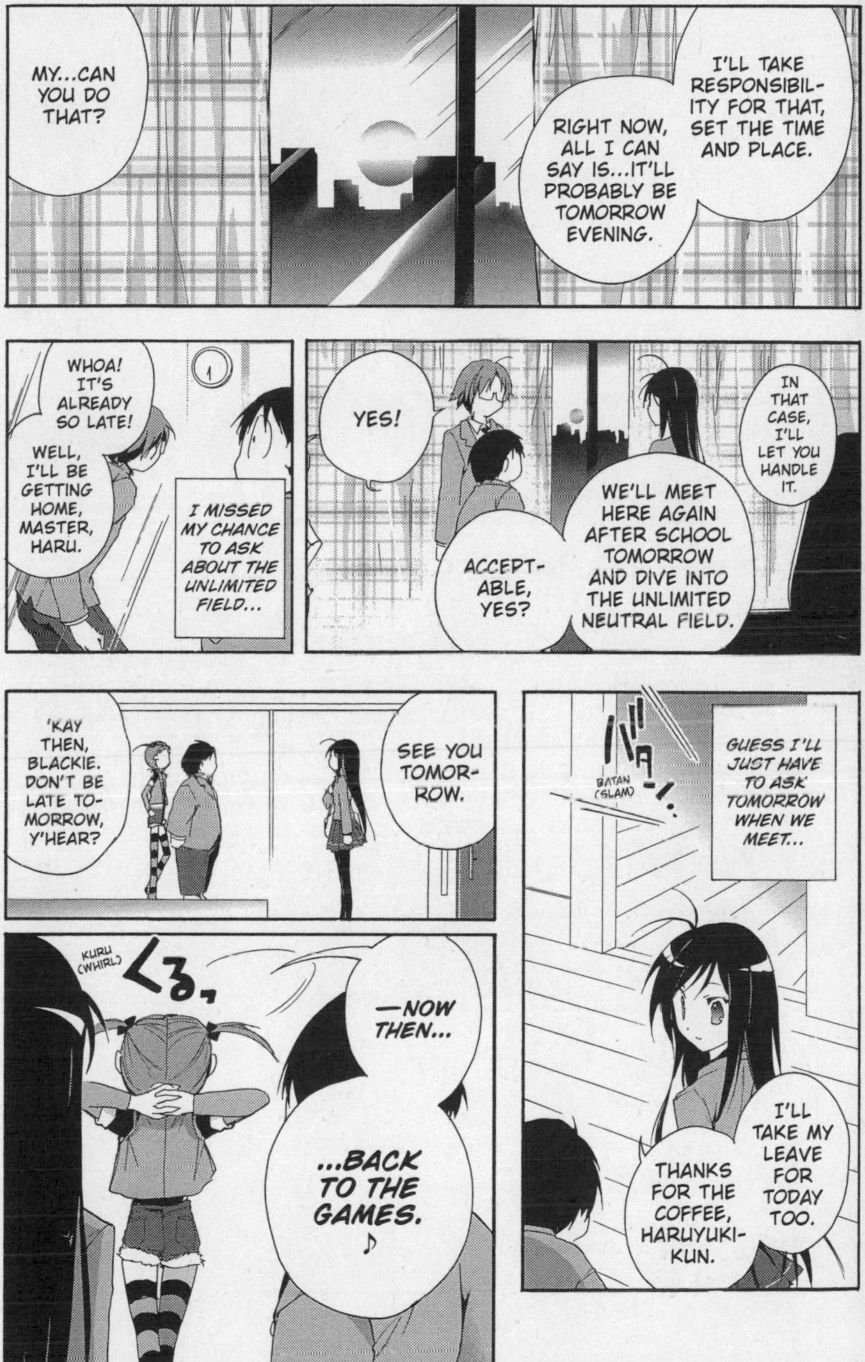
I'LL TAKE RESPONSIBILITY FOR THAT, SET THE TIME AND PLACE.
RIGHT NOW, ALL I CAN SAY IS...IT'LL PROBABLY BE TOMORROW EVENING.
MY...CAN YOU DO THAT?
IN THAT CASE, I'LL LET YOU HANDLE IT.
WE'LL MEET HERE AGAIN AFTER SCHOOL TOMORROW AND DIVE INTO THE UNLIMITED NEUTRAL FIELD.
ACCEPTABLE, YES?
YES!
WHOA! IT'S ALREADY SO LATE!
WELL, I'LL BE GETTING HOME, MASTER, HARU.
I MISSED MY CHANCE TO ASK ABOUT THE UNLIMITED FIELD...
BATAN (SLAM)
GUESS I'LL JUST HAVE TO ASK TOMORROW WHEN WE MEET...
I'LL TAKE MY LEAVE FOR TODAY TOO.
THANKS FOR THE COFFEE, HARUYUKI-KUN.
SEE YOU TOMORROW.
'KAY THEN, BLACKIE. DON'T BE LATE TOMORROW, Y'HEAR?
KURU (WHIRL)
—NOW THEN...
...BACK TO THE GAMES. ♪

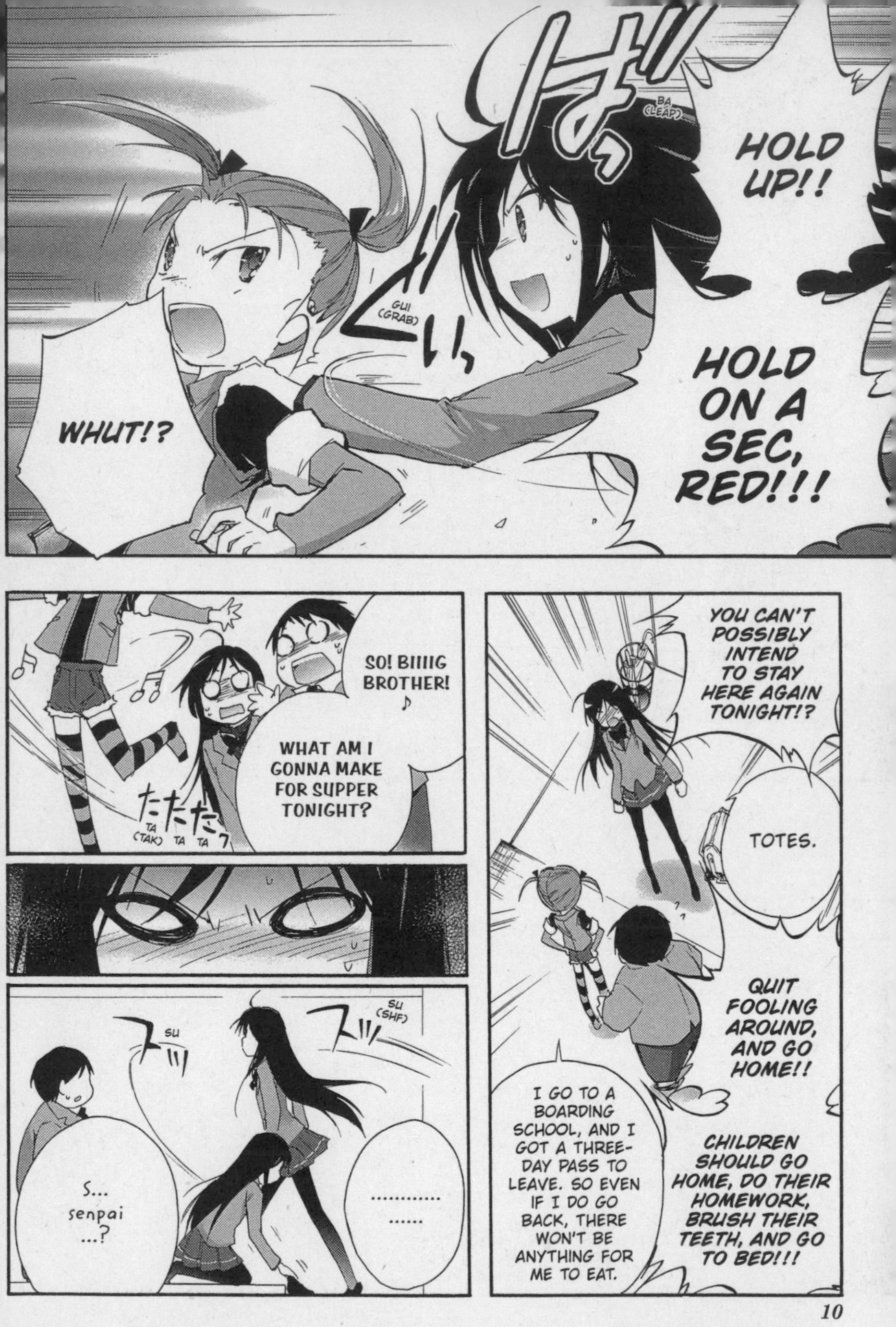
BA (LEAP)
HOLD UP!!
HOLD ON A SEC, RED!!!
GUI (GRAB)
WHUT!?
YOU CAN'T POSSIBLY INTEND TO STAY HERE AGAIN TONIGHT!?
TOTES.
QUIT FOOLING AROUND, AND GO HOME!!
CHILDREN SHOULD GO HOME, DO THEIR HOMEWORK, BRUSH THEIR TEETH, AND GO TO BED!!!
I GO TO A BOARDING SCHOOL, AND I GOT A THREE-DAY PASS TO LEAVE. SO EVEN IF I DO GO BACK, THERE WON'T BE ANYTHING FOR ME TO EAT.
SO! BIIIIG BROTHER! ♪
WHAT AM I GONNA MAKE FOR SUPPER TONIGHT?
たたた
TA (TAK) TA TA
SU (SHF)
SU
....
......
S... senpai ...?

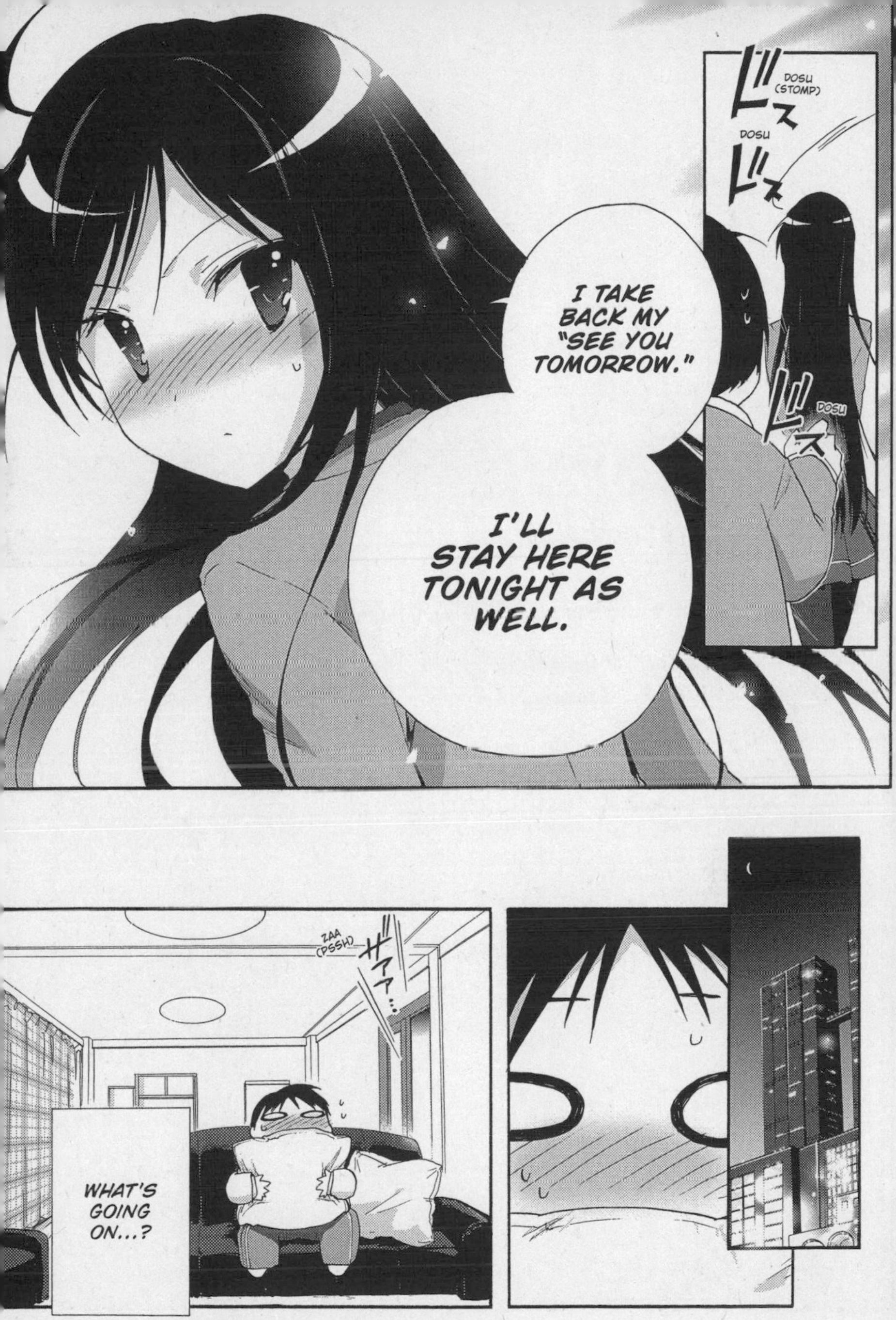
DOSU (STOMP)
DOSU
DOSU
I TAKE BACK MY "SEE YOU TOMORROW."
I'LL STAY HERE TONIGHT AS WELL.
ZAA (PSSH)
WHAT'S GOING ON...?

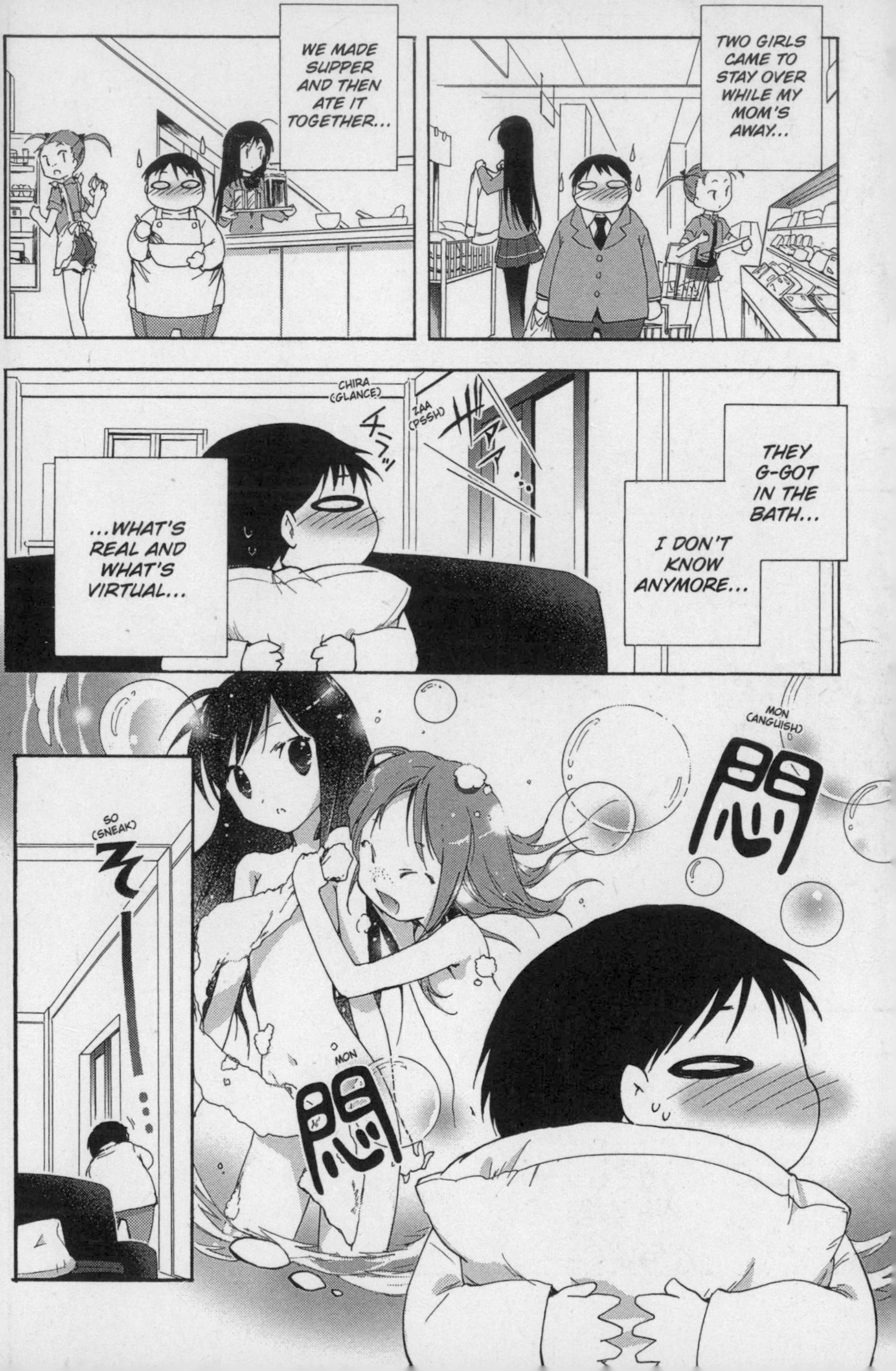
TWO GIRLS CAME TO STAY OVER WHILE MY MOM'S AWAY...
WE MADE SUPPER AND THEN ATE IT TOGETHER...
THEY G-GOT IN THE BATH...
I DON'T KNOW ANYMORE...
ZAA (PSSH)
CHIRA (GLANCE)
...WHAT'S REAL AND WHAT'S VIRTUAL...
MON (ANGUISH)
悶
MON
悶
SO (SNEAK)

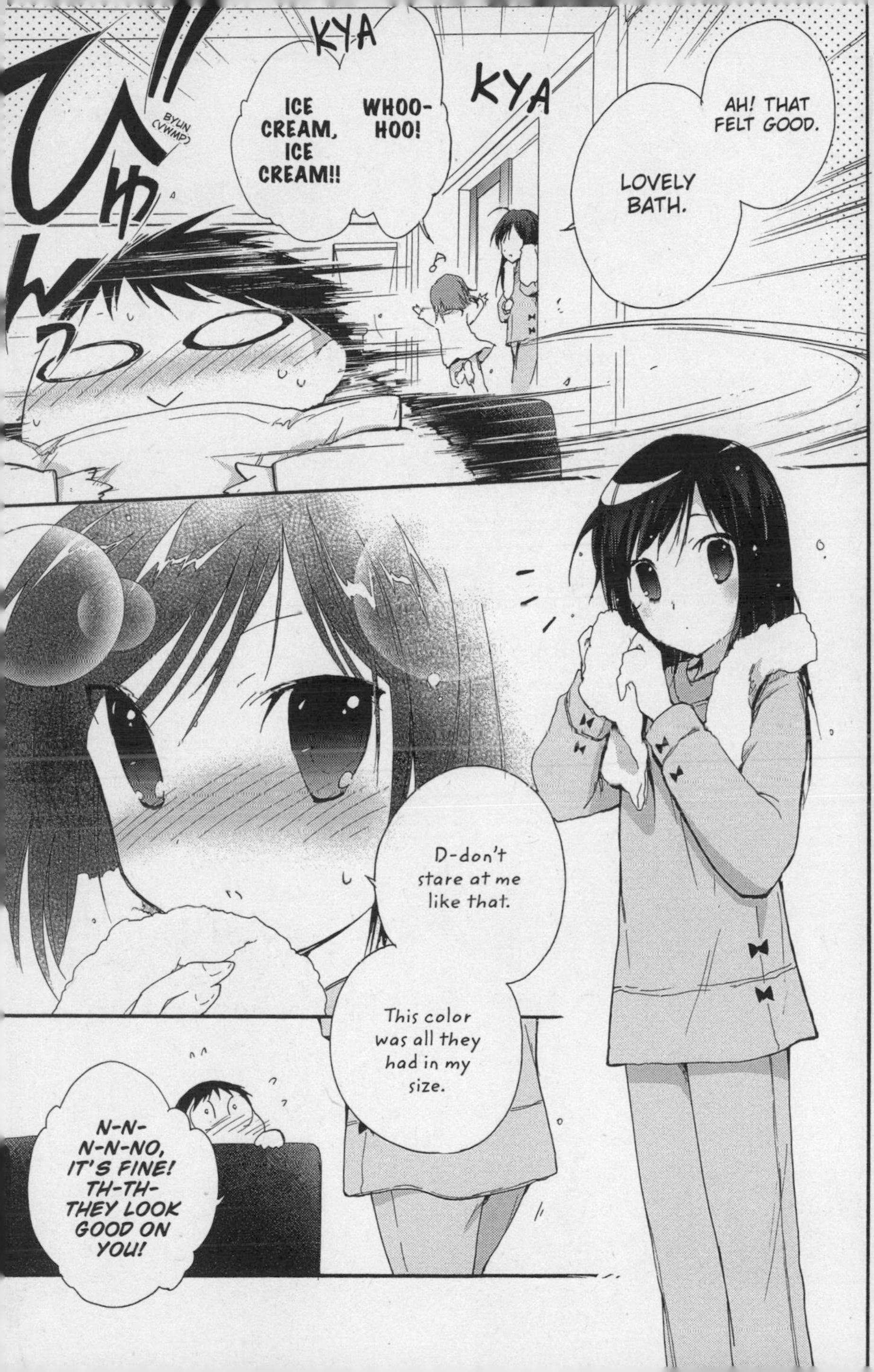
AH! THAT FELT GOOD.
LOVELY BATH.
KYA
KYA
WHOO-HOO!
ICE CREAM, ICE CREAM!!
BYUN (VWMP)
D-don't stare at me like that.
This color was all they had in my size.
N-N-N-N-NO, IT'S FINE! TH-TH-THEY LOOK GOOD ON YOU!

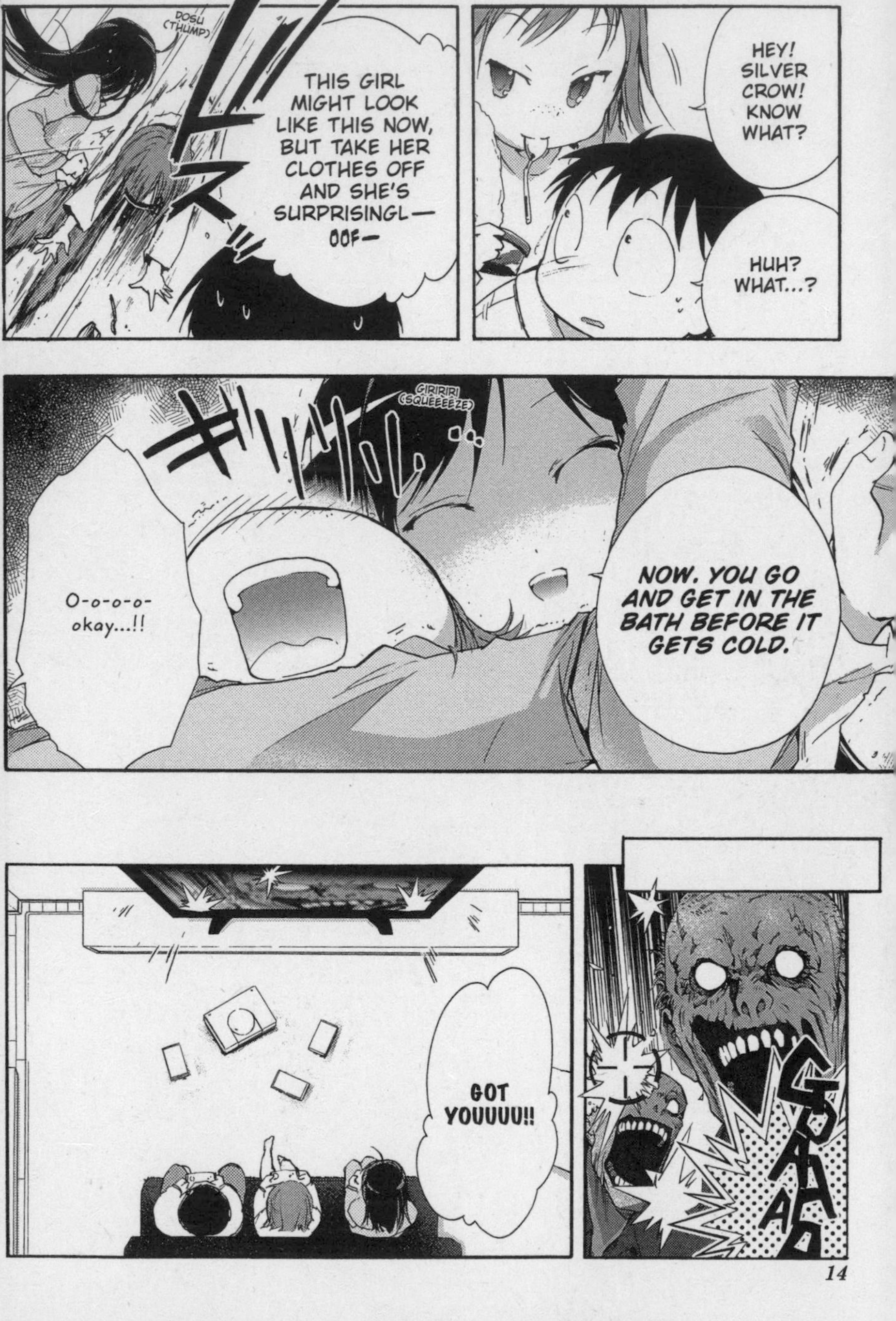
HEY! SILVER CROW! KNOW WHAT?
HUH? WHAT...?
THIS GIRL MIGHT LOOK LIKE THIS NOW, BUT TAKE HER CLOTHES OFF AND SHE'S SURPRISINGL— OOF—
DOSU (THUMP)
GIRIRIRI (SQUEEEEEZE)
NOW. YOU GO AND GET IN THE BATH BEFORE IT GETS COLD.
O-o-o-o-okay...!!
GAAAA
GOT YOUUUU!!

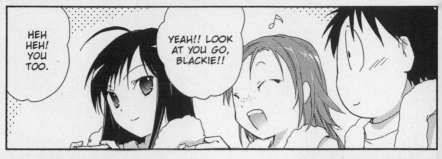

YEAH!! LOOK AT YOU GO, BLACKIE!!
HEH HEH! YOU TOO.
THIS IS REALLY WEIRD SOMEHOW.
WE'RE ONLY CONNECTED...
...THROUGH THE VR GAME BRAIN BURST.
BUT TODAY WE...
...MADE SUPPER TOGETHER, ATE IT TOGETHER, TOOK TURNS IN THE BATH...
...AND NOW WE'RE HERE— SO CLOSE, WE CAN EVEN FEEL EACH OTHER'S BODY HEAT.
IN THIS WORLD WHERE THE BORDER BETWEEN REAL AND VIRTUAL IS ENDLESSLY BLURRED...
...AND WE CAN'T EVEN TELL HOW MUCH OF THE INFORMATION FROM OUR SENSES IS ANALOG AND HOW MUCH IS DIGITAL...

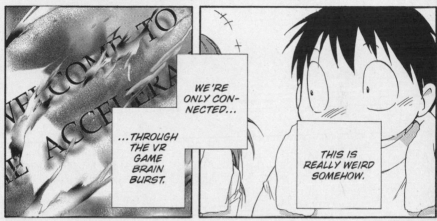

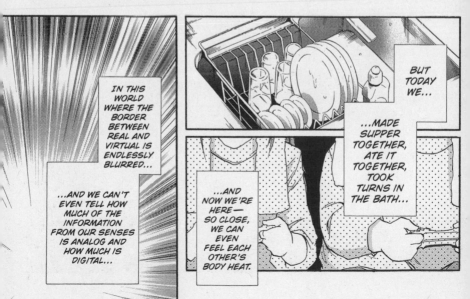

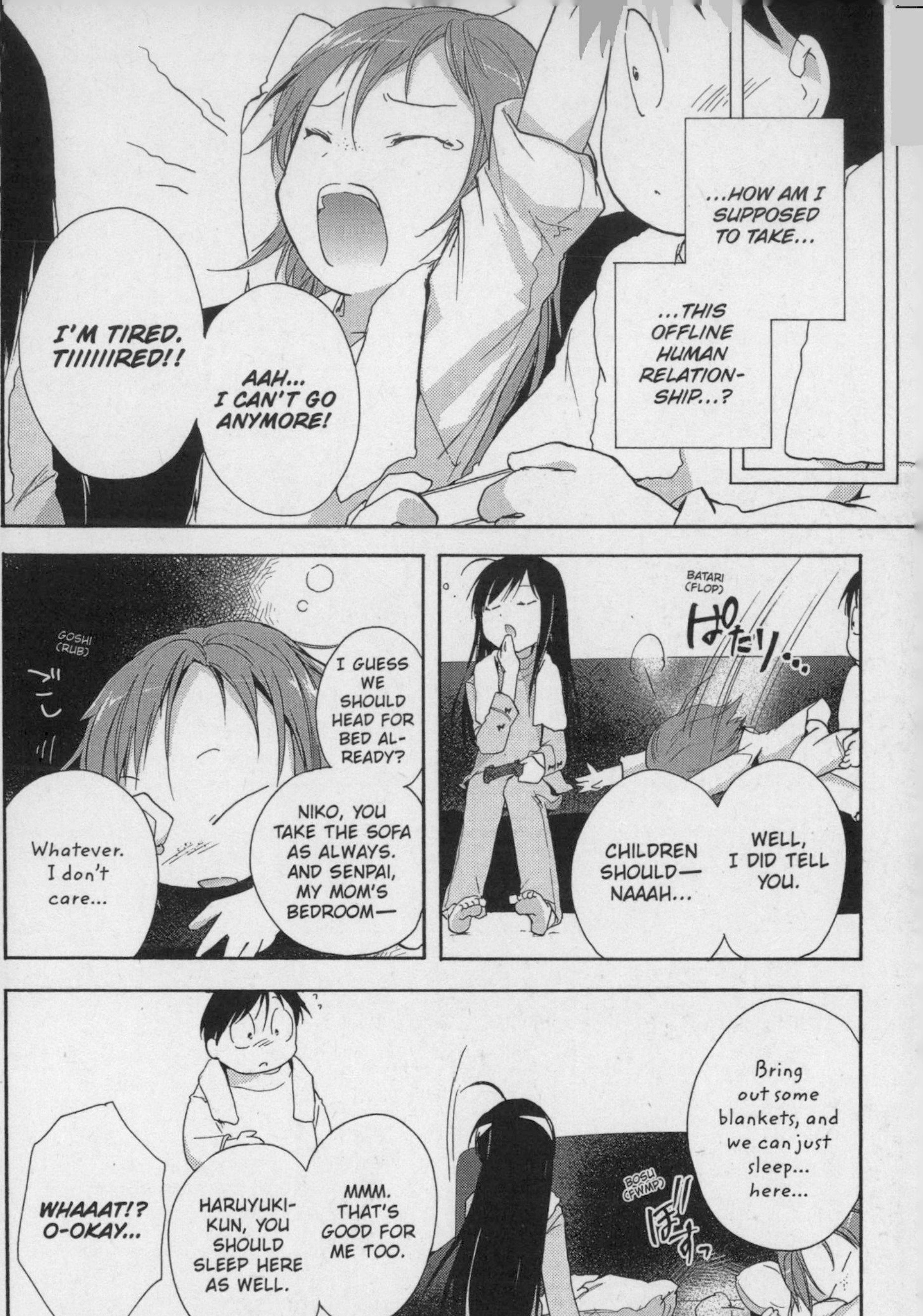
...HOW AM I SUPPOSED TO TAKE...
...THIS OFFLINE HUMAN RELATION-SHIP...?
AAH... I CAN'T GO ANYMORE!
I'M TIRED. TIIIIIIRED!!
BATARI (FLOP)
WELL, I DID TELL YOU.
CHILDREN SHOULD— NAAAH...
I GUESS WE SHOULD HEAD FOR BED AL-READY?
NIKO, YOU TAKE THE SOFA AS ALWAYS. AND SENPAI, MY MOM'S BEDROOM—
GOSHI (RUB)
Whatever. I don't care...
Bring out some blankets, and we can just sleep... here...
BOSU (FWMP)
MMM. THAT'S GOOD FOR ME TOO.
HARUYUKI-KUN, YOU SHOULD SLEEP HERE AS WELL.
WHAAAT!? O-OKAY...

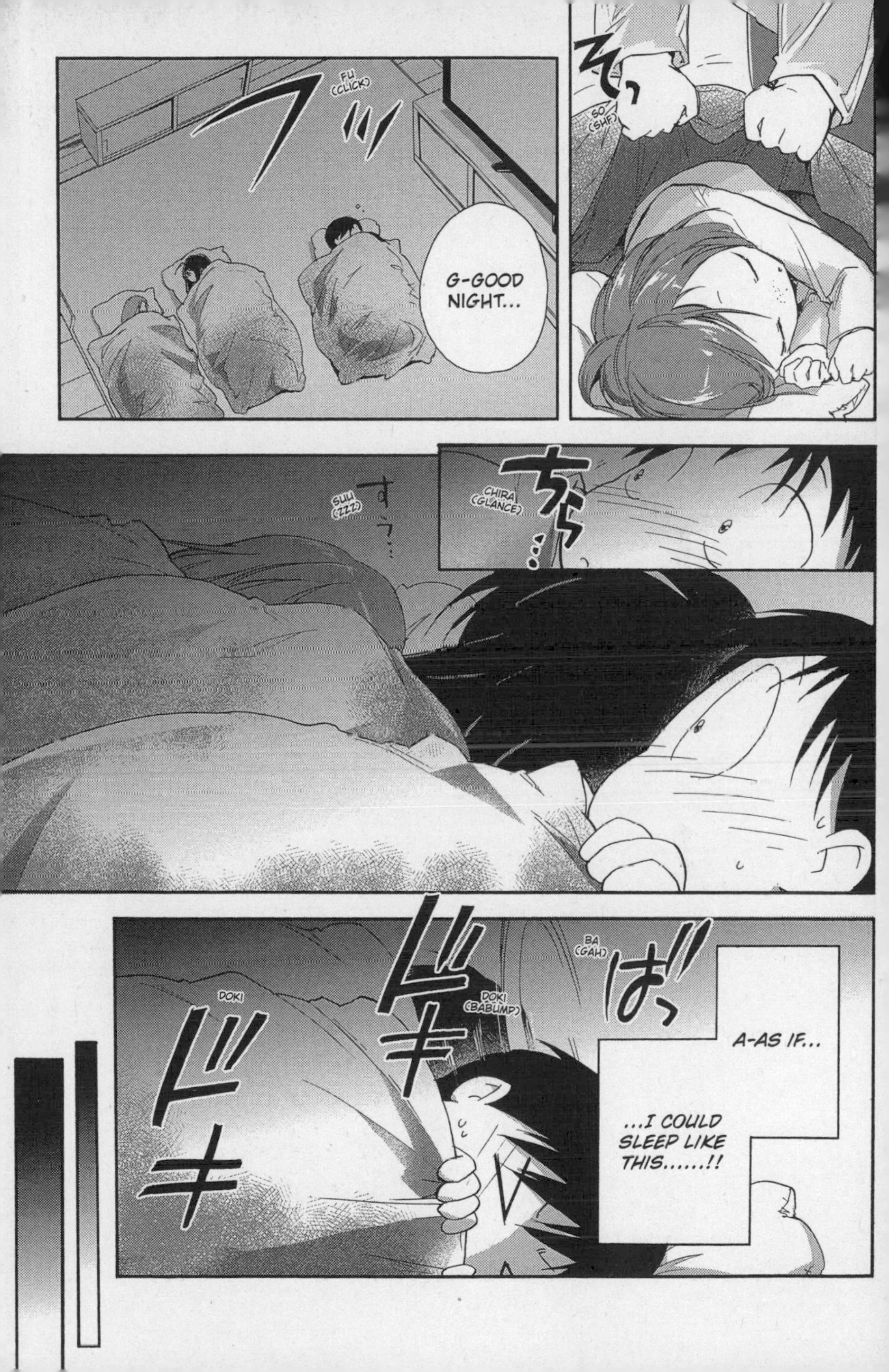

SO (SHF)
FU (CLICK)
G-GOOD NIGHT...
CHIRA (GLANCE)
SUU (ZZZ)
BA (GAH)
A-AS IF...
...I COULD SLEEP LIKE THIS......!!
DOKI (BABUMP)
DOKI

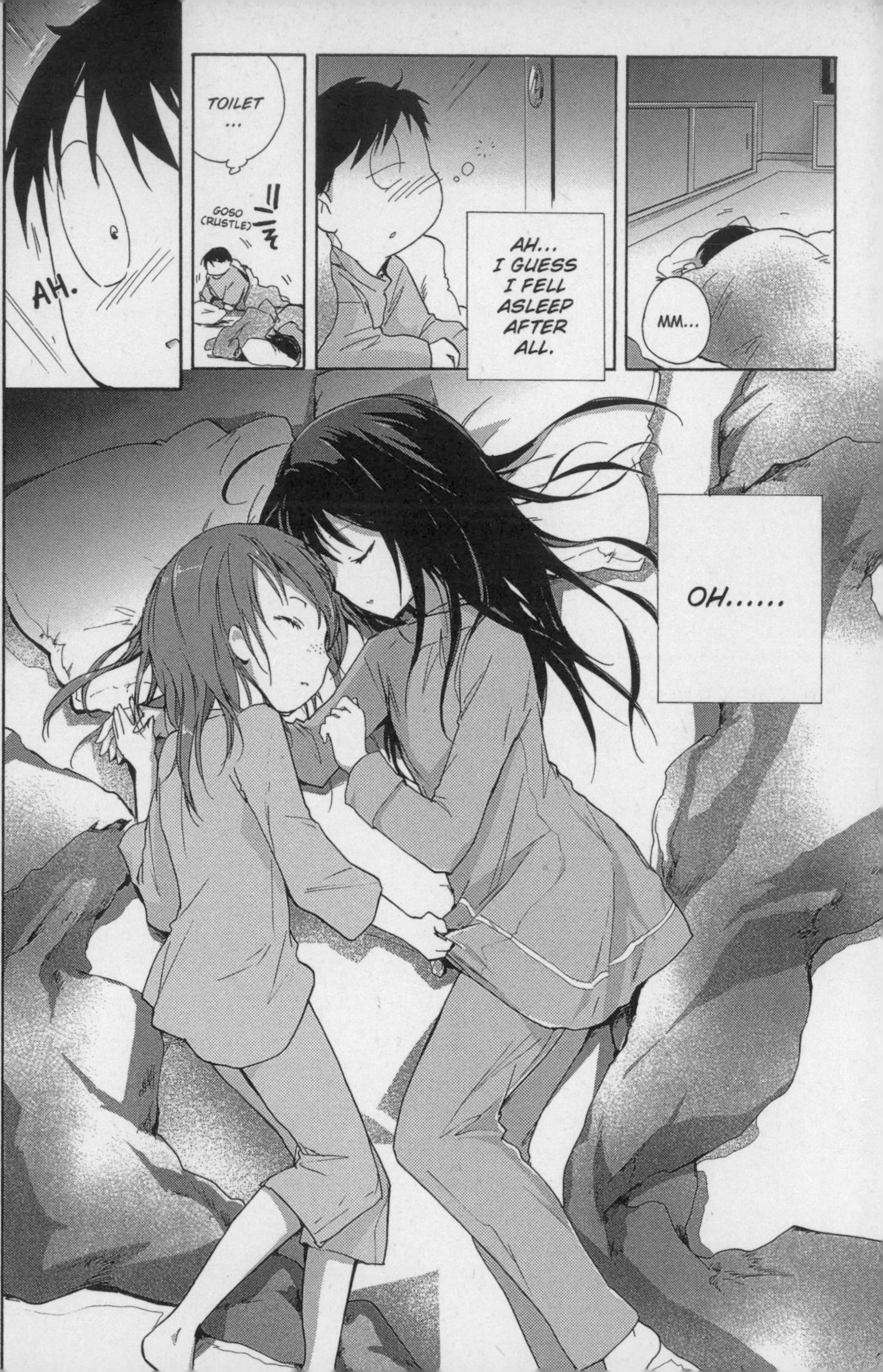
MM...
AH... I GUESS I FELL ASLEEP AFTER ALL.
TOILET ...
GOSO (RUSTLE)
AH.
OH......

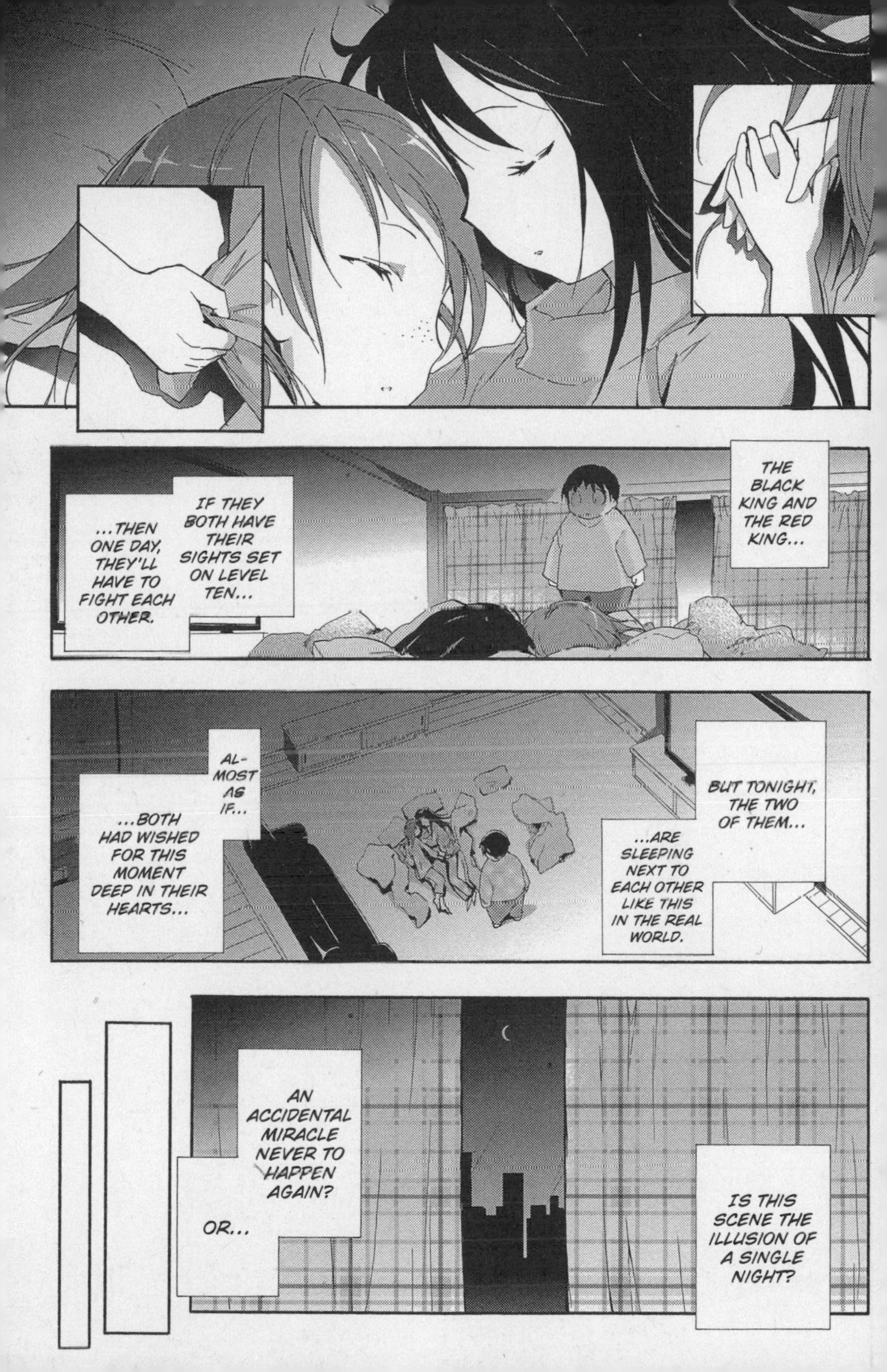
THE BLACK KING AND THE RED KING...
IF THEY BOTH HAVE THEIR SIGHTS SET ON LEVEL TEN...
...THEN ONE DAY, THEY'LL HAVE TO FIGHT EACH OTHER.
BUT TONIGHT, THE TWO OF THEM...
...ARE SLEEPING NEXT TO EACH OTHER LIKE THIS IN THE REAL WORLD.
AL-MOST AS IF...
...BOTH HAD WISHED FOR THIS MOMENT DEEP IN THEIR HEARTS...
IS THIS SCENE THE ILLUSION OF A SINGLE NIGHT?
AN ACCIDENTAL MIRACLE NEVER TO HAPPEN AGAIN?
OR...

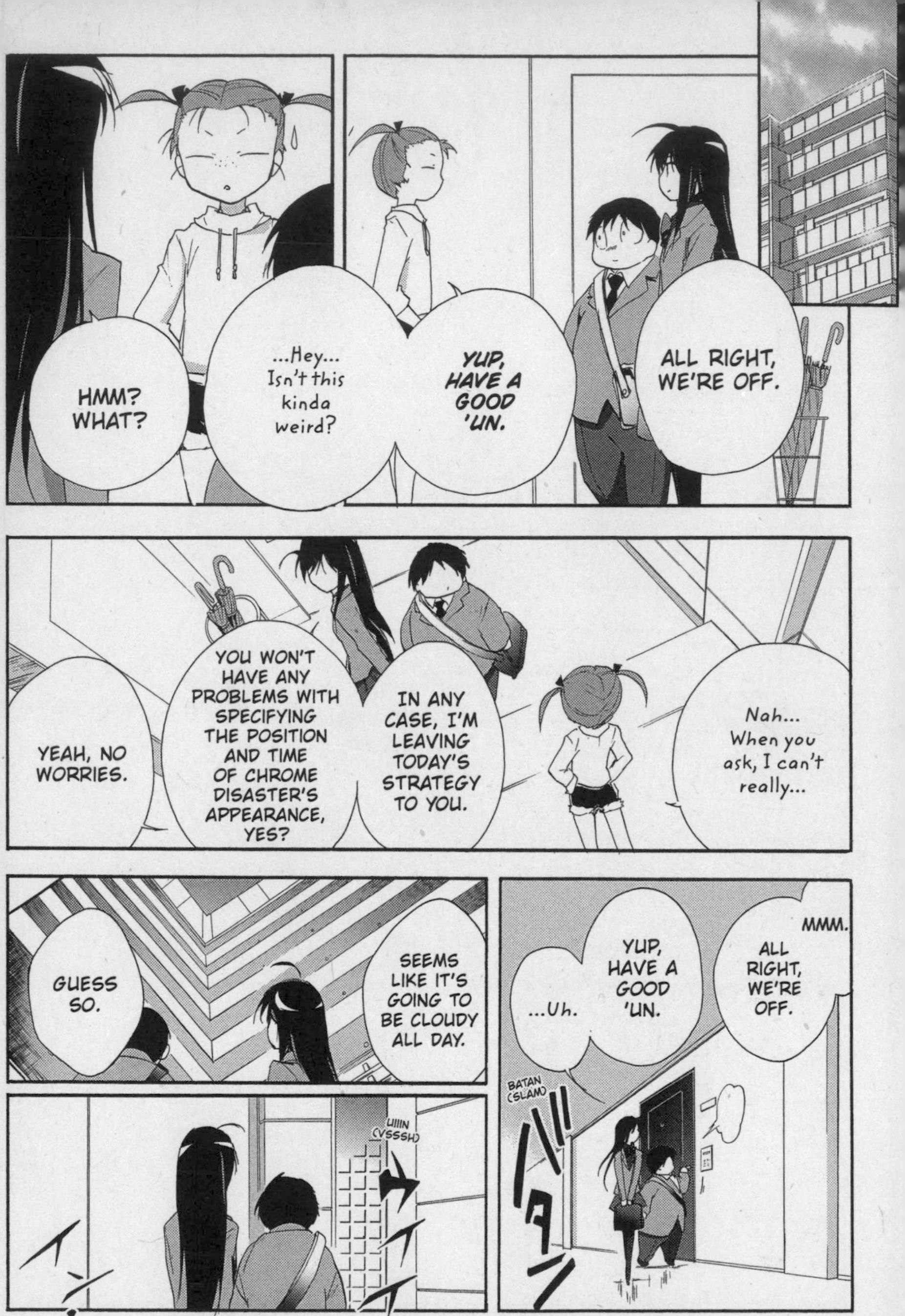
ALL RIGHT, WE'RE OFF.
YUP, HAVE A GOOD 'UN.
...Hey... Isn't this kinda weird?
HMM? WHAT?
Nah... When you ask, I can't really...
IN ANY CASE, I'M LEAVING TODAY'S STRATEGY TO YOU.
YOU WON'T HAVE ANY PROBLEMS WITH SPECIFYING THE POSITION AND TIME OF CHROME DISASTER'S APPEARANCE, YES?
YEAH, NO WORRIES.
MMM.
ALL RIGHT, WE'RE OFF.
YUP, HAVE A GOOD 'UN.
...Uh.
BATAN (SLAM)
SEEMS LIKE IT'S GOING TO BE CLOUDY ALL DAY.
GUESS SO.
UIIIN (VSSSH)

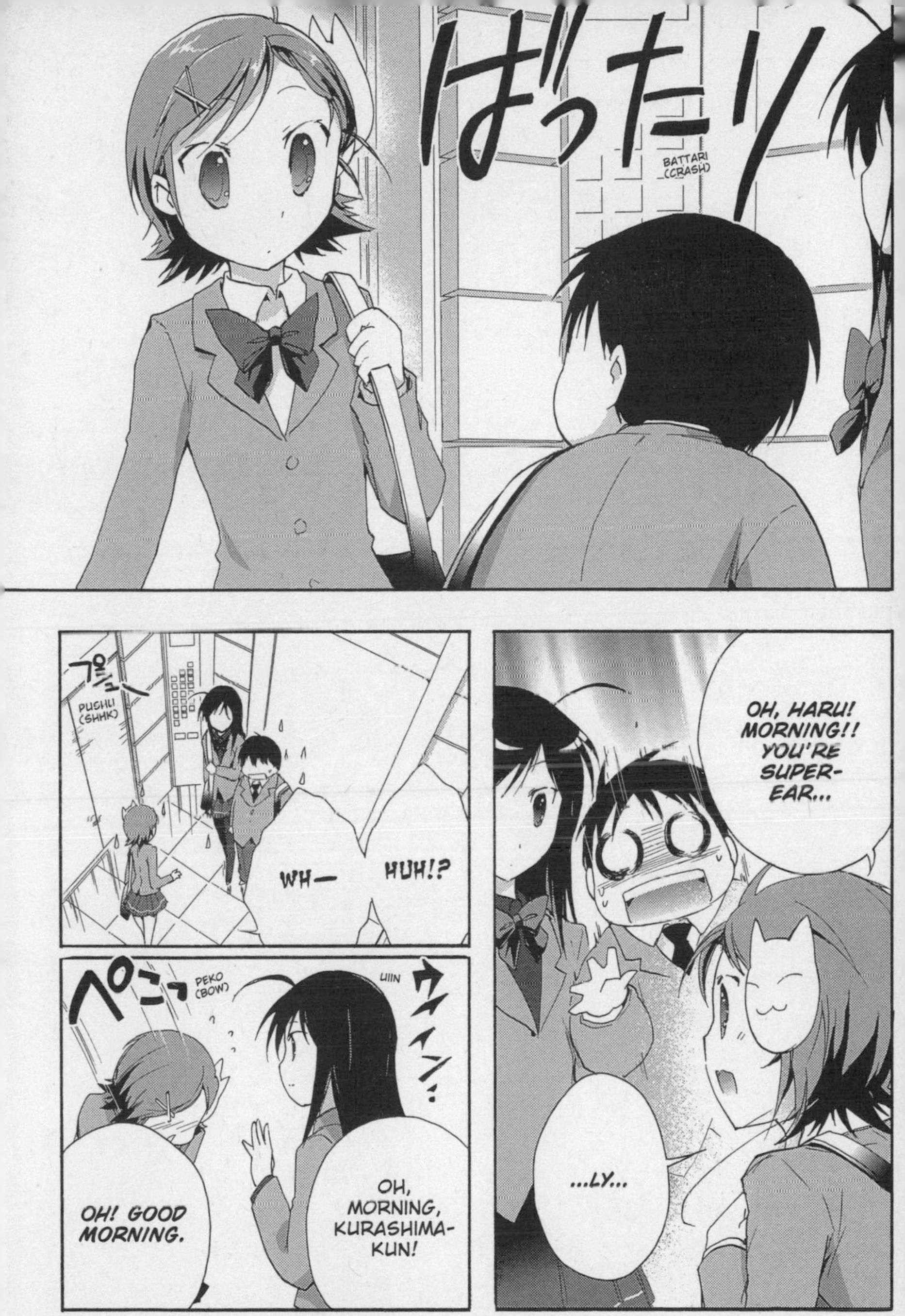
ばったり
BATTARI (CRASH)
OH, HARU! MORNING!! YOU'RE SUPER-EAR...
...LY...
プシュー
PUSHU (SHHK)
WH— HUH!?
ウイイン
UIIN
ペコッ
PEKO (BOW)
OH, MORNING, KURASHIMA-KUN!
OH! GOOD MORNING.

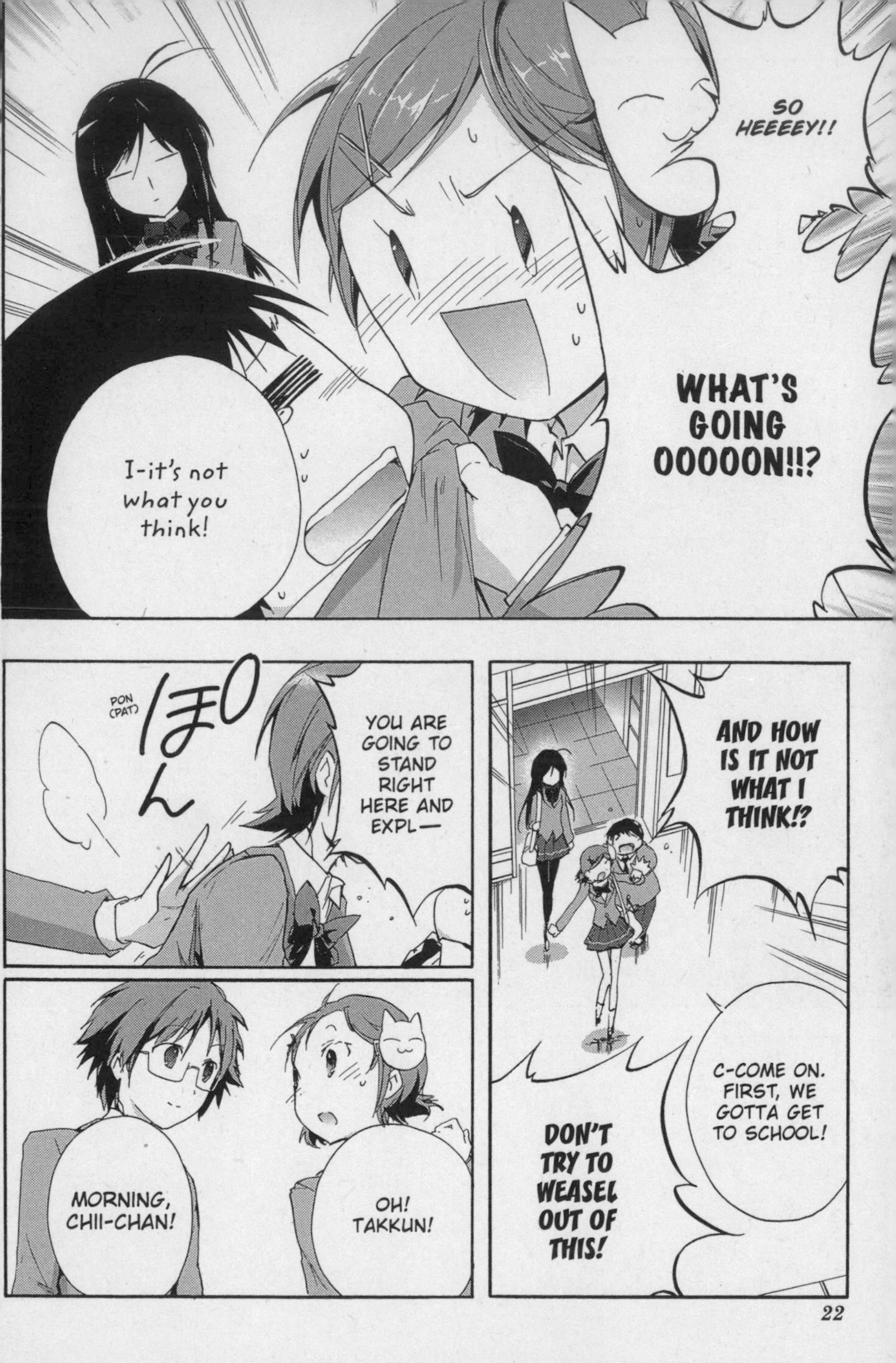
SO HEEEEY!!
WHAT'S GOING OOOOON!!?
I-it's not what you think!
AND HOW IS IT NOT WHAT I THINK!?
C-COME ON. FIRST, WE GOTTA GET TO SCHOOL!
DON'T TRY TO WEASEL OUT OF THIS!
YOU ARE GOING TO STAND RIGHT HERE AND EXPL—
ぽん
PON (PAT)
OH! TAKKUN!
MORNING, CHII-CHAN!

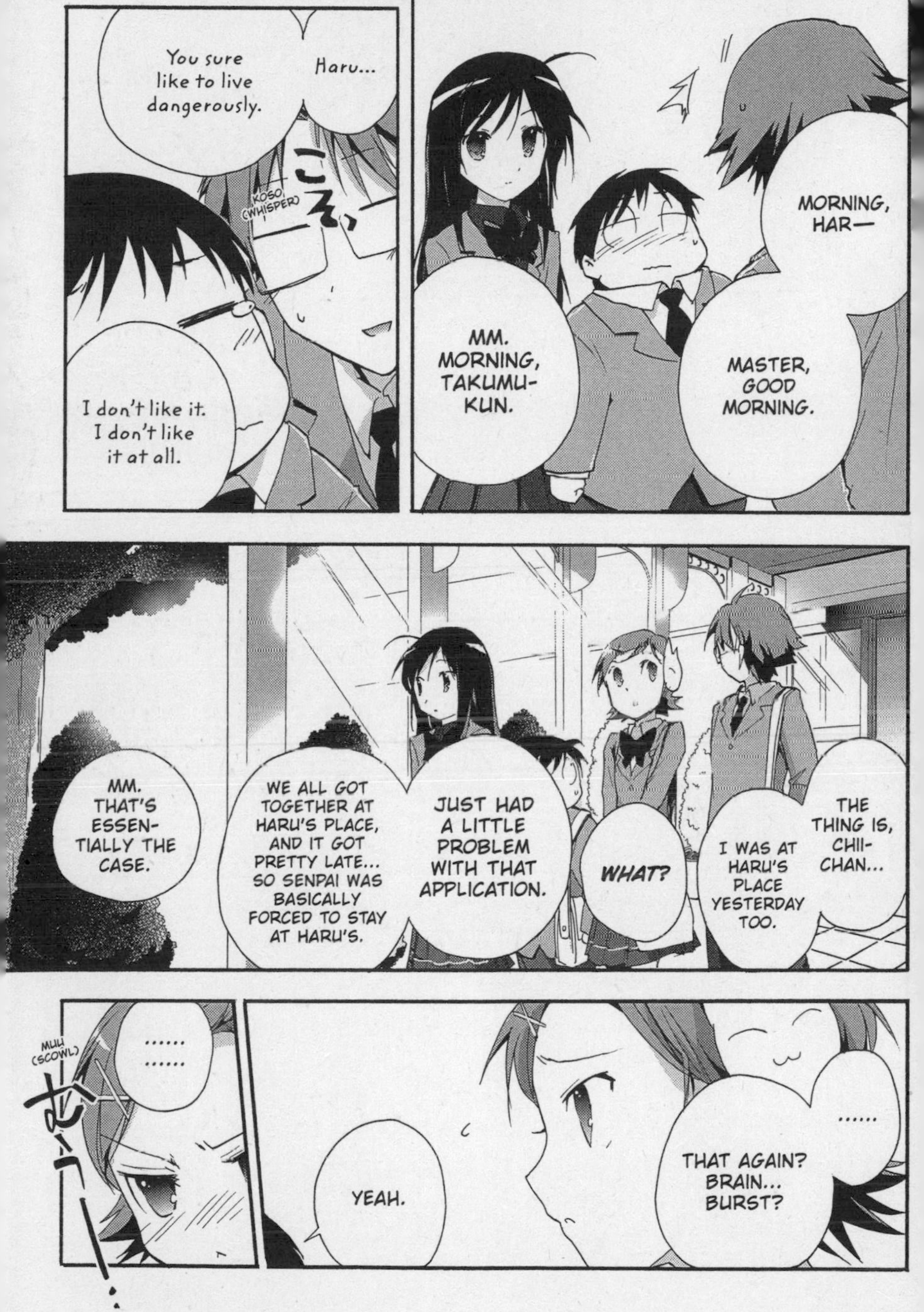
MORNING, HAR—
MASTER, GOOD MORNING.
MM. MORNING, TAKUMU-KUN.
Haru...
You sure like to live dangerously.
KOSO (WHISPER)
I don't like it. I don't like it at all.
THE THING IS, CHII-CHAN...
I WAS AT HARU'S PLACE YESTERDAY TOO.
WHAT?
JUST HAD A LITTLE PROBLEM WITH THAT APPLICATION.
WE ALL GOT TOGETHER AT HARU'S PLACE, AND IT GOT PRETTY LATE... SO SENPAI WAS BASICALLY FORCED TO STAY AT HARU'S.
MM. THAT'S ESSENTIALLY THE CASE.
......
THAT AGAIN? BRAIN... BURST?
YEAH.
....
MUU (SCOWL)

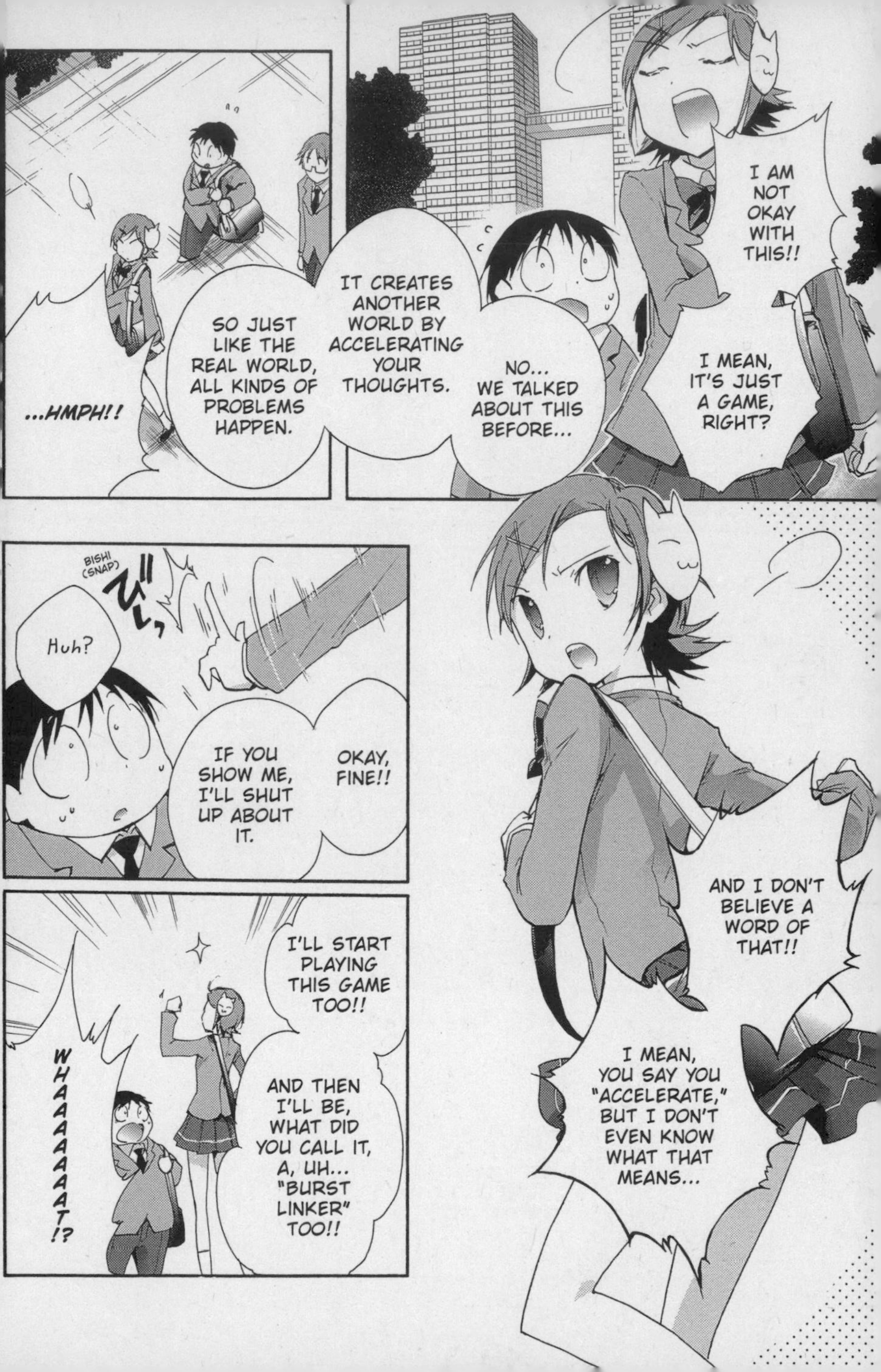
I AM NOT OKAY WITH THIS!!
I MEAN, IT'S JUST A GAME, RIGHT?
NO... WE TALKED ABOUT THIS BEFORE...
IT CREATES ANOTHER WORLD BY ACCELERATING YOUR THOUGHTS.
SO JUST LIKE THE REAL WORLD, ALL KINDS OF PROBLEMS HAPPEN.
...HMPH!!
AND I DON'T BELIEVE A WORD OF THAT!!
I MEAN, YOU SAY YOU "ACCELERATE," BUT I DON'T EVEN KNOW WHAT THAT MEANS...
BISHI (SNAP)
OKAY, FINE!!
IF YOU SHOW ME, I'LL SHUT UP ABOUT IT.
Huh?
I'LL START PLAYING THIS GAME TOO!!
AND THEN I'LL BE, WHAT DID YOU CALL IT, A, UH... "BURST LINKER" TOO!!
WHAAAAAAAAT!?

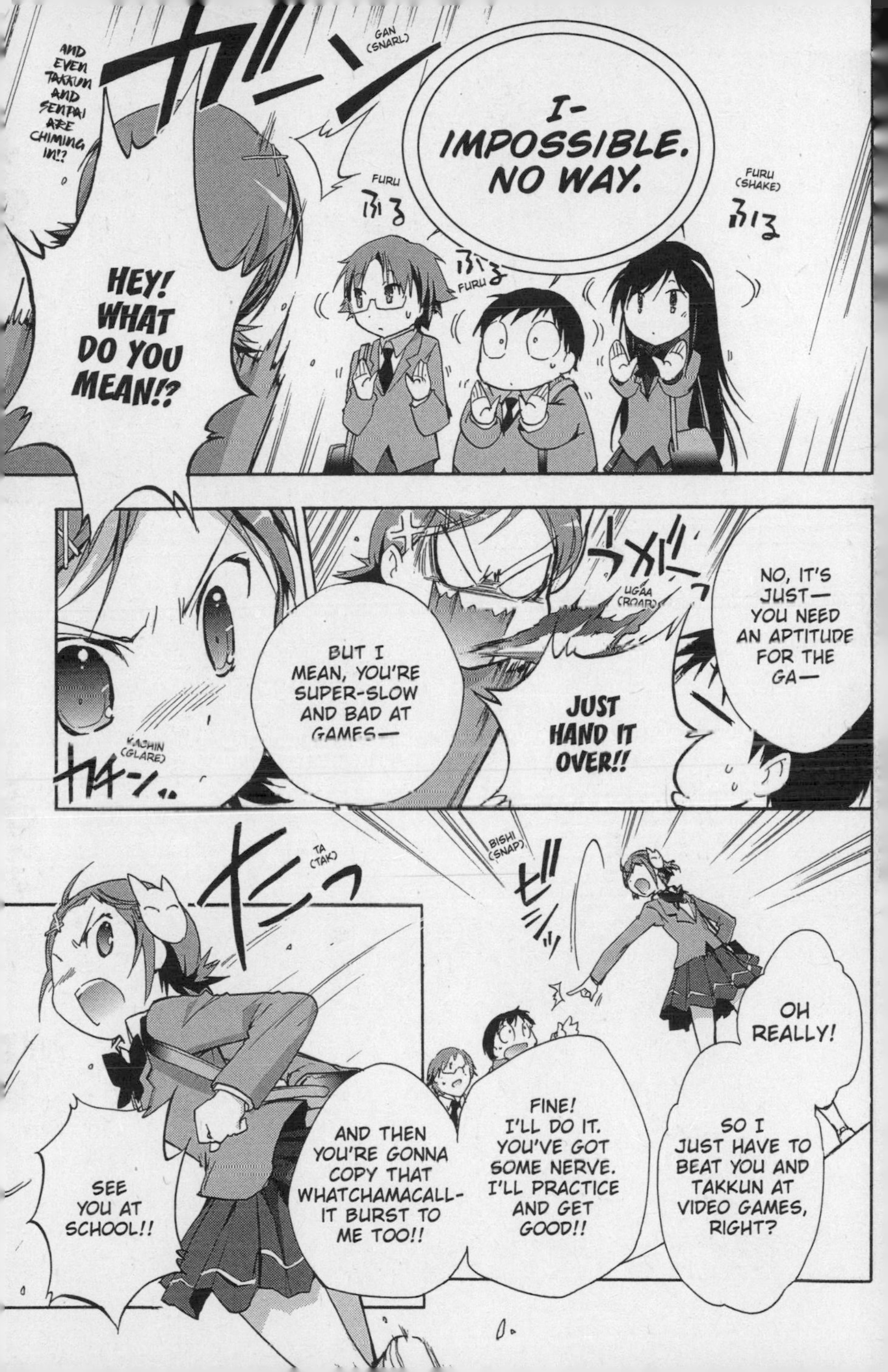

FURU (SHAKE)
ふる
I- IMPOSSIBLE. NO WAY.
FURU
ふる
ふる
FURU
GAN (SNARL)
AND EVEN TAKKUN AND SENPAI ARE CHIMING IN!?
HEY! WHAT DO YOU MEAN!?
NO, IT'S JUST— YOU NEED AN APTITUDE FOR THE GA—
UGAA (ROAR)
JUST HAND IT OVER!!
BUT I MEAN, YOU'RE SUPER-SLOW AND BAD AT GAMES—
KACHIN (GLARE)
BISHI (SNAP)
OH REALLY!
SO I JUST HAVE TO BEAT YOU AND TAKKUN AT VIDEO GAMES, RIGHT?
FINE! I'LL DO IT. YOU'VE GOT SOME NERVE. I'LL PRACTICE AND GET GOOD!!
AND THEN YOU'RE GONNA COPY THAT WHATCHAMACALL-IT BURST TO ME TOO!!
TA (TAK)
SEE YOU AT SCHOOL!!

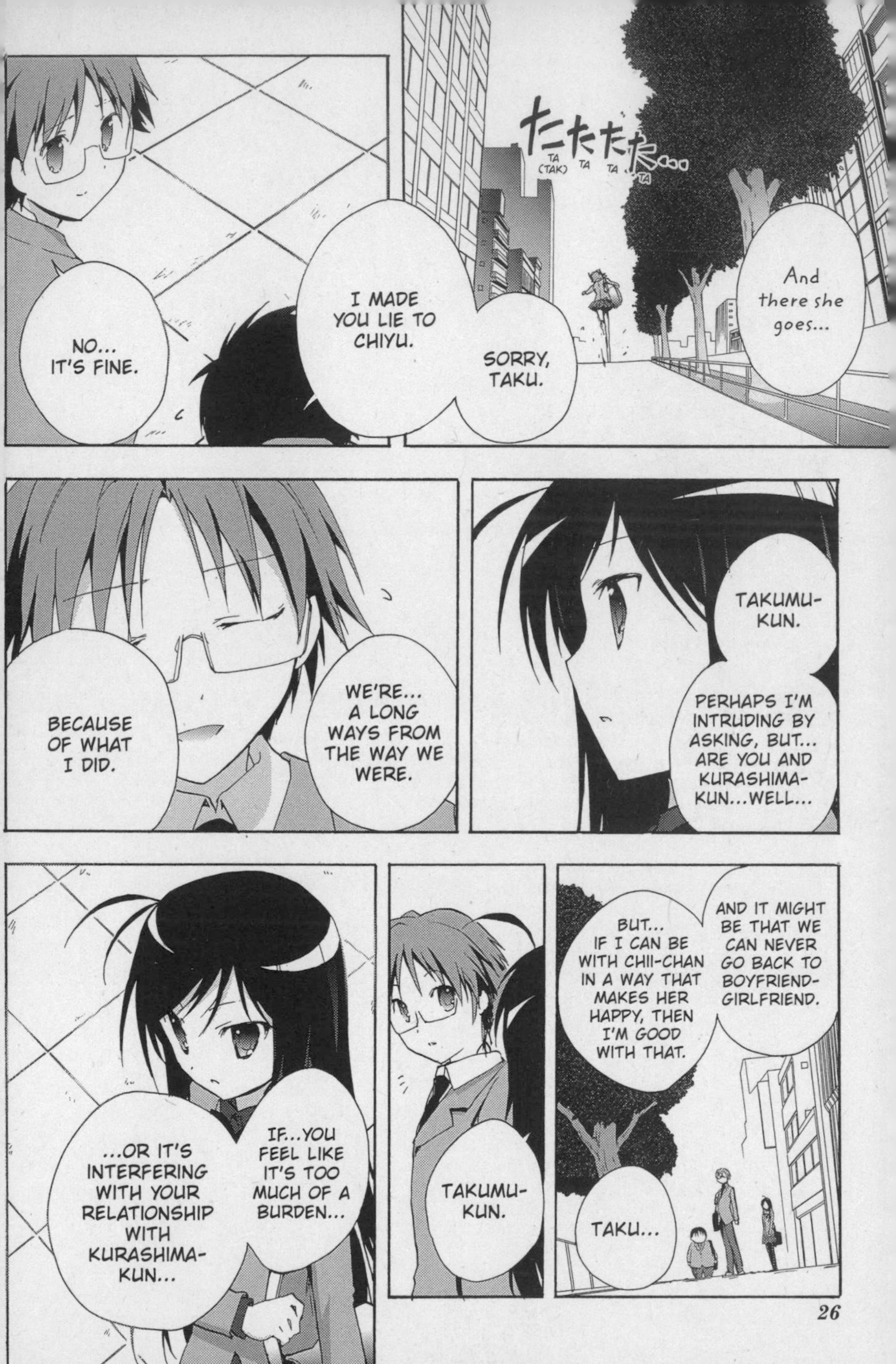
たーたたた…
TA (TAK) TA TA TA
And there she goes...
SORRY, TAKU.
I MADE YOU LIE TO CHIYU.
NO... IT'S FINE.
TAKUMU-KUN.
PERHAPS I'M INTRUDING BY ASKING, BUT... ARE YOU AND KURASHIMA-KUN...WELL...
WE'RE... A LONG WAYS FROM THE WAY WE WERE.
BECAUSE OF WHAT I DID.
AND IT MIGHT BE THAT WE CAN NEVER GO BACK TO BOYFRIEND-GIRLFRIEND.
BUT... IF I CAN BE WITH CHII-CHAN IN A WAY THAT MAKES HER HAPPY, THEN I'M GOOD WITH THAT.
TAKU...
TAKUMU-KUN.
IF...YOU FEEL LIKE IT'S TOO MUCH OF A BURDEN...
...OR IT'S INTERFERING WITH YOUR RELATIONSHIP WITH KURASHIMA-KUN...

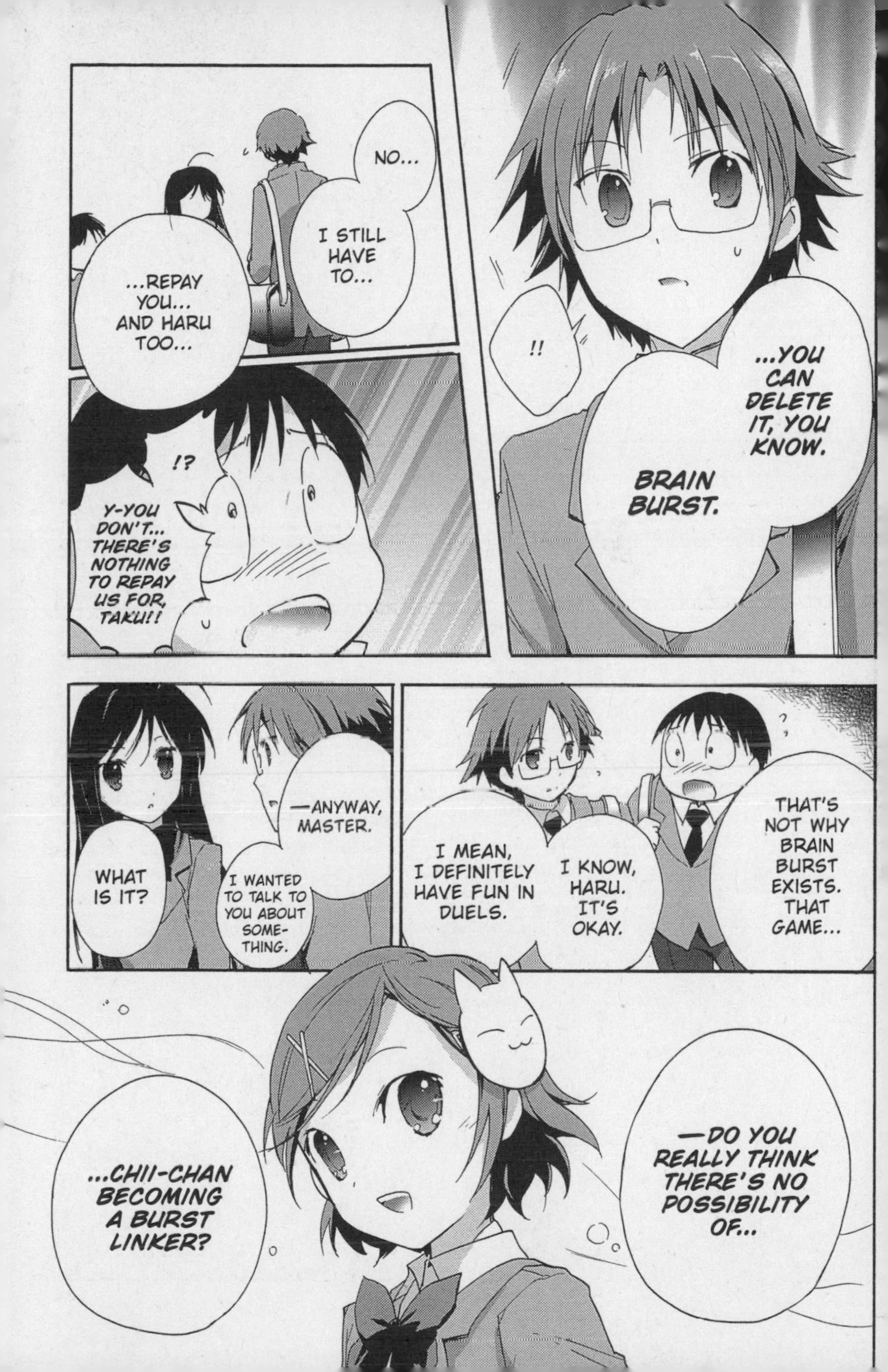
...YOU CAN DELETE IT, YOU KNOW.
BRAIN BURST.
!!
NO...
I STILL HAVE TO...
...REPAY YOU... AND HARU TOO...
!?
Y-YOU DON'T... THERE'S NOTHING TO REPAY US FOR, TAKU!!
THAT'S NOT WHY BRAIN BURST EXISTS. THAT GAME...
I KNOW, HARU. IT'S OKAY.
I MEAN, I DEFINITELY HAVE FUN IN DUELS.
—ANYWAY, MASTER.
I WANTED TO TALK TO YOU ABOUT SOME-THING.
WHAT IS IT?
—DO YOU REALLY THINK THERE'S NO POSSIBILITY OF...
...CHII-CHAN BECOMING A BURST LINKER?

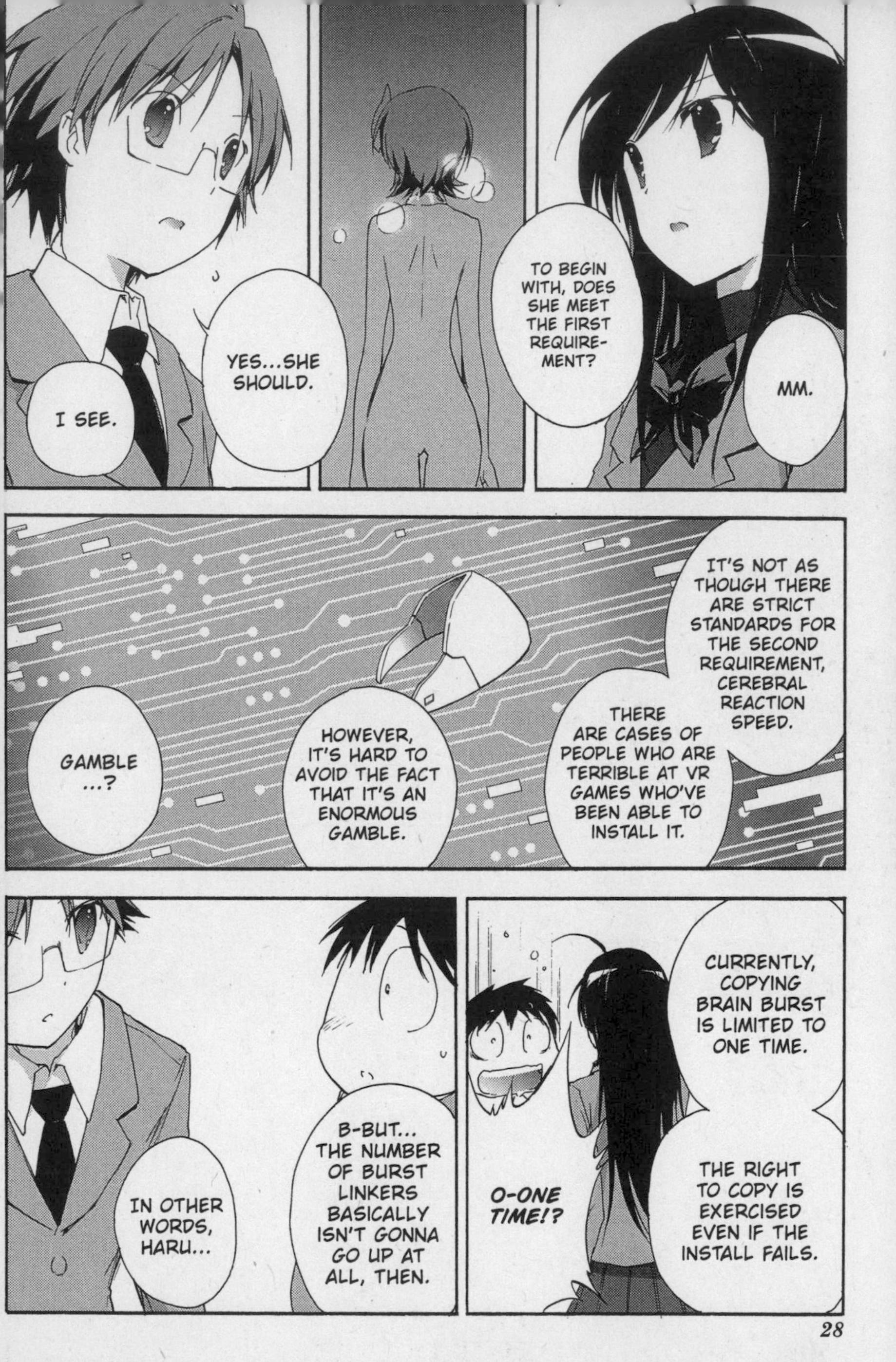
MM.
TO BEGIN WITH, DOES SHE MEET THE FIRST REQUIRE-MENT?
YES...SHE SHOULD.
I SEE.
IT'S NOT AS THOUGH THERE ARE STRICT STANDARDS FOR THE SECOND REQUIREMENT, CEREBRAL REACTION SPEED.
THERE ARE CASES OF PEOPLE WHO ARE TERRIBLE AT VR GAMES WHO'VE BEEN ABLE TO INSTALL IT.
HOWEVER, IT'S HARD TO AVOID THE FACT THAT IT'S AN ENORMOUS GAMBLE.
GAMBLE ...?
CURRENTLY, COPYING BRAIN BURST IS LIMITED TO ONE TIME.
THE RIGHT TO COPY IS EXERCISED EVEN IF THE INSTALL FAILS.
O-ONE TIME!?
B-BUT... THE NUMBER OF BURST LINKERS BASICALLY ISN'T GONNA GO UP AT ALL, THEN.
IN OTHER WORDS, HARU...

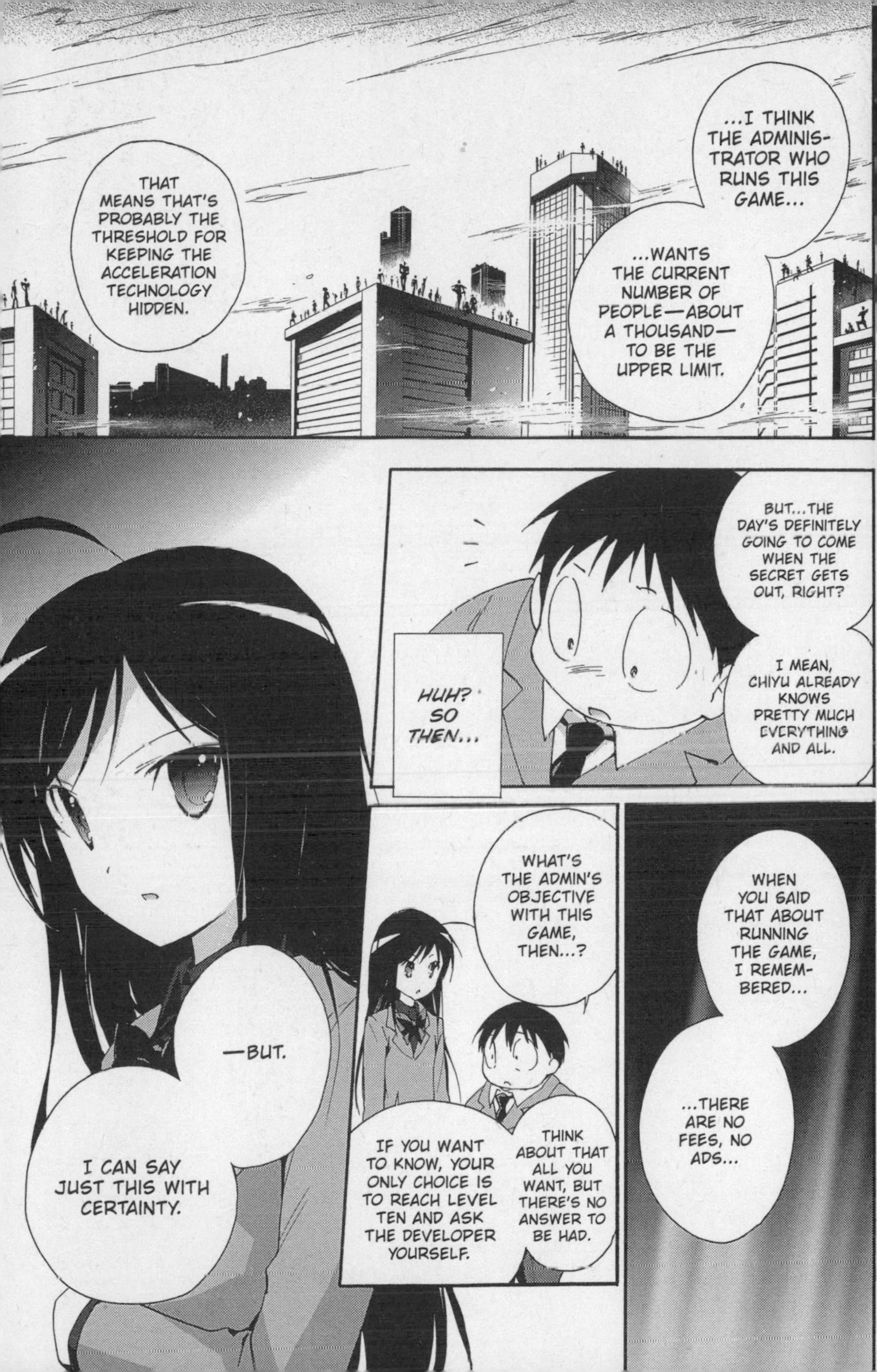
...I THINK THE ADMINISTRATOR WHO RUNS THIS GAME...
...WANTS THE CURRENT NUMBER OF PEOPLE—ABOUT A THOUSAND—TO BE THE UPPER LIMIT.
THAT MEANS THAT'S PROBABLY THE THRESHOLD FOR KEEPING THE ACCELERATION TECHNOLOGY HIDDEN.
BUT...THE DAY'S DEFINITELY GOING TO COME WHEN THE SECRET GETS OUT, RIGHT?
I MEAN, CHIYU ALREADY KNOWS PRETTY MUCH EVERYTHING AND ALL.
HUH? SO THEN...
WHEN YOU SAID THAT ABOUT RUNNING THE GAME, I REMEMBERED...
...THERE ARE NO FEES, NO ADS...
WHAT'S THE ADMIN'S OBJECTIVE WITH THIS GAME, THEN...?
THINK ABOUT THAT ALL YOU WANT, BUT THERE'S NO ANSWER TO BE HAD.
IF YOU WANT TO KNOW, YOUR ONLY CHOICE IS TO REACH LEVEL TEN AND ASK THE DEVELOPER YOURSELF.
—BUT.
I CAN SAY JUST THIS WITH CERTAINTY.

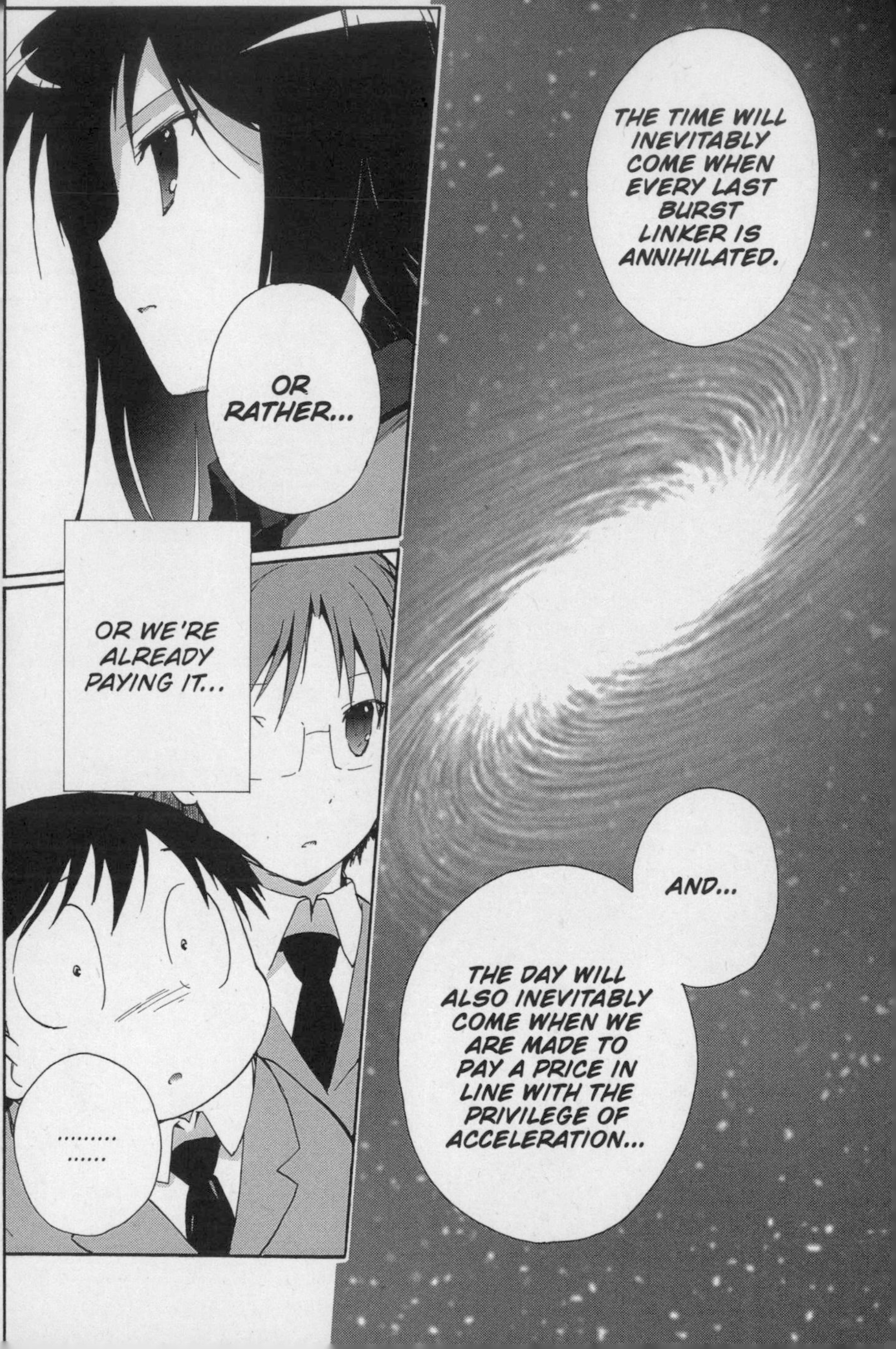
THE TIME WILL INEVITABLY COME WHEN EVERY LAST BURST LINKER IS ANNIHILATED.
AND...
THE DAY WILL ALSO INEVITABLY COME WHEN WE ARE MADE TO PAY A PRICE IN LINE WITH THE PRIVILEGE OF ACCELERATION...
OR RATHER...
OR WE'RE ALREADY PAYING IT...
....
......

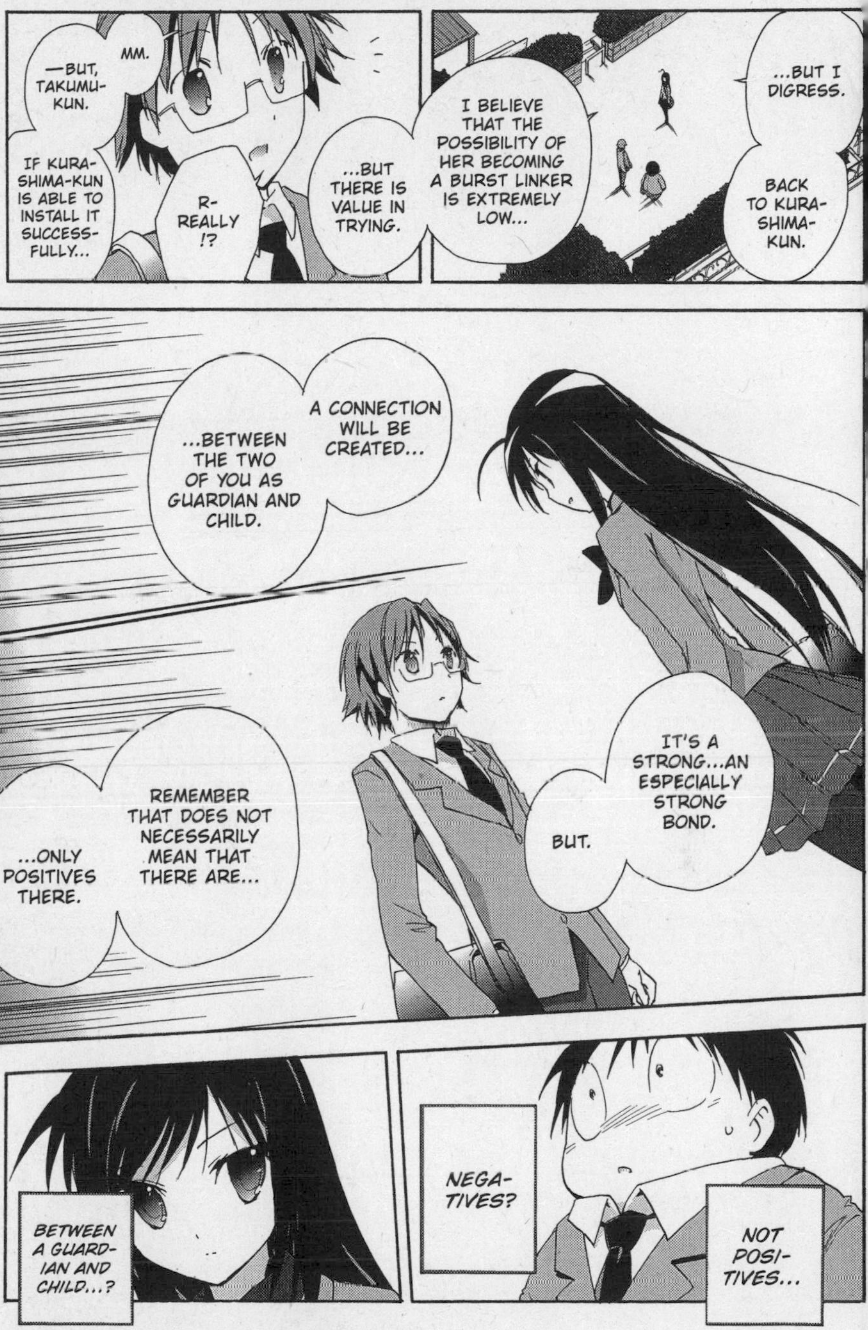
...BUT I DIGRESS.
BACK TO KURASHIMA-KUN.
I BELIEVE THAT THE POSSIBILITY OF HER BECOMING A BURST LINKER IS EXTREMELY LOW...
...BUT THERE IS VALUE IN TRYING.
R-REALLY!?
MM.
—BUT, TAKUMU-KUN.
IF KURASHIMA-KUN IS ABLE TO INSTALL IT SUCCESSFULLY...
A CONNECTION WILL BE CREATED...
...BETWEEN THE TWO OF YOU AS GUARDIAN AND CHILD.
IT'S A STRONG...AN ESPECIALLY STRONG BOND.
BUT.
REMEMBER THAT DOES NOT NECESSARILY MEAN THAT THERE ARE...
...ONLY POSITIVES THERE.
NOT POSITIVES...
NEGATIVES?
BETWEEN A GUARDIAN AND CHILD...?

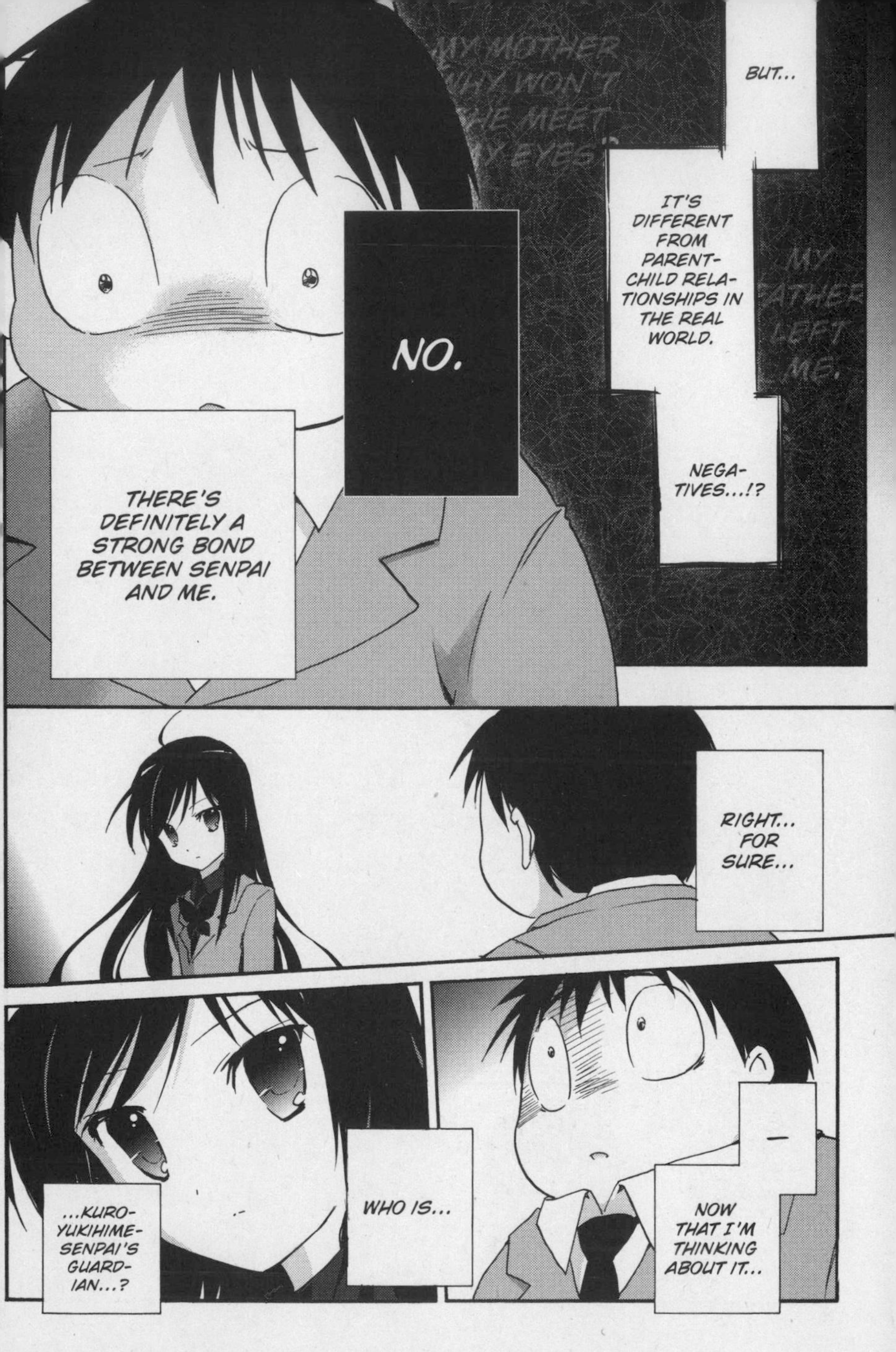
BUT...
MY FATHER LEFT ME.
IT'S DIFFERENT FROM PARENT-CHILD RELATIONSHIPS IN THE REAL WORLD.
MY MOTHER
NEGATIVES...!?
NO.
THERE'S DEFINITELY A STRONG BOND BETWEEN SENPAI AND ME.
RIGHT... FOR SURE...
NOW THAT I'M THINKING ABOUT IT...
WHO IS...
...KUROYUKIHIME-SENPAI'S GUARDIAN...?

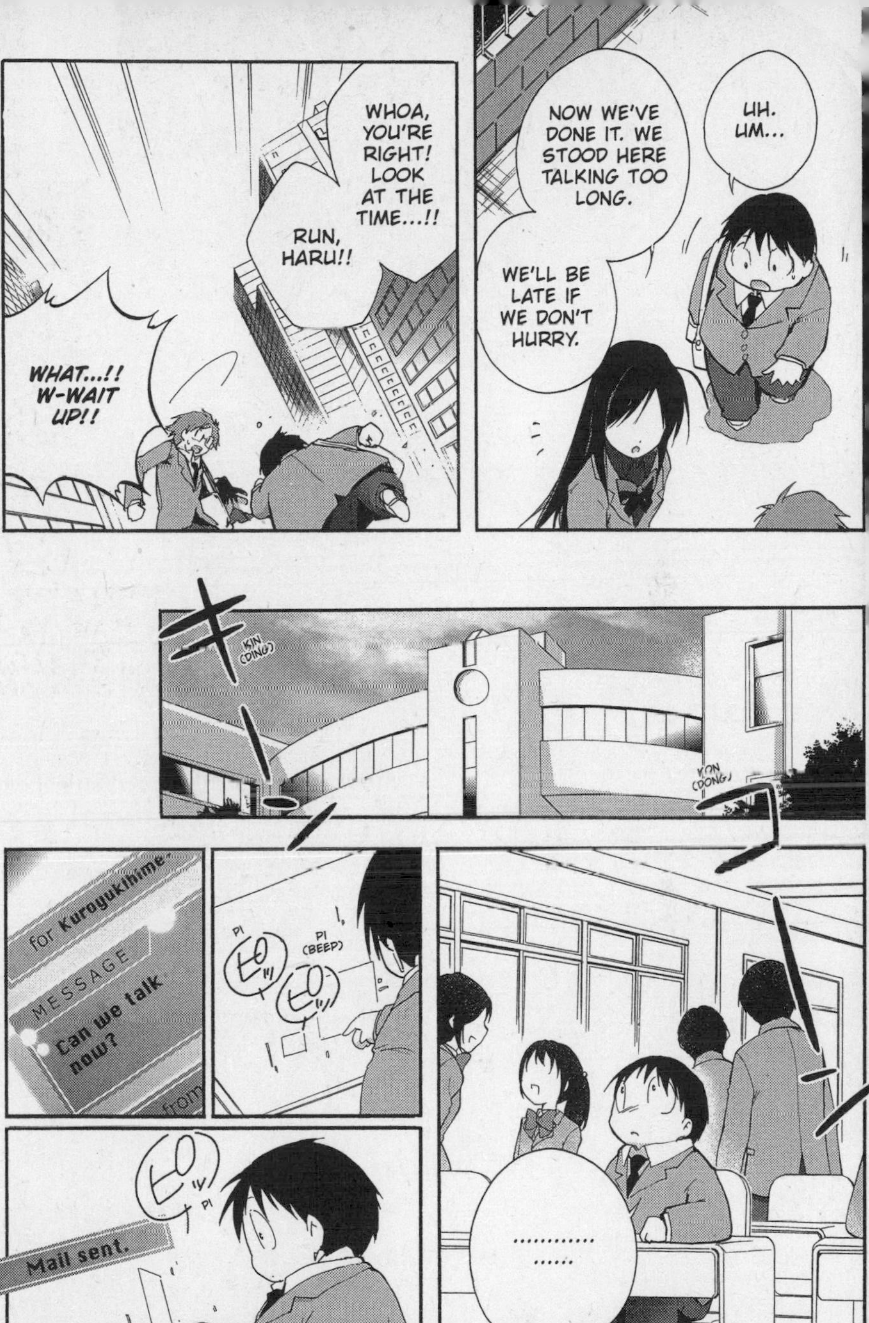

UH. UM...
NOW WE'VE DONE IT. WE STOOD HERE TALKING TOO LONG.
WE'LL BE LATE IF WE DON'T HURRY.
WHOA, YOU'RE RIGHT! LOOK AT THE TIME...!!
RUN, HARU!!
WHAT...!! W-WAIT UP!!
KIN (DING)
KON (DONG)
....
......
PI
PI (BEEP)
for Kuroyukihime
MESSAGE
Can we talk now?
from
PI
Mail sent.

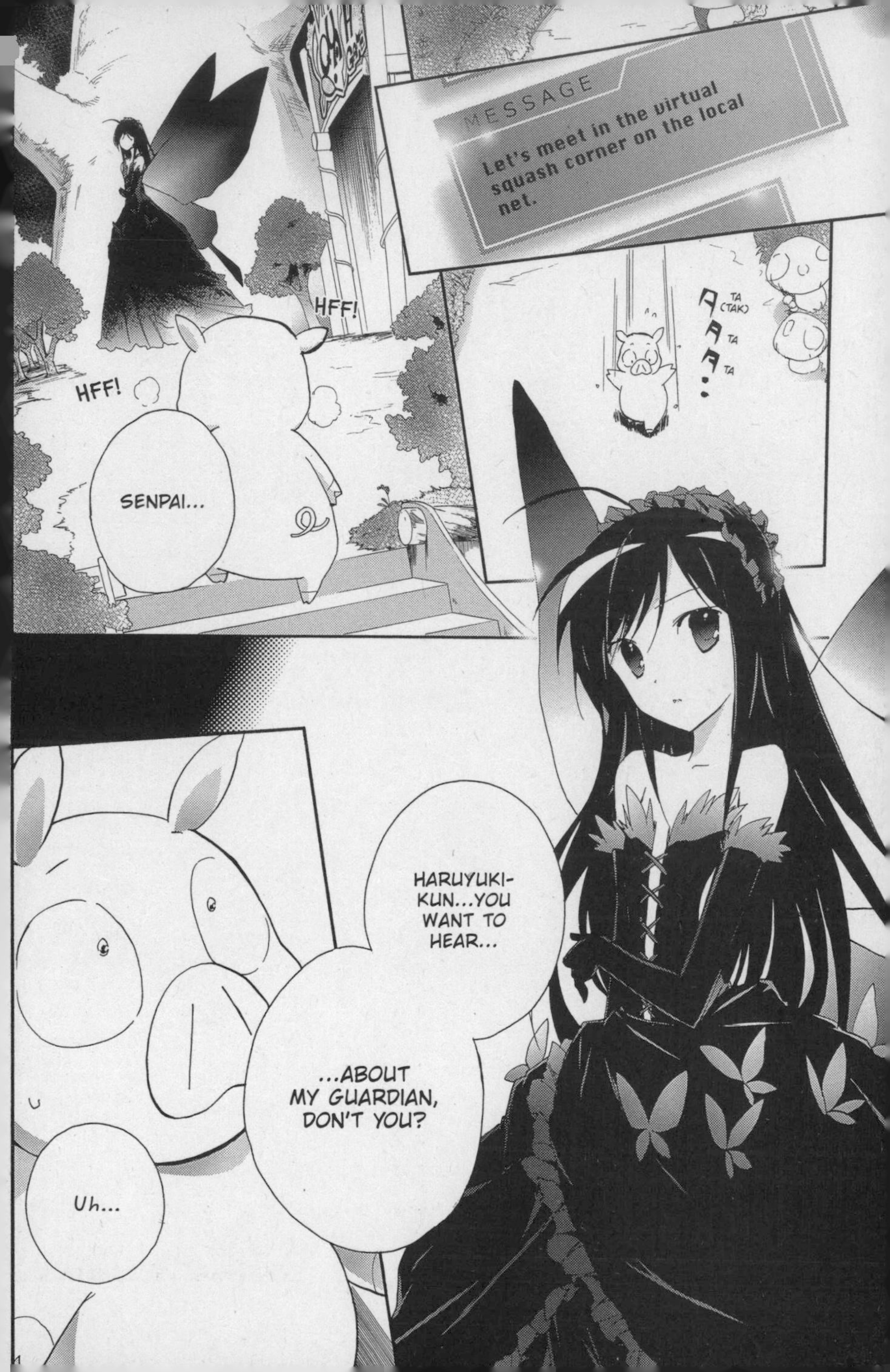
MESSAGE
Let's meet in the virtual squash corner on the local net.
TA (TAK)
TA
TA
HFF!
HFF!
SENPAI...
HARUYUKI-KUN...YOU WANT TO HEAR...
...ABOUT MY GUARDIAN, DON'T YOU?
Uh...

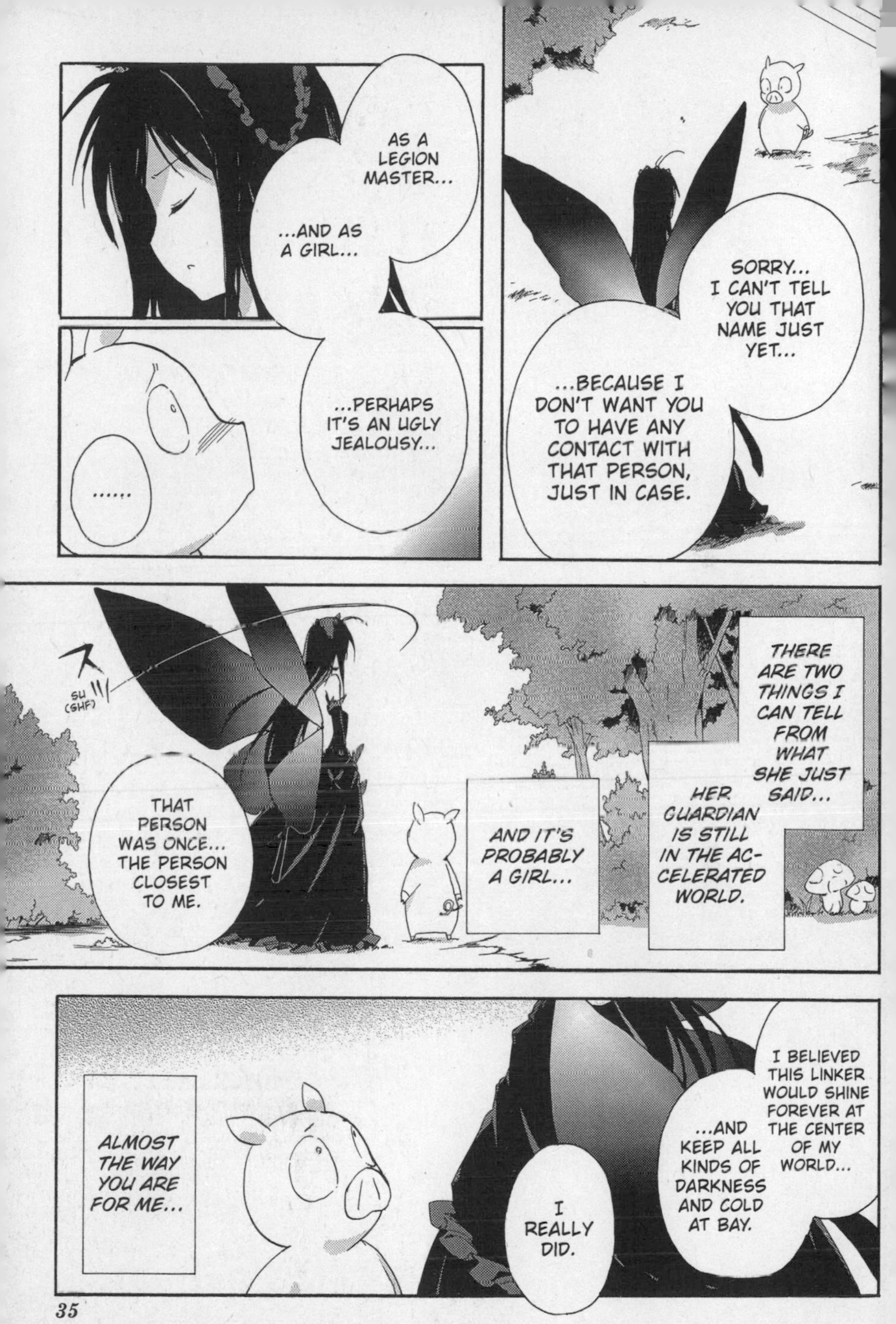
SORRY... I CAN'T TELL YOU THAT NAME JUST YET...
...BECAUSE I DON'T WANT YOU TO HAVE ANY CONTACT WITH THAT PERSON, JUST IN CASE.
AS A LEGION MASTER...
...AND AS A GIRL...
...PERHAPS IT'S AN UGLY JEALOUSY...
......
THERE ARE TWO THINGS I CAN TELL FROM WHAT SHE JUST SAID...
HER GUARDIAN IS STILL IN THE AC-CELERATED WORLD.
AND IT'S PROBABLY A GIRL...
ス
SU (SHF)
THAT PERSON WAS ONCE... THE PERSON CLOSEST TO ME.
I BELIEVED THIS LINKER WOULD SHINE FOREVER AT THE CENTER OF MY WORLD...
...AND KEEP ALL KINDS OF DARKNESS AND COLD AT BAY.
I REALLY DID.
ALMOST THE WAY YOU ARE FOR ME...

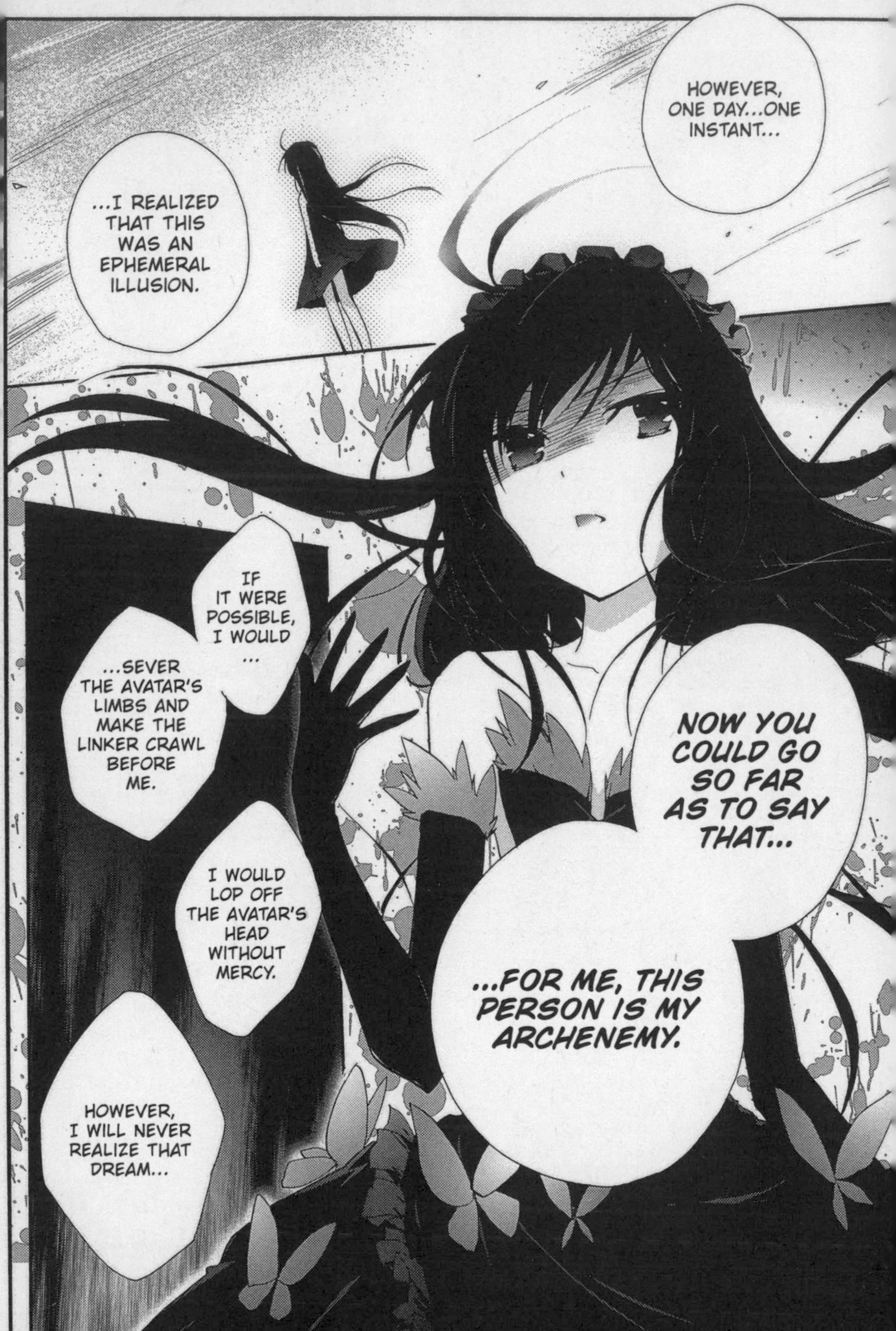
HOWEVER, ONE DAY...ONE INSTANT...
...I REALIZED THAT THIS WAS AN EPHEMERAL ILLUSION.
NOW YOU COULD GO SO FAR AS TO SAY THAT...
...FOR ME, THIS PERSON IS MY ARCHENEMY.
IF IT WERE POSSIBLE, I WOULD ...
...SEVER THE AVATAR'S LIMBS AND MAKE THE LINKER CRAWL BEFORE ME.
I WOULD LOP OFF THE AVATAR'S HEAD WITHOUT MERCY.
HOWEVER, I WILL NEVER REALIZE THAT DREAM...

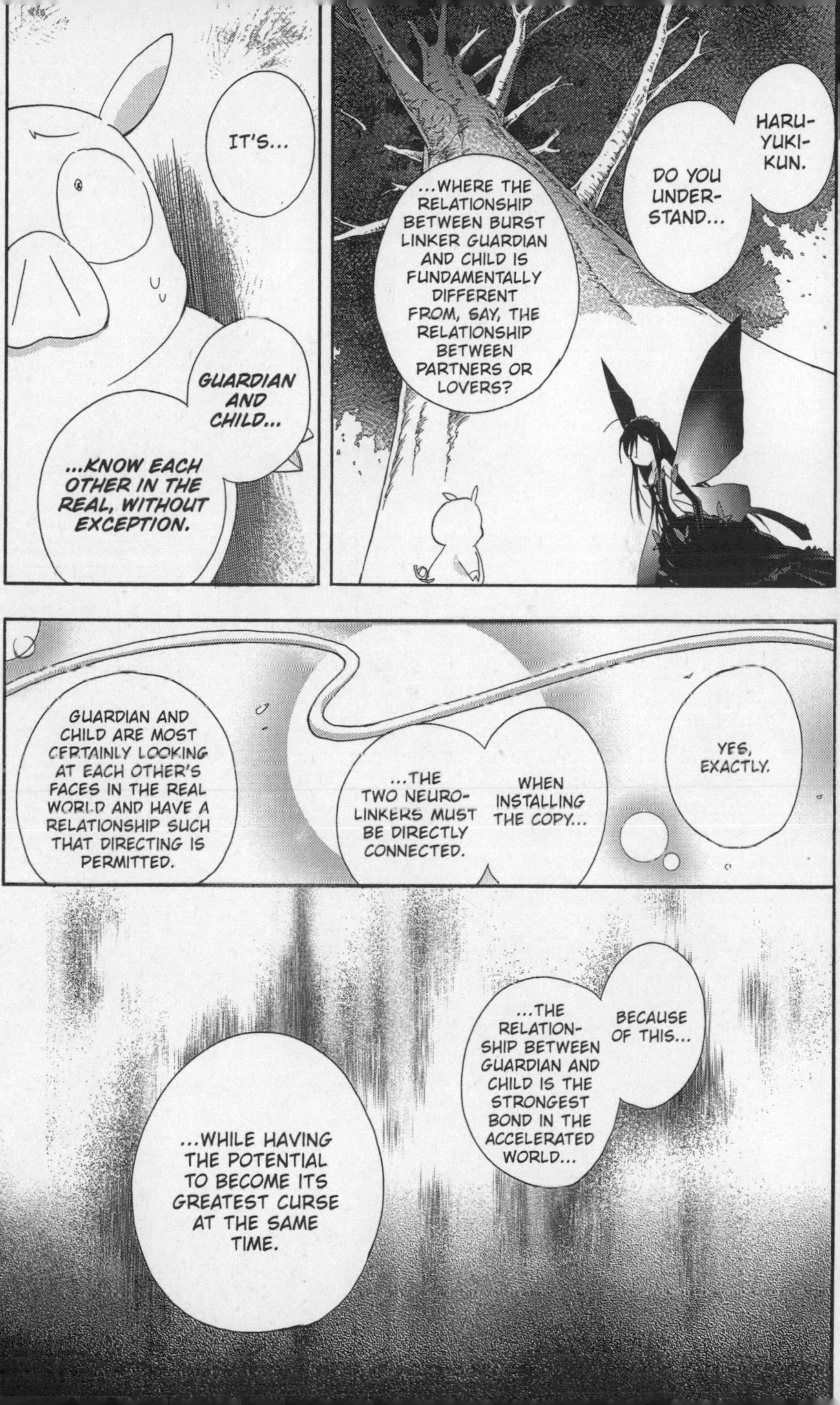
HARU-YUKI-KUN.
DO YOU UNDERSTAND...
...WHERE THE RELATIONSHIP BETWEEN BURST LINKER GUARDIAN AND CHILD IS FUNDAMENTALLY DIFFERENT FROM, SAY, THE RELATIONSHIP BETWEEN PARTNERS OR LOVERS?
IT'S...
GUARDIAN AND CHILD...
...KNOW EACH OTHER IN THE REAL, WITHOUT EXCEPTION.
YES, EXACTLY.
WHEN INSTALLING THE COPY...
...THE TWO NEURO-LINKERS MUST BE DIRECTLY CONNECTED.
GUARDIAN AND CHILD ARE MOST CERTAINLY LOOKING AT EACH OTHER'S FACES IN THE REAL WORLD AND HAVE A RELATIONSHIP SUCH THAT DIRECTING IS PERMITTED.
BECAUSE OF THIS...
...THE RELATION-SHIP BETWEEN GUARDIAN AND CHILD IS THE STRONGEST BOND IN THE ACCELERATED WORLD...
...WHILE HAVING THE POTENTIAL TO BECOME ITS GREATEST CURSE AT THE SAME TIME.

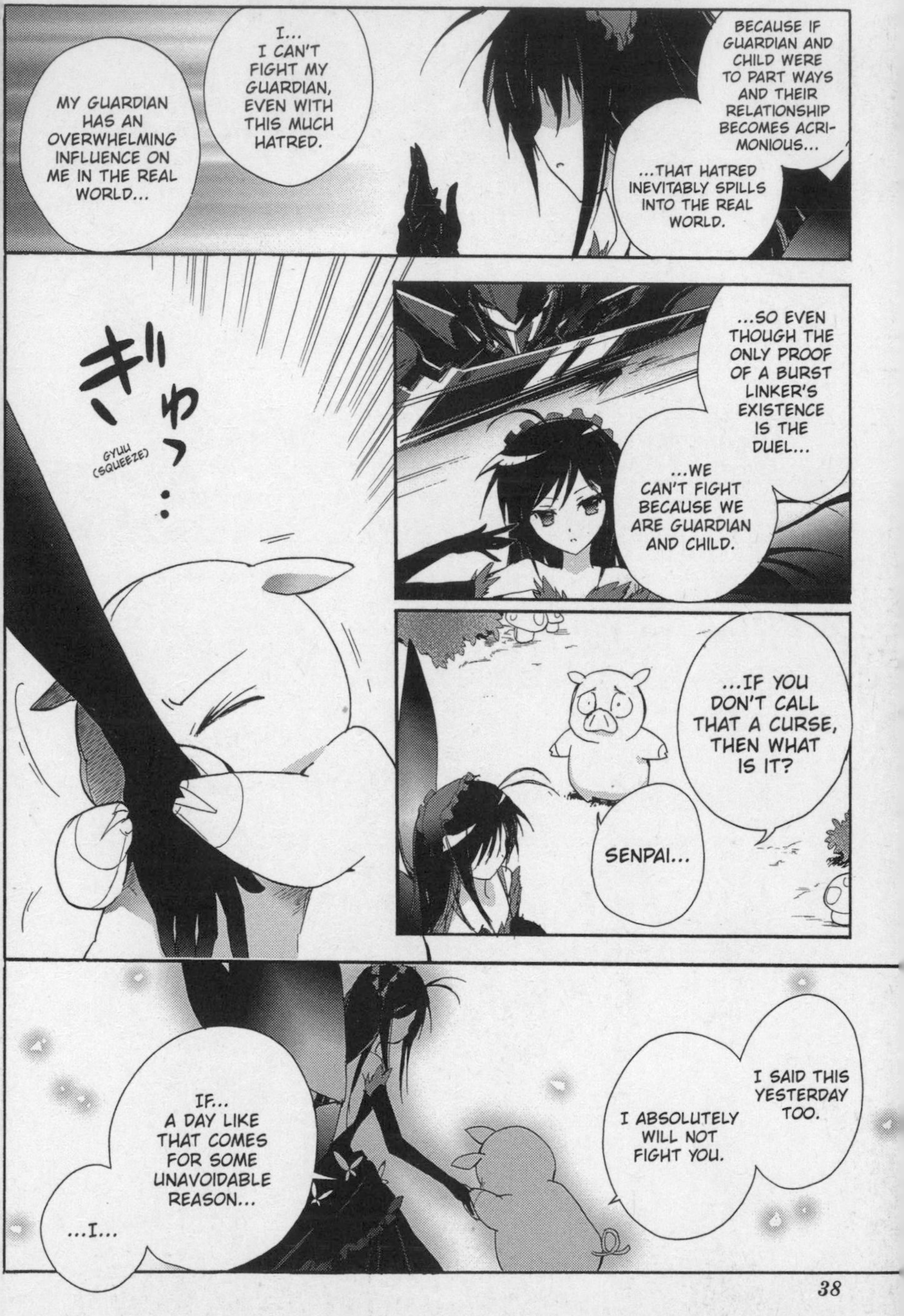
BECAUSE IF GUARDIAN AND CHILD WERE TO PART WAYS AND THEIR RELATIONSHIP BECOMES ACRI-MONIOUS...
...THAT HATRED INEVITABLY SPILLS INTO THE REAL WORLD.
I... I CAN'T FIGHT MY GUARDIAN, EVEN WITH THIS MUCH HATRED.
MY GUARDIAN HAS AN OVERWHELMING INFLUENCE ON ME IN THE REAL WORLD...
...SO EVEN THOUGH THE ONLY PROOF OF A BURST LINKER'S EXISTENCE IS THE DUEL...
...WE CAN'T FIGHT BECAUSE WE ARE GUARDIAN AND CHILD.
...IF YOU DON'T CALL THAT A CURSE, THEN WHAT IS IT?
SENPAI...
ぎゅっ
GYUU (SQUEEZE)
I SAID THIS YESTERDAY TOO.
I ABSOLUTELY WILL NOT FIGHT YOU.
IF... A DAY LIKE THAT COMES FOR SOME UNAVOIDABLE REASON...
...I...

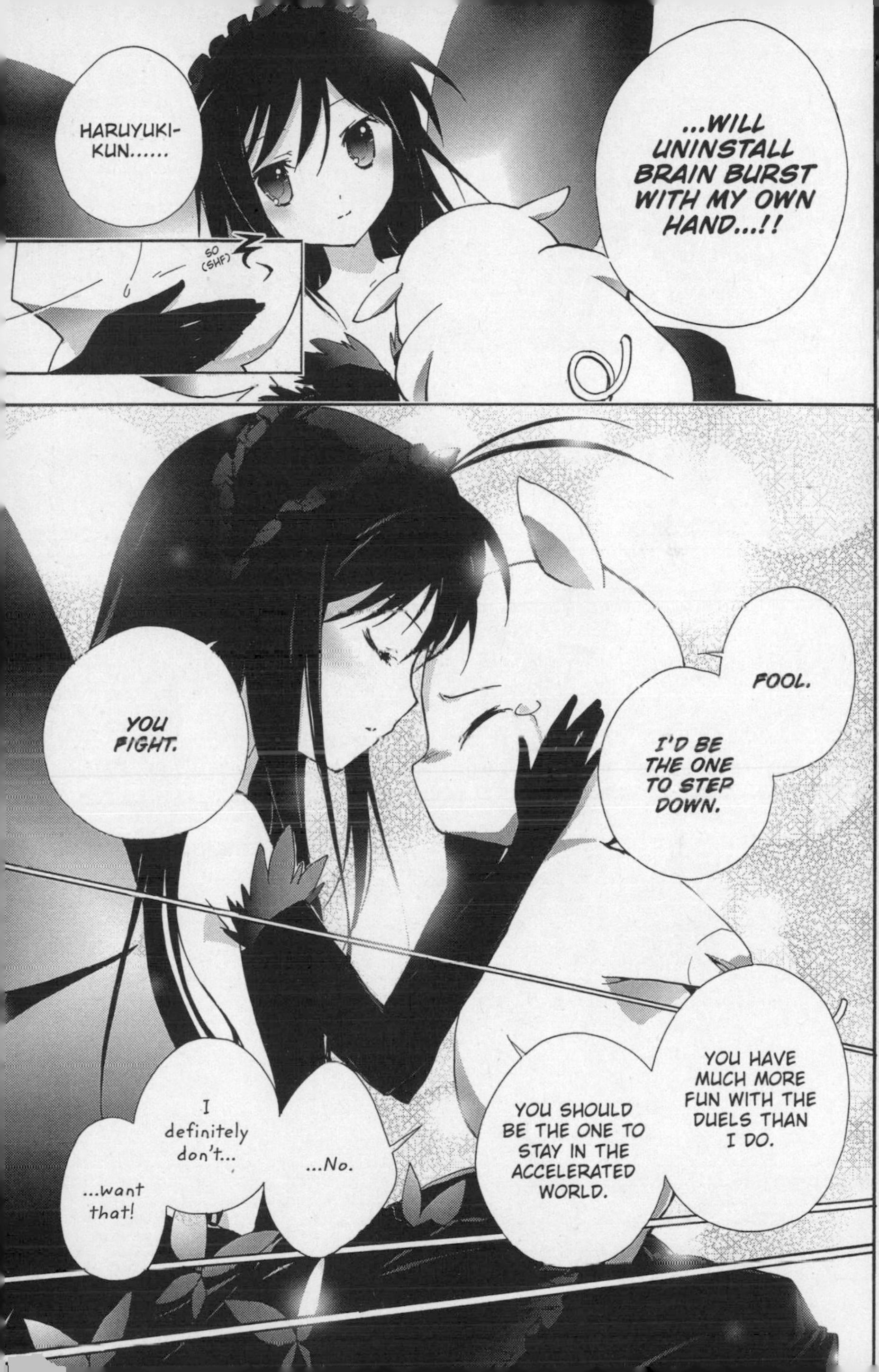
...WILL UNINSTALL BRAIN BURST WITH MY OWN HAND...!!
HARUYUKI-KUN......
SO (SHF)
FOOL.
I'D BE THE ONE TO STEP DOWN.
YOU FIGHT.
YOU HAVE MUCH MORE FUN WITH THE DUELS THAN I DO.
YOU SHOULD BE THE ONE TO STAY IN THE ACCELERATED WORLD.
...No.
I definitely don't...
...want that!

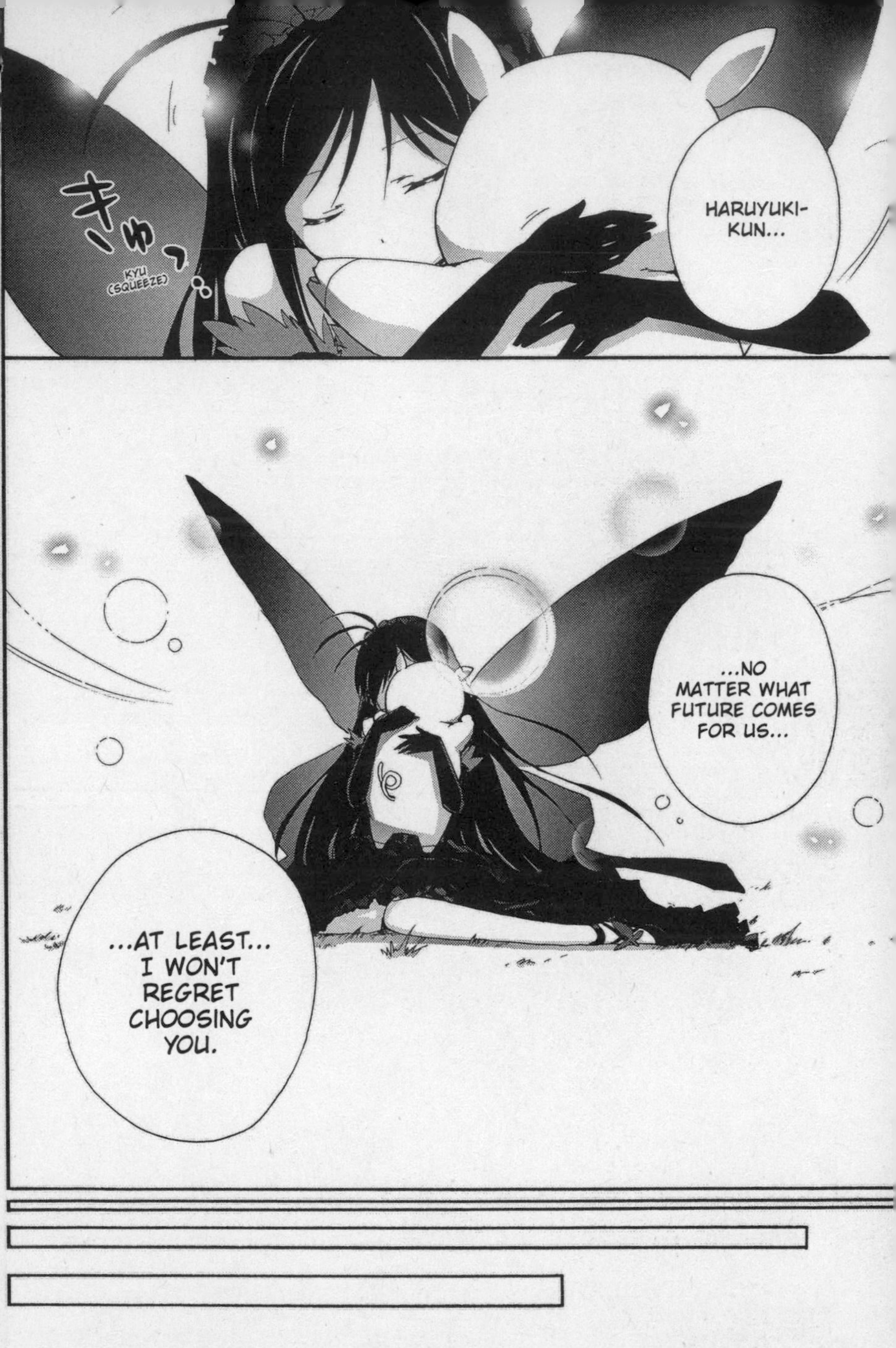
HARUYUKI-KUN...
きゅっ
KYU (SQUEEZE)
...NO MATTER WHAT FUTURE COMES FOR US...
...AT LEAST... I WON'T REGRET CHOOSING YOU.

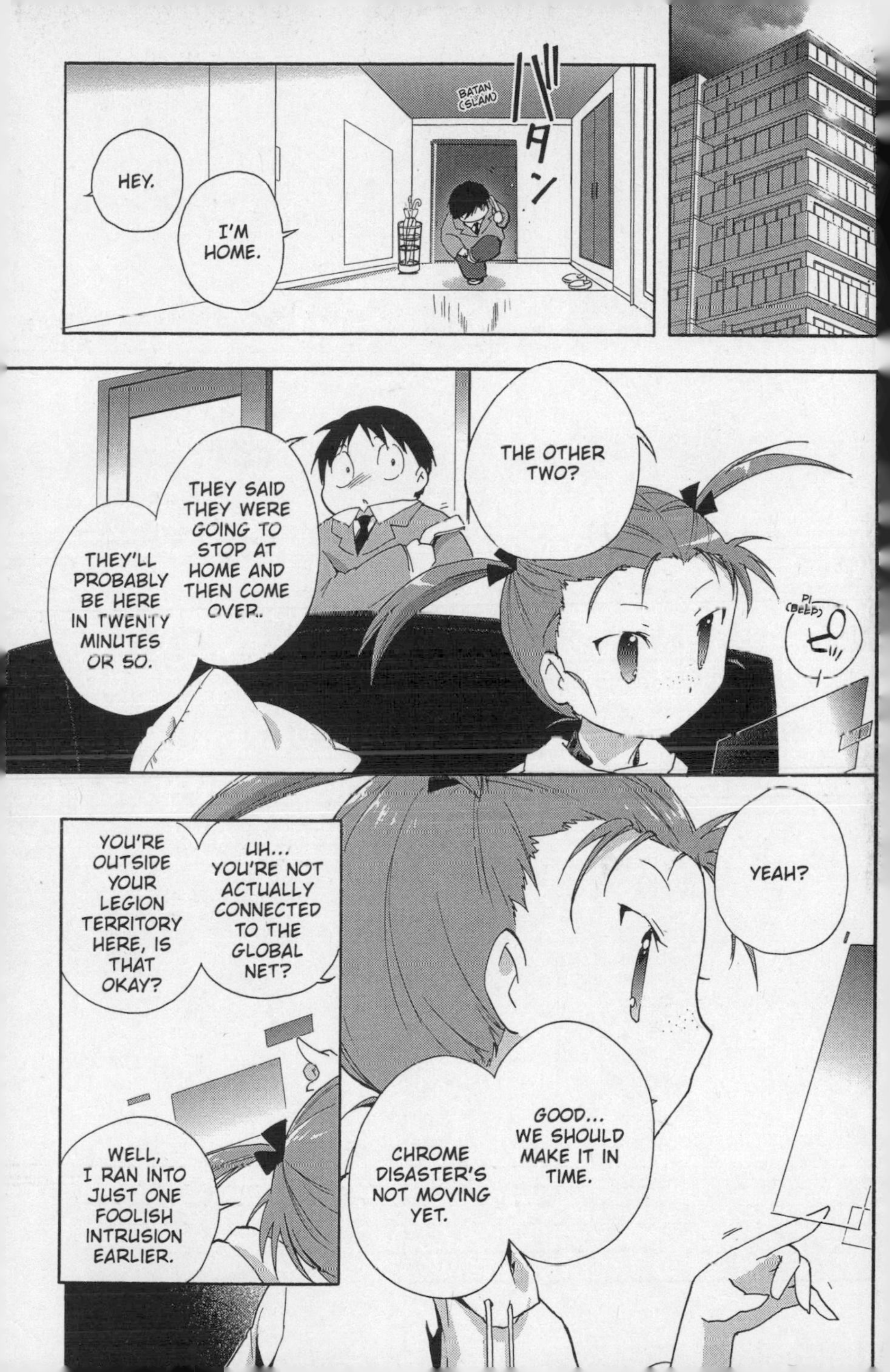
BATAN (SLAM)
HEY.
I'M HOME.
PI (BEEP)
THE OTHER TWO?
THEY SAID THEY WERE GOING TO STOP AT HOME AND THEN COME OVER.
THEY'LL PROBABLY BE HERE IN TWENTY MINUTES OR SO.
YEAH?
UH... YOU'RE NOT ACTUALLY CONNECTED TO THE GLOBAL NET?
YOU'RE OUTSIDE YOUR LEGION TERRITORY HERE, IS THAT OKAY?
GOOD... WE SHOULD MAKE IT IN TIME.
CHROME DISASTER'S NOT MOVING YET.
WELL, I RAN INTO JUST ONE FOOLISH INTRUSION EARLIER.

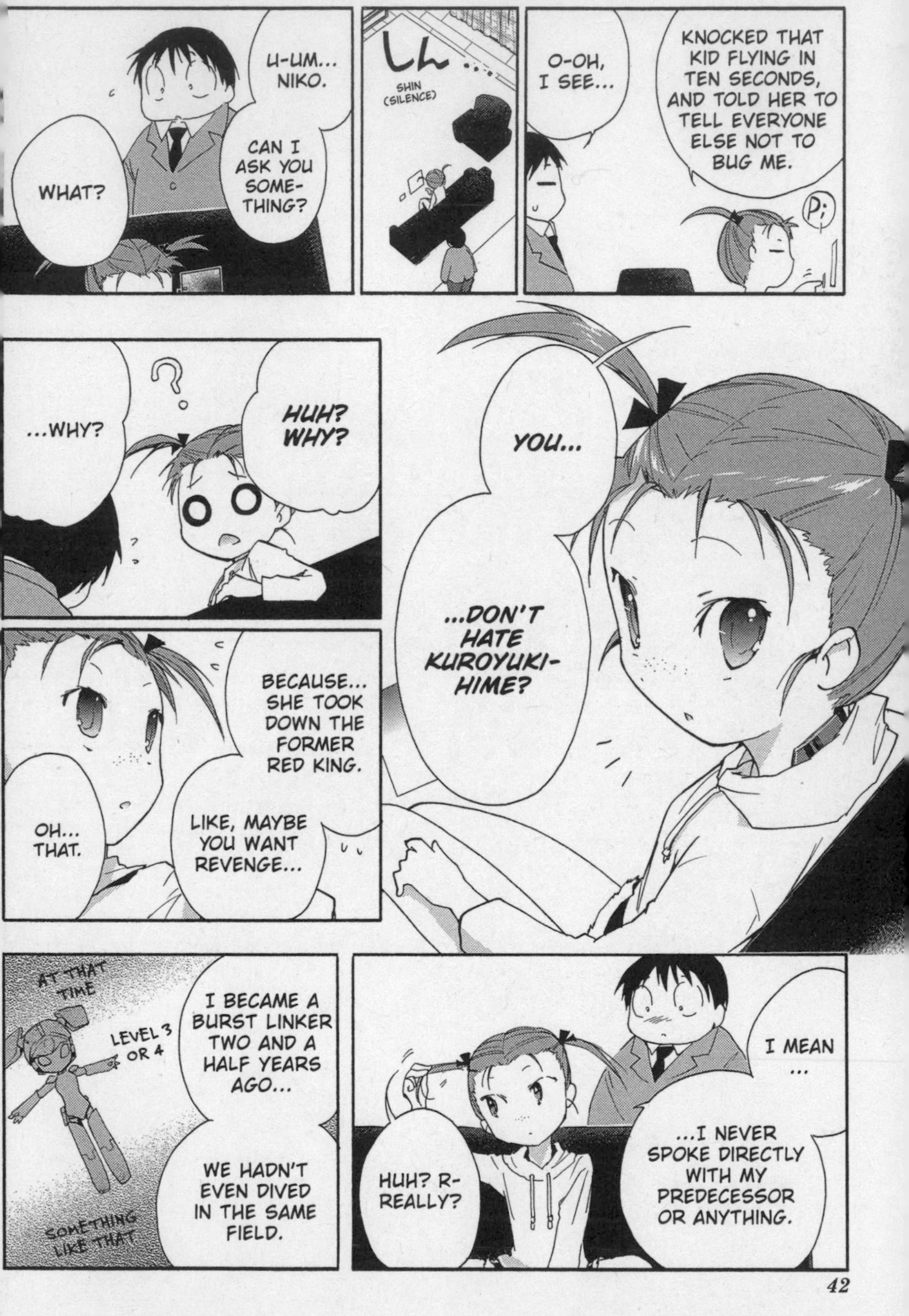
KNOCKED THAT KID FLYING IN TEN SECONDS, AND TOLD HER TO TELL EVERYONE ELSE NOT TO BUG ME.
Pi
O-OH, I SEE...
しん
SHIN (SILENCE)
U-UM... NIKO.
CAN I ASK YOU SOMETHING?
WHAT?
YOU...
...DON'T HATE KUROYUKI-HIME?
HUH? WHY?
...WHY?
BECAUSE... SHE TOOK DOWN THE FORMER RED KING.
LIKE, MAYBE YOU WANT REVENGE...
OH... THAT.
I MEAN ...
...I NEVER SPOKE DIRECTLY WITH MY PREDECESSOR OR ANYTHING.
HUH? R-REALLY?
I BECAME A BURST LINKER TWO AND A HALF YEARS AGO...
WE HADN'T EVEN DIVED IN THE SAME FIELD.
AT THAT TIME
LEVEL 3 OR 4
SOMETHING LIKE THAT

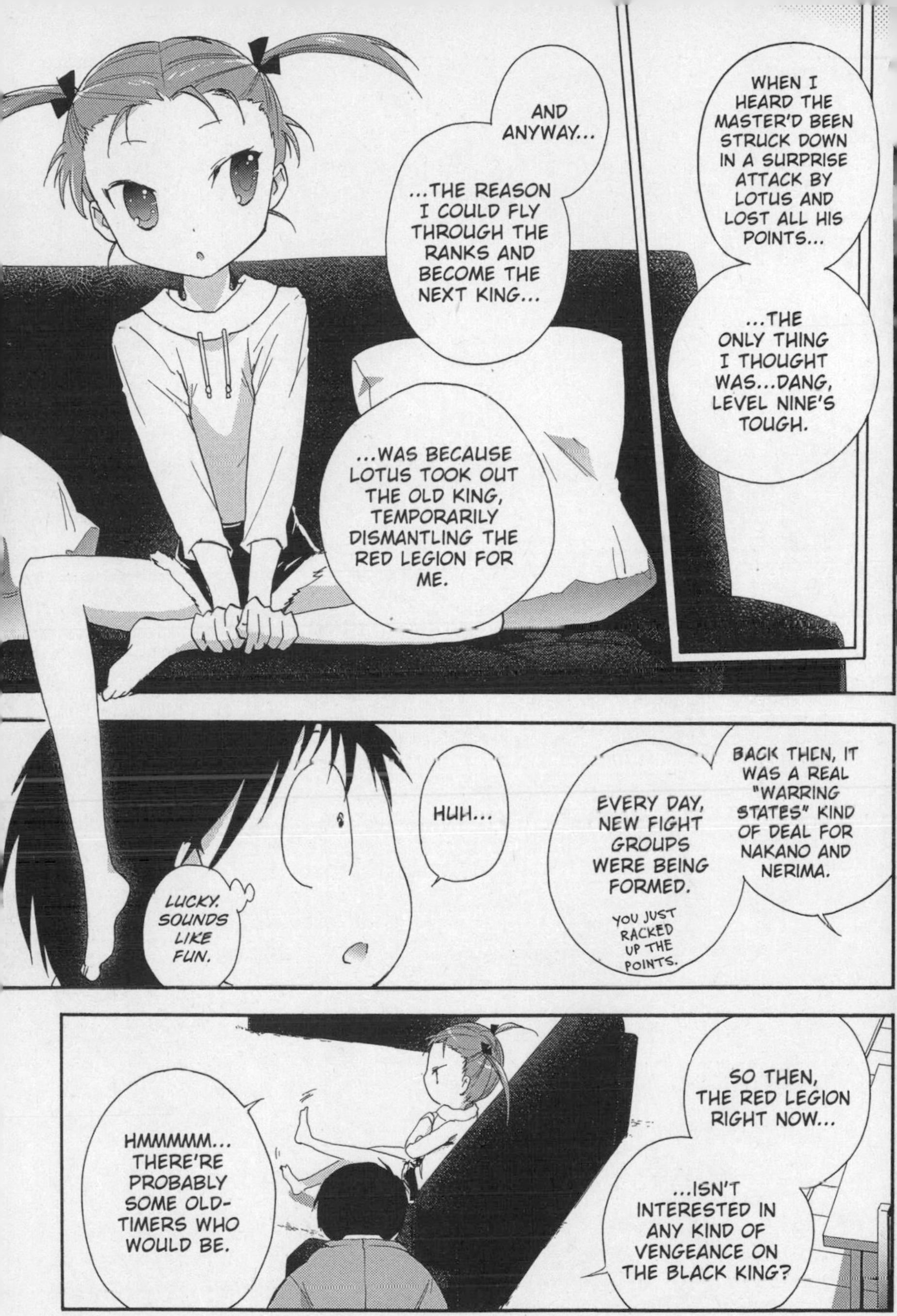
WHEN I HEARD THE MASTER'D BEEN STRUCK DOWN IN A SURPRISE ATTACK BY LOTUS AND LOST ALL HIS POINTS...
...THE ONLY THING I THOUGHT WAS...DANG, LEVEL NINE'S TOUGH.
AND ANYWAY...
...THE REASON I COULD FLY THROUGH THE RANKS AND BECOME THE NEXT KING...
...WAS BECAUSE LOTUS TOOK OUT THE OLD KING, TEMPORARILY DISMANTLING THE RED LEGION FOR ME.
BACK THEN, IT WAS A REAL "WARRING STATES" KIND OF DEAL FOR NAKANO AND NERIMA.
EVERY DAY, NEW FIGHT GROUPS WERE BEING FORMED.
YOU JUST RACKED UP THE POINTS.
HUH...
LUCKY. SOUNDS LIKE FUN.
SO THEN, THE RED LEGION RIGHT NOW...
...ISN'T INTERESTED IN ANY KIND OF VENGEANCE ON THE BLACK KING?
HMMMMM... THERE'RE PROBABLY SOME OLD-TIMERS WHO WOULD BE.

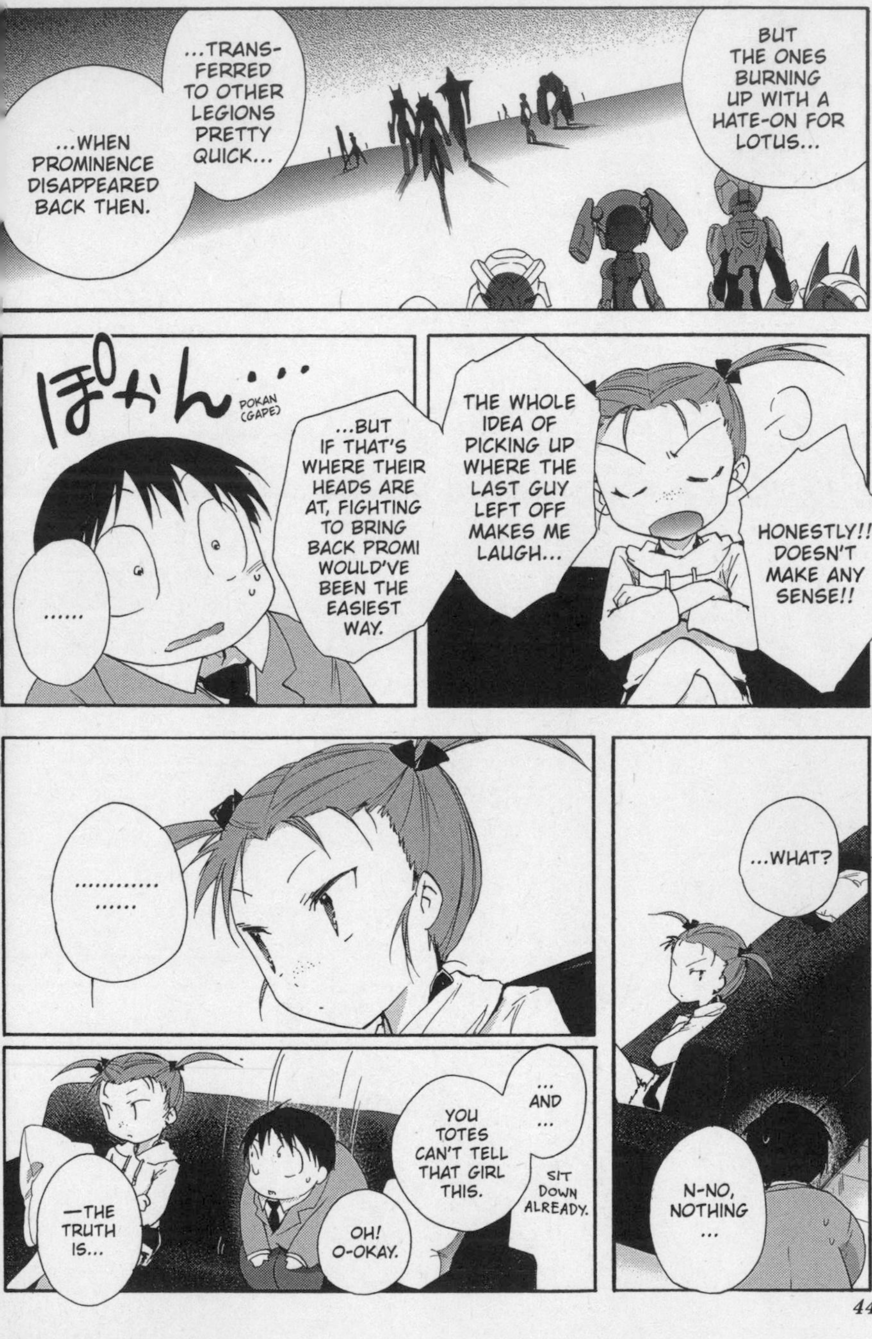
BUT THE ONES BURNING UP WITH A HATE-ON FOR LOTUS...
...TRANS-FERRED TO OTHER LEGIONS PRETTY QUICK...
...WHEN PROMINENCE DISAPPEARED BACK THEN.
HONESTLY!! DOESN'T MAKE ANY SENSE!!
THE WHOLE IDEA OF PICKING UP WHERE THE LAST GUY LEFT OFF MAKES ME LAUGH...
...BUT IF THAT'S WHERE THEIR HEADS ARE AT, FIGHTING TO BRING BACK PROMI WOULD'VE BEEN THE EASIEST WAY.
ぽかん…
POKAN (GAPE)
......
...WHAT?
N-NO, NOTHING ...
....
... AND ...
YOU TOTES CAN'T TELL THAT GIRL THIS.
SIT DOWN ALREADY.
OH! O-OKAY.
—THE TRUTH IS...

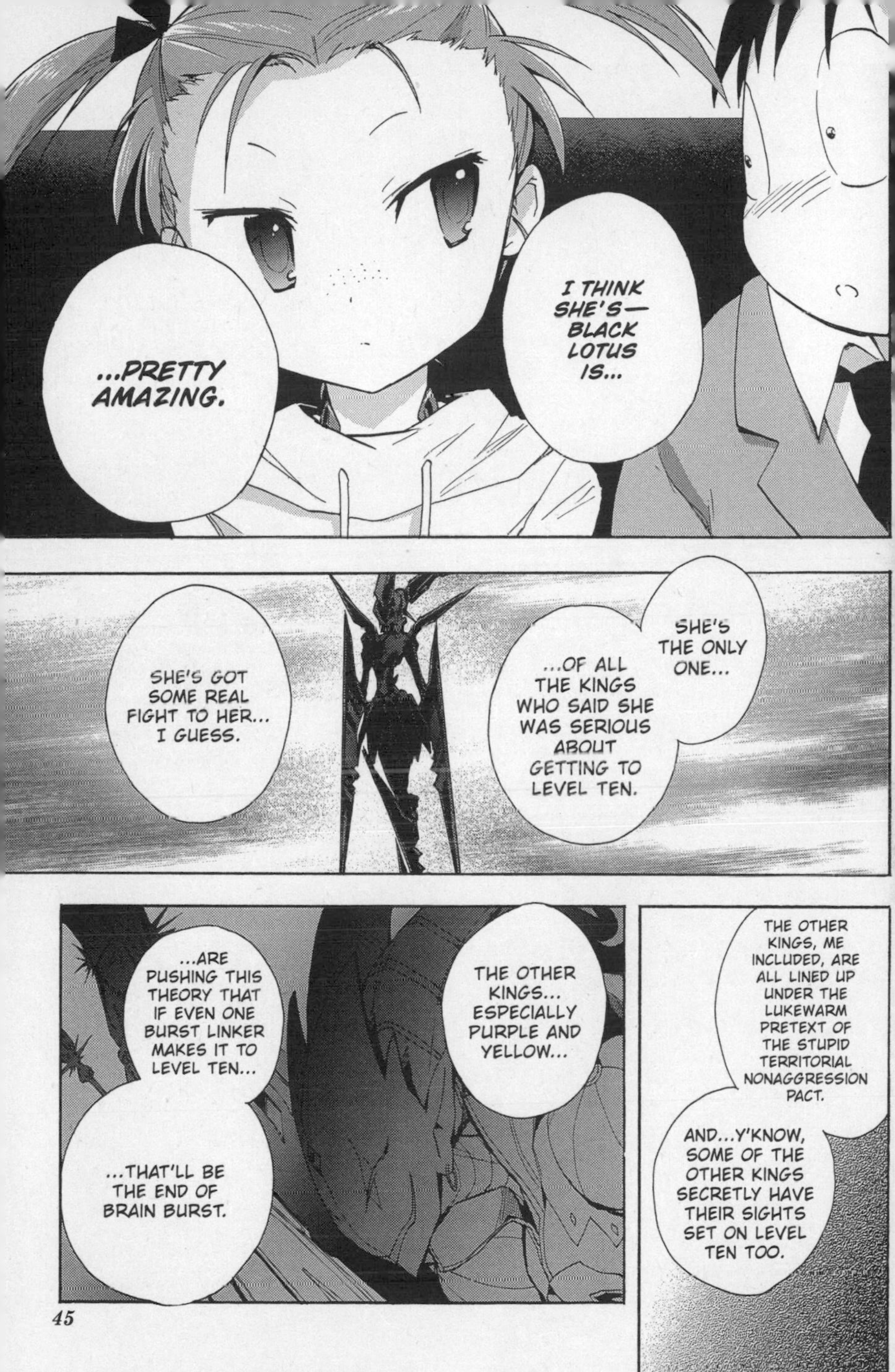
I THINK SHE'S— BLACK LOTUS IS...
...PRETTY AMAZING.
SHE'S THE ONLY ONE...
...OF ALL THE KINGS WHO SAID SHE WAS SERIOUS ABOUT GETTING TO LEVEL TEN.
SHE'S GOT SOME REAL FIGHT TO HER... I GUESS.
THE OTHER KINGS, ME INCLUDED, ARE ALL LINED UP UNDER THE LUKEWARM PRETEXT OF THE STUPID TERRITORIAL NONAGGRESSION PACT.
AND...Y'KNOW, SOME OF THE OTHER KINGS SECRETLY HAVE THEIR SIGHTS SET ON LEVEL TEN TOO.
THE OTHER KINGS... ESPECIALLY PURPLE AND YELLOW...
...ARE PUSHING THIS THEORY THAT IF EVEN ONE BURST LINKER MAKES IT TO LEVEL TEN...
...THAT'LL BE THE END OF BRAIN BURST.

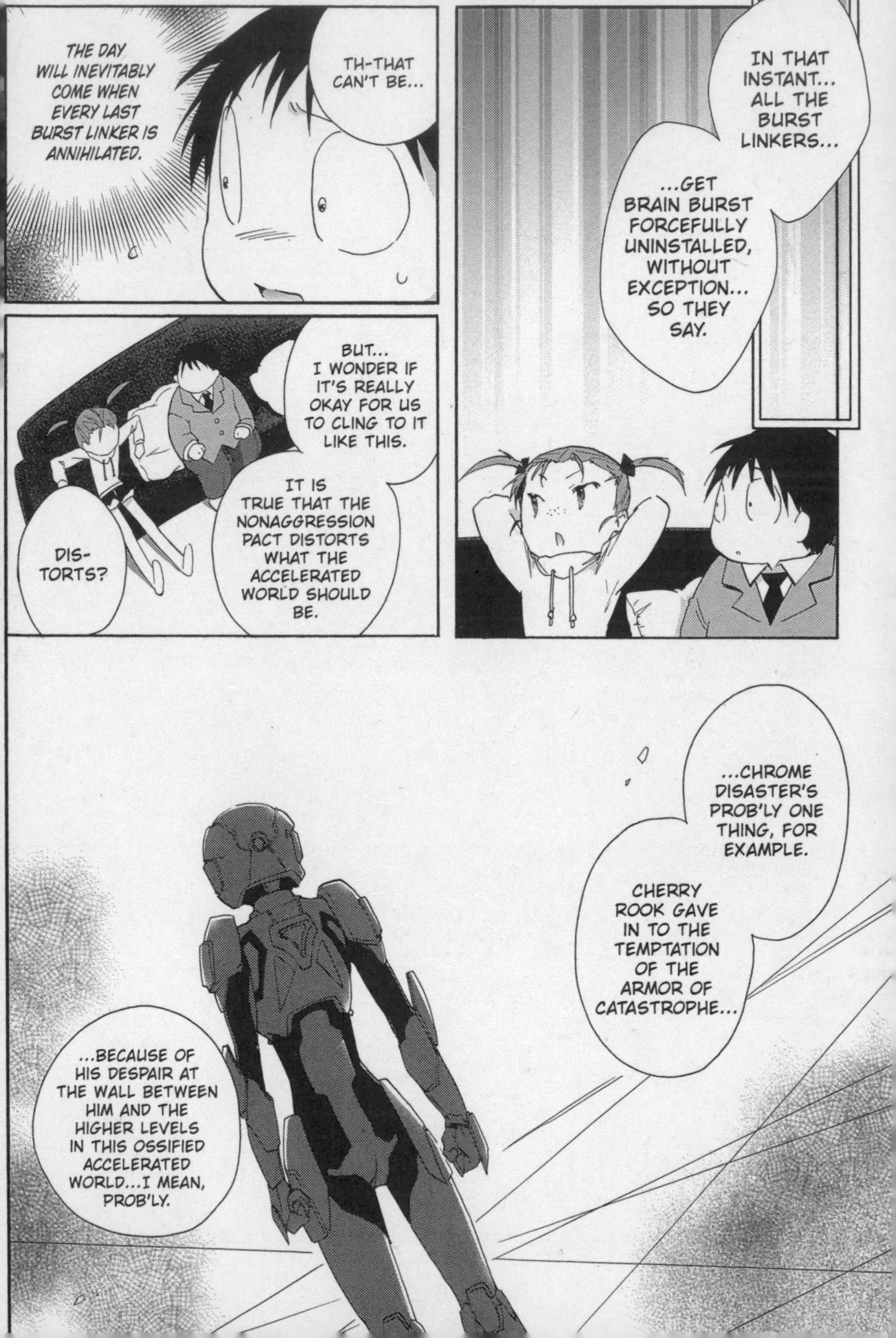
IN THAT INSTANT... ALL THE BURST LINKERS...
...GET BRAIN BURST FORCEFULLY UNINSTALLED, WITHOUT EXCEPTION... SO THEY SAY.
TH-THAT CAN'T BE...
THE DAY WILL INEVITABLY COME WHEN EVERY LAST BURST LINKER IS ANNIHILATED.
BUT... I WONDER IF IT'S REALLY OKAY FOR US TO CLING TO IT LIKE THIS.
IT IS TRUE THAT THE NONAGGRESSION PACT DISTORTS WHAT THE ACCELERATED WORLD SHOULD BE.
DIS-TORTS?
...CHROME DISASTER'S PROB'LY ONE THING, FOR EXAMPLE.
CHERRY ROOK GAVE IN TO THE TEMPTATION OF THE ARMOR OF CATASTROPHE...
...BECAUSE OF HIS DESPAIR AT THE WALL BETWEEN HIM AND THE HIGHER LEVELS IN THIS OSSIFIED ACCELERATED WORLD...I MEAN, PROB'LY.

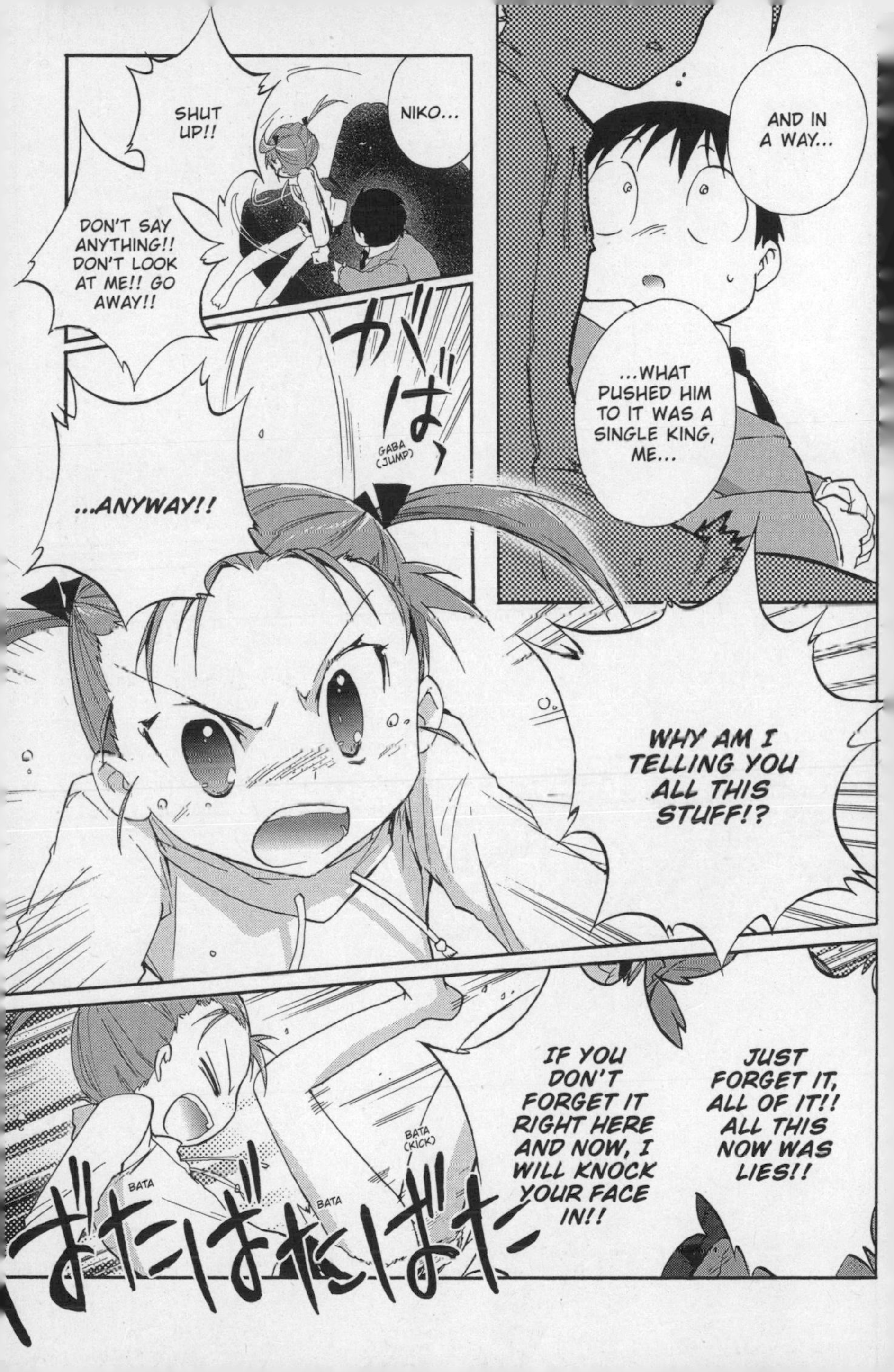

AND IN A WAY...
...WHAT PUSHED HIM TO IT WAS A SINGLE KING, ME...
NIKO...
SHUT UP!!
DON'T SAY ANYTHING!! DON'T LOOK AT ME!! GO AWAY!!
GABA (JUMP)
...ANYWAY!!
WHY AM I TELLING YOU ALL THIS STUFF!?
JUST FORGET IT, ALL OF IT!! ALL THIS NOW WAS LIES!!
IF YOU DON'T FORGET IT RIGHT HERE AND NOW, I WILL KNOCK YOUR FACE IN!!
BATA (KICK)
BATA
BATA

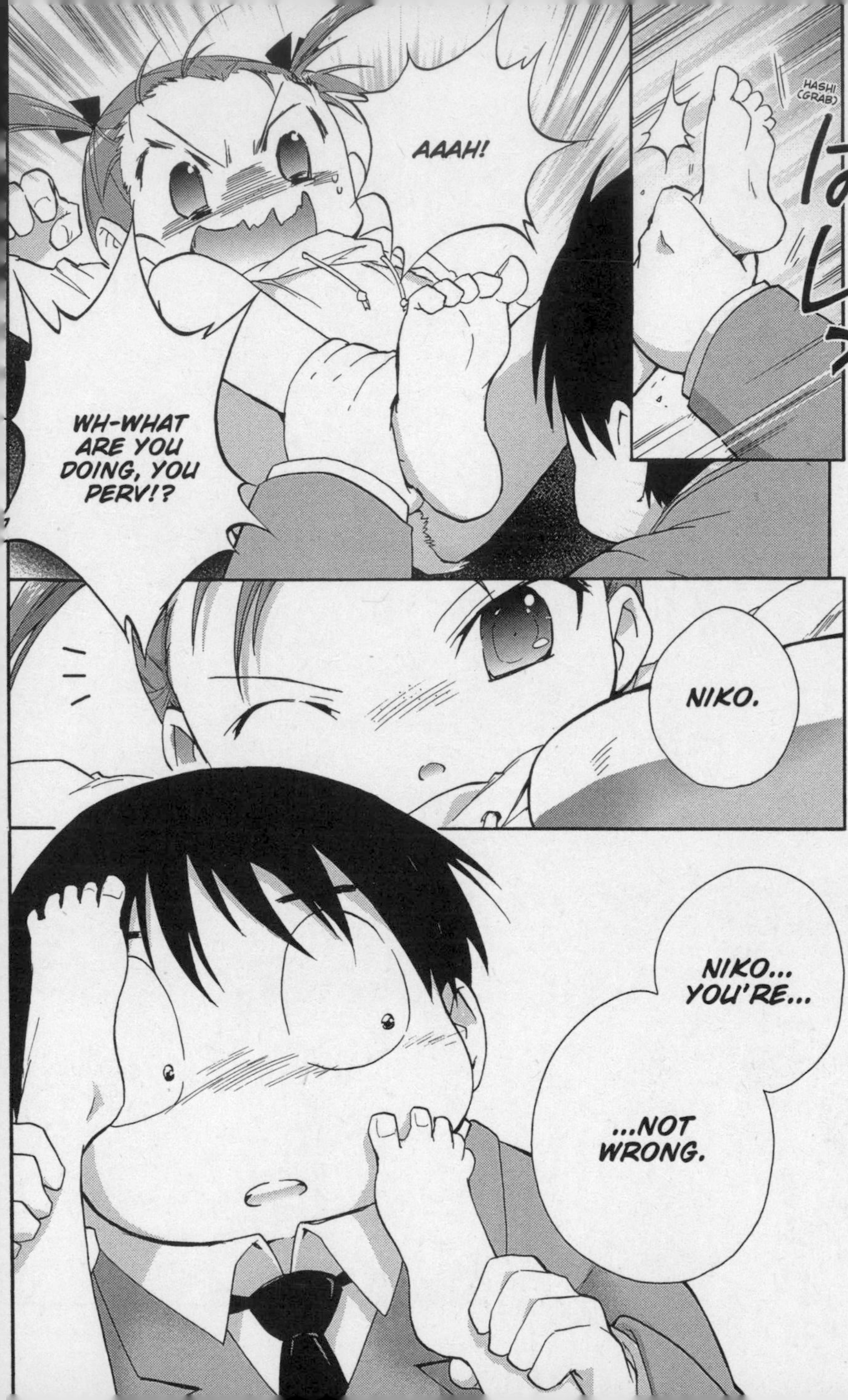
HASHI (GRAB)
はしっ
AAAH!
WH-WHAT ARE YOU DOING, YOU PERV!?
NIKO.
NIKO... YOU'RE...
...NOT WRONG.

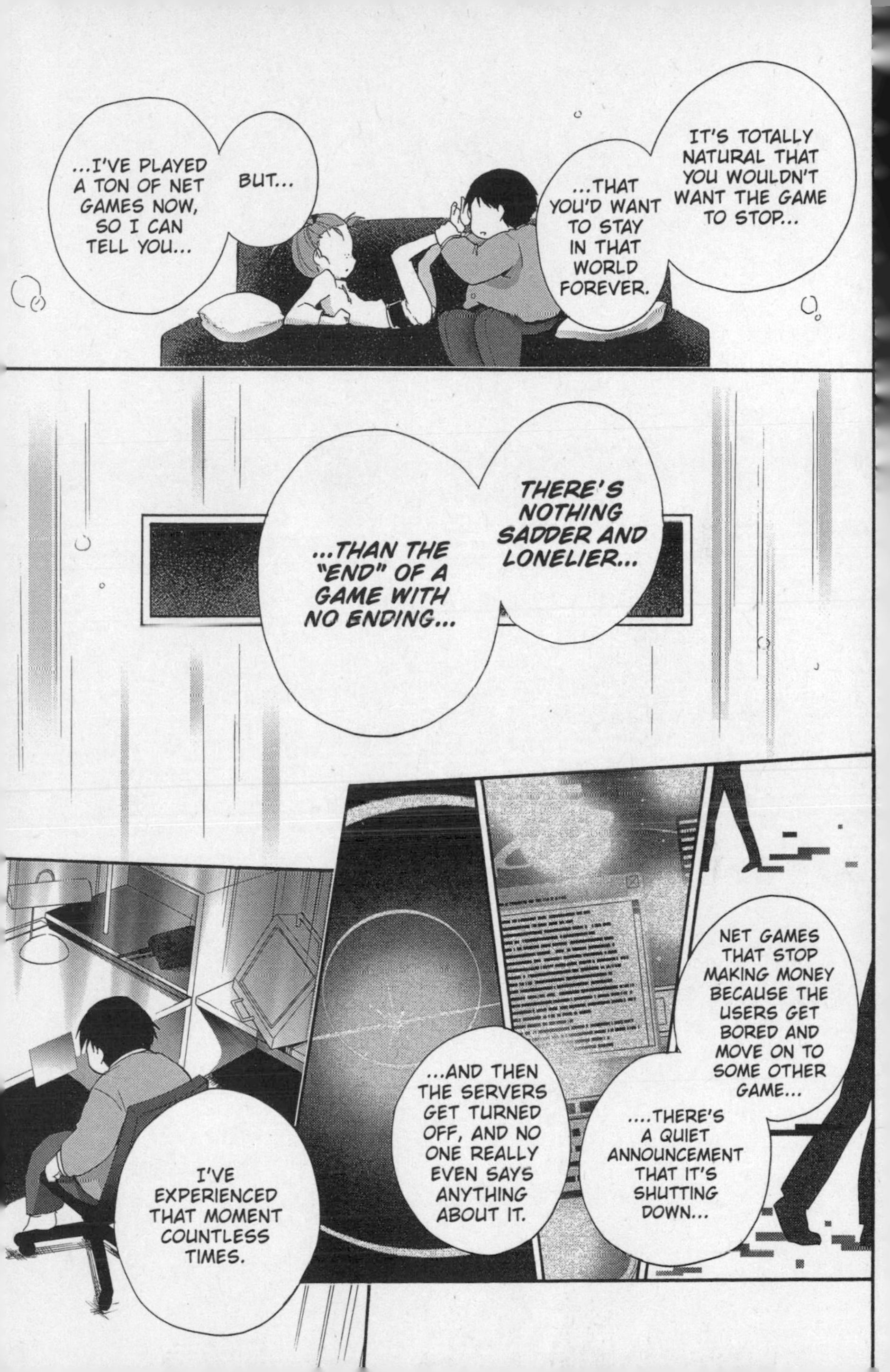
IT'S TOTALLY NATURAL THAT YOU WOULDN'T WANT THE GAME TO STOP...
...THAT YOU'D WANT TO STAY IN THAT WORLD FOREVER.
BUT...
...I'VE PLAYED A TON OF NET GAMES NOW, SO I CAN TELL YOU...
THERE'S NOTHING SADDER AND LONELIER...
...THAN THE "END" OF A GAME WITH NO ENDING...
NET GAMES THAT STOP MAKING MONEY BECAUSE THE USERS GET BORED AND MOVE ON TO SOME OTHER GAME...
....THERE'S A QUIET ANNOUNCEMENT THAT IT'S SHUTTING DOWN...
...AND THEN THE SERVERS GET TURNED OFF, AND NO ONE REALLY EVEN SAYS ANYTHING ABOUT IT.
I'VE EXPERIENCED THAT MOMENT COUNTLESS TIMES.

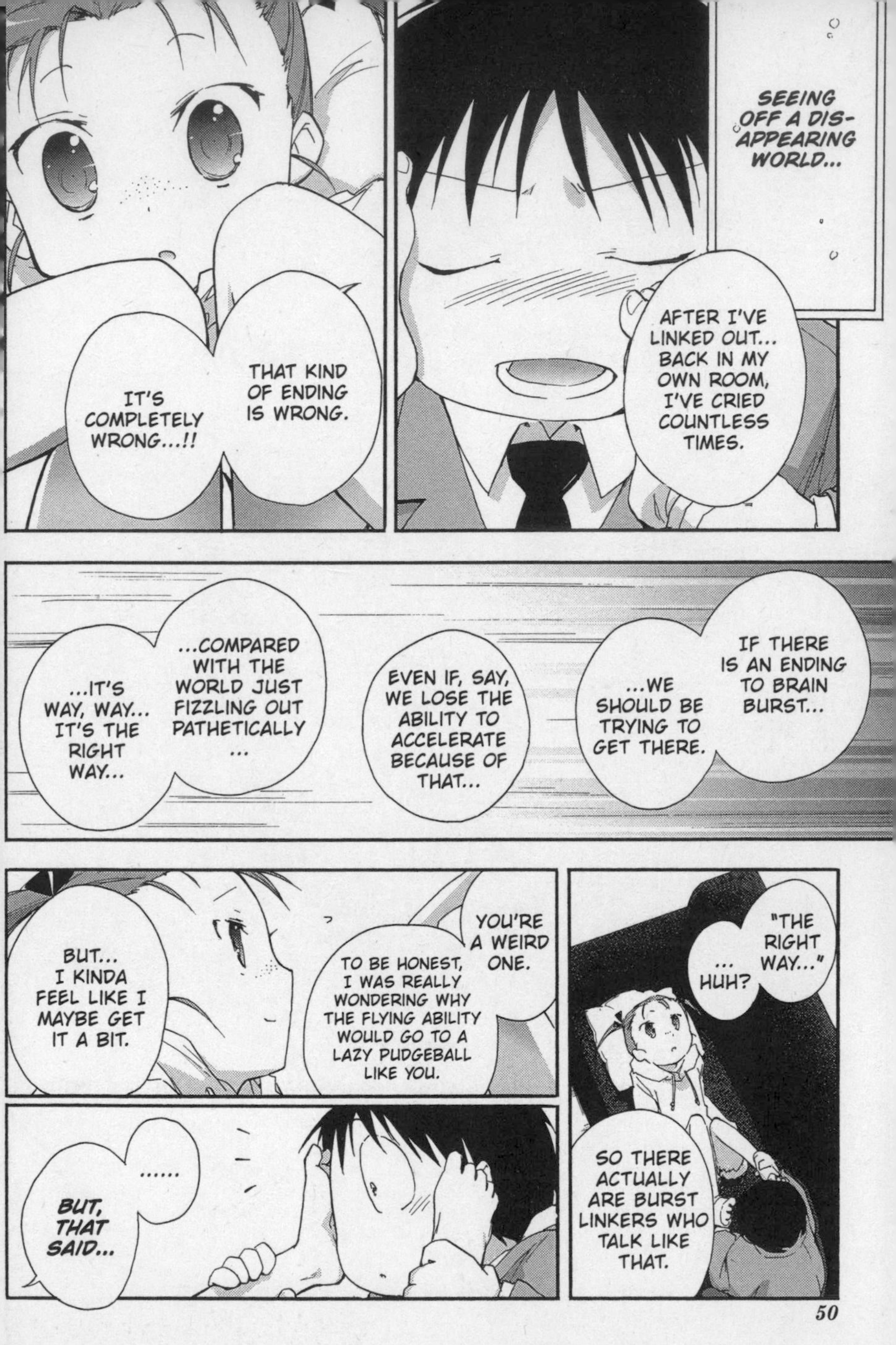
SEEING OFF A DIS-APPEARING WORLD...
AFTER I'VE LINKED OUT... BACK IN MY OWN ROOM, I'VE CRIED COUNTLESS TIMES.
THAT KIND OF ENDING IS WRONG.
IT'S COMPLETELY WRONG...!!
IF THERE IS AN ENDING TO BRAIN BURST...
...WE SHOULD BE TRYING TO GET THERE.
EVEN IF, SAY, WE LOSE THE ABILITY TO ACCELERATE BECAUSE OF THAT...
...COMPARED WITH THE WORLD JUST FIZZLING OUT PATHETICALLY ...
...IT'S WAY, WAY... IT'S THE RIGHT WAY...
"THE RIGHT WAY..."
... HUH?
SO THERE ACTUALLY ARE BURST LINKERS WHO TALK LIKE THAT.
YOU'RE A WEIRD ONE.
TO BE HONEST, I WAS REALLY WONDERING WHY THE FLYING ABILITY WOULD GO TO A LAZY PUDGEBALL LIKE YOU.
BUT... I KINDA FEEL LIKE I MAYBE GET IT A BIT.
......
BUT, THAT SAID...

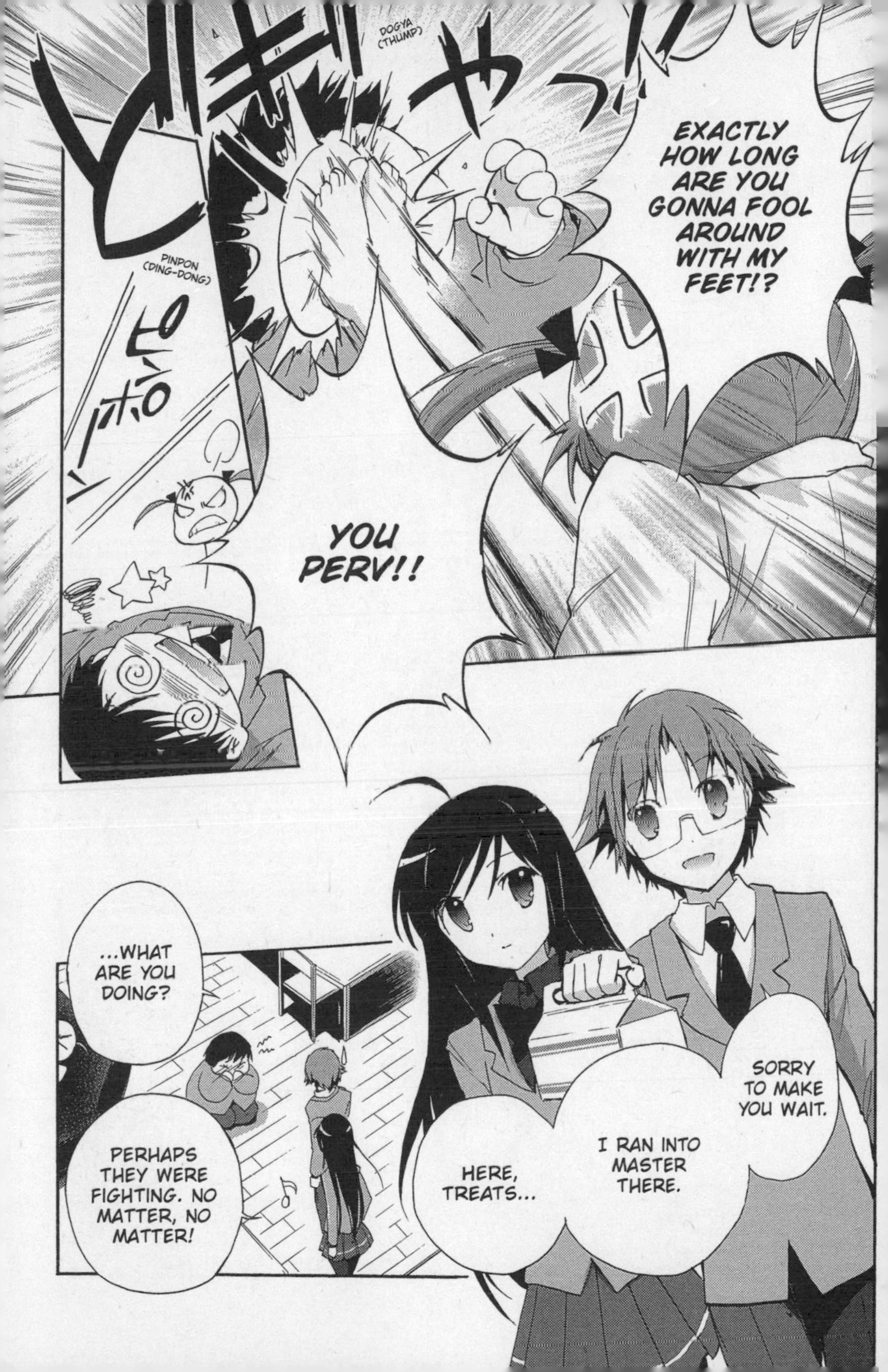
DOGYA (THUMP)
EXACTLY HOW LONG ARE YOU GONNA FOOL AROUND WITH MY FEET!?
YOU PERV!!
PINPON (DING-DONG)
SORRY TO MAKE YOU WAIT.
I RAN INTO MASTER THERE.
HERE, TREATS...
...WHAT ARE YOU DOING?
PERHAPS THEY WERE FIGHTING. NO MATTER, NO MATTER!

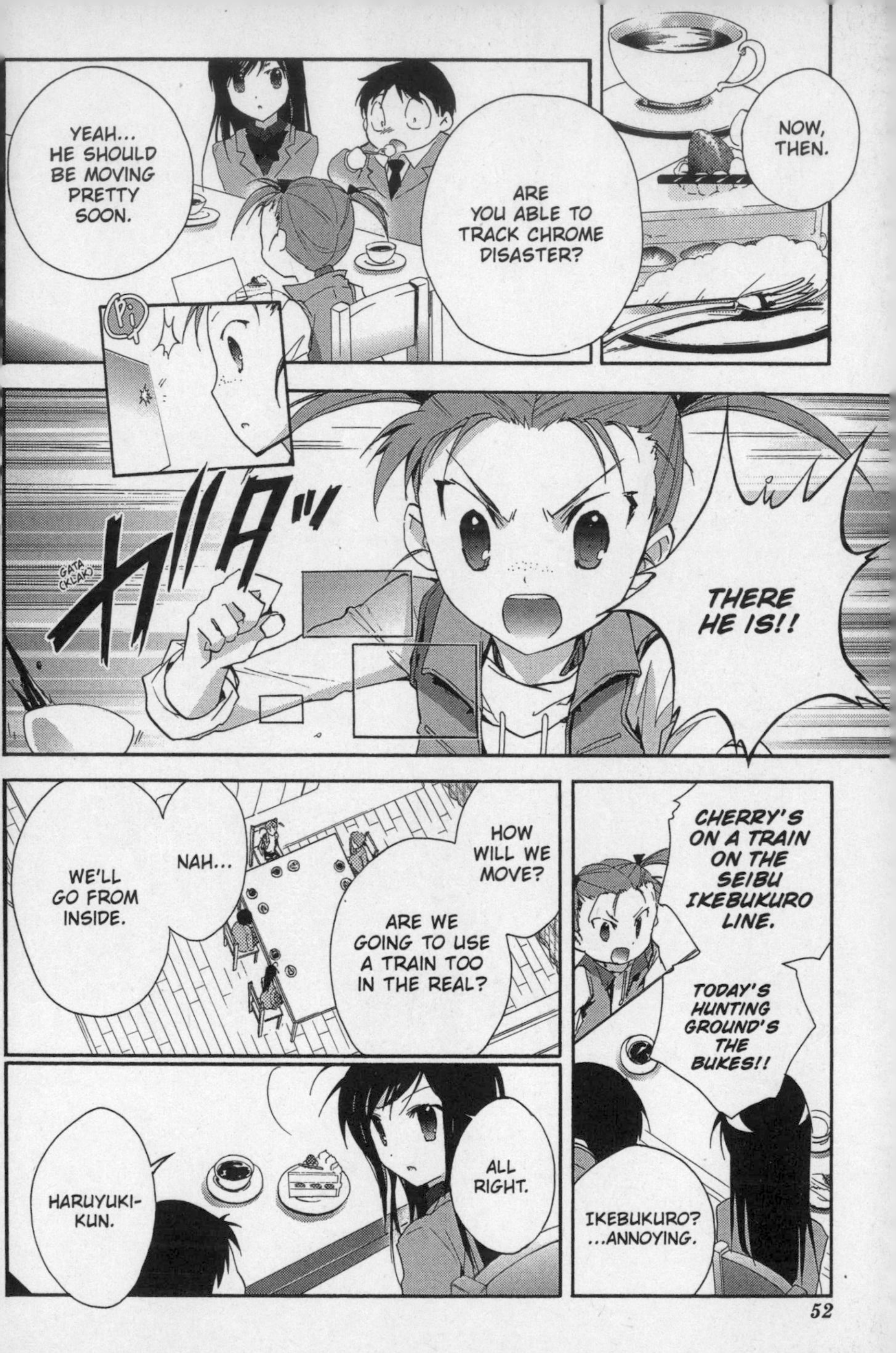
NOW, THEN.
ARE YOU ABLE TO TRACK CHROME DISASTER?
YEAH... HE SHOULD BE MOVING PRETTY SOON.
Pi
GATA (KLAK)
THERE HE IS!!
CHERRY'S ON A TRAIN ON THE SEIBU IKEBUKURO LINE.
HOW WILL WE MOVE?
ARE WE GOING TO USE A TRAIN TOO IN THE REAL?
NAH...
WE'LL GO FROM INSIDE.
TODAY'S HUNTING GROUND'S THE BUKES!!
IKEBUKURO? ...ANNOYING.
ALL RIGHT.
HARUYUKI-KUN.

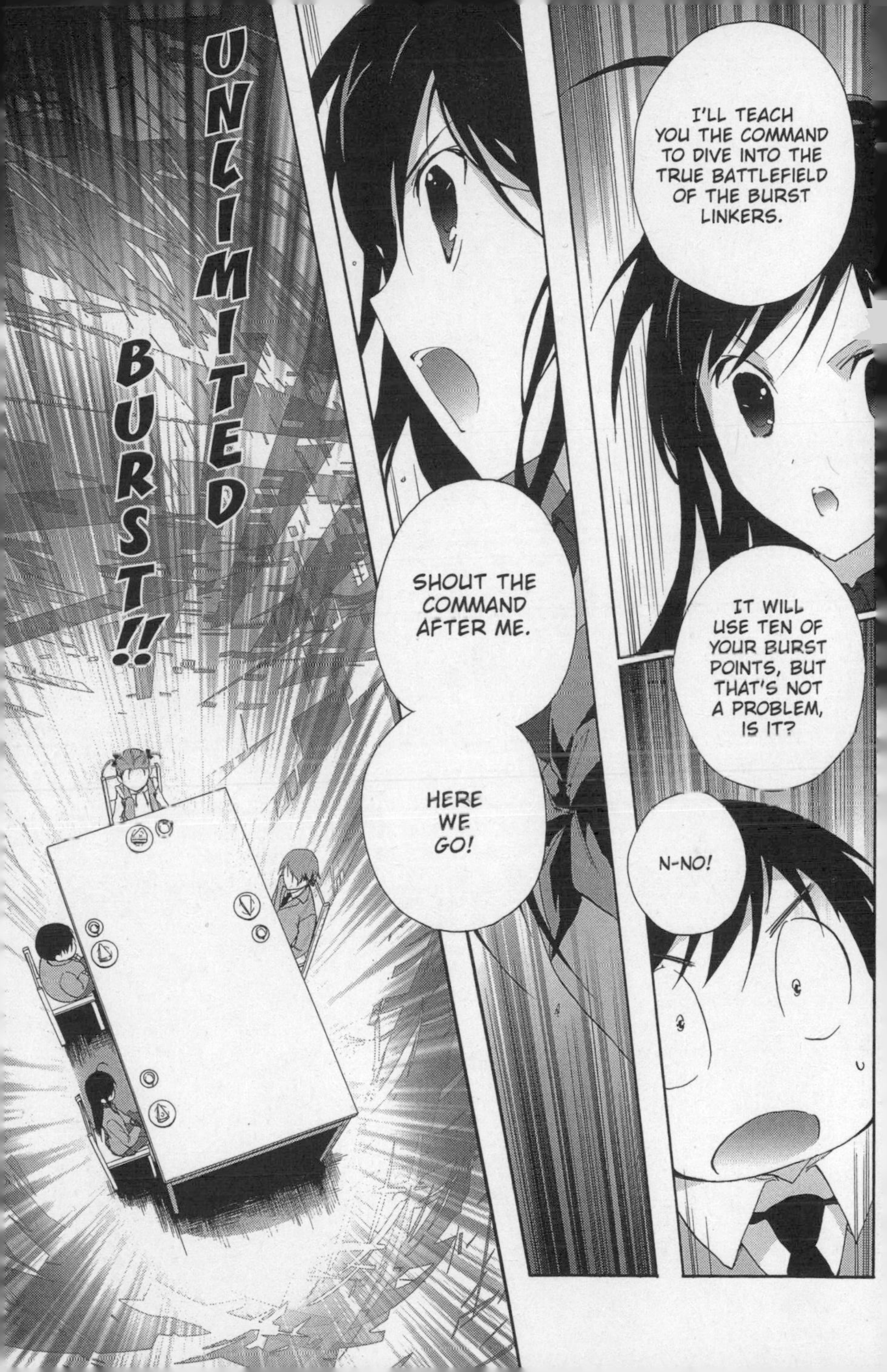
I'LL TEACH YOU THE COMMAND TO DIVE INTO THE TRUE BATTLEFIELD OF THE BURST LINKERS.
IT WILL USE TEN OF YOUR BURST POINTS, BUT THAT'S NOT A PROBLEM, IS IT?
N-NO!
SHOUT THE COMMAND AFTER ME.
HERE WE GO!
UNLIMITED BURST!!

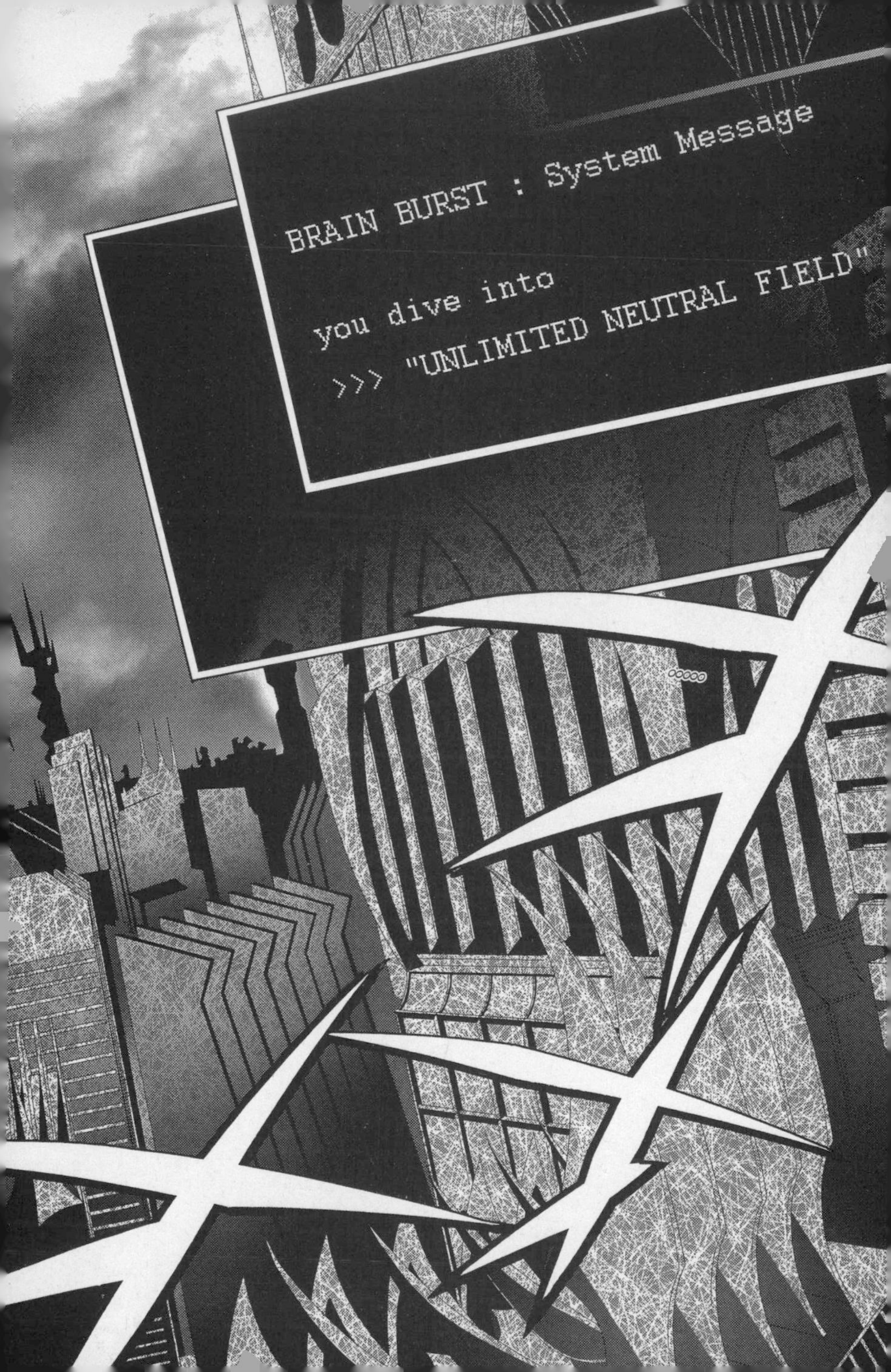

BRAIN BURST : System Message
you dive into
>>> "UNLIMITED NEUTRAL FIELD"

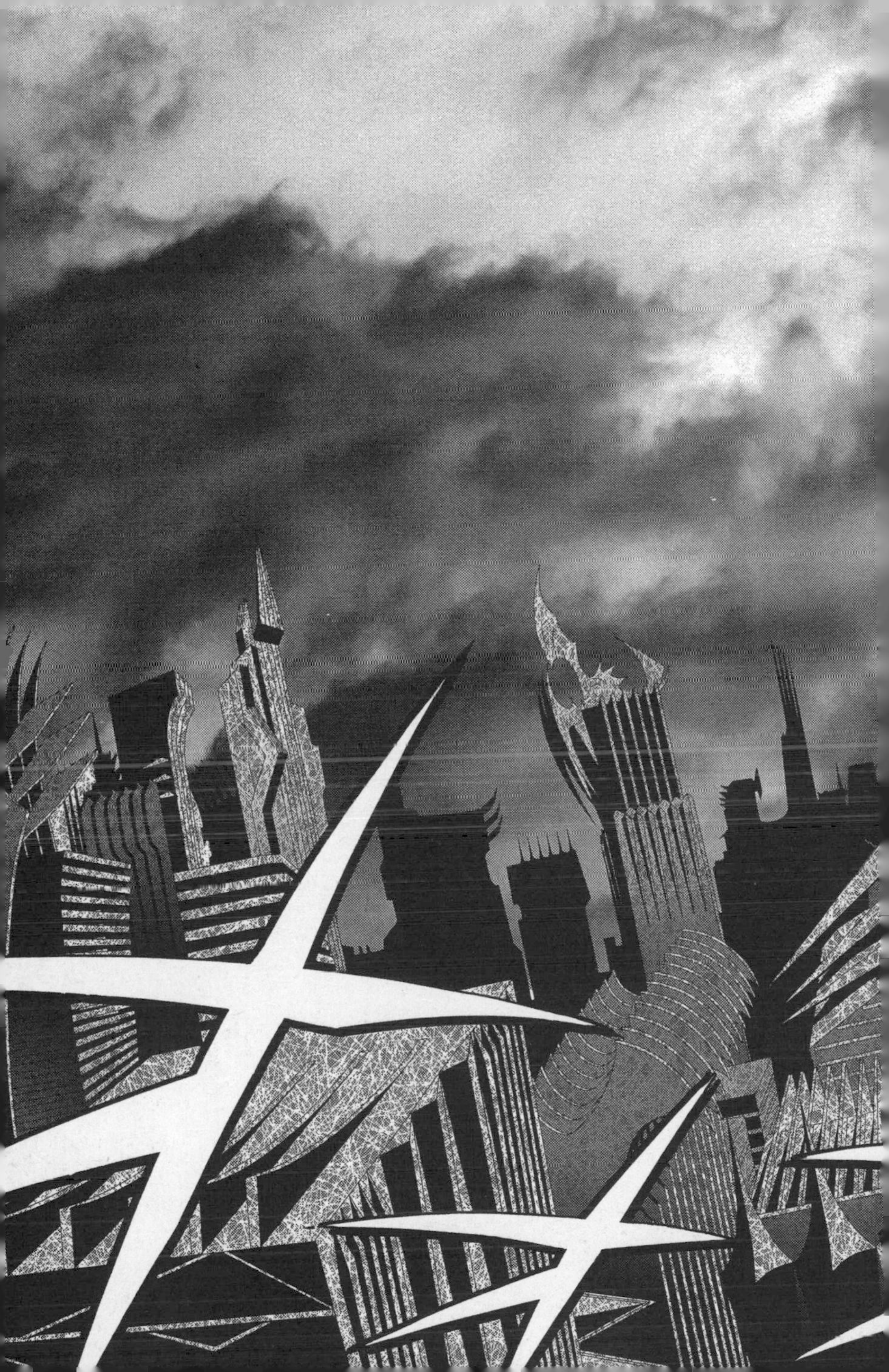

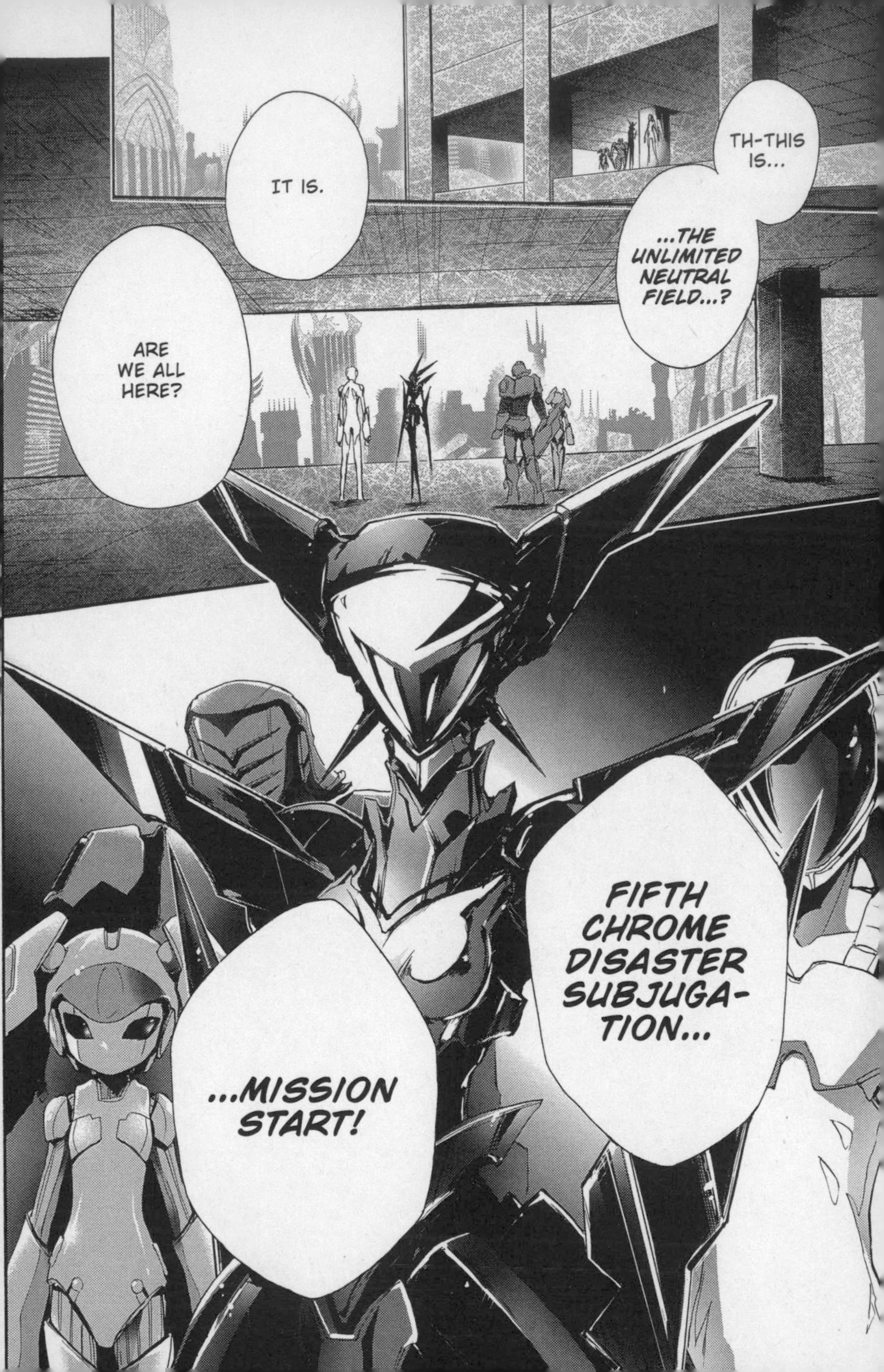
TH-THIS IS...
...THE UNLIMITED NEUTRAL FIELD...?
IT IS.
ARE WE ALL HERE?
FIFTH CHROME DISASTER SUBJUGA-TION...
...MISSION START!

▶▶▶ *ACCEL·WORLD*

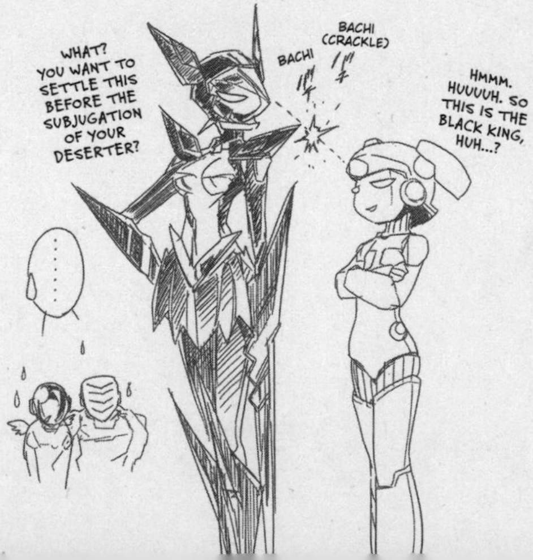
HMMM. HUUUUH. SO THIS IS THE BLACK KING, HUH...?
BACHI (CRACKLE)
BACHI
WHAT? YOU WANT TO SETTLE THIS BEFORE THE SUBJUGATION OF YOUR DESERTER?
......

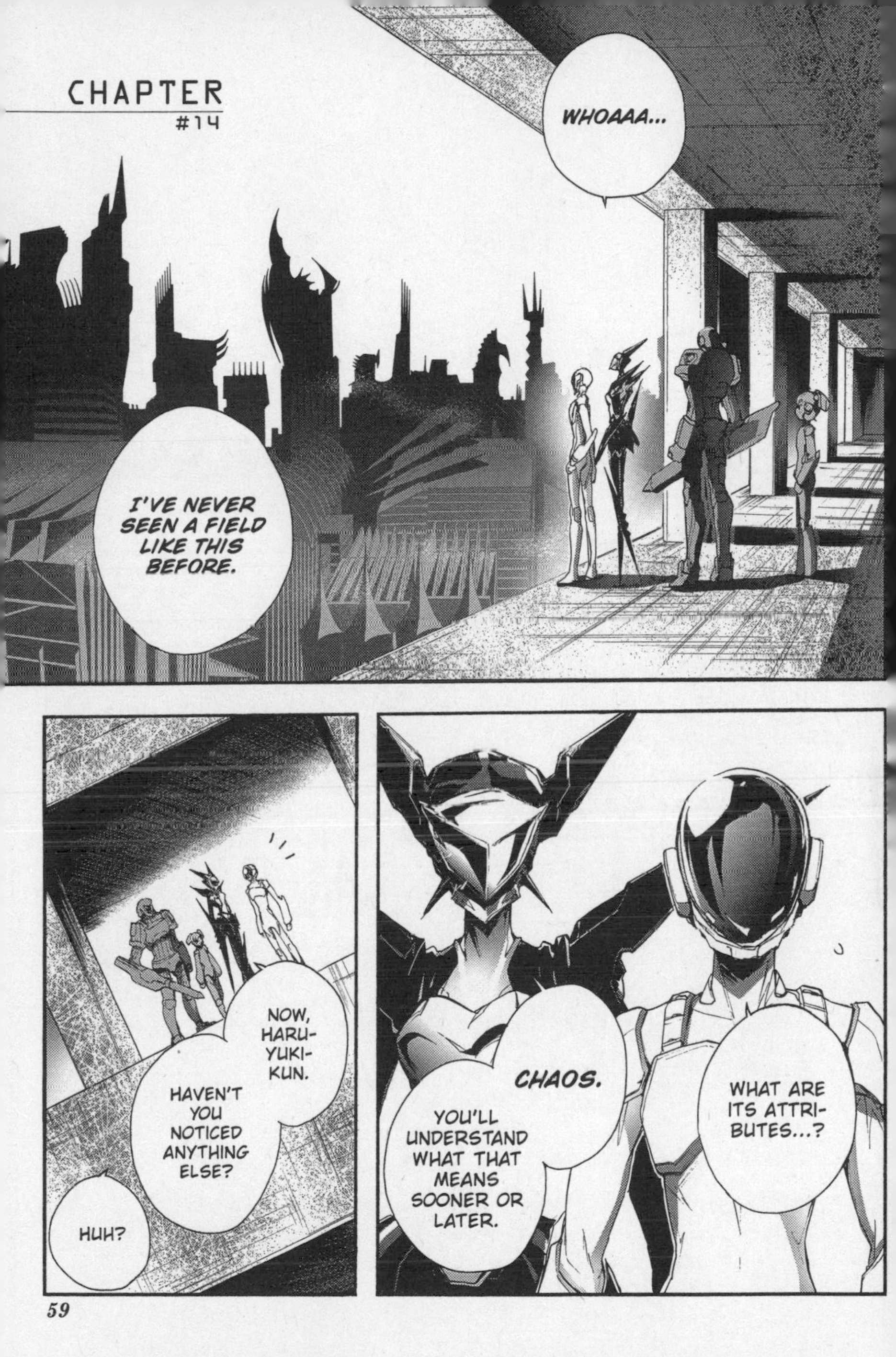
CHAPTER #14
WHOAAA...
I'VE NEVER SEEN A FIELD LIKE THIS BEFORE.
WHAT ARE ITS ATTRI-BUTES...?
CHAOS.
YOU'LL UNDERSTAND WHAT THAT MEANS SOONER OR LATER.
NOW, HARU-YUKI-KUN.
HAVEN'T YOU NOTICED ANYTHING ELSE?
HUH?

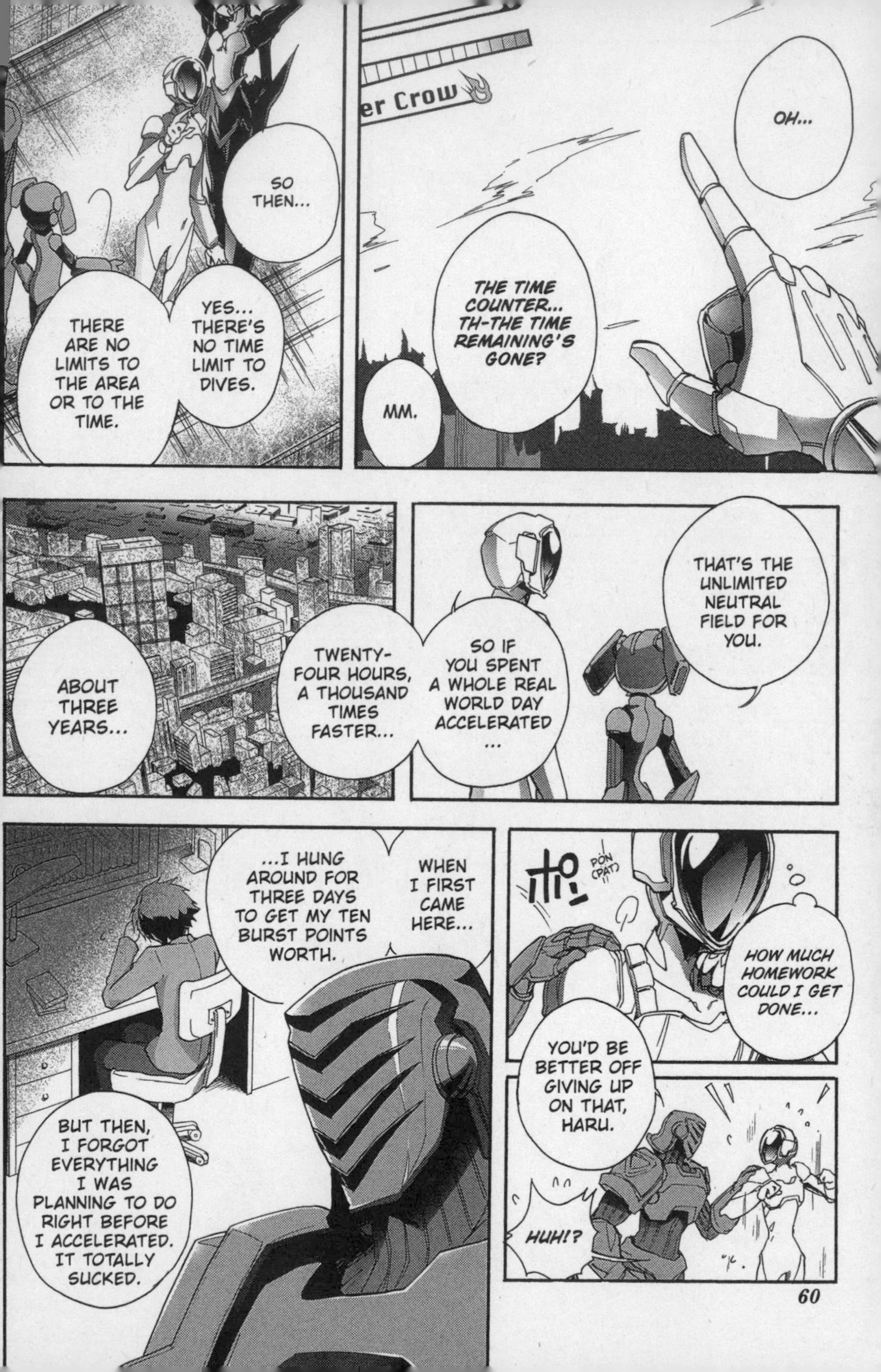

er Crow
OH...
THE TIME COUNTER... TH-THE TIME REMAINING'S GONE?
MM.
SO THEN...
YES... THERE'S NO TIME LIMIT TO DIVES.
THERE ARE NO LIMITS TO THE AREA OR TO THE TIME.
THAT'S THE UNLIMITED NEUTRAL FIELD FOR YOU.
SO IF YOU SPENT A WHOLE REAL WORLD DAY ACCELERATED...
TWENTY-FOUR HOURS, A THOUSAND TIMES FASTER...
ABOUT THREE YEARS...
PON (PAT)
HOW MUCH HOMEWORK COULD I GET DONE...
YOU'D BE BETTER OFF GIVING UP ON THAT, HARU.
HUH!?
WHEN I FIRST CAME HERE...
...I HUNG AROUND FOR THREE DAYS TO GET MY TEN BURST POINTS WORTH.
BUT THEN, I FORGOT EVERYTHING I WAS PLANNING TO DO RIGHT BEFORE I ACCELERATED. IT TOTALLY SUCKED.

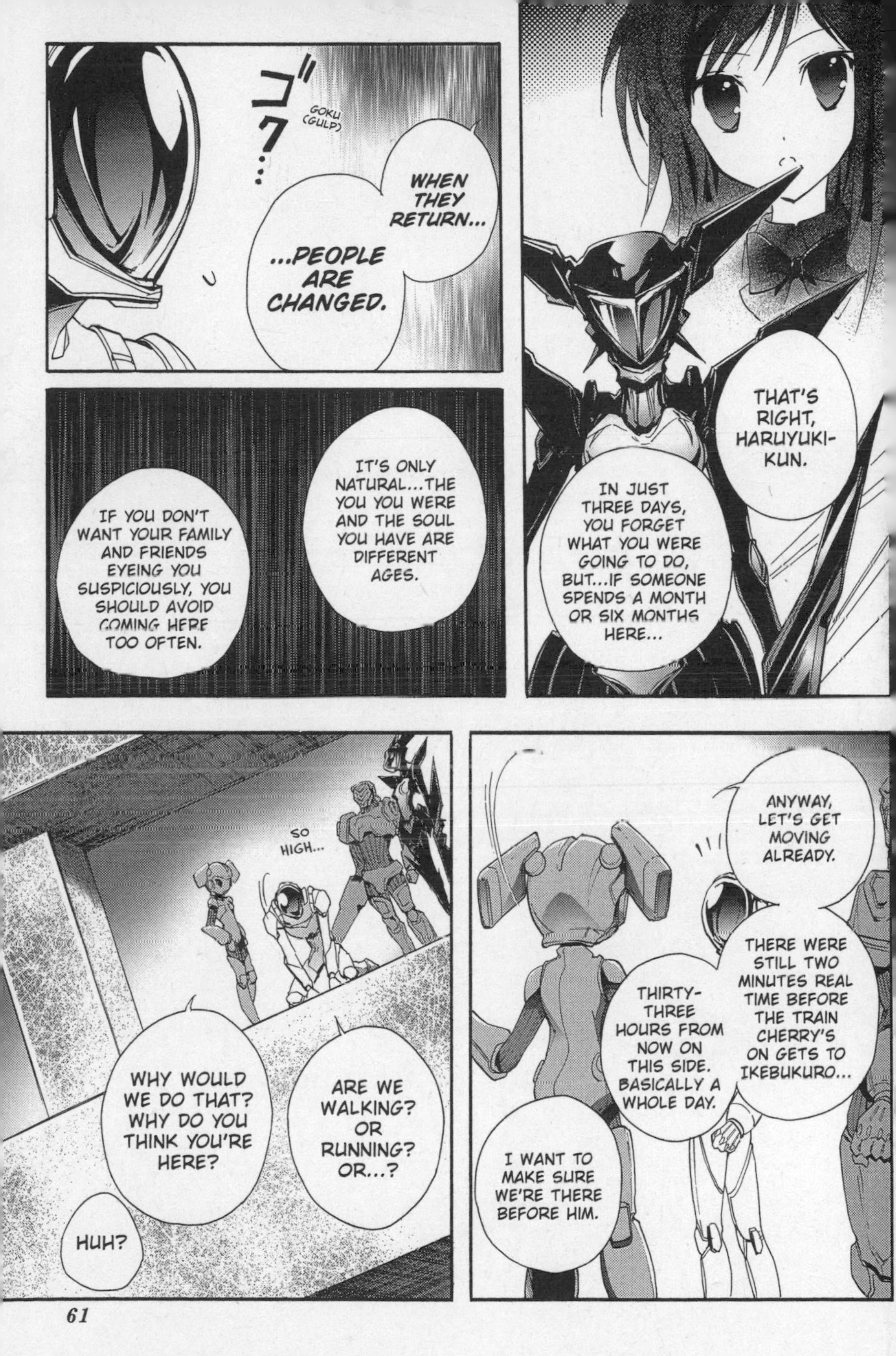
THAT'S RIGHT, HARUYUKI-KUN.
IN JUST THREE DAYS, YOU FORGET WHAT YOU WERE GOING TO DO, BUT...IF SOMEONE SPENDS A MONTH OR SIX MONTHS HERE...
ゴク…
GOKU (GULP)
WHEN THEY RETURN...
...PEOPLE ARE CHANGED.
IT'S ONLY NATURAL...THE YOU YOU WERE AND THE SOUL YOU HAVE ARE DIFFERENT AGES.
IF YOU DON'T WANT YOUR FAMILY AND FRIENDS EYEING YOU SUSPICIOUSLY, YOU SHOULD AVOID COMING HERE TOO OFTEN.
ANYWAY, LET'S GET MOVING ALREADY.
THERE WERE STILL TWO MINUTES REAL TIME BEFORE THE TRAIN CHERRY'S ON GETS TO IKEBUKURO...
THIRTY-THREE HOURS FROM NOW ON THIS SIDE. BASICALLY A WHOLE DAY.
I WANT TO MAKE SURE WE'RE THERE BEFORE HIM.
SO HIGH...
ARE WE WALKING? OR RUNNING? OR...?
WHY WOULD WE DO THAT? WHY DO YOU THINK YOU'RE HERE?
HUH?

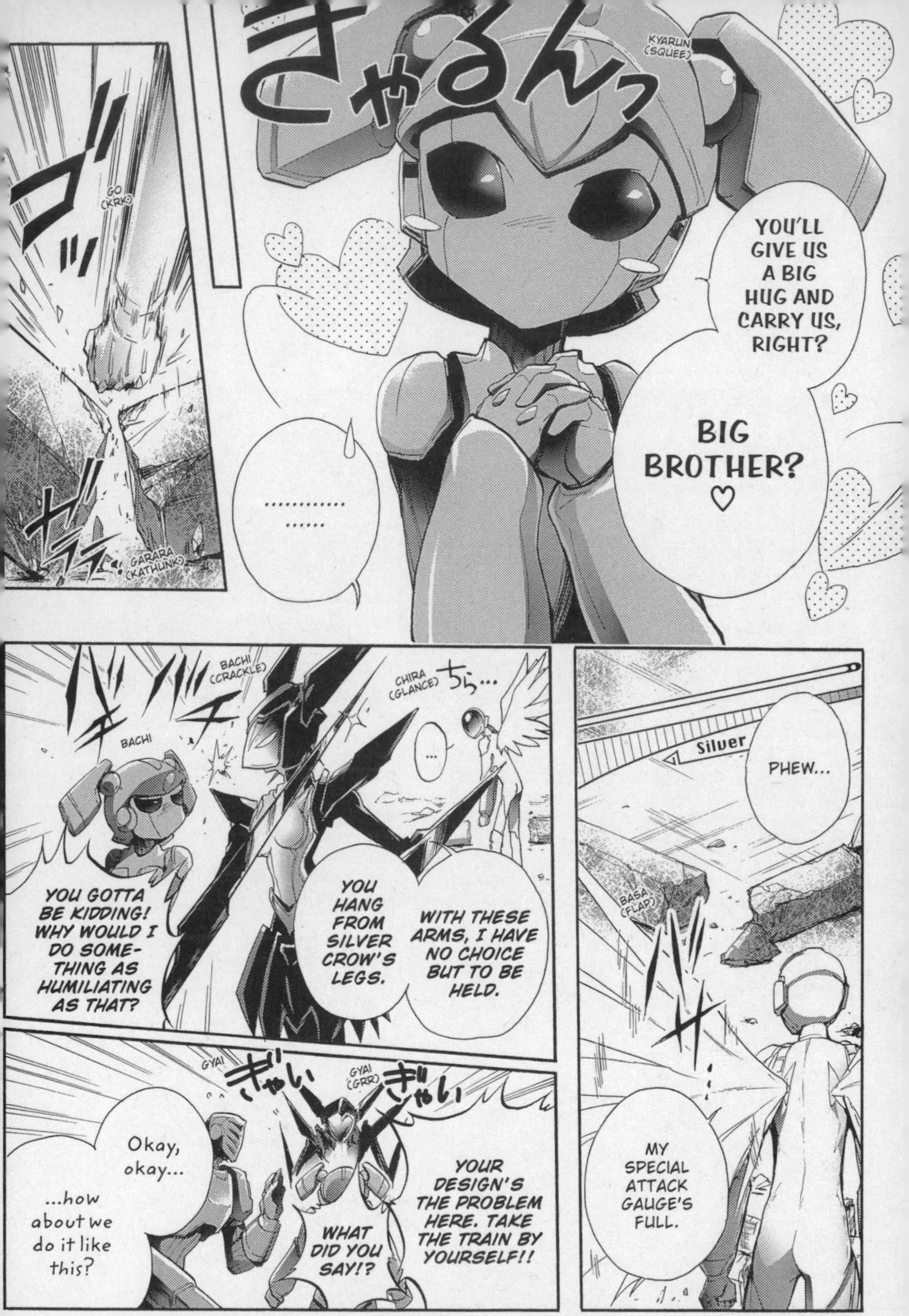

KYARUN (SQUEE)
きゃるんっ
YOU'LL GIVE US A BIG HUG AND CARRY US, RIGHT?
BIG BROTHER? ♡
....
GO (KRK)
GARARA (KATHUNK)
Silver
PHEW...
BASA (FLAP)
MY SPECIAL ATTACK GAUGE'S FULL.
BACHI (CRACKLE)
CHIRA (GLANCE) ちら...
...
WITH THESE ARMS, I HAVE NO CHOICE BUT TO BE HELD.
YOU HANG FROM SILVER CROW'S LEGS.
BACHI
YOU GOTTA BE KIDDING! WHY WOULD I DO SOME-THING AS HUMILIATING AS THAT?
GYAI (GRR) ぎゃい
GYAI ぎゃい
YOUR DESIGN'S THE PROBLEM HERE. TAKE THE TRAIN BY YOURSELF!!
WHAT DID YOU SAY!?
Okay, okay...
...how about we do it like this?

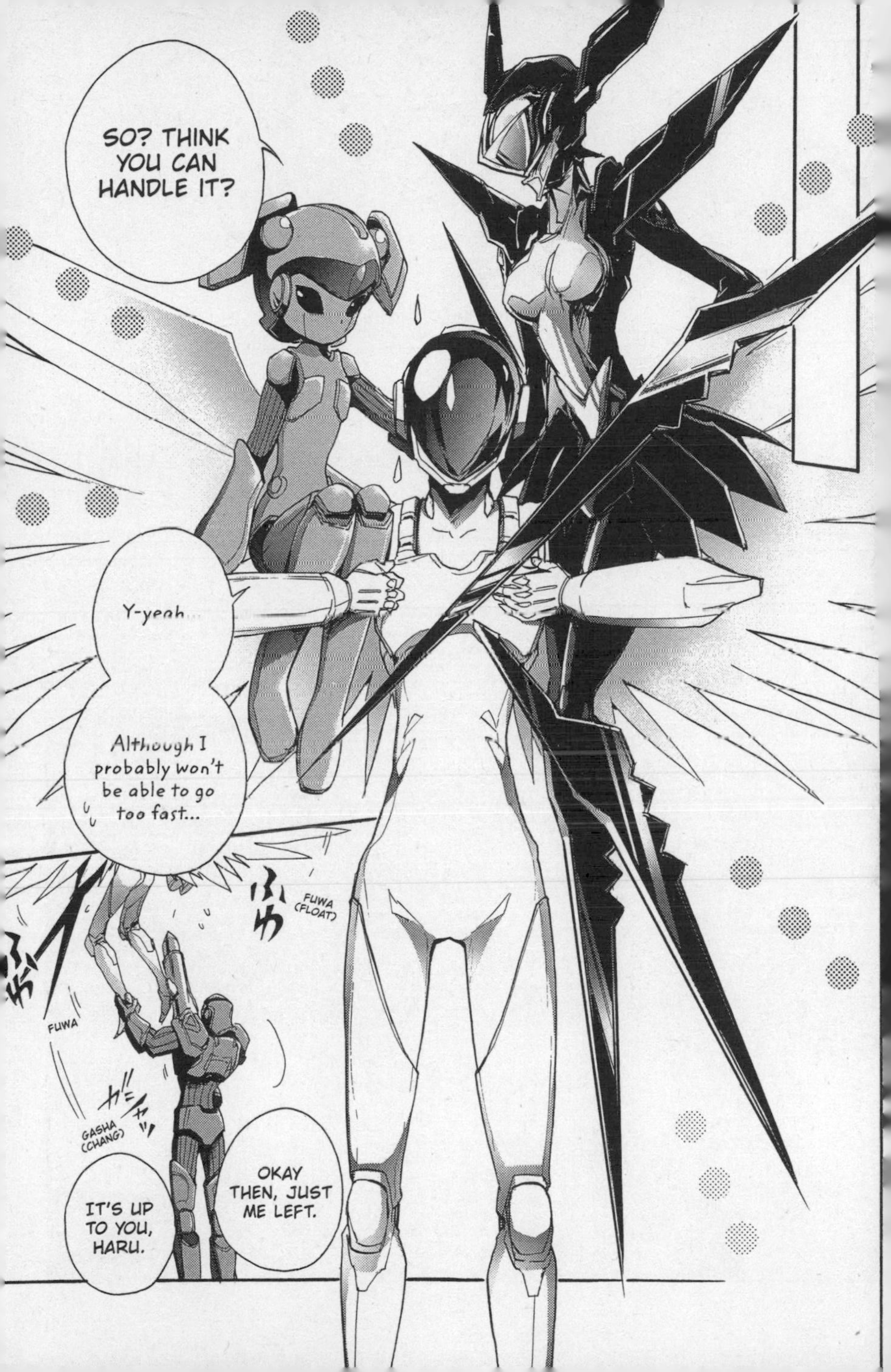
SO? THINK YOU CAN HANDLE IT?
Y-yeah...
Although I probably won't be able to go too fast...
FUWA (FLOAT)
FUWA
GASHA (CHANG)
OKAY THEN, JUST ME LEFT.
IT'S UP TO YOU, HARU.

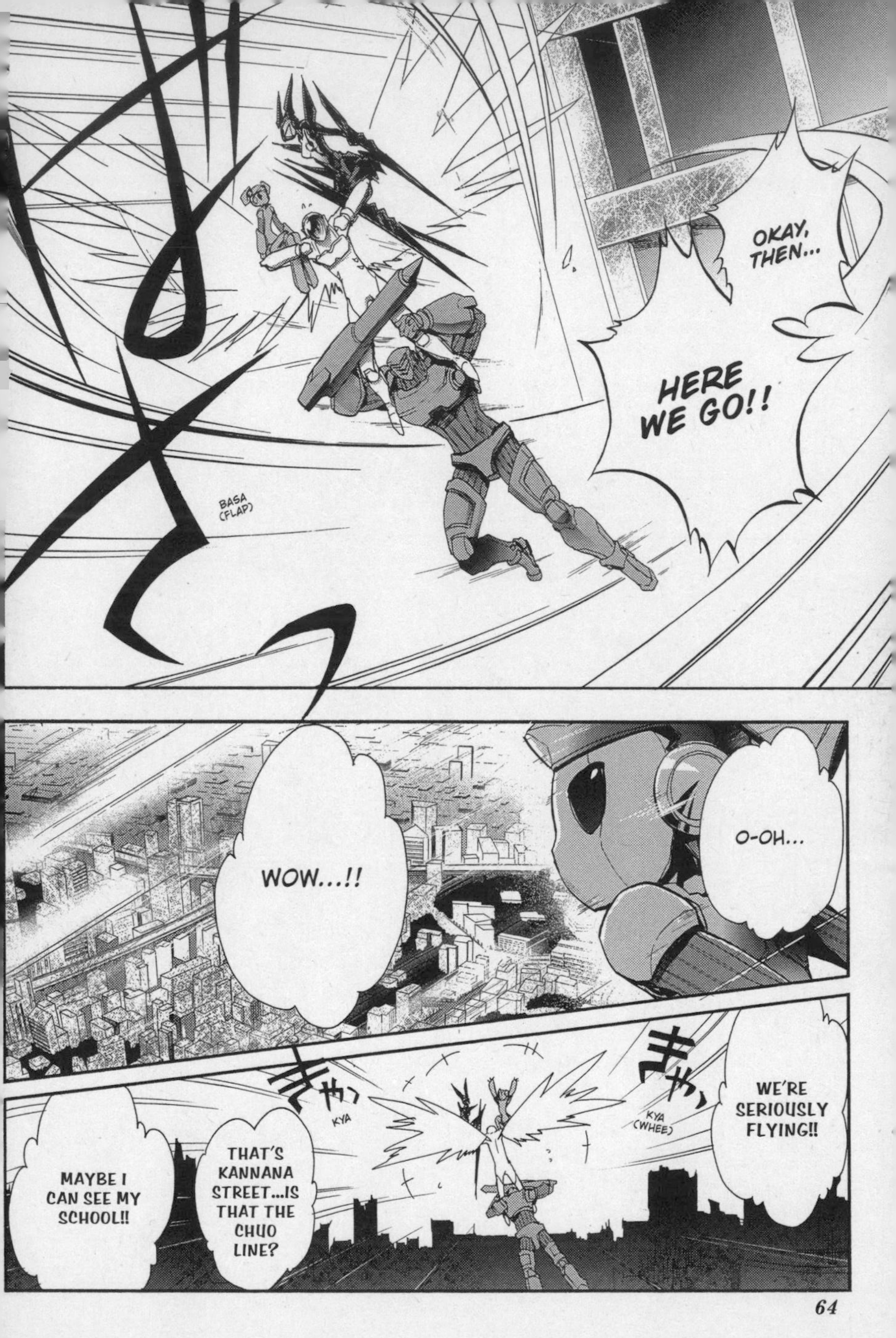
OKAY, THEN...
HERE WE GO!!
BASA (FLAP)
O-OH...
WOW...!!
WE'RE SERIOUSLY FLYING!!
KYA (WHEE)
KYA
THAT'S KANNANA STREET...IS THAT THE CHUO LINE?
MAYBE I CAN SEE MY SCHOOL!!

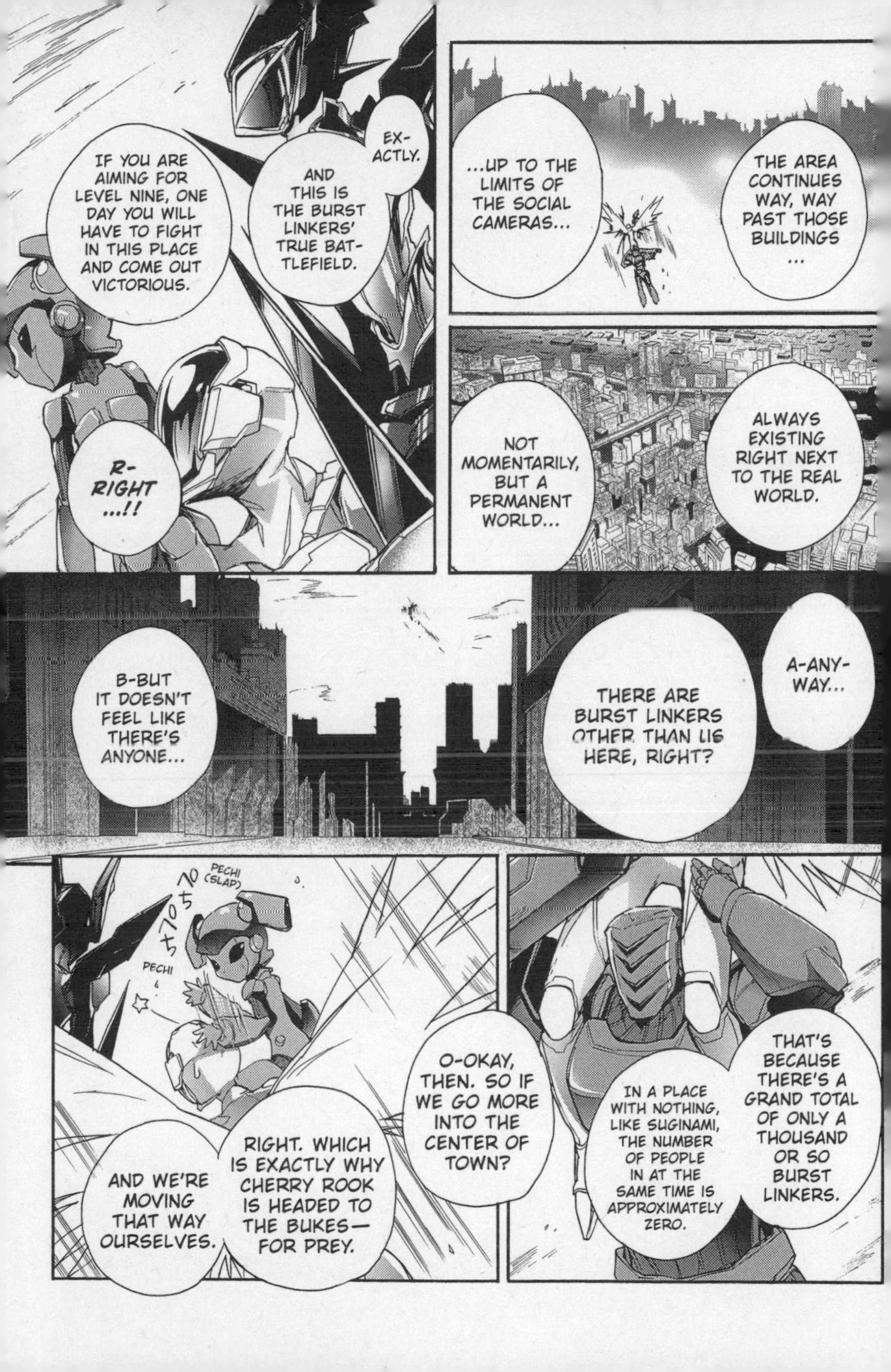

THE AREA CONTINUES WAY, WAY PAST THOSE BUILDINGS...
...UP TO THE LIMITS OF THE SOCIAL CAMERAS...
ALWAYS EXISTING RIGHT NEXT TO THE REAL WORLD.
NOT MOMENTARILY, BUT A PERMANENT WORLD...
EX-ACTLY.
AND THIS IS THE BURST LINKERS' TRUE BAT-TLEFIELD.
IF YOU ARE AIMING FOR LEVEL NINE, ONE DAY YOU WILL HAVE TO FIGHT IN THIS PLACE AND COME OUT VICTORIOUS.
R-RIGHT ...!!
A-ANY-WAY...
THERE ARE BURST LINKERS OTHER THAN US HERE, RIGHT?
B-BUT IT DOESN'T FEEL LIKE THERE'S ANYONE...
THAT'S BECAUSE THERE'S A GRAND TOTAL OF ONLY A THOUSAND OR SO BURST LINKERS.
IN A PLACE WITH NOTHING, LIKE SUGINAMI, THE NUMBER OF PEOPLE IN AT THE SAME TIME IS APPROXIMATELY ZERO.
O-OKAY, THEN. SO IF WE GO MORE INTO THE CENTER OF TOWN?
PECHI (SLAP)
PECHI
RIGHT. WHICH IS EXACTLY WHY CHERRY ROOK IS HEADED TO THE BUKES—FOR PREY.
AND WE'RE MOVING THAT WAY OURSELVES.

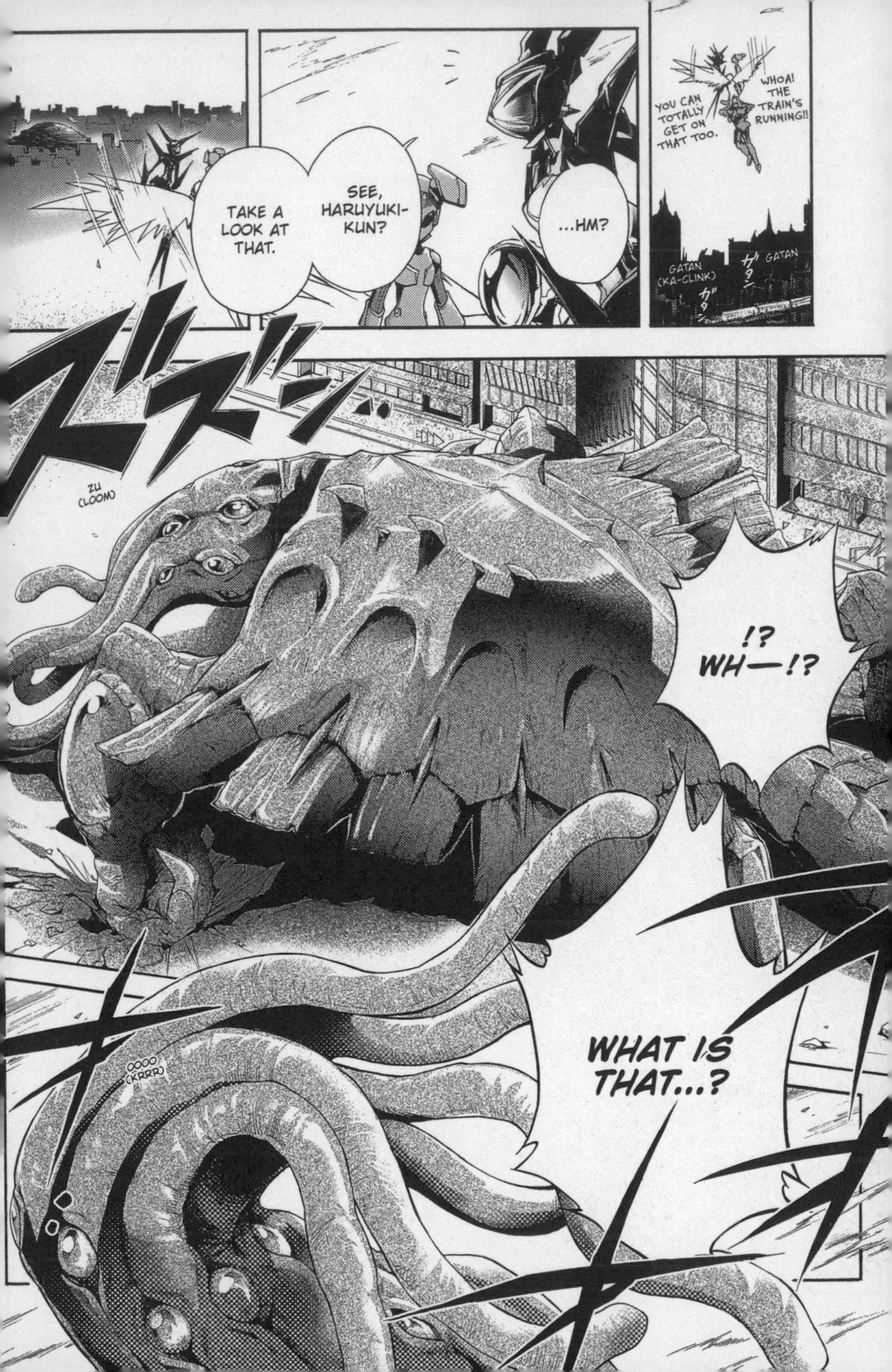
WHOA! THE TRAIN'S RUNNING!!
YOU CAN TOTALLY GET ON THAT TOO.
GATAN
GATAN (KA-CLINK)
...HM?
SEE, HARUYUKI-KUN?
TAKE A LOOK AT THAT.
ZU (LOOM)
!? WH—!?
WHAT IS THAT...?
OOOO (KRRR)

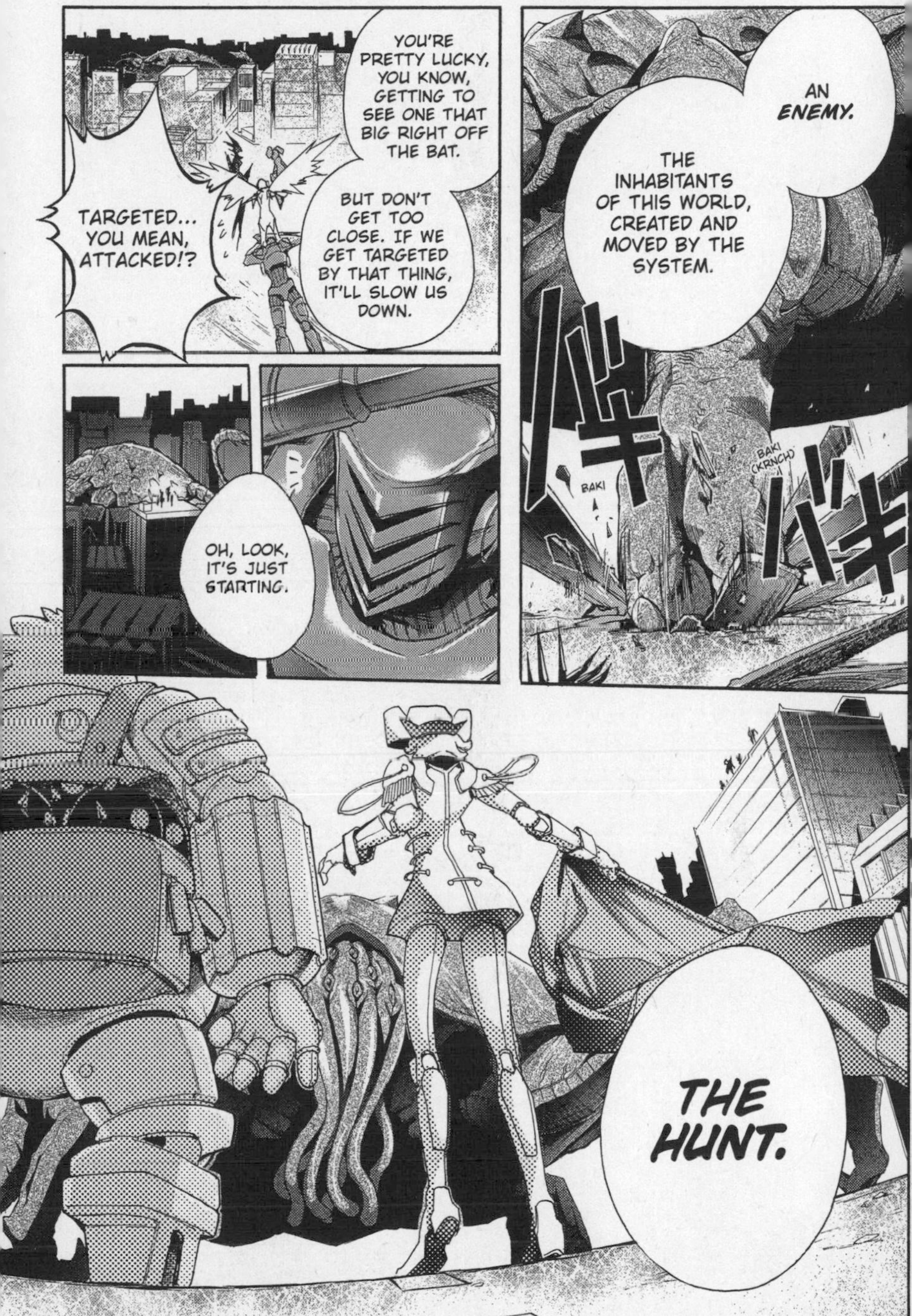
AN *ENEMY.*
THE INHABITANTS OF THIS WORLD, CREATED AND MOVED BY THE SYSTEM.
BAKI (KRNCH)
バキ
BAKI
バキ
YOU'RE PRETTY LUCKY, YOU KNOW, GETTING TO SEE ONE THAT BIG RIGHT OFF THE BAT.
BUT DON'T GET TOO CLOSE. IF WE GET TARGETED BY THAT THING, IT'LL SLOW US DOWN.
TARGETED... YOU MEAN, ATTACKED!?
OH, LOOK, IT'S JUST STARTING.
THE HUNT.

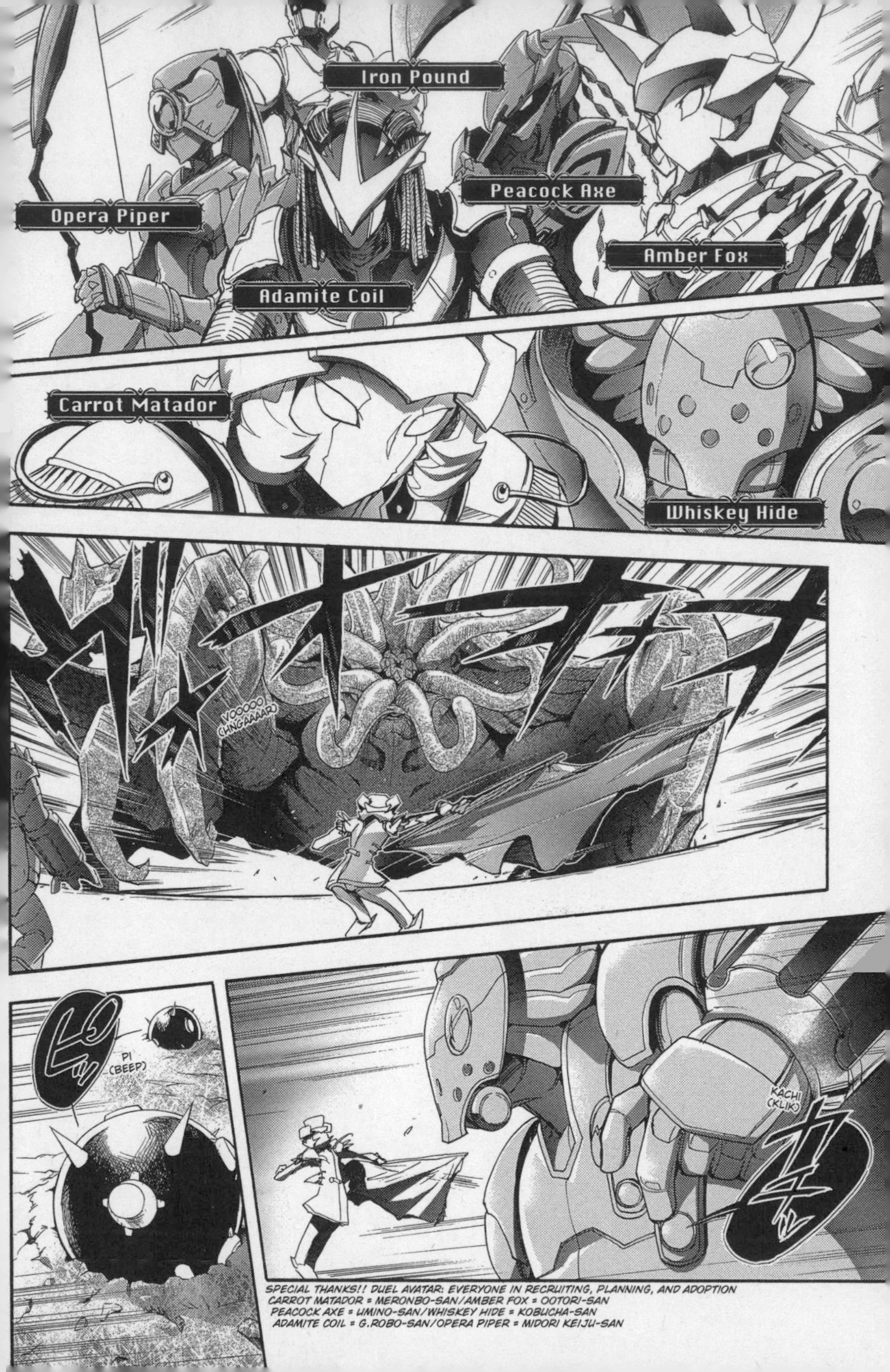
Iron Pound
Peacock Axe
Amber Fox
Opera Piper
Adamite Coil
Whiskey Hide
Carrot Matador
VOOOOO (HNGAAAAR)
KACHI (KLIK)
PI (BEEP)

SPECIAL THANKS!! DUEL AVATAR: EVERYONE IN RECRUITING, PLANNING, AND ADOPTION
CARROT MATADOR = MERONBO-SAN/AMBER FOX = OOTORI-SAN
PEACOCK AXE = UMINO-SAN/WHISKEY HIDE = KOBUCHA-SAN
ADAMITE COIL = G.ROBO-SAN/OPERA PIPER = MIDORI KEIJU-SAN

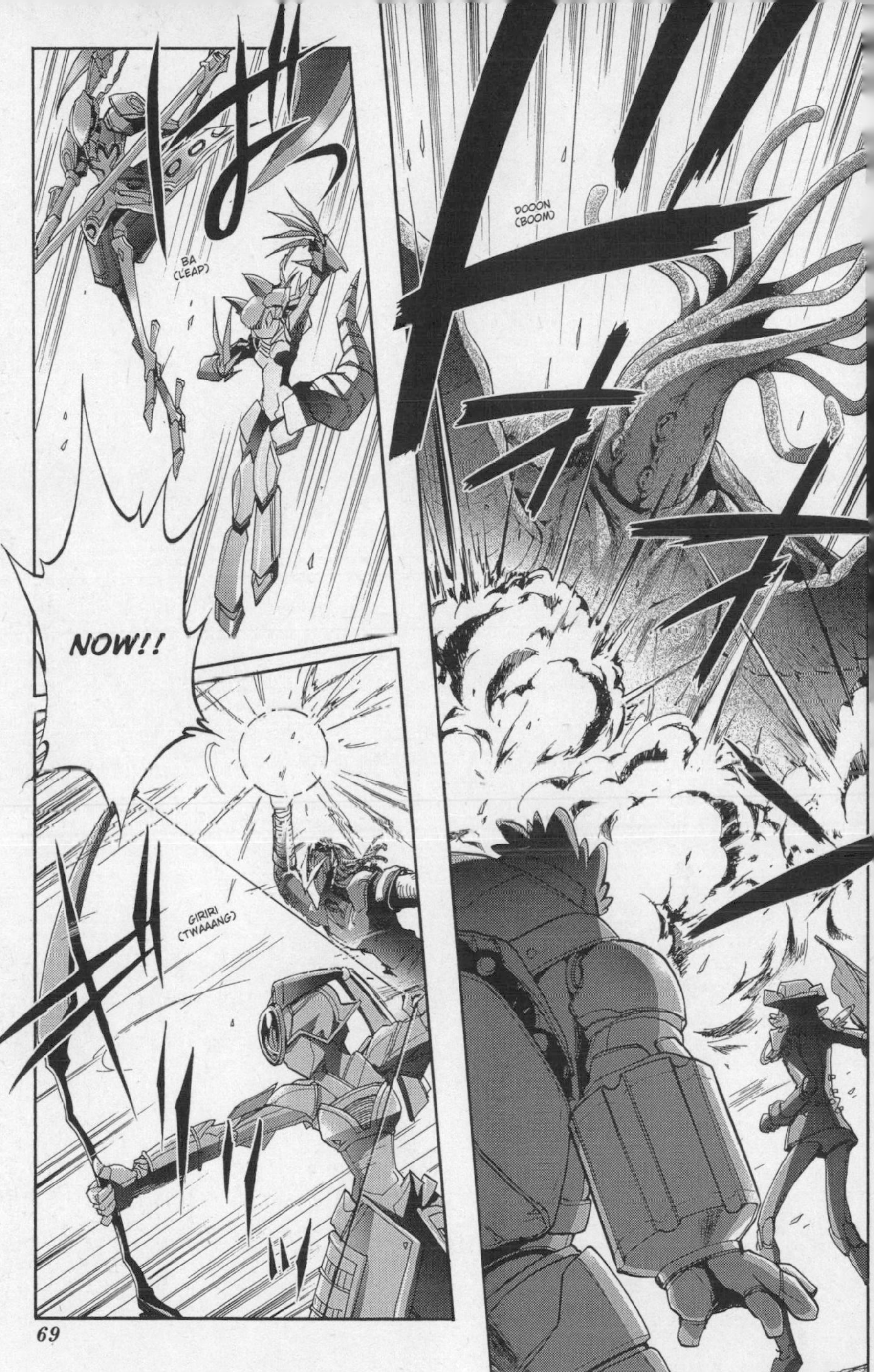
DOOON
(BOOM)
BA
(LEAP)
NOW!!
GIRIRI
(TWAAANG)

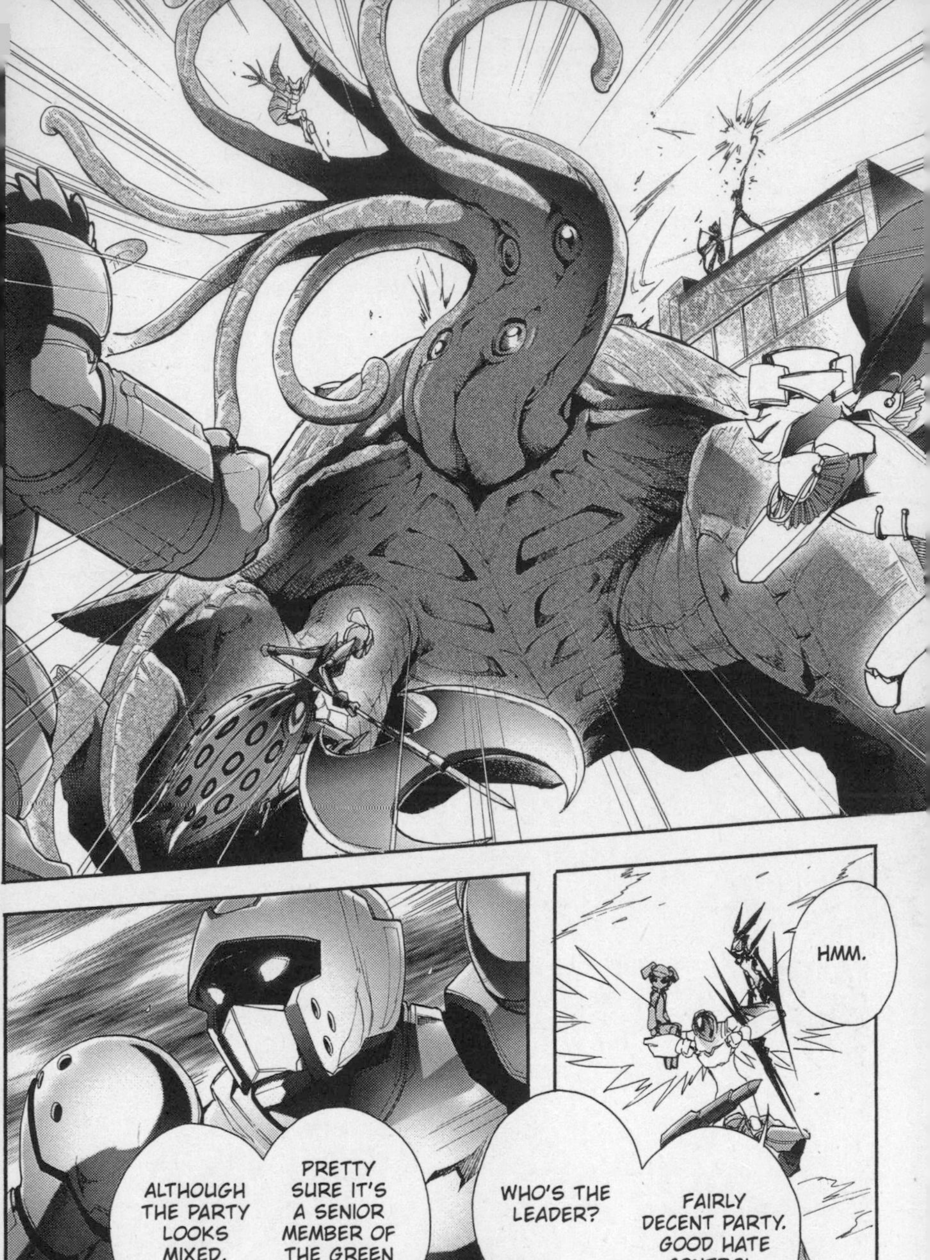
HMM.
FAIRLY DECENT PARTY. GOOD HATE CONTROL.
WHO'S THE LEADER?
PRETTY SURE IT'S A SENIOR MEMBER OF THE GREEN LEGION.
ALTHOUGH THE PARTY LOOKS MIXED.

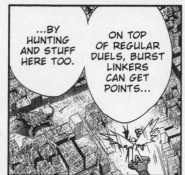

THAT'S A "HUNT"...
YUP.
ON TOP OF REGULAR DUELS, BURST LINKERS CAN GET POINTS...
...BY HUNTING AND STUFF HERE TOO.
BUT...IT'S REMARKABLY INEFFICIENT.
EVEN IF YOU'RE WILLING TO RISK THE ANNIHILATION TO HUNT A LARGE MONSTER AT THAT LEVEL...
...IF YOU'RE LUCKY, YOU GET WHAT YOU'D GET FOR WINNING A DUEL.
BRAIN BURST IS ESSENTIALLY A ONE-ON-ONE FIGHTING GAME...
THERE'S NO AVOIDING THAT.
SO HUNTING IS A SUPPLE-MENTARY MEANS OF POINT SUPPLY.
HOW-EVER...

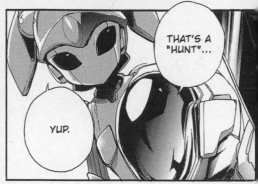

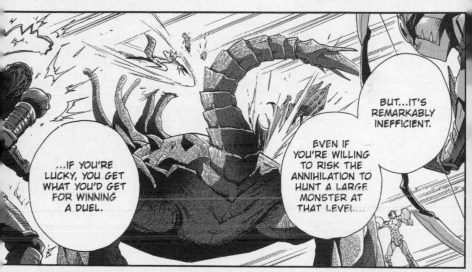

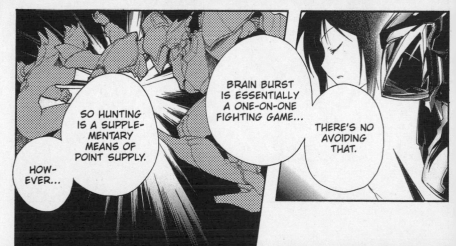

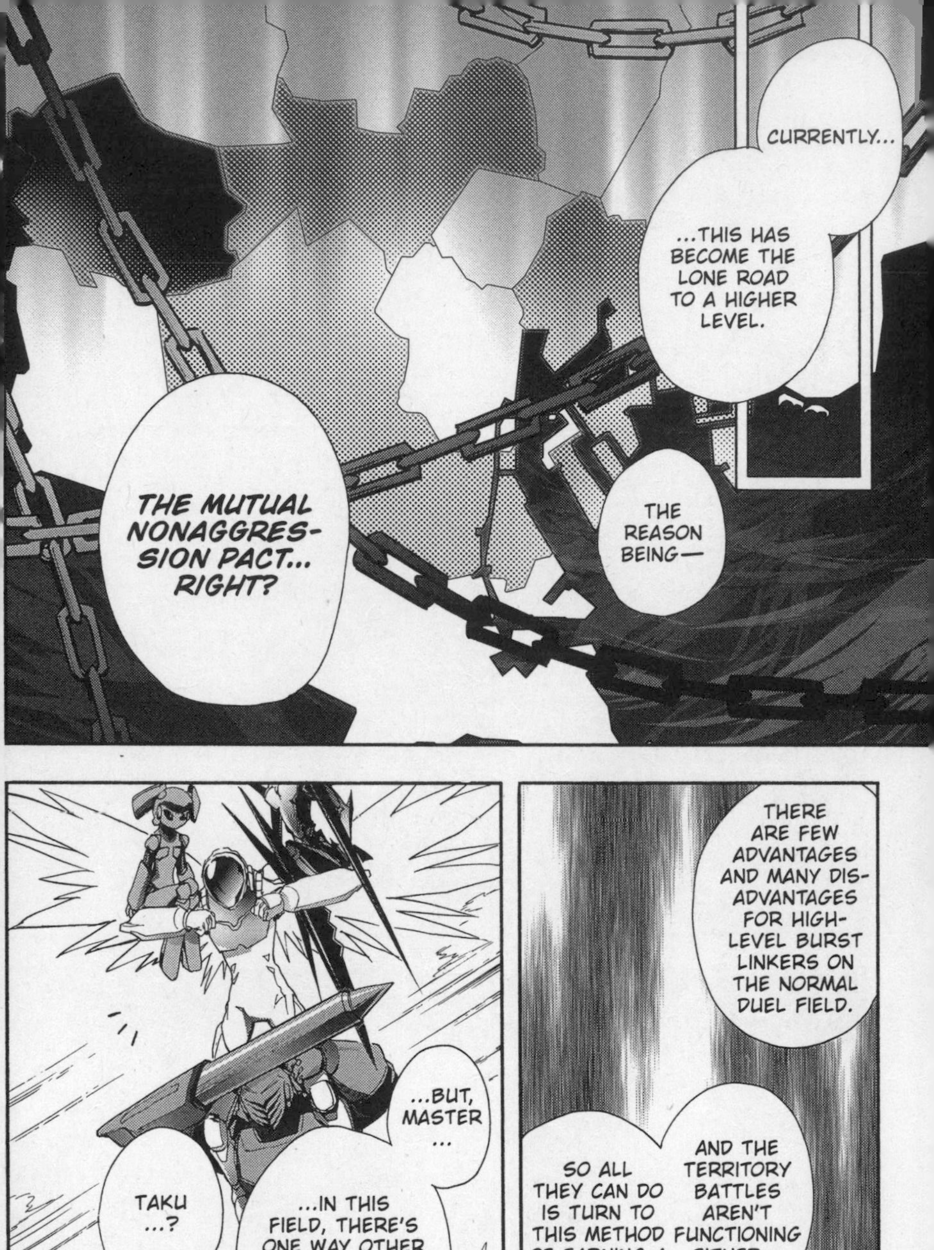
CURRENTLY...
...THIS HAS BECOME THE LONE ROAD TO A HIGHER LEVEL.
THE REASON BEING—
THE MUTUAL NONAGGRES-SION PACT... RIGHT?
THERE ARE FEW ADVANTAGES AND MANY DIS-ADVANTAGES FOR HIGH-LEVEL BURST LINKERS ON THE NORMAL DUEL FIELD.
AND THE TERRITORY BATTLES AREN'T FUNCTIONING EITHER...
SO ALL THEY CAN DO IS TURN TO THIS METHOD OF EARNING A FEW POINTS AT LEAST.
...BUT, MASTER...
...IN THIS FIELD, THERE'S ONE WAY OTHER THAN HUNTING, ISN'T THERE?
TAKU...?

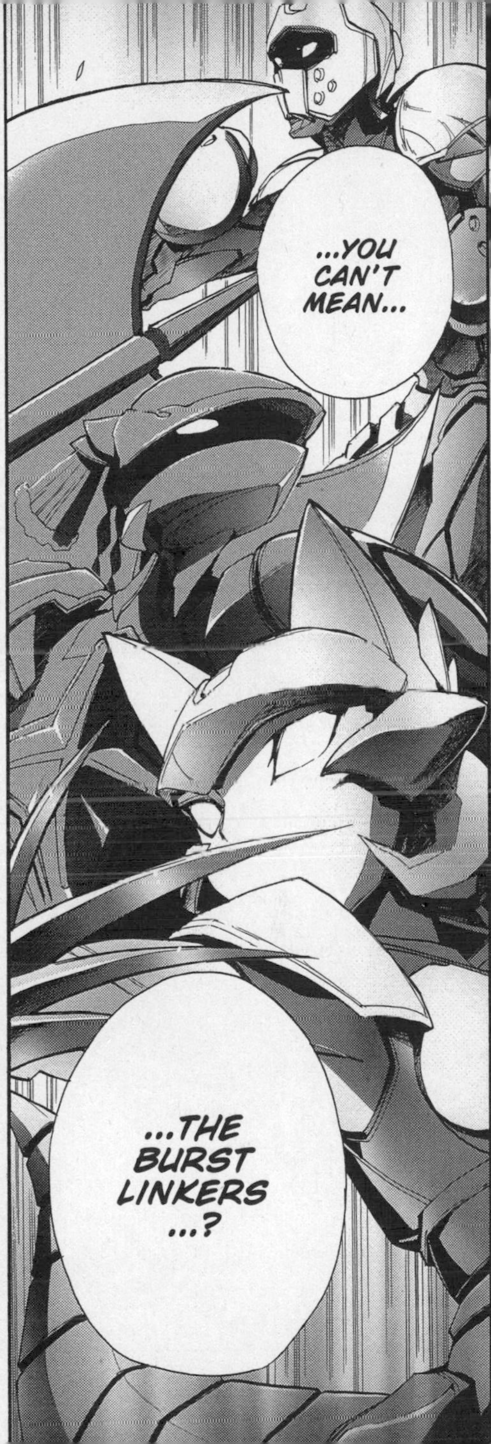
...YOU CAN'T MEAN...
...THE BURST LINKERS ...?
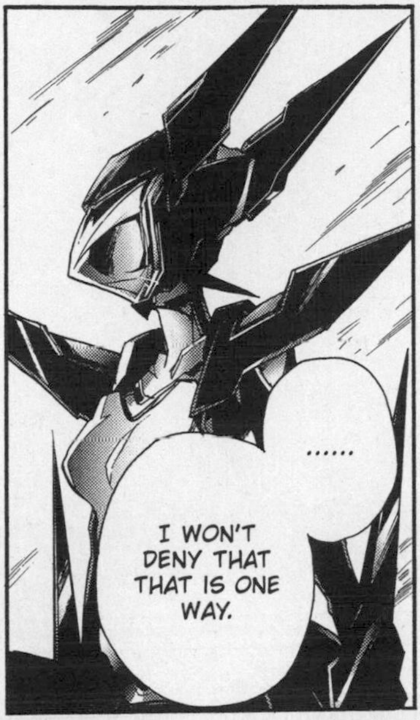
......
I WON'T DENY THAT THAT IS ONE WAY.
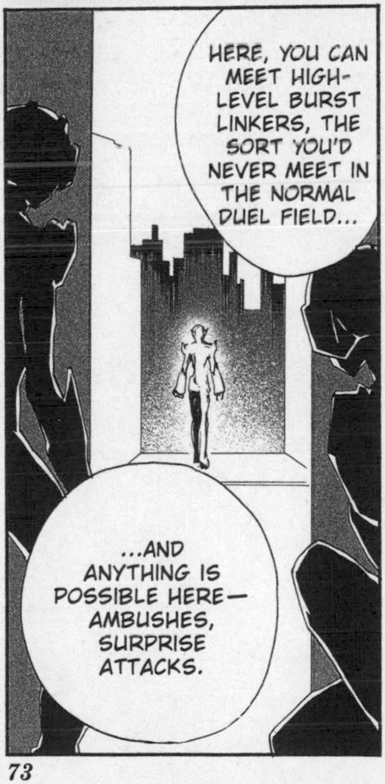
HERE, YOU CAN MEET HIGH-LEVEL BURST LINKERS, THE SORT YOU'D NEVER MEET IN THE NORMAL DUEL FIELD...
...AND ANYTHING IS POSSIBLE HERE—AMBUSHES, SURPRISE ATTACKS.

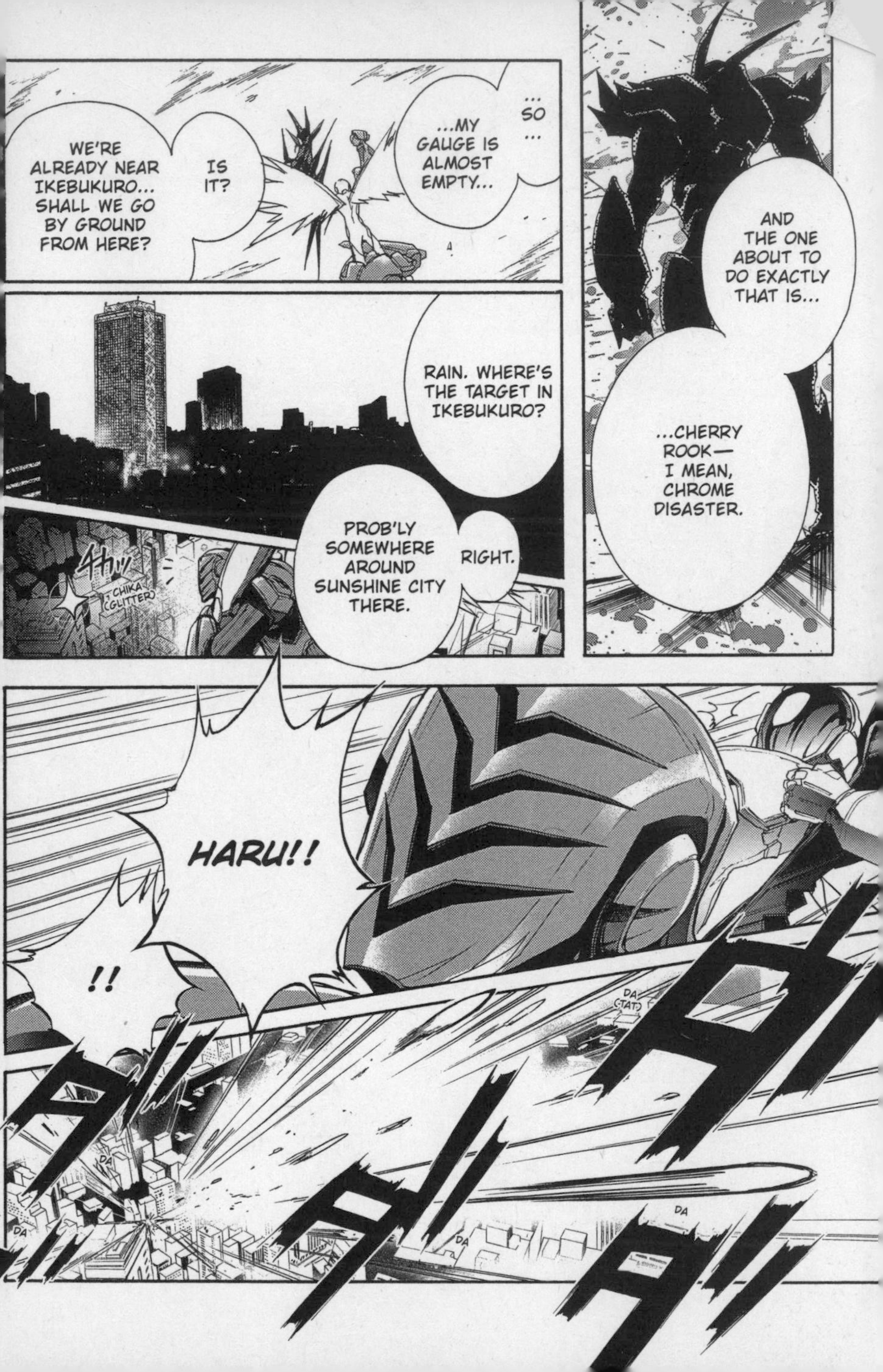
AND THE ONE ABOUT TO DO EXACTLY THAT IS...
...CHERRY ROOK— I MEAN, CHROME DISASTER.
...SO...
...MY GAUGE IS ALMOST EMPTY...
IS IT?
WE'RE ALREADY NEAR IKEBUKURO... SHALL WE GO BY GROUND FROM HERE?
RAIN. WHERE'S THE TARGET IN IKEBUKURO?
RIGHT.
PROB'LY SOMEWHERE AROUND SUNSHINE CITY THERE.
CHIKA (GLITTER)
HARU!!
!!
DA (TAT)
DA
DA
DA
DA

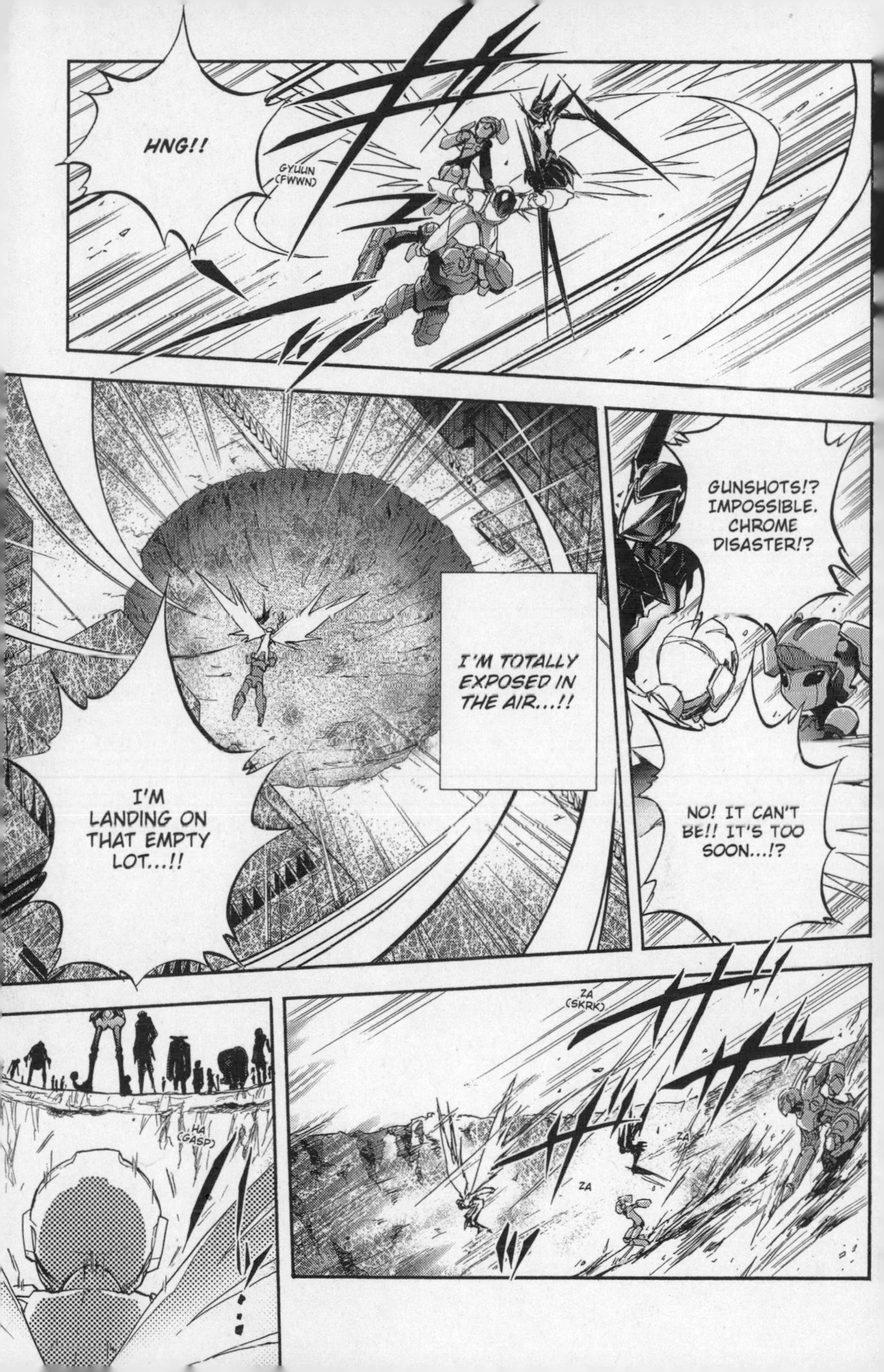
HNG!!
GYUUN (FWWN)
GUNSHOTS!? IMPOSSIBLE. CHROME DISASTER!?
NO! IT CAN'T BE!! IT'S TOO SOON...!?
I'M TOTALLY EXPOSED IN THE AIR...!!
I'M LANDING ON THAT EMPTY LOT...!!
ZA (SKRK)
ZA
ZA
HA (GASP)

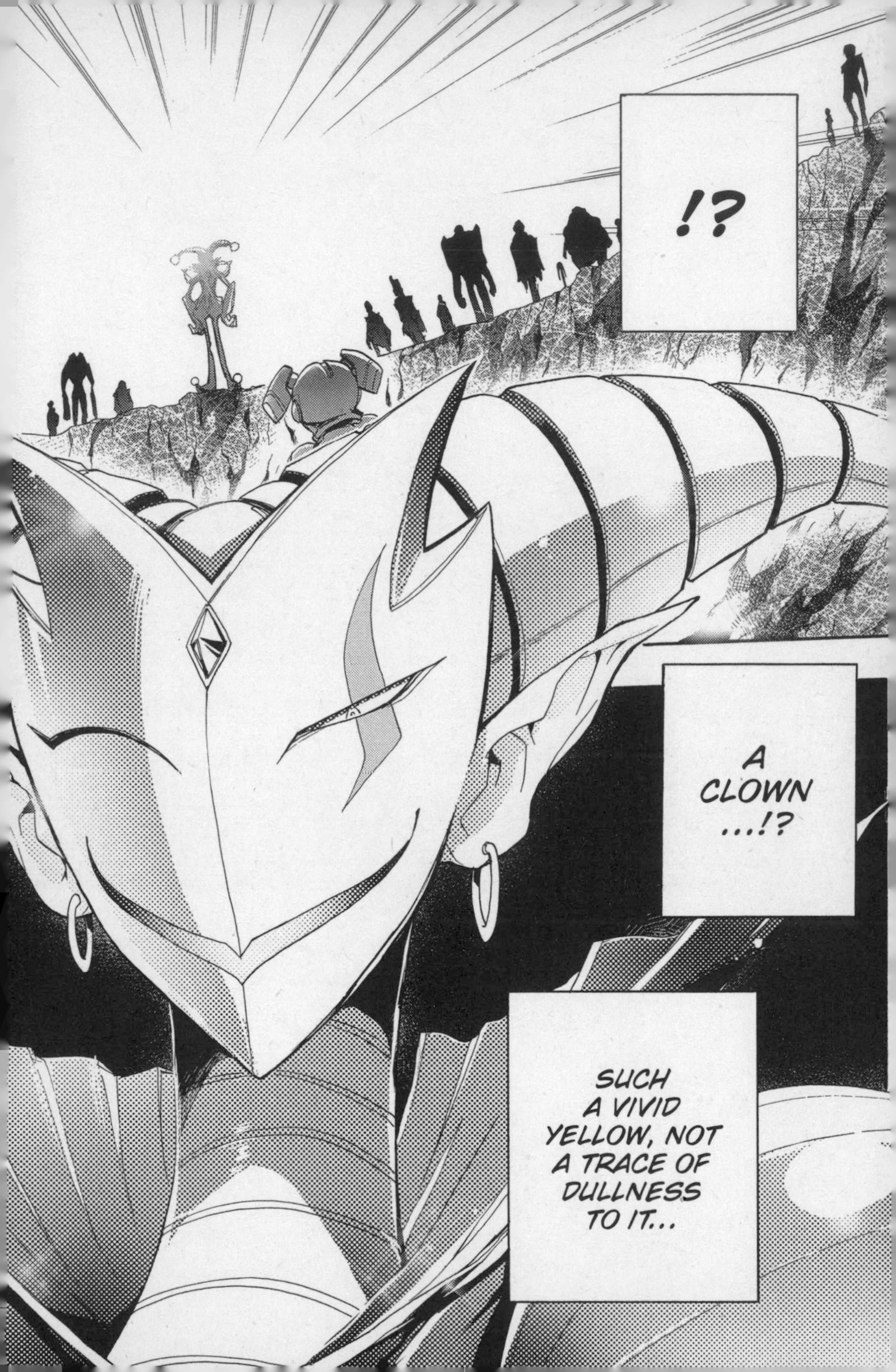
!?
A CLOWN ...!?
SUCH A VIVID YELLOW, NOT A TRACE OF DULLNESS TO IT...

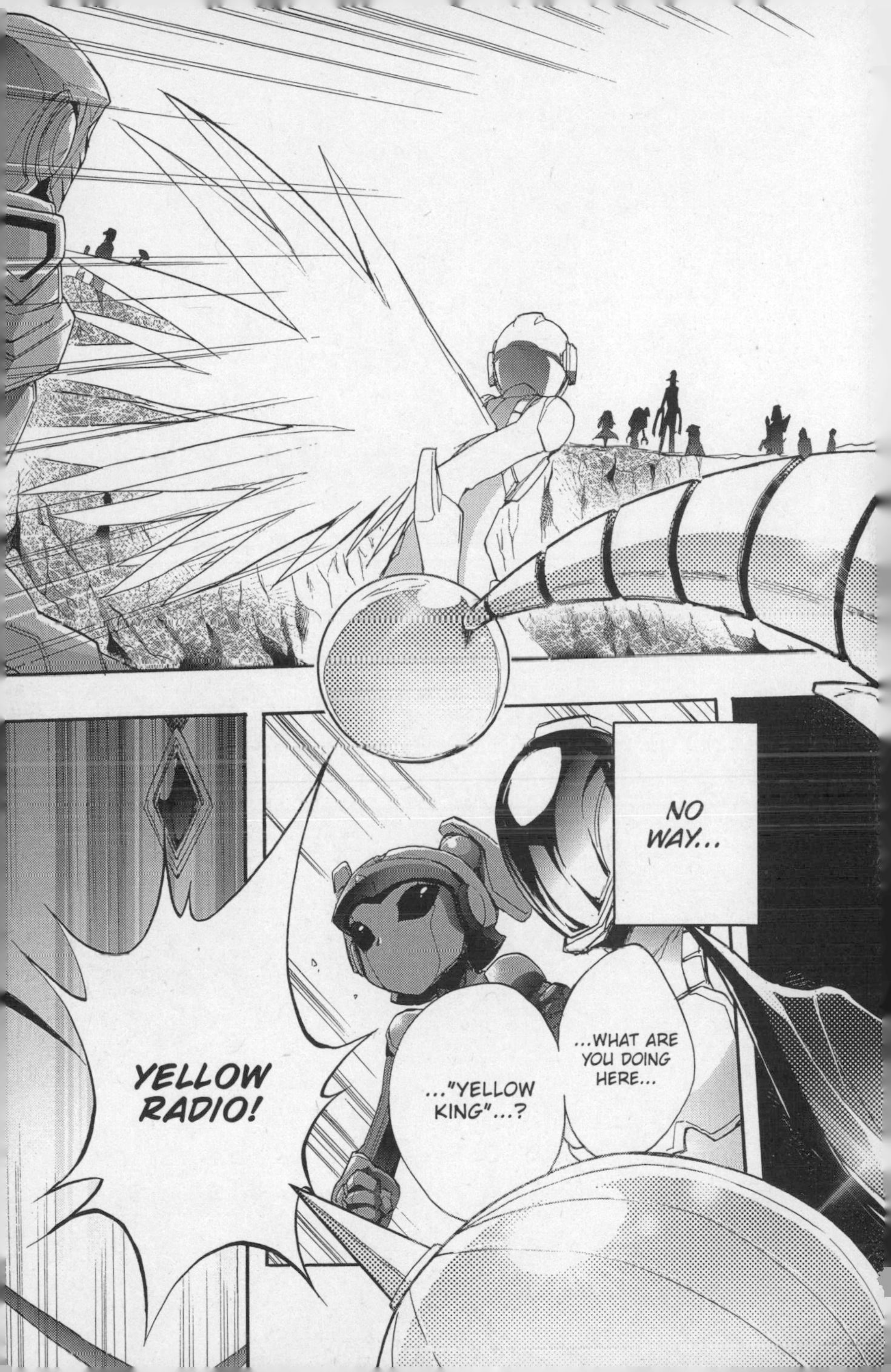
NO WAY...
...WHAT ARE YOU DOING HERE...
..."YELLOW KING"...?
YELLOW RADIO!

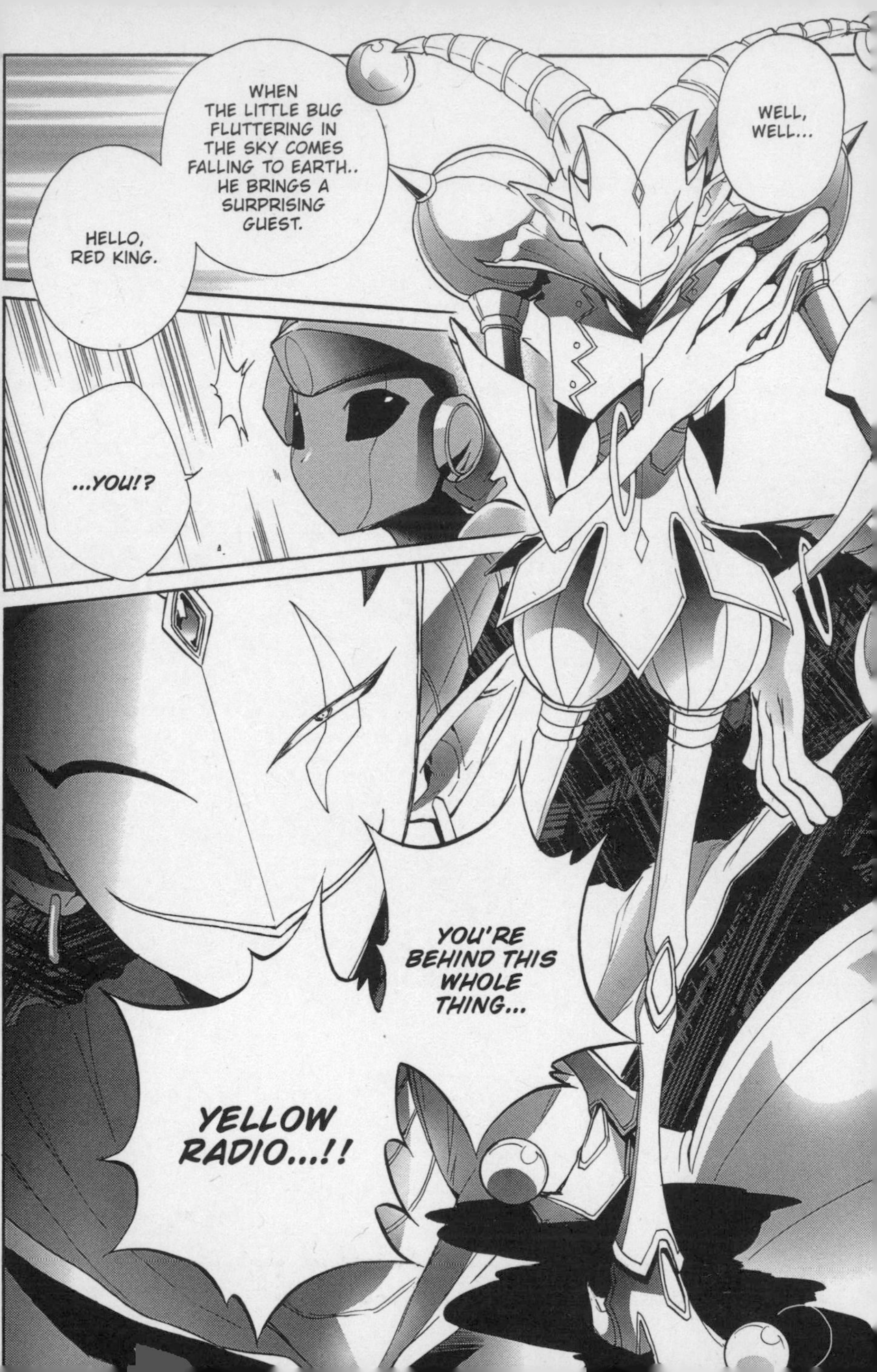
WELL, WELL...
WHEN THE LITTLE BUG FLUTTERING IN THE SKY COMES FALLING TO EARTH.. HE BRINGS A SURPRISING GUEST.
HELLO, RED KING.
...YOU!?
YOU'RE BEHIND THIS WHOLE THING...
YELLOW RADIO...!!

►►► *ACCEL·WORLD*

CHAPTER #15

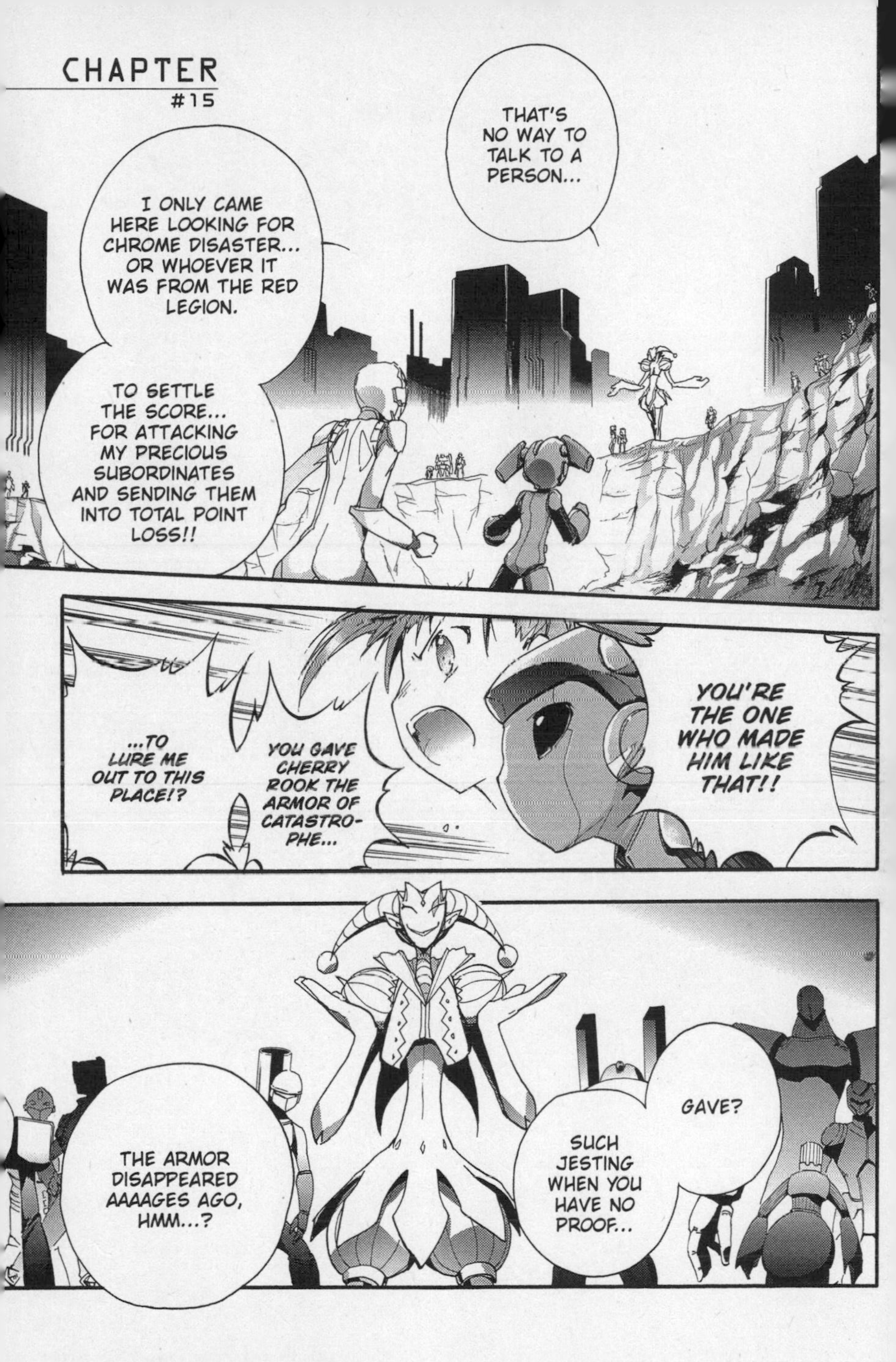

THAT'S NO WAY TO TALK TO A PERSON...
I ONLY CAME HERE LOOKING FOR CHROME DISASTER... OR WHOEVER IT WAS FROM THE RED LEGION.
TO SETTLE THE SCORE... FOR ATTACKING MY PRECIOUS SUBORDINATES AND SENDING THEM INTO TOTAL POINT LOSS!!
YOU'RE THE ONE WHO MADE HIM LIKE THAT!!
YOU GAVE CHERRY ROOK THE ARMOR OF CATASTRO-PHE...
...TO LURE ME OUT TO THIS PLACE!?
GAVE?
SUCH JESTING WHEN YOU HAVE NO PROOF...
THE ARMOR DISAPPEARED AAAAGES AGO, HMM...?

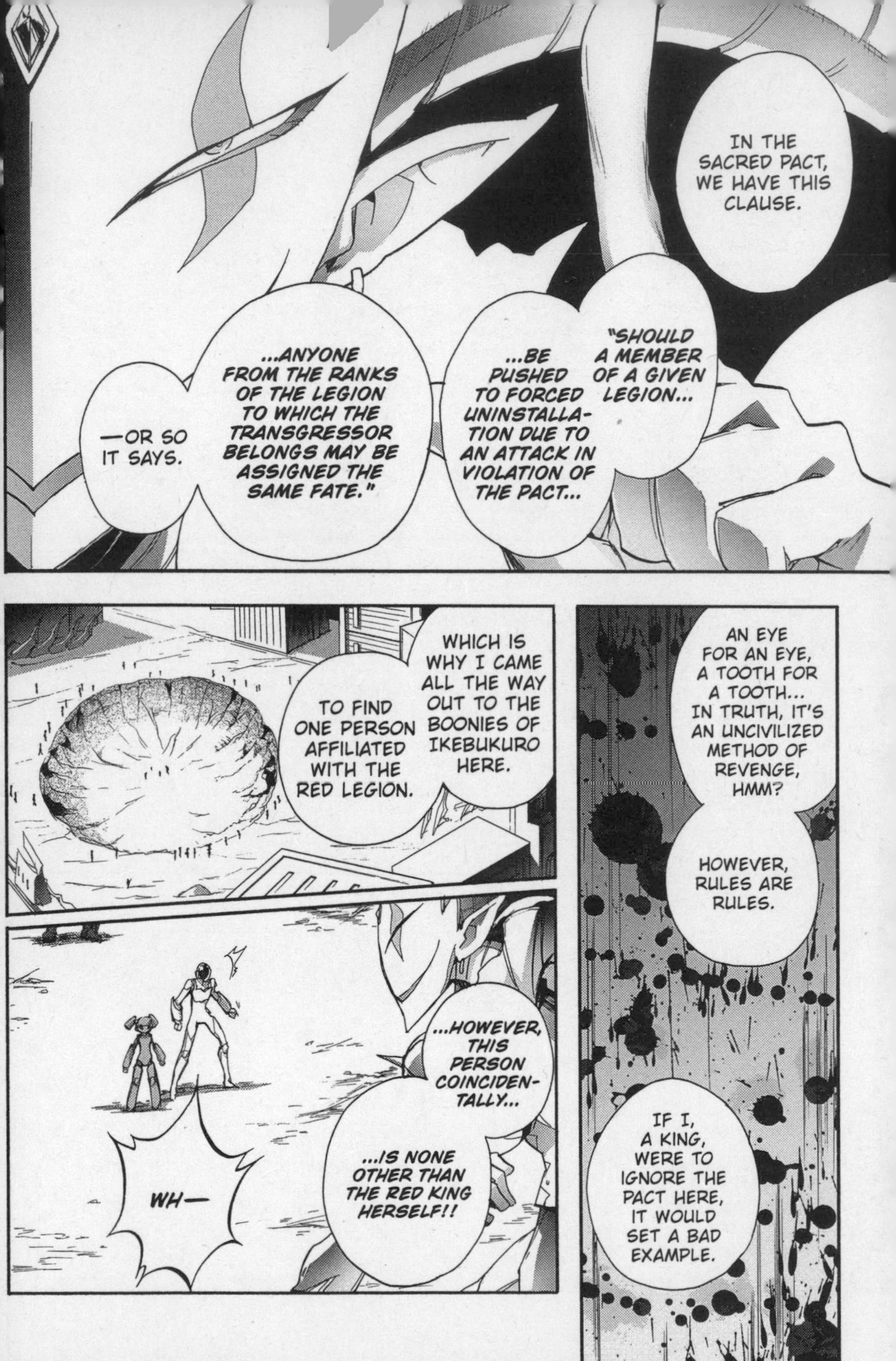
IN THE SACRED PACT, WE HAVE THIS CLAUSE.
"SHOULD A MEMBER OF A GIVEN LEGION...
...BE PUSHED TO FORCED UNINSTALLATION DUE TO AN ATTACK IN VIOLATION OF THE PACT...
...ANYONE FROM THE RANKS OF THE LEGION TO WHICH THE TRANSGRESSOR BELONGS MAY BE ASSIGNED THE SAME FATE."
—OR SO IT SAYS.
AN EYE FOR AN EYE, A TOOTH FOR A TOOTH... IN TRUTH, IT'S AN UNCIVILIZED METHOD OF REVENGE, HMM?
HOWEVER, RULES ARE RULES.
IF I, A KING, WERE TO IGNORE THE PACT HERE, IT WOULD SET A BAD EXAMPLE.
WHICH IS WHY I CAME ALL THE WAY OUT TO THE BOONIES OF IKEBUKURO HERE.
TO FIND ONE PERSON AFFILIATED WITH THE RED LEGION.
...HOWEVER, THIS PERSON COINCIDENTALLY...
...IS NONE OTHER THAN THE RED KING HERSELF!!
WH—

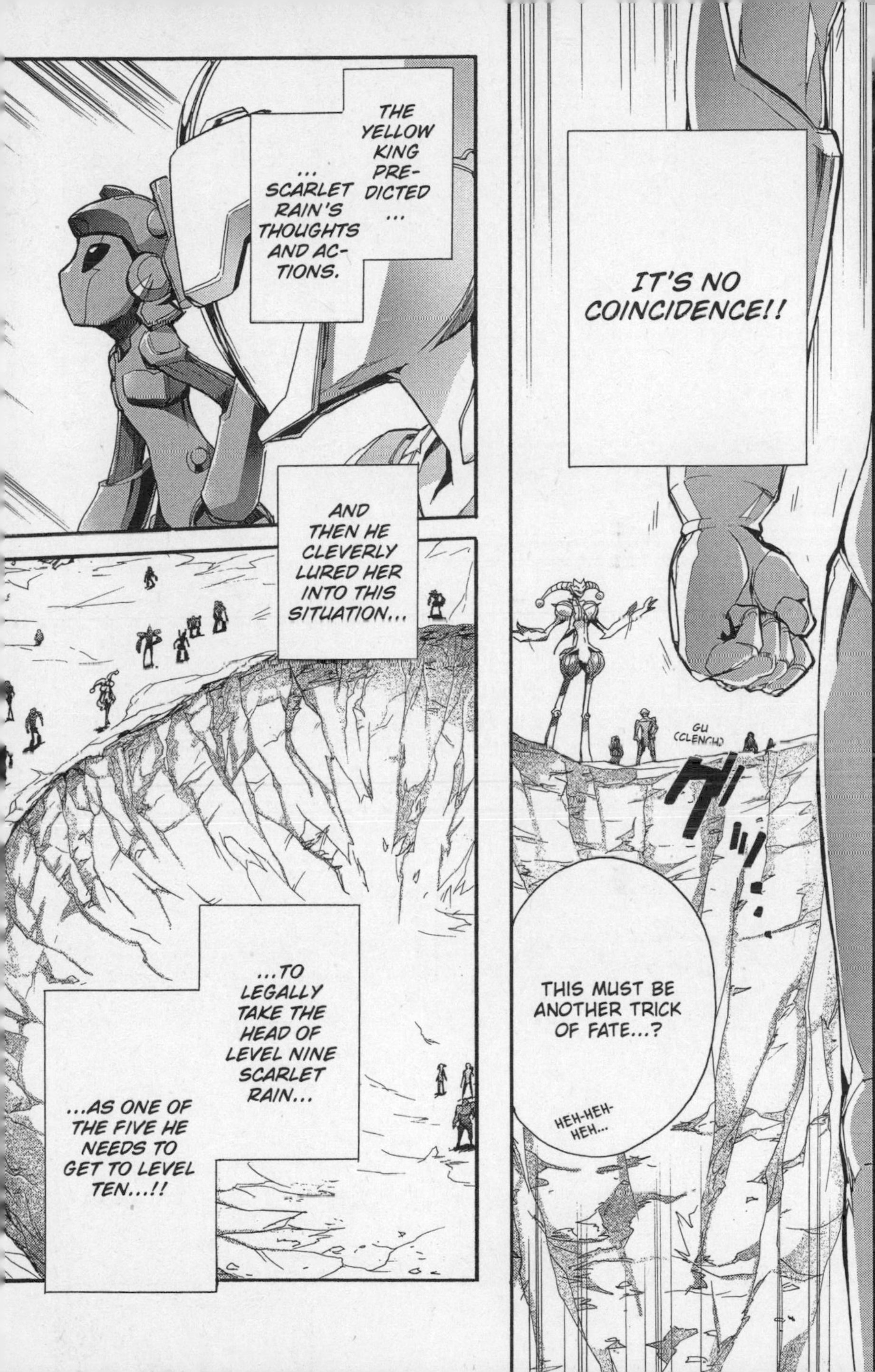
IT'S NO COINCIDENCE!!
GU (CLENCH)
THIS MUST BE ANOTHER TRICK OF FATE...?
HEH-HEH-HEH...
THE YELLOW KING PREDICTED...
...SCARLET RAIN'S THOUGHTS AND ACTIONS.
AND THEN HE CLEVERLY LURED HER INTO THIS SITUATION...
...TO LEGALLY TAKE THE HEAD OF LEVEL NINE SCARLET RAIN...
...AS ONE OF THE FIVE HE NEEDS TO GET TO LEVEL TEN...!!

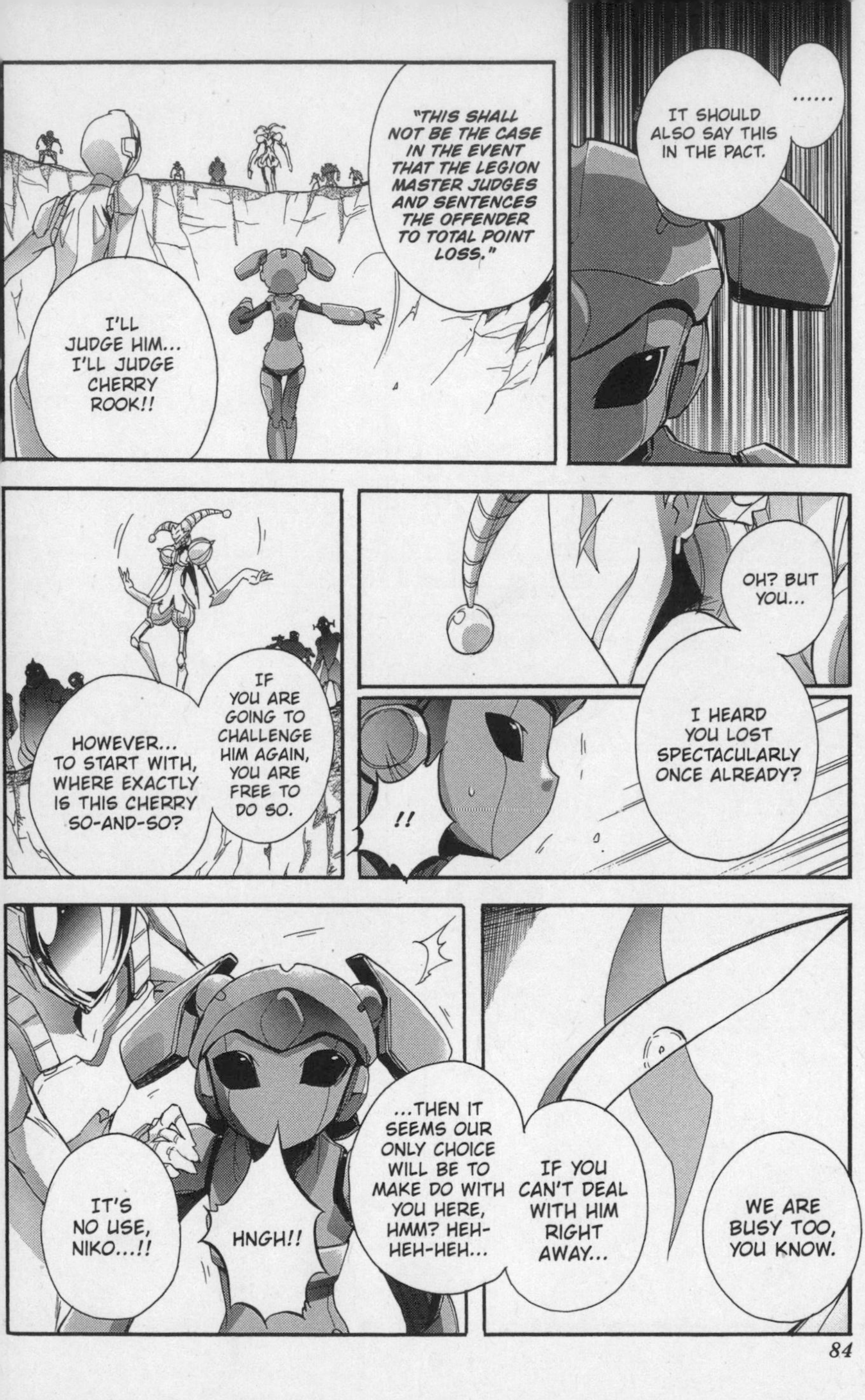
......
IT SHOULD ALSO SAY THIS IN THE PACT.
"THIS SHALL NOT BE THE CASE IN THE EVENT THAT THE LEGION MASTER JUDGES AND SENTENCES THE OFFENDER TO TOTAL POINT LOSS."
I'LL JUDGE HIM... I'LL JUDGE CHERRY ROOK!!
OH? BUT YOU...
I HEARD YOU LOST SPECTACULARLY ONCE ALREADY?
!!
IF YOU ARE GOING TO CHALLENGE HIM AGAIN, YOU ARE FREE TO DO SO.
HOWEVER... TO START WITH, WHERE EXACTLY IS THIS CHERRY SO-AND-SO?
WE ARE BUSY TOO, YOU KNOW.
IF YOU CAN'T DEAL WITH HIM RIGHT AWAY...
...THEN IT SEEMS OUR ONLY CHOICE WILL BE TO MAKE DO WITH YOU HERE, HMM? HEH-HEH-HEH...
HNGH!!
IT'S NO USE, NIKO...!!

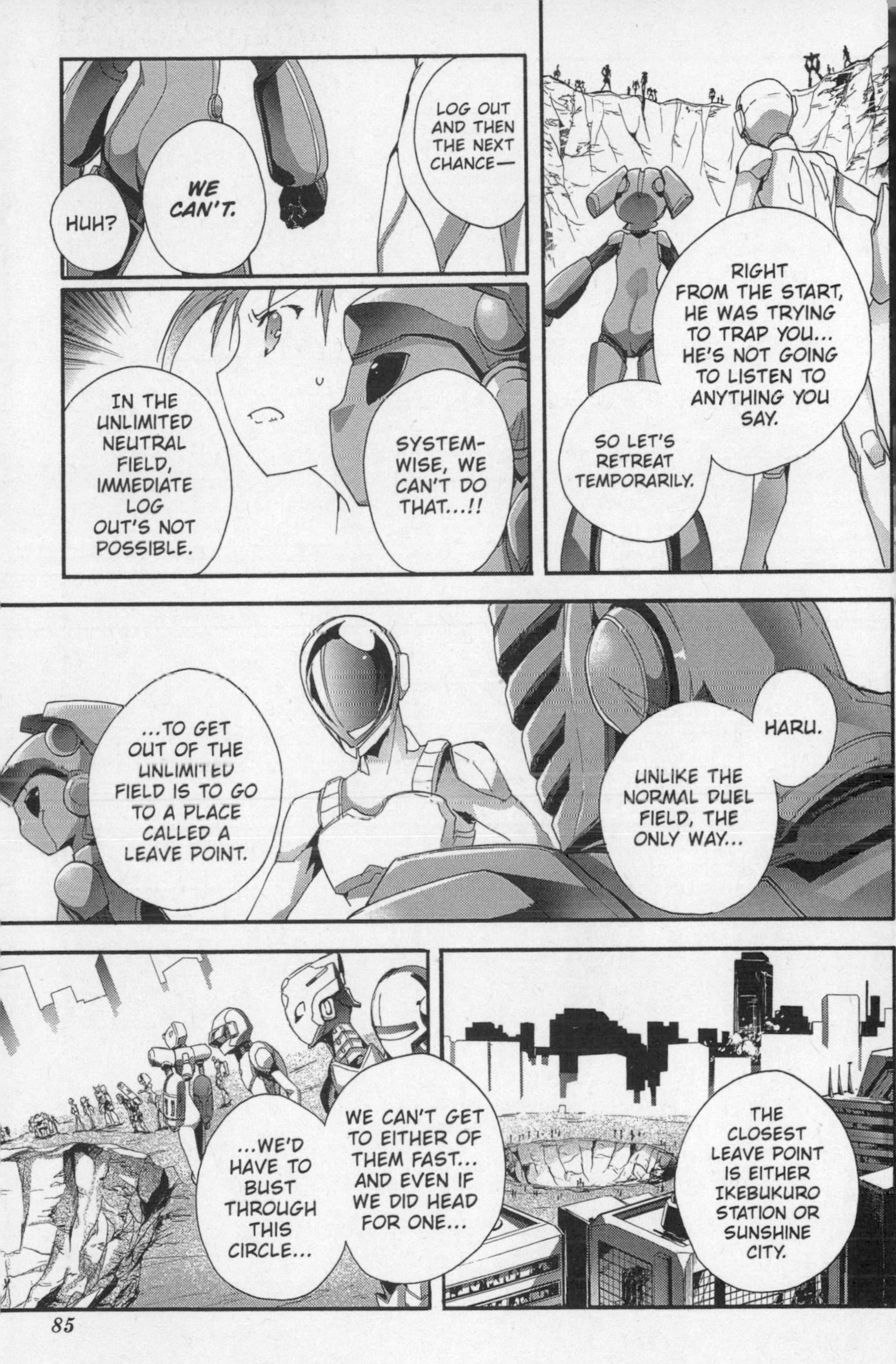
RIGHT FROM THE START, HE WAS TRYING TO TRAP YOU... HE'S NOT GOING TO LISTEN TO ANYTHING YOU SAY.
SO LET'S RETREAT TEMPORARILY.
LOG OUT AND THEN THE NEXT CHANCE—
WE CAN'T.
HUH?
SYSTEM-WISE, WE CAN'T DO THAT...!!
IN THE UNLIMITED NEUTRAL FIELD, IMMEDIATE LOG OUT'S NOT POSSIBLE.
HARU.
UNLIKE THE NORMAL DUEL FIELD, THE ONLY WAY...
...TO GET OUT OF THE UNLIMITED FIELD IS TO GO TO A PLACE CALLED A LEAVE POINT.
THE CLOSEST LEAVE POINT IS EITHER IKEBUKURO STATION OR SUNSHINE CITY.
WE CAN'T GET TO EITHER OF THEM FAST... AND EVEN IF WE DID HEAD FOR ONE...
...WE'D HAVE TO BUST THROUGH THIS CIRCLE...

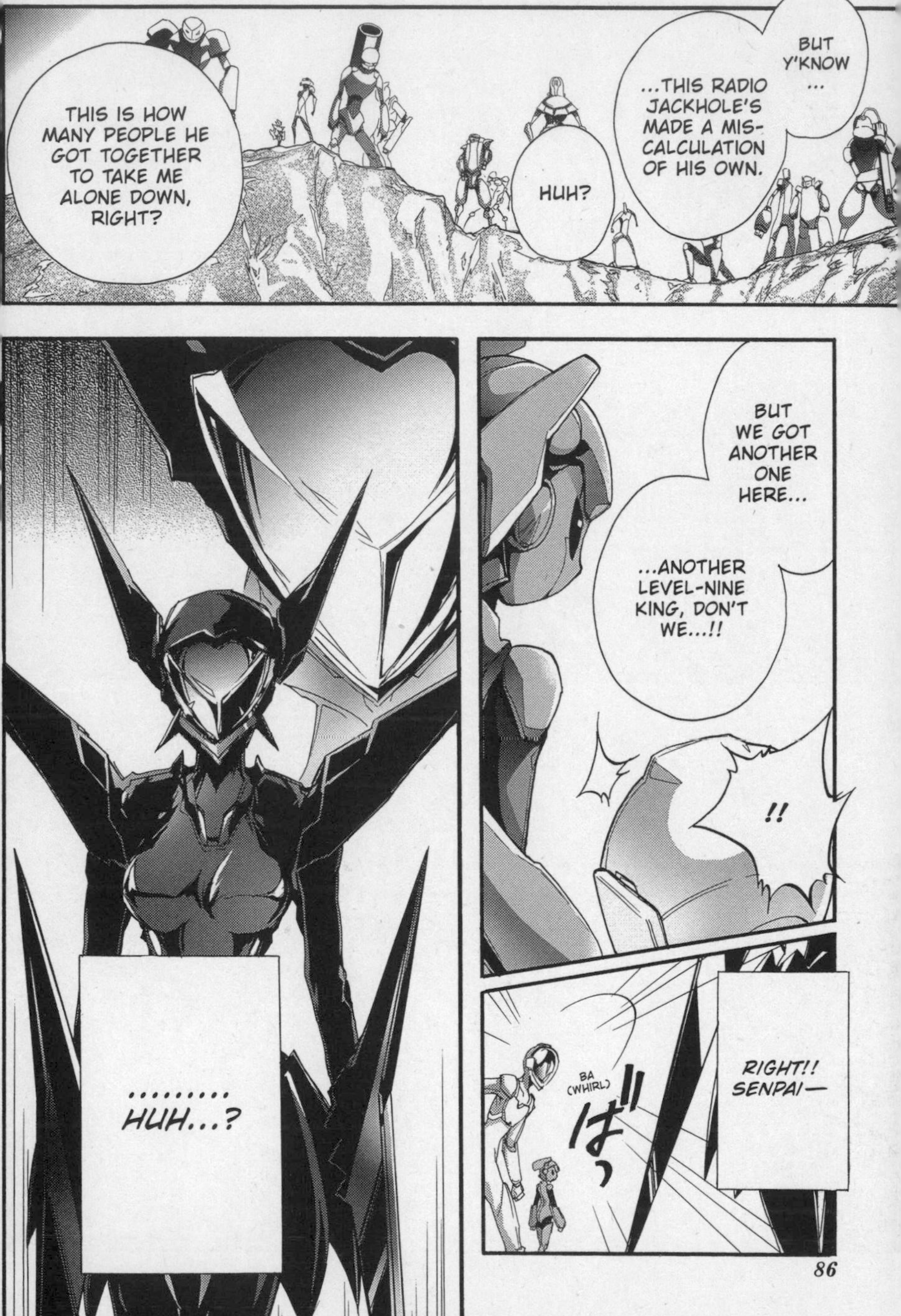
BUT Y'KNOW ...
...THIS RADIO JACKHOLE'S MADE A MIS-CALCULATION OF HIS OWN.
HUH?
THIS IS HOW MANY PEOPLE HE GOT TOGETHER TO TAKE ME ALONE DOWN, RIGHT?
BUT WE GOT ANOTHER ONE HERE...
...ANOTHER LEVEL-NINE KING, DON'T WE...!!
!!
RIGHT!! SENPAI—
BA (WHIRL)
ばっ
.... HUH...?

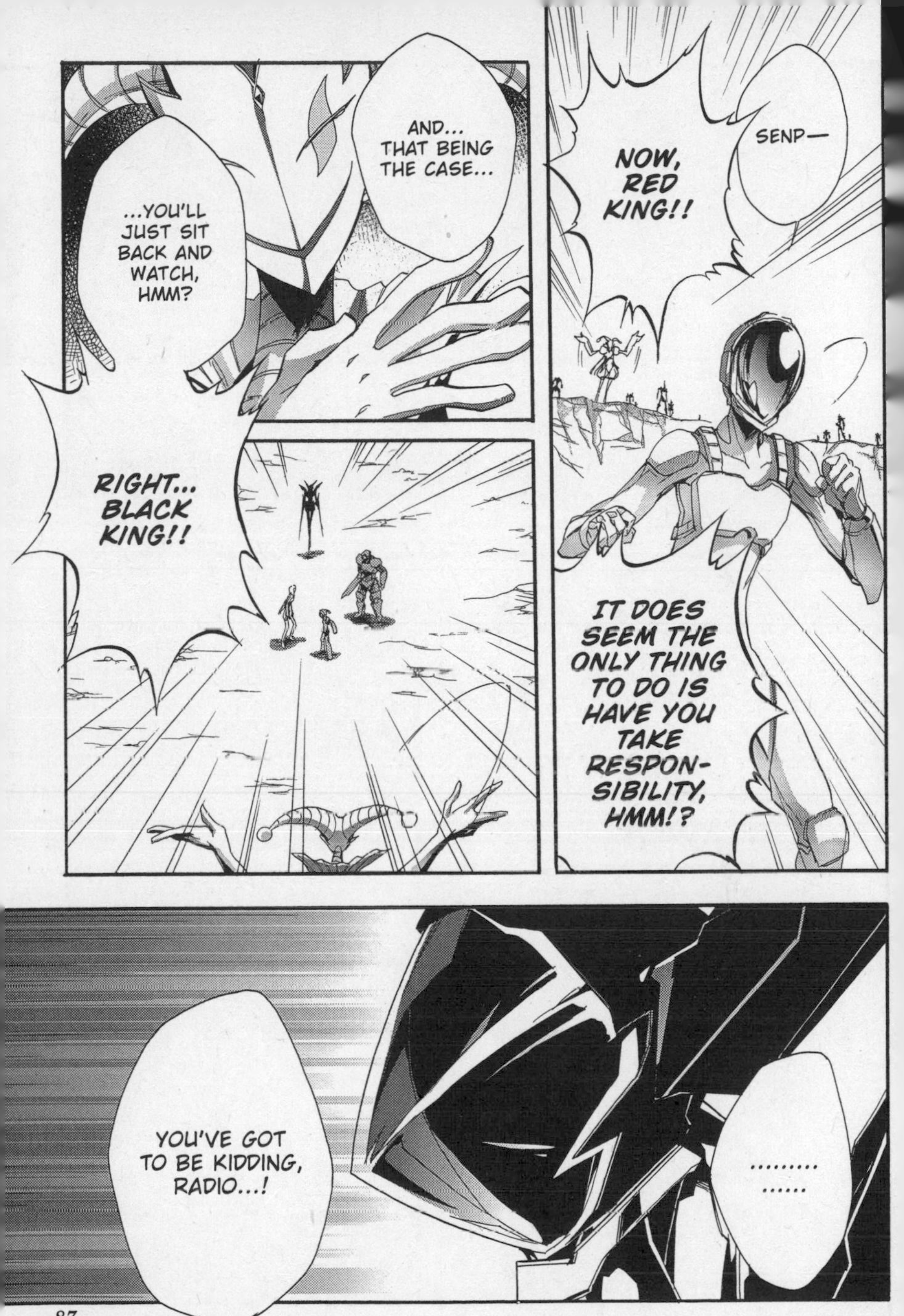
SENP—
NOW, RED KING!!
IT DOES SEEM THE ONLY THING TO DO IS HAVE YOU TAKE RESPON-SIBILITY, HMM!?
AND... THAT BEING THE CASE...
...YOU'LL JUST SIT BACK AND WATCH, HMM?
RIGHT... BLACK KING!!
....
......
YOU'VE GOT TO BE KIDDING, RADIO...!

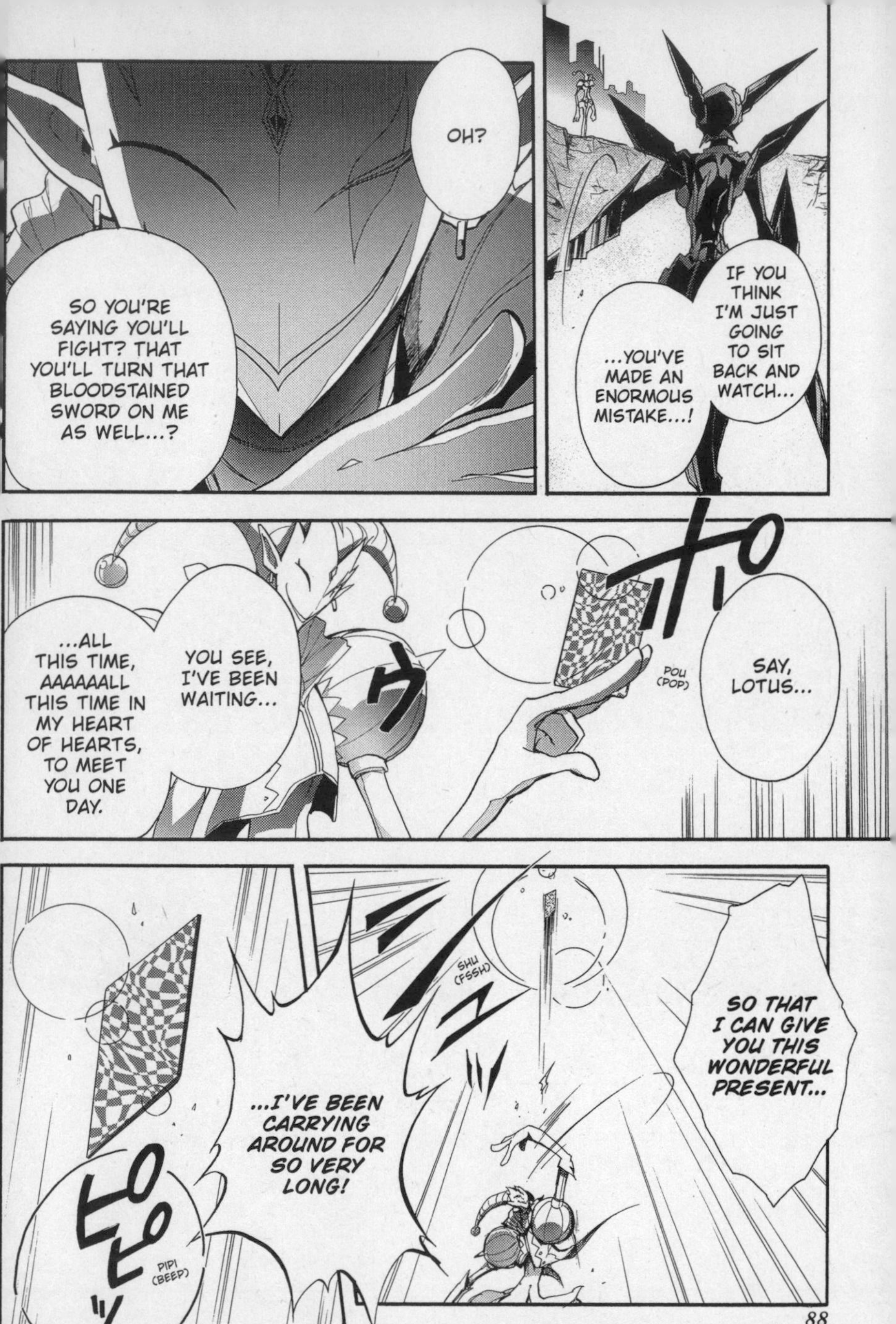
IF YOU THINK I'M JUST GOING TO SIT BACK AND WATCH...
...YOU'VE MADE AN ENORMOUS MISTAKE...!
OH?
SO YOU'RE SAYING YOU'LL FIGHT? THAT YOU'LL TURN THAT BLOODSTAINED SWORD ON ME AS WELL...?
SAY, LOTUS...
POU (POP)
YOU SEE, I'VE BEEN WAITING...
...ALL THIS TIME, AAAAAALL THIS TIME IN MY HEART OF HEARTS, TO MEET YOU ONE DAY.
SO THAT I CAN GIVE YOU THIS WONDERFUL PRESENT...
SHU (FSSH)
...I'VE BEEN CARRYING AROUND FOR SO VERY LONG!
PIPI (BEEP)

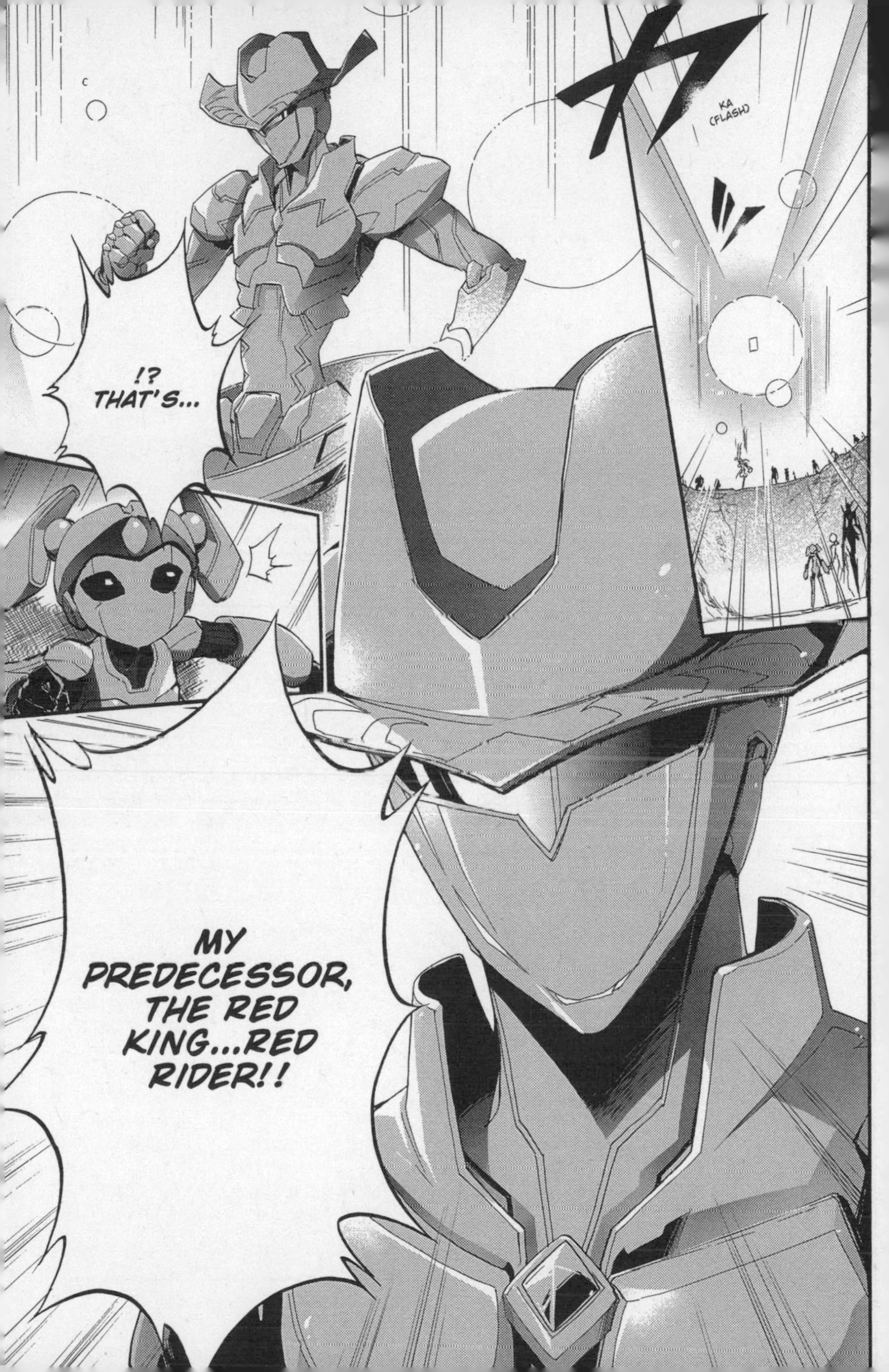
KA (FLASH)
!? THAT'S...
MY PREDECESSOR, THE RED KING...RED RIDER!!

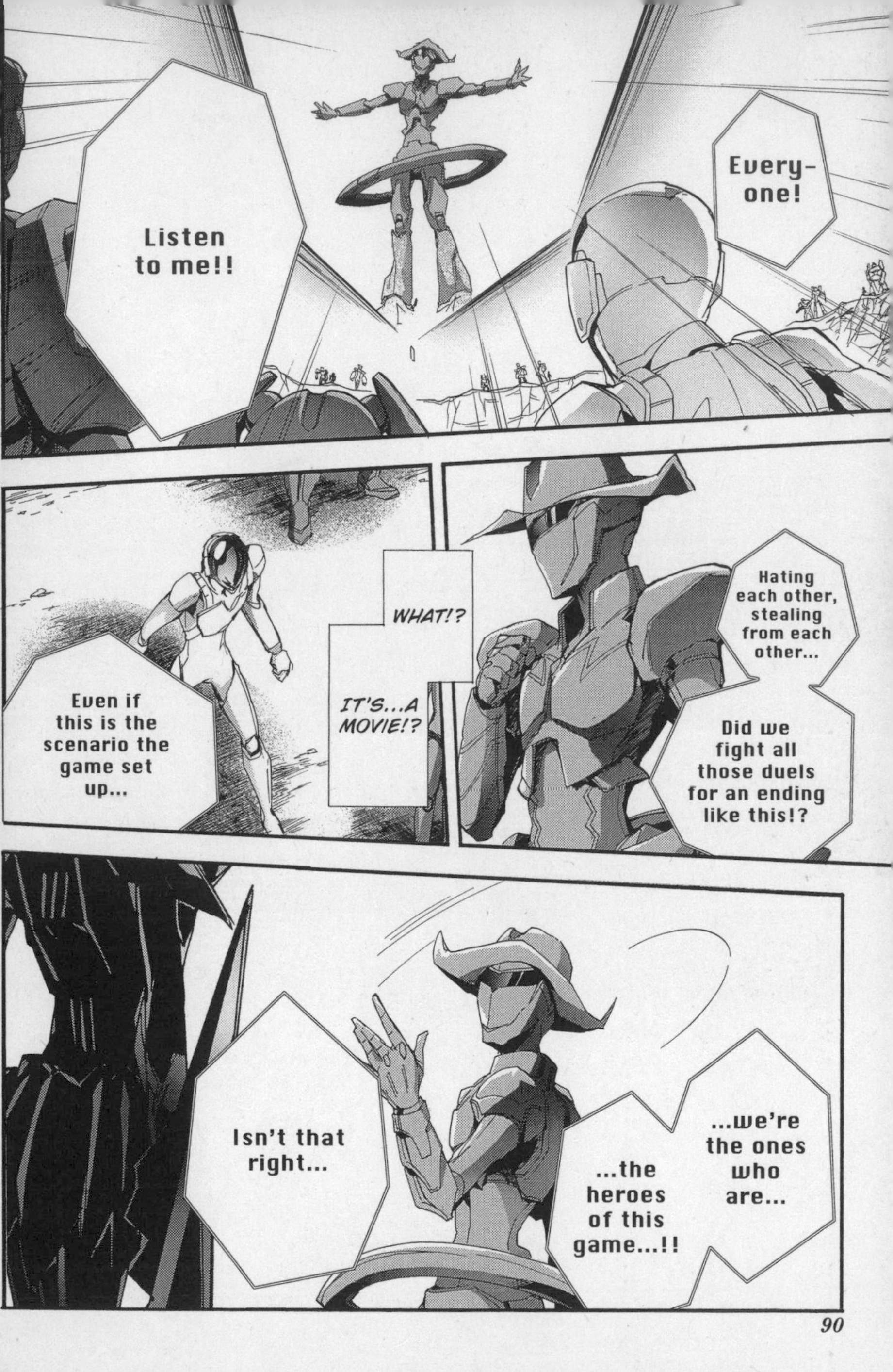
Every-one!
Listen to me!!
Hating each other, stealing from each other...
Did we fight all those duels for an ending like this!?
WHAT!?
IT'S...A MOVIE!?
Even if this is the scenario the game set up...
...we're the ones who are...
...the heroes of this game...!!
Isn't that right...

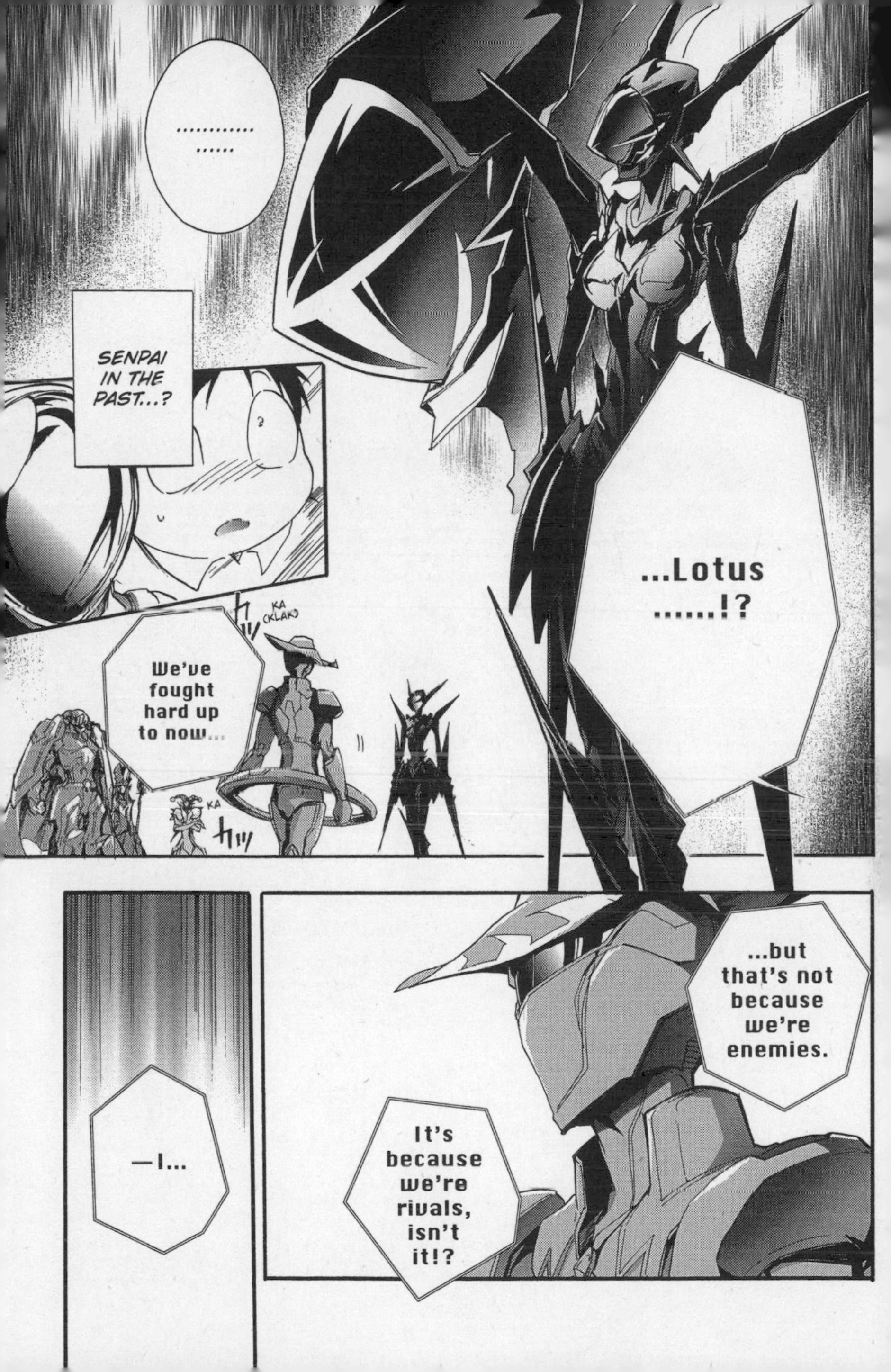
....
......
...Lotus
......!?
SENPAI IN THE PAST...?
KA (KLAK)
We've fought hard up to now...
KA
...but that's not because we're enemies.
It's because we're rivals, isn't it!?
—I...

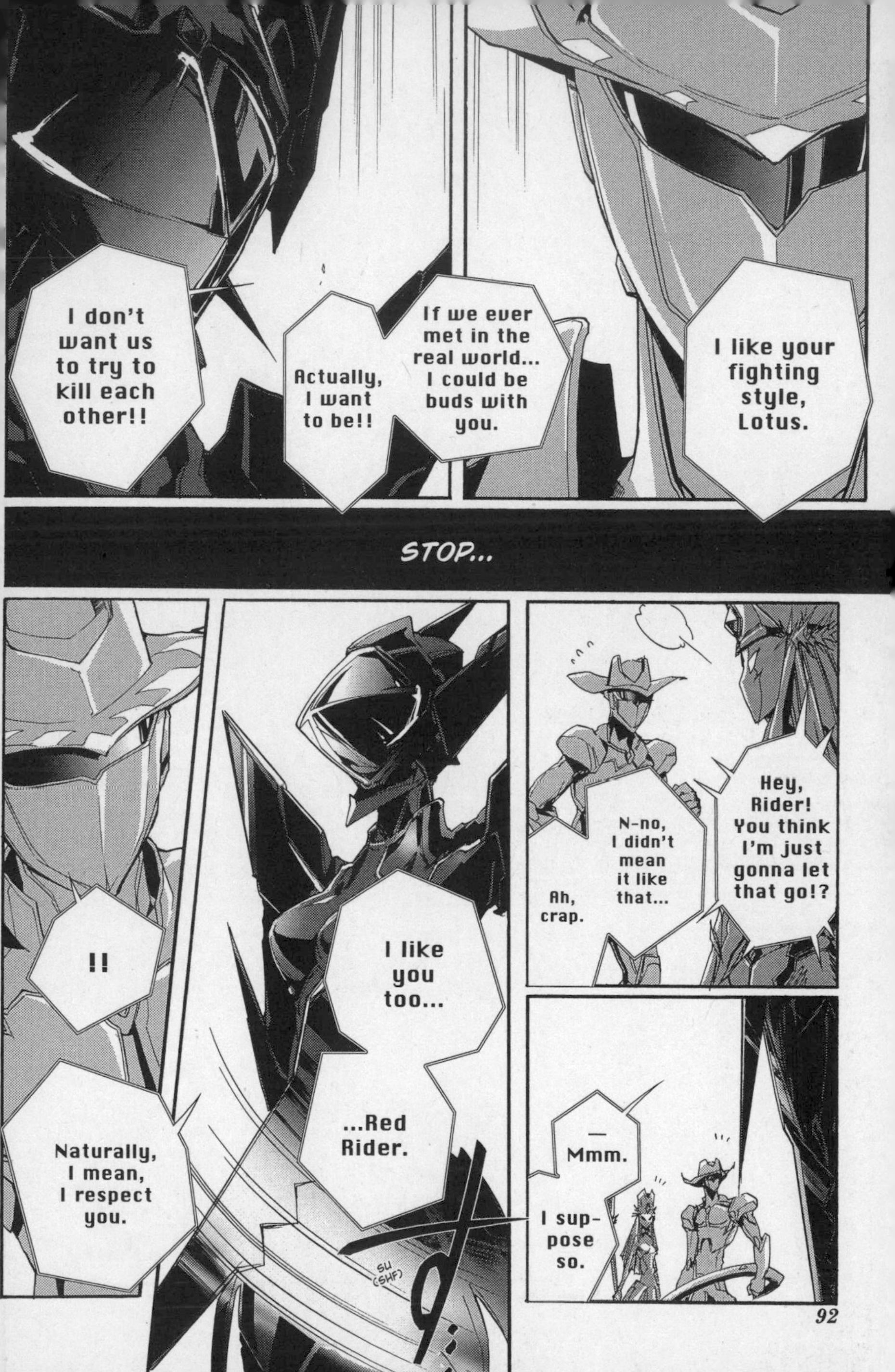
I like your fighting style, Lotus.
If we ever met in the real world... I could be buds with you.
Actually, I want to be!!
I don't want us to try to kill each other!!
STOP...
Hey, Rider! You think I'm just gonna let that go!?
N-no, I didn't mean it like that...
Ah, crap.
—Mmm.
I sup-pose so.
I like you too...
...Red Rider.
SU (SHF)
!!
Naturally, I mean, I respect you.

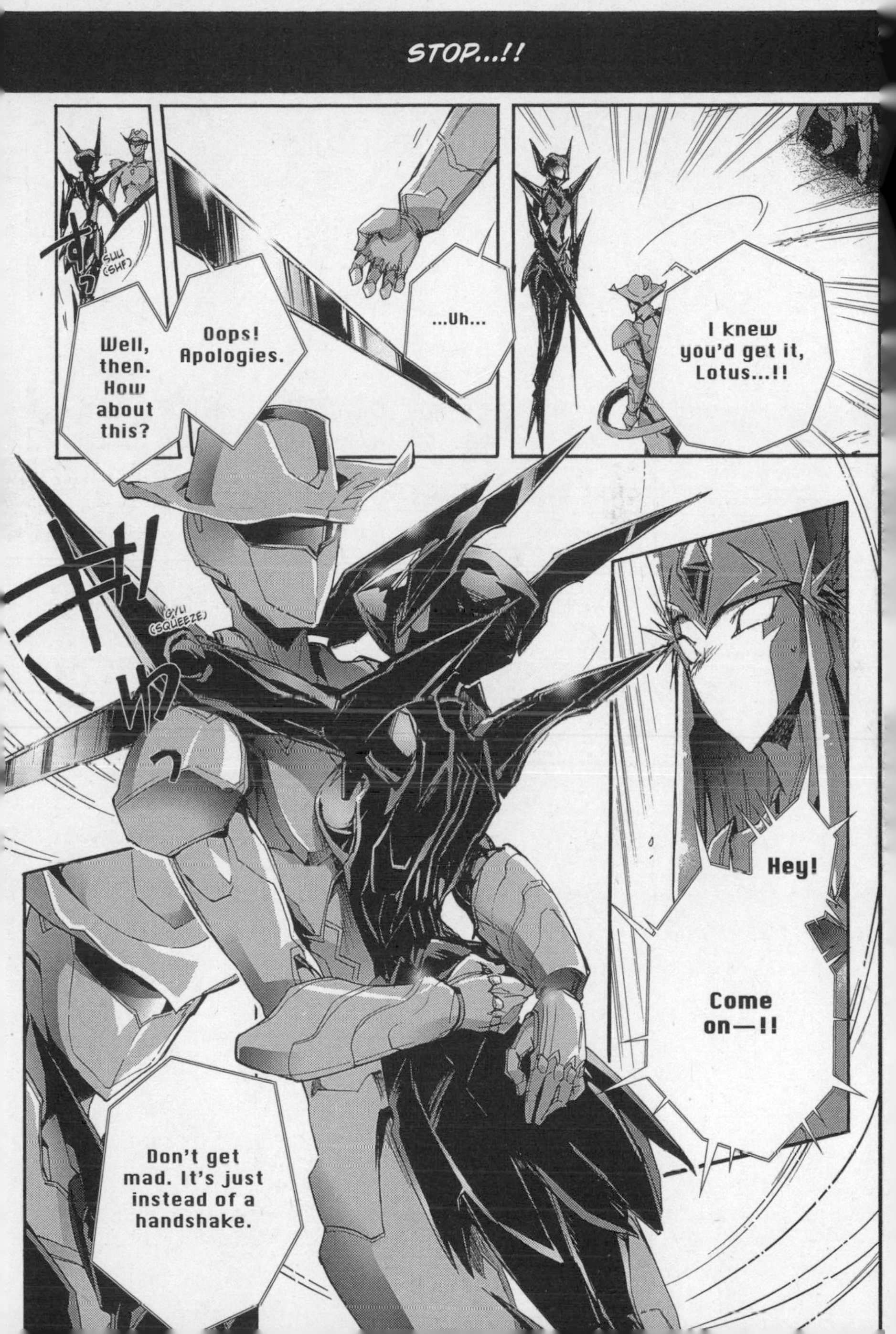
STOP...!!
I knew you'd get it, Lotus...!!
...Uh...
Oops! Apologies.
SUU (SHF)
Well, then. How about this?
GYU (SQUEEZE)
Hey!
Come on—!!
Don't get mad. It's just instead of a handshake.

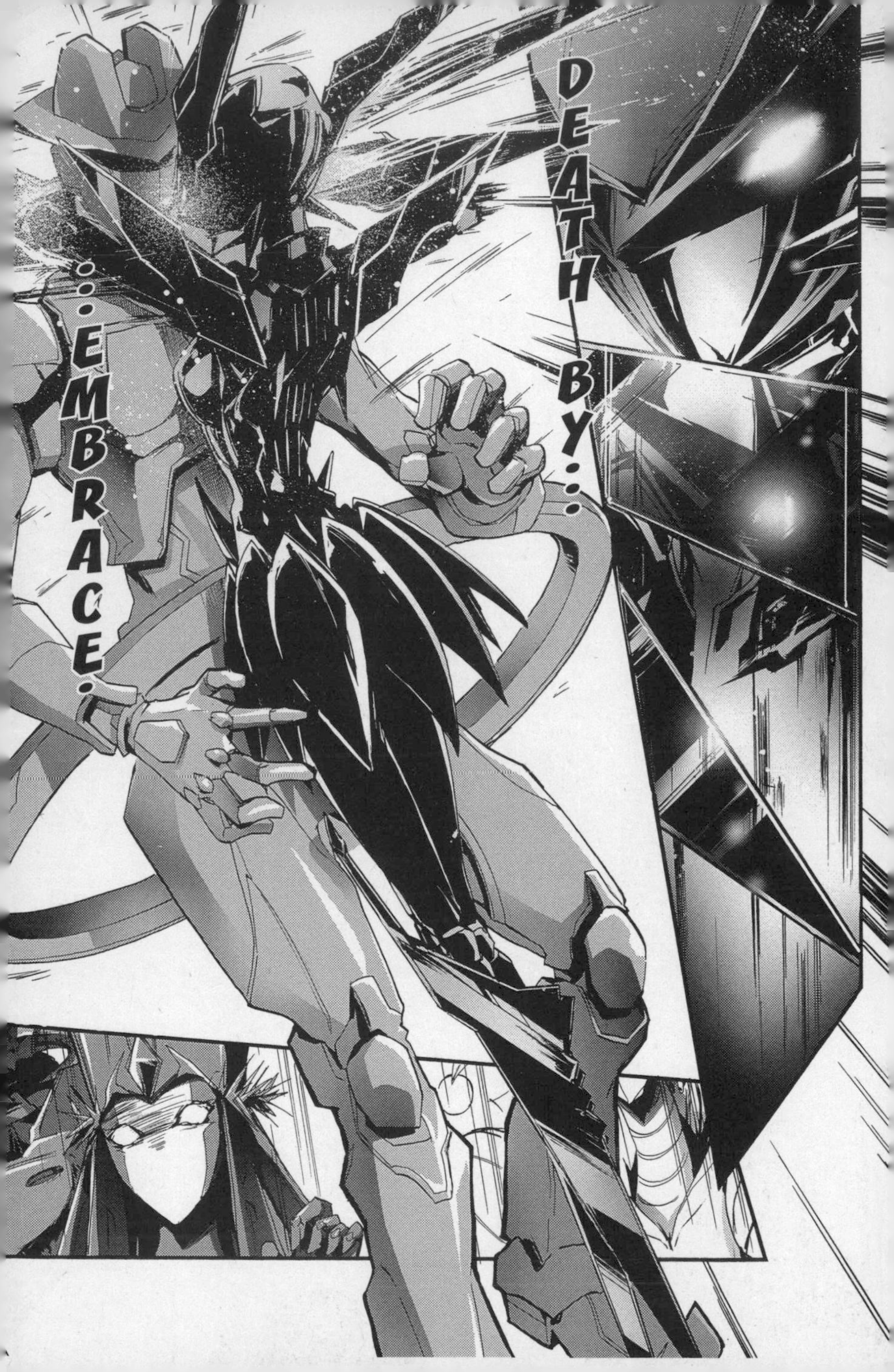
DEATH BY...
...EMBRACE.

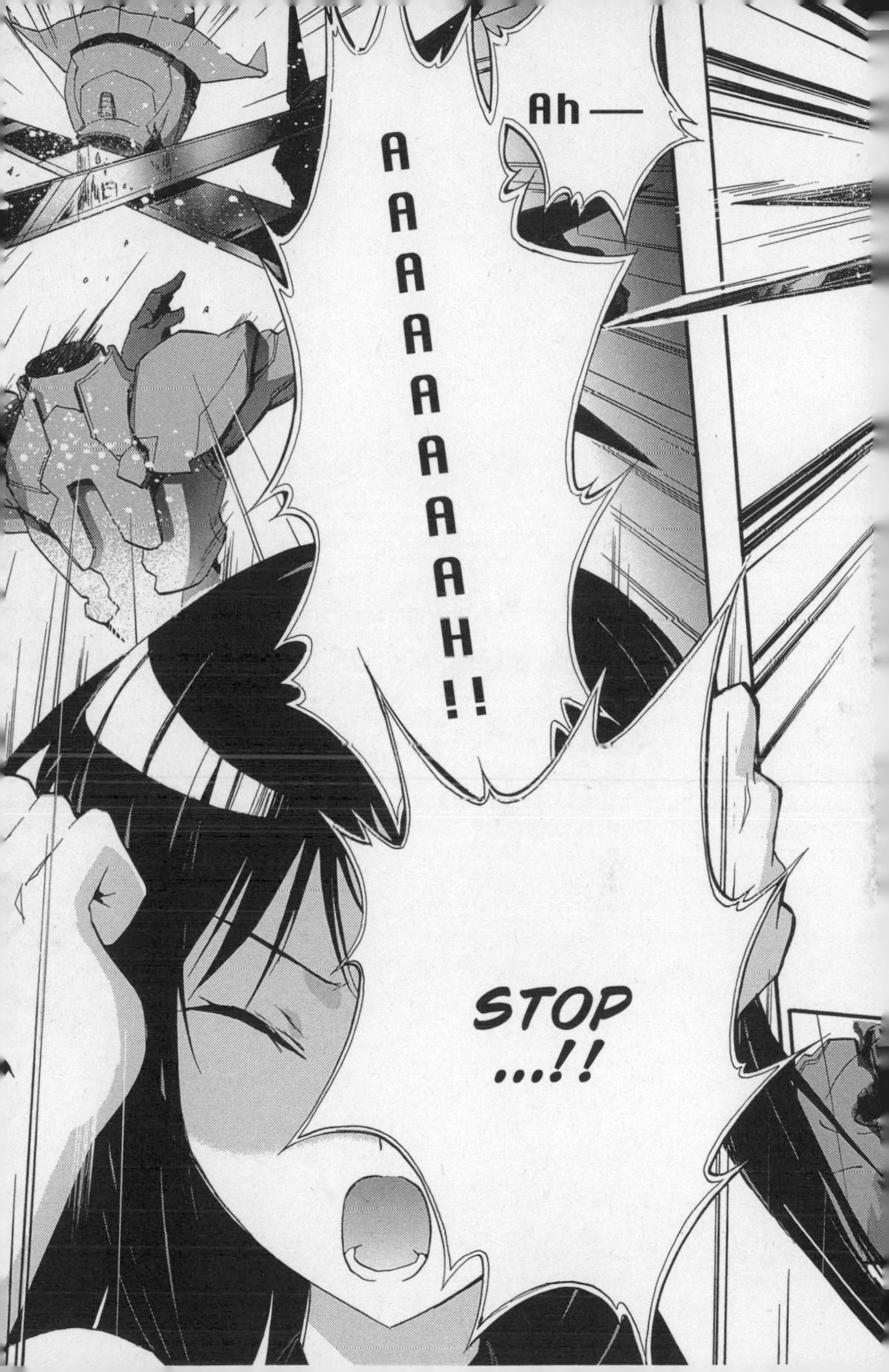
Ah—
AAAAAAAAH!!
STOP ...!!

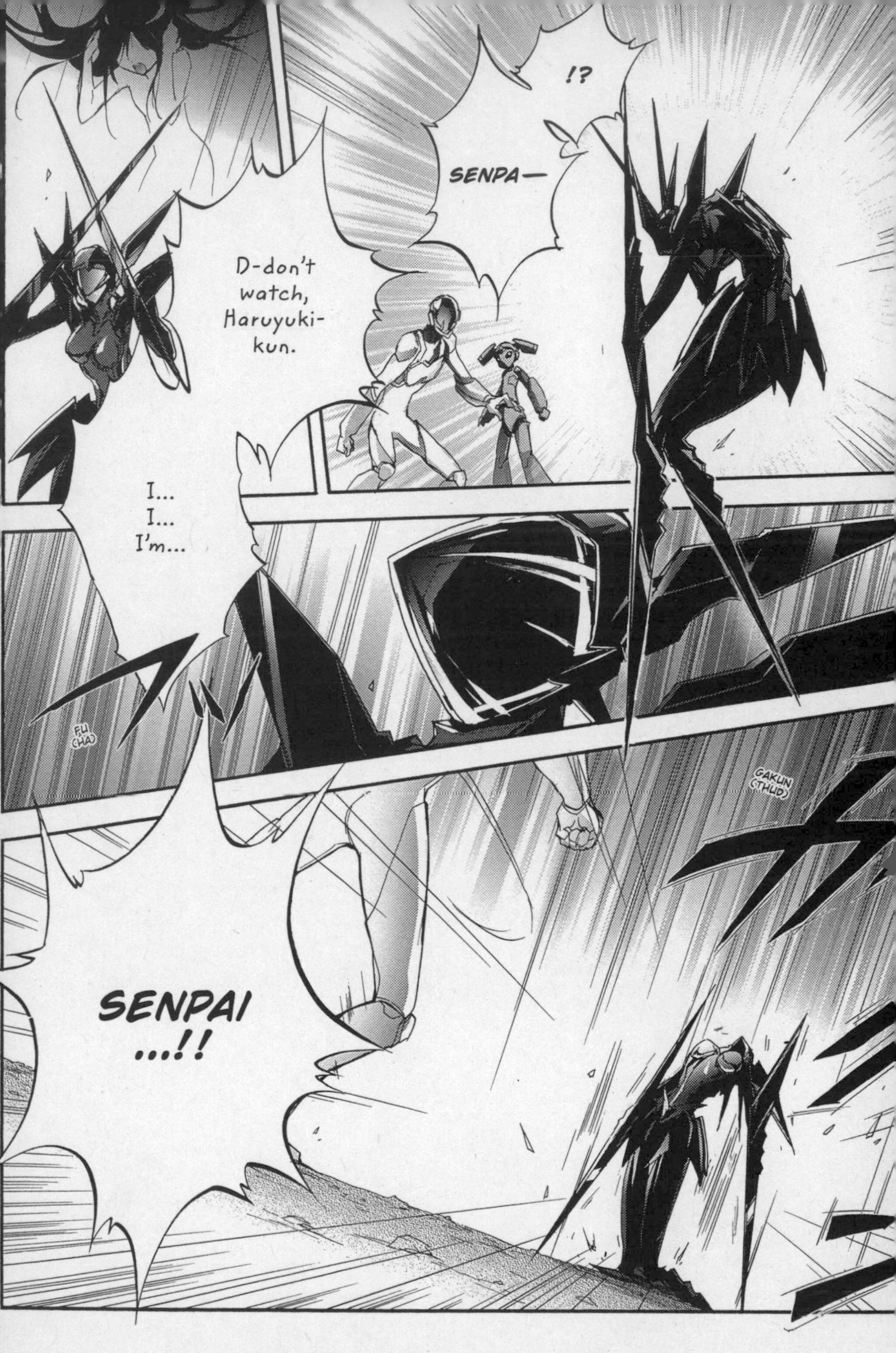

!?
SENPA—
D-don't watch, Haruyuki-kun.
I... I... I'm...
FU CHA
GAKUN (THUD)
SENPAI ...!!

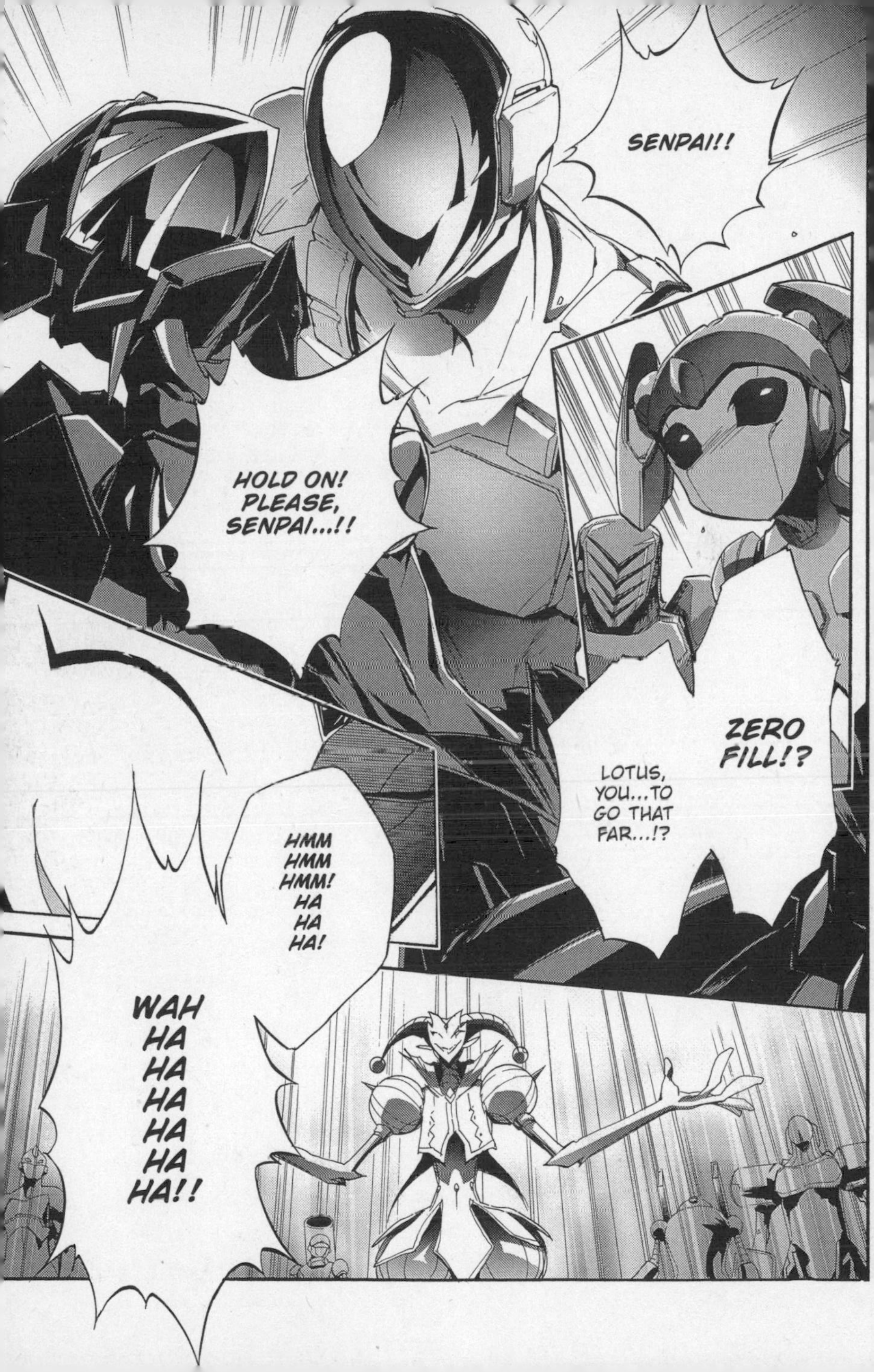
SENPAI!!
HOLD ON! PLEASE, SENPAI...!!
ZERO FILL!?
LOTUS, YOU...TO GO THAT FAR...!?
HMM HMM HMM! HA HA HA!
WAH HA HA HA HA HA HA!!

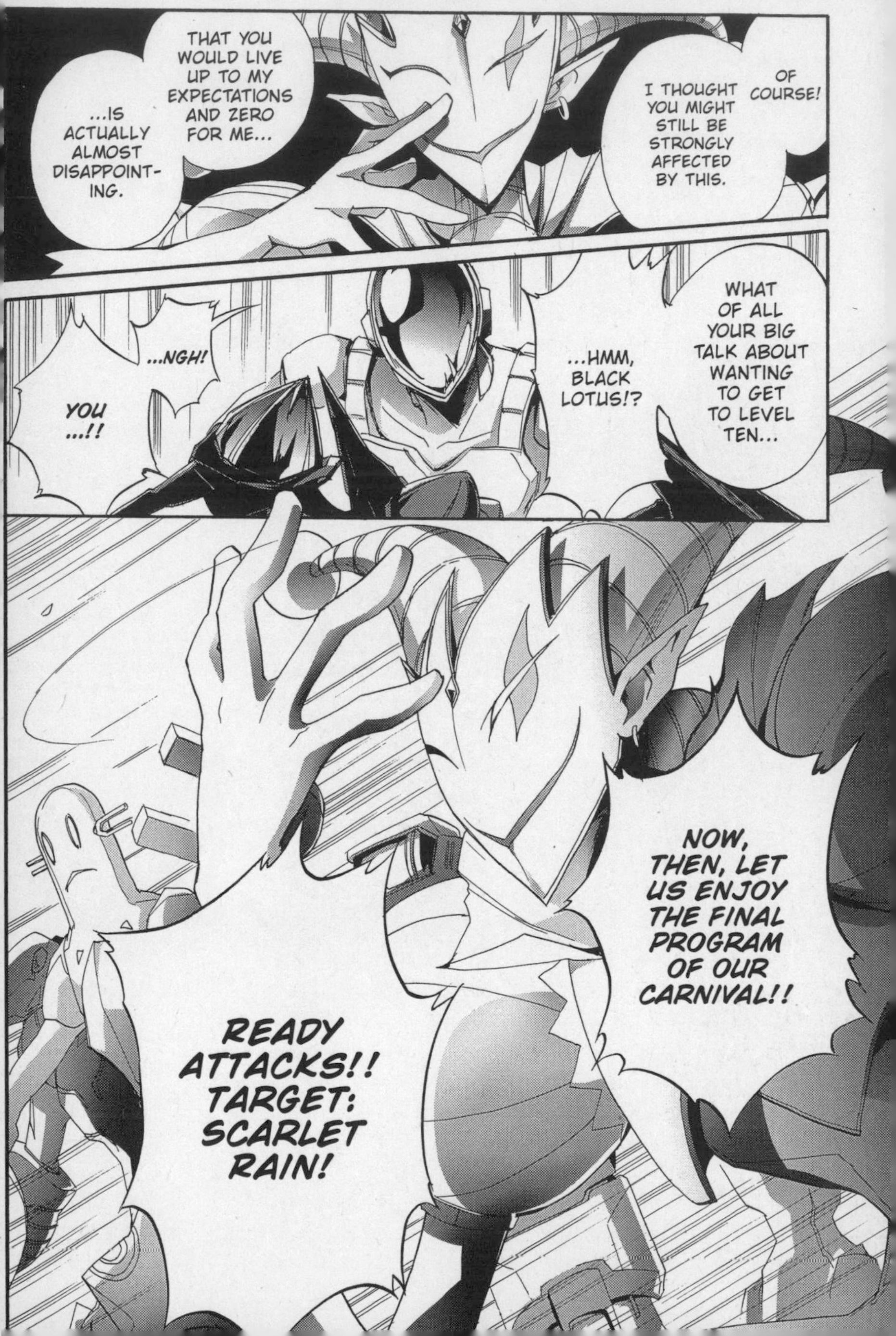
OF COURSE!
I THOUGHT YOU MIGHT STILL BE STRONGLY AFFECTED BY THIS.
THAT YOU WOULD LIVE UP TO MY EXPECTATIONS AND ZERO FOR ME...
...IS ACTUALLY ALMOST DISAPPOINT-ING.
WHAT OF ALL YOUR BIG TALK ABOUT WANTING TO GET TO LEVEL TEN...
...HMM, BLACK LOTUS!?
...NGH!
YOU ...!!
NOW, THEN, LET US ENJOY THE FINAL PROGRAM OF OUR CARNIVAL!!
READY ATTACKS!! TARGET: SCARLET RAIN!

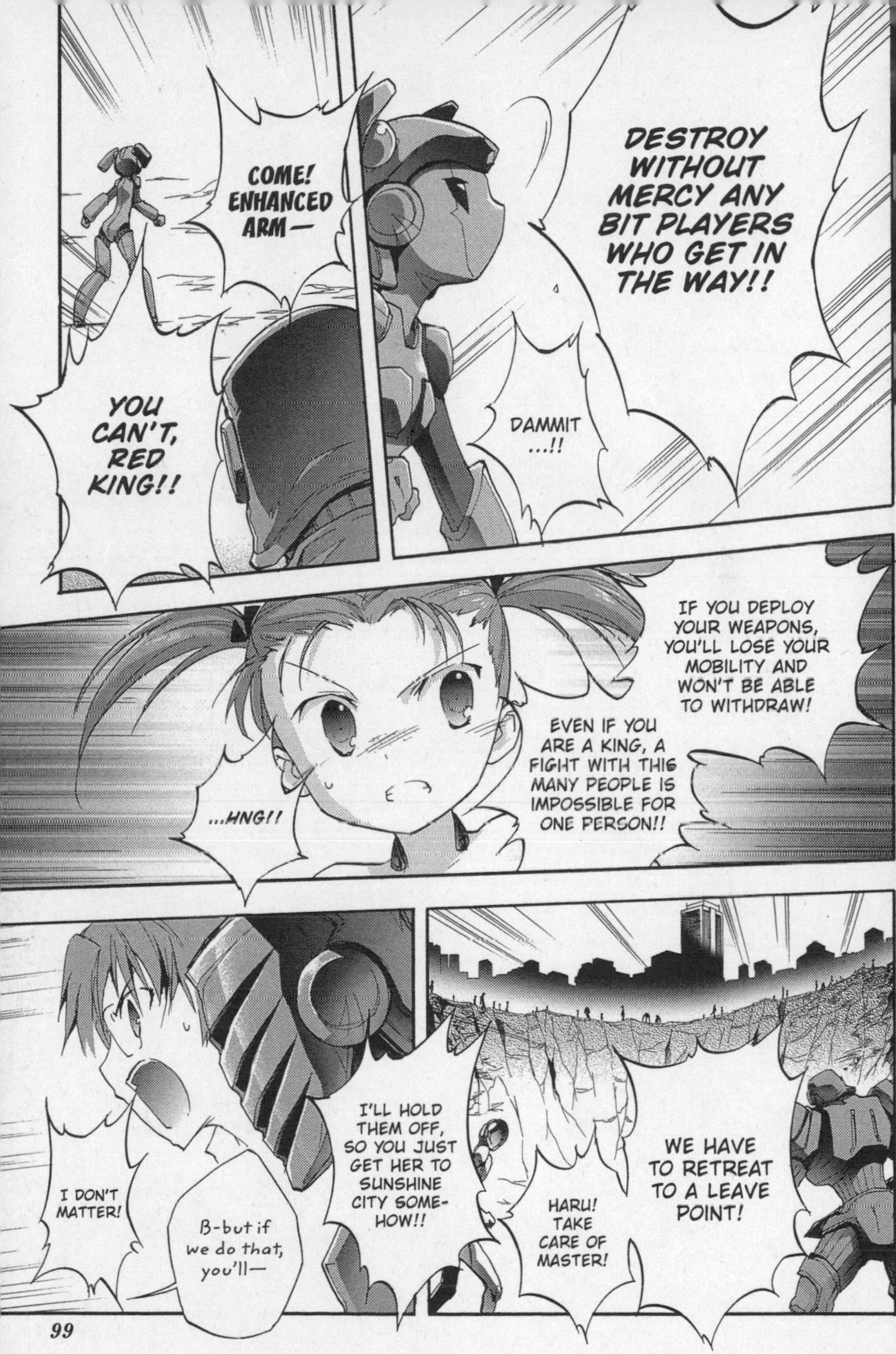
DESTROY WITHOUT MERCY ANY BIT PLAYERS WHO GET IN THE WAY!!
DAMMIT ...!!
COME! ENHANCED ARM—
YOU CAN'T, RED KING!!
IF YOU DEPLOY YOUR WEAPONS, YOU'LL LOSE YOUR MOBILITY AND WON'T BE ABLE TO WITHDRAW!
EVEN IF YOU ARE A KING, A FIGHT WITH THIS MANY PEOPLE IS IMPOSSIBLE FOR ONE PERSON!!
...HNG!!
WE HAVE TO RETREAT TO A LEAVE POINT!
HARU! TAKE CARE OF MASTER!
I'LL HOLD THEM OFF, SO YOU JUST GET HER TO SUNSHINE CITY SOME-HOW!!
B-but if we do that, you'll—
I DON'T MATTER!

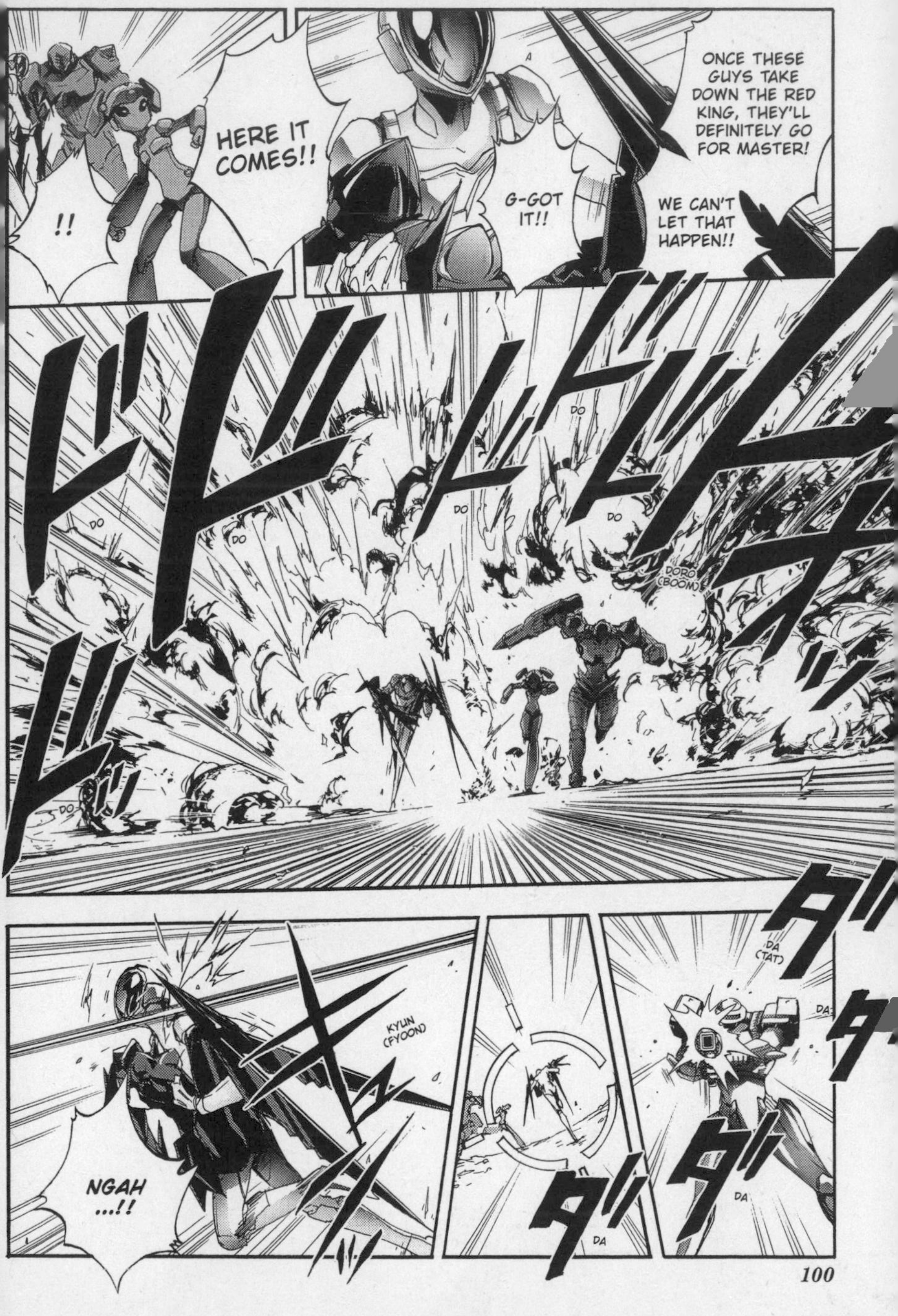

ONCE THESE GUYS TAKE DOWN THE RED KING, THEY'LL DEFINITELY GO FOR MASTER!
WE CAN'T LET THAT HAPPEN!!
G-GOT IT!!
HERE IT COMES!!
!!
DO
DORO (BOOM)
DO
DO
DO
DO
DO
DA (TAT)
DA
DA
DA
KYUN (FYOON)
NGAH ...!!

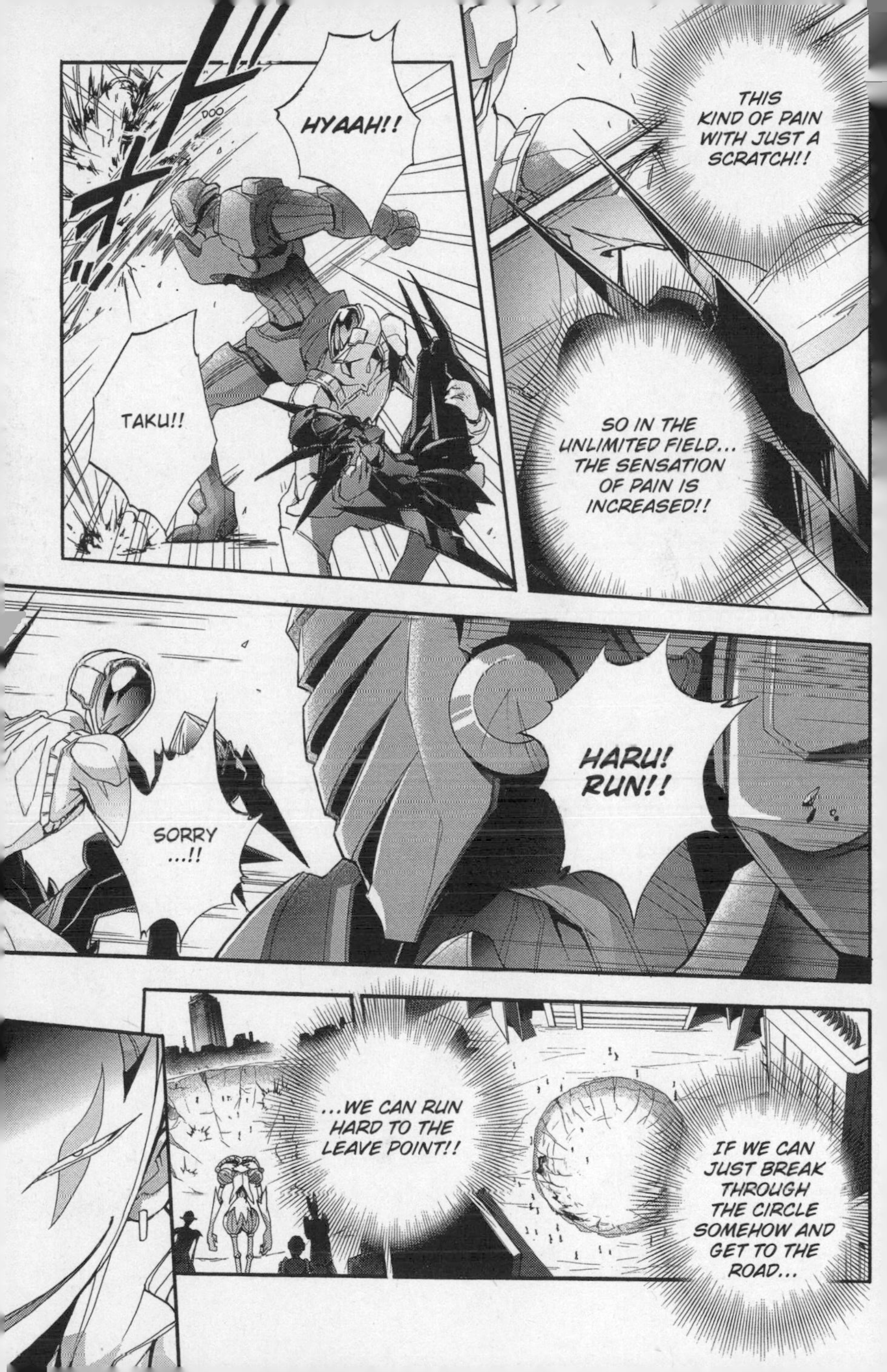
THIS KIND OF PAIN WITH JUST A SCRATCH!!
SO IN THE UNLIMITED FIELD... THE SENSATION OF PAIN IS INCREASED!!
DOO
HYAAH!!
TAKU!!
HARU! RUN!!
SORRY ...!!
IF WE CAN JUST BREAK THROUGH THE CIRCLE SOMEHOW AND GET TO THE ROAD...
...WE CAN RUN HARD TO THE LEAVE POINT!!

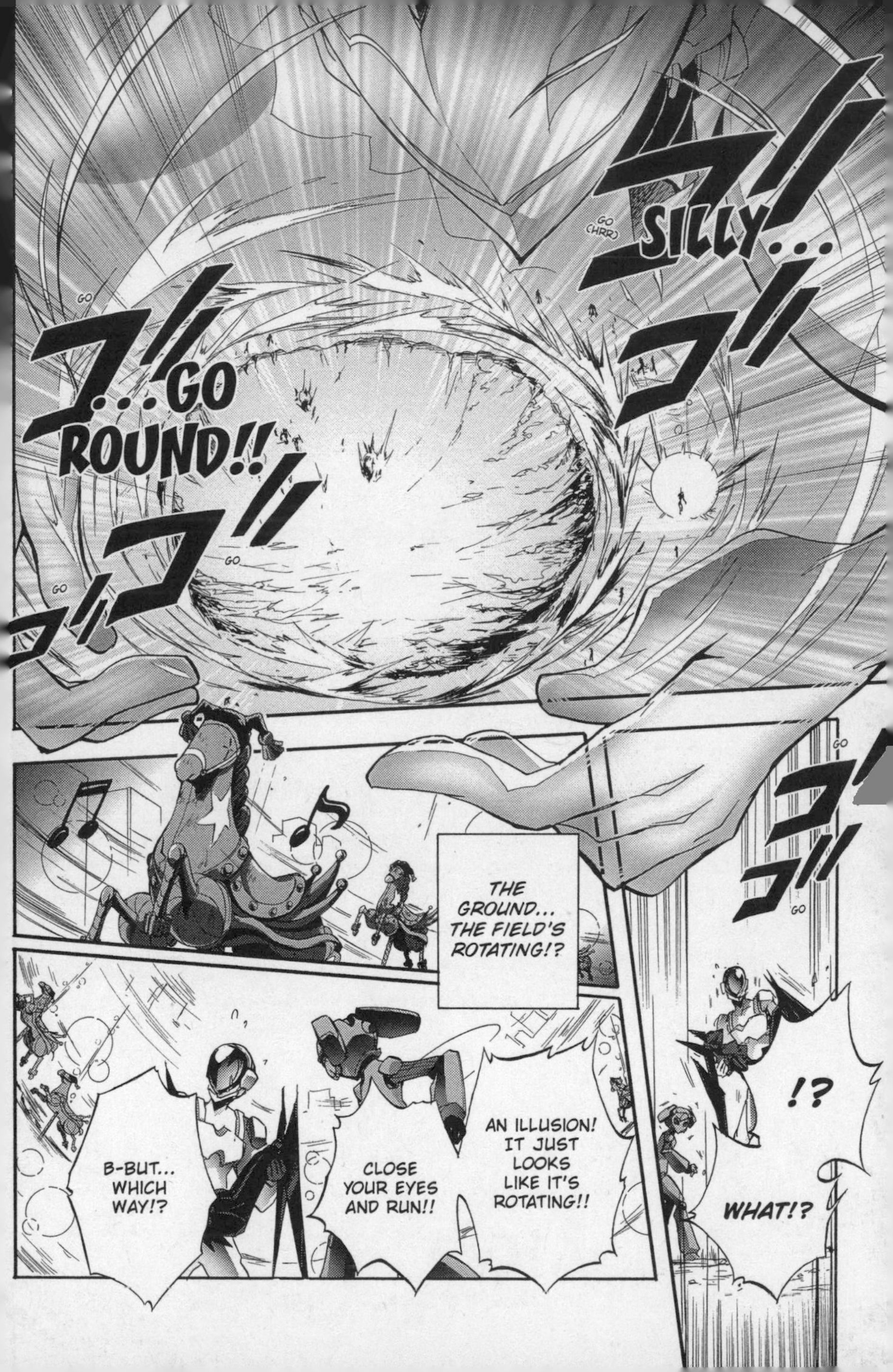
GO (HRR)
SILLY...
GO
GO... GO ROUND!!
GO
GO
GO
GO
THE GROUND... THE FIELD'S ROTATING!?
!?
WHAT!?
AN ILLUSION! IT JUST LOOKS LIKE IT'S ROTATING!!
CLOSE YOUR EYES AND RUN!!
B-BUT... WHICH WAY!?

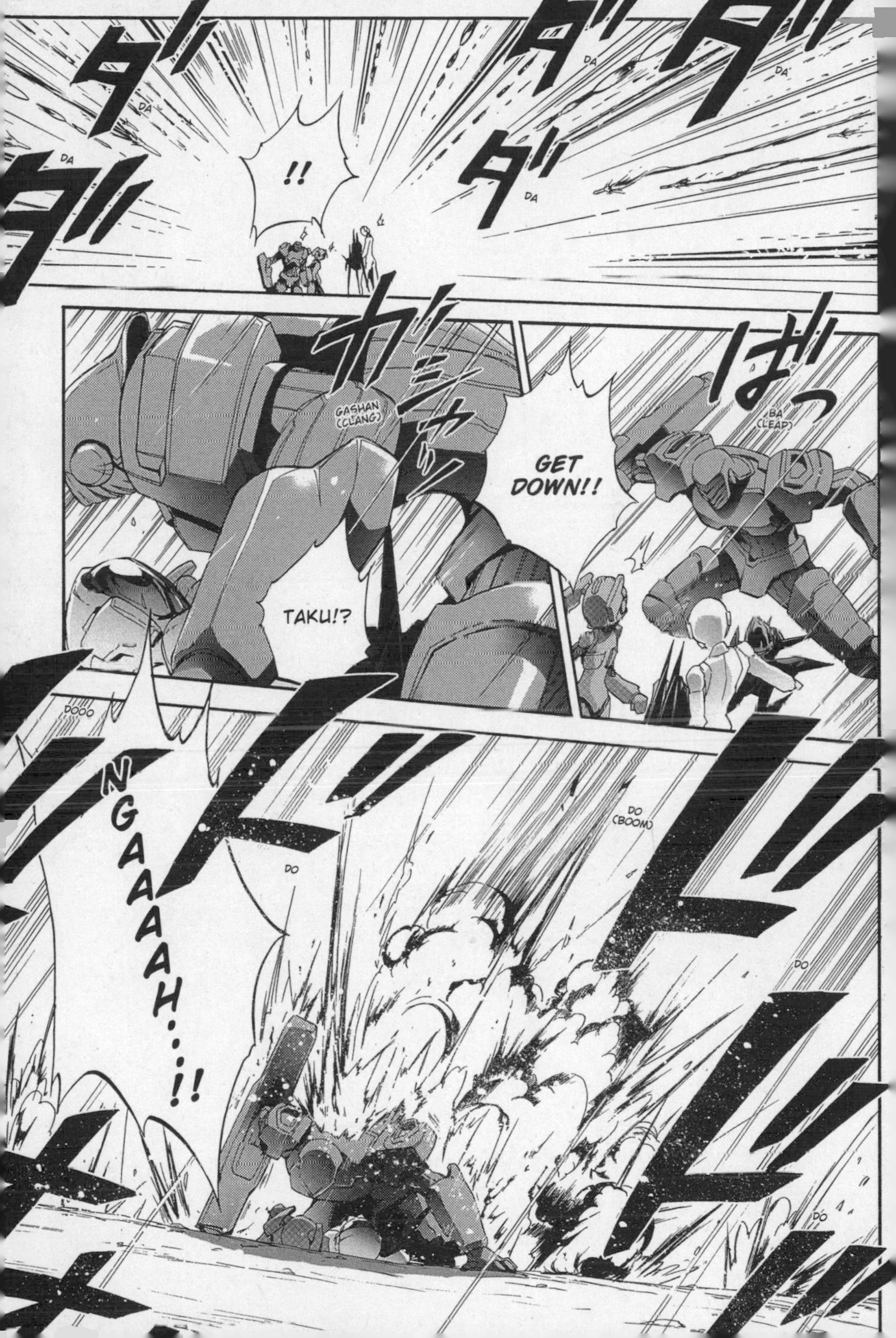
DA
DA
DA
!!
DA
DA
BA (LEAP)
GET DOWN!!
GASHAN (CLANG)
TAKU!?
DO (BOOM)
DO
DO
DO
DOOO
NGAAAAH...!!

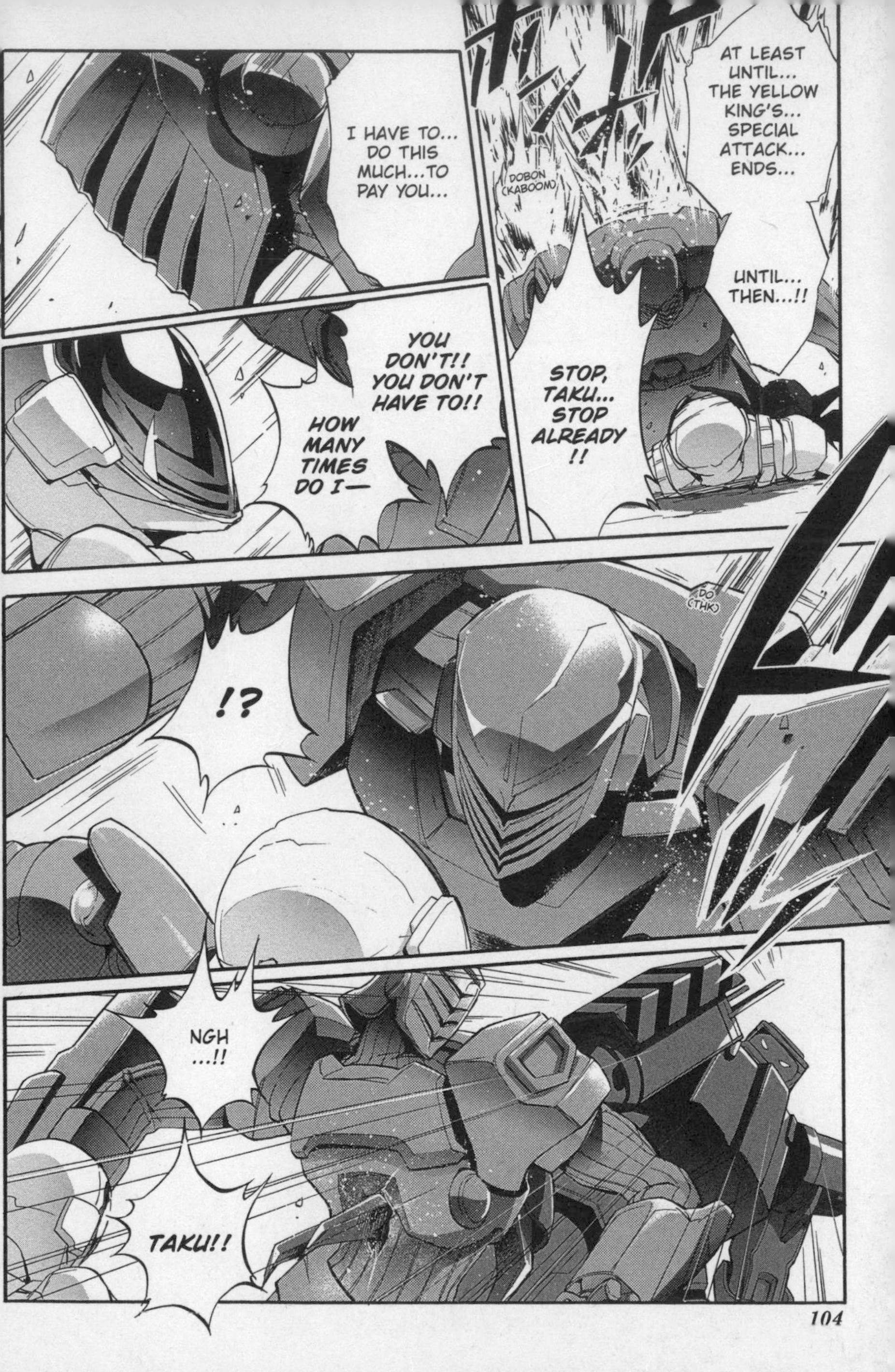
AT LEAST UNTIL... THE YELLOW KING'S... SPECIAL ATTACK... ENDS...
DOBON (KABOOM)
UNTIL... THEN...!!
STOP, TAKU... STOP ALREADY !!
I HAVE TO... DO THIS MUCH...TO PAY YOU...
YOU DON'T!! YOU DON'T HAVE TO!!
HOW MANY TIMES DO I—
DO (THK)
!?
NGH ...!!
TAKU!!

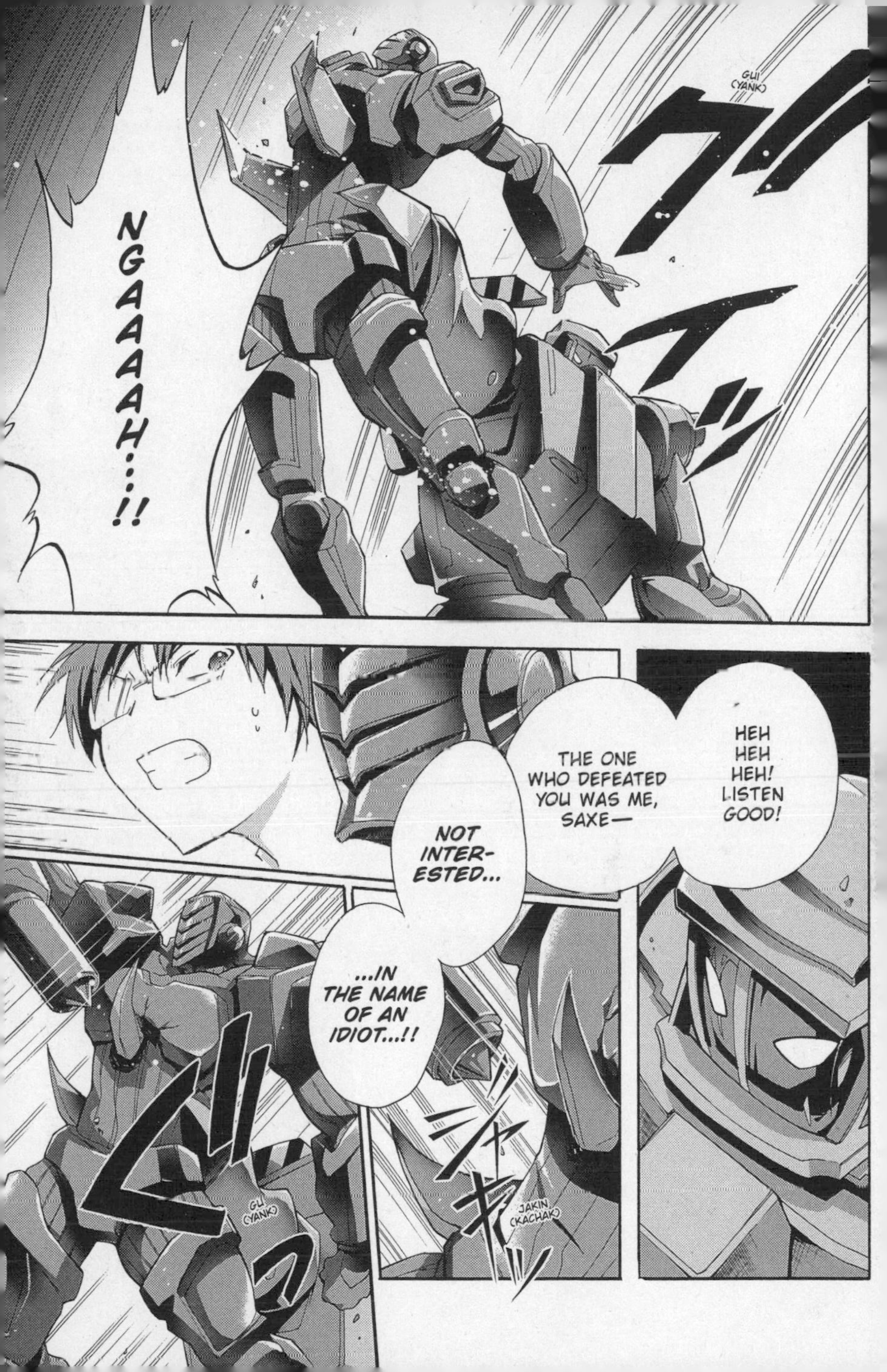
GUI (YANK)
NGAAAAAH...!!
HEH HEH HEH! LISTEN GOOD!
THE ONE WHO DEFEATED YOU WAS ME, SAXE—
NOT INTERESTED...
...IN THE NAME OF AN IDIOT...!!
JAKIN (KACHAK)
GUI (YANK)

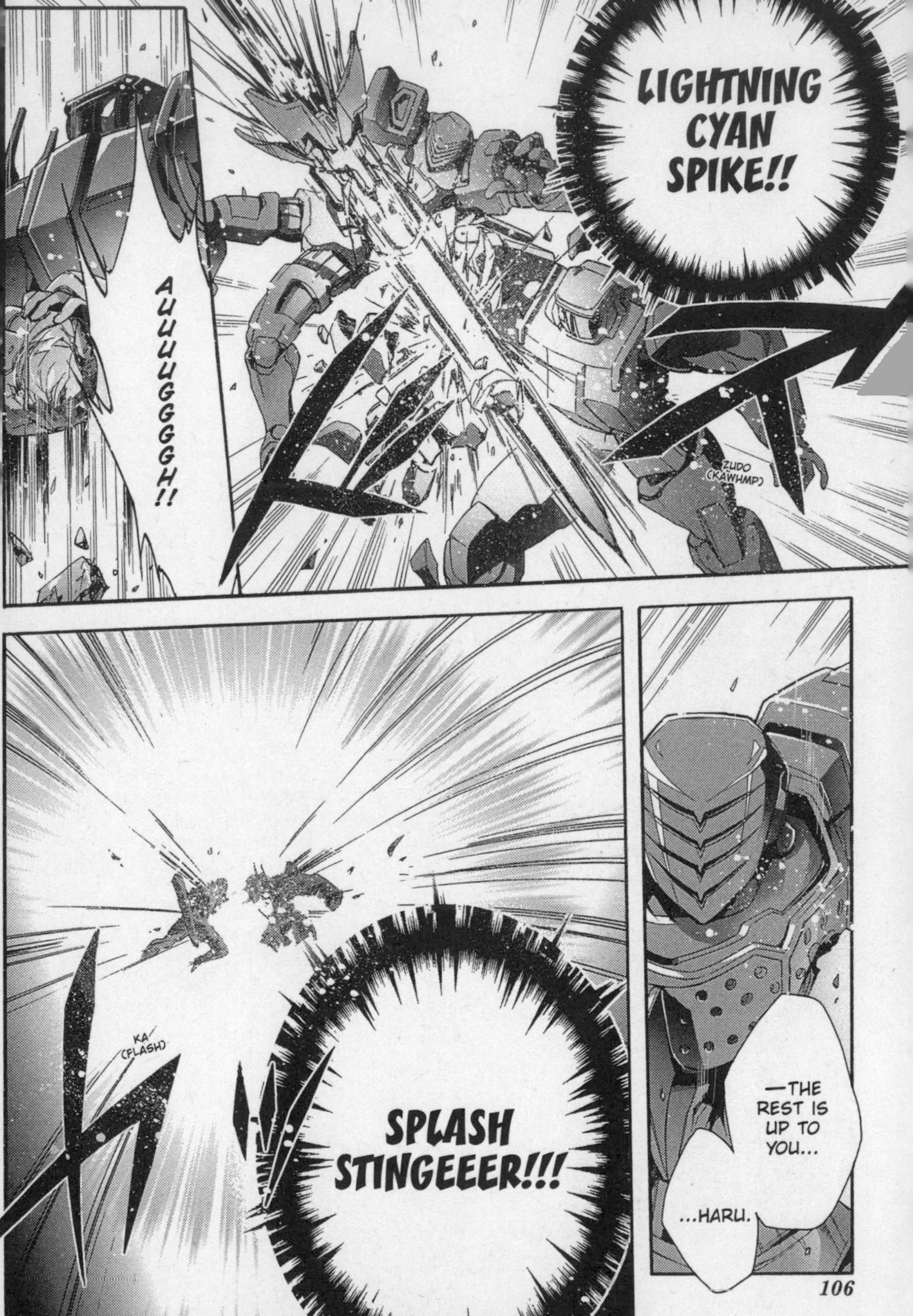
LIGHTNING CYAN SPIKE!!
ZUDO (KAWHMP)
AUUUUGGGGH!!
—THE REST IS UP TO YOU...
...HARU.
SPLASH STINGEEER!!!
KA (FLASH)

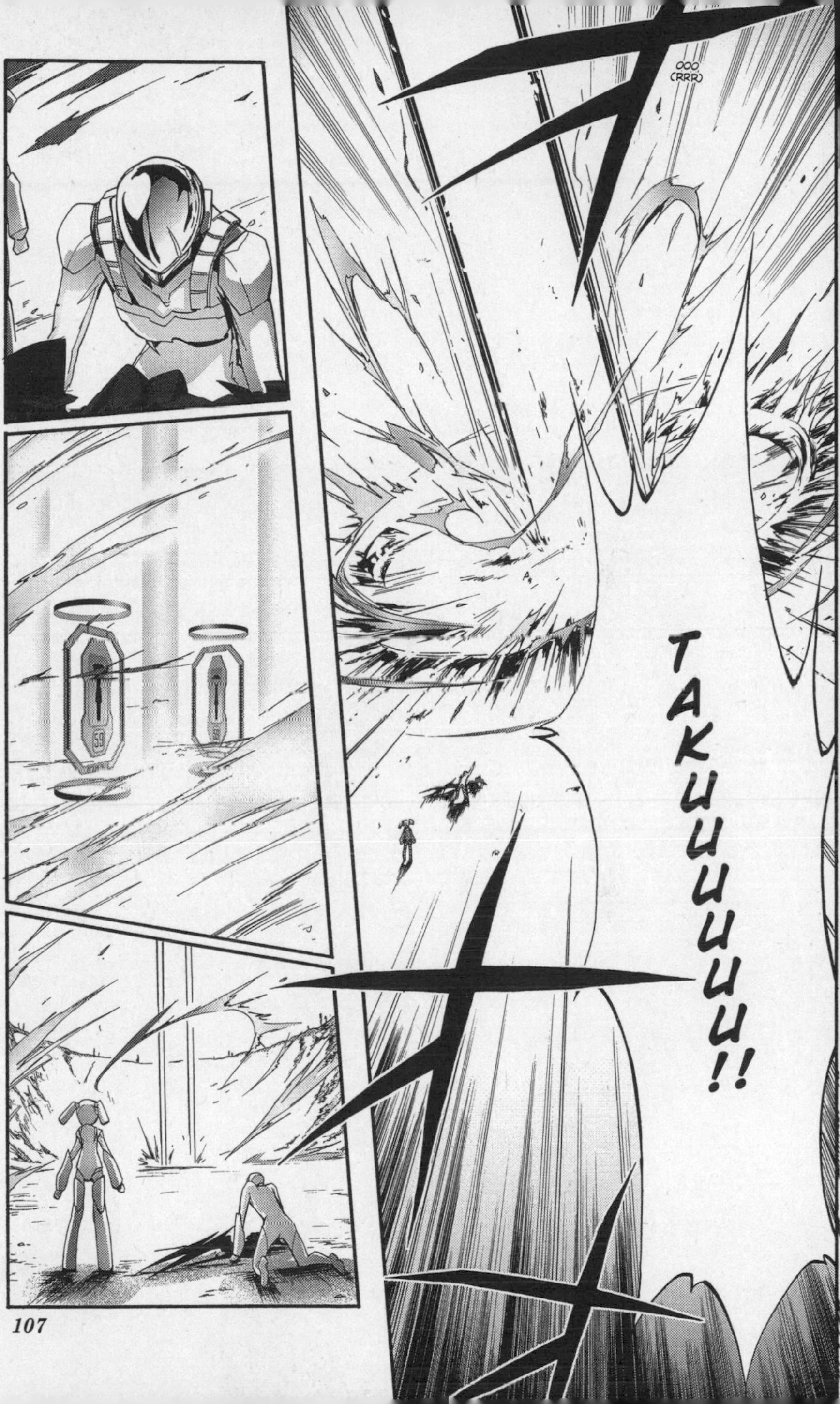
OOO
(RRR)
TAKUUUUUU!!

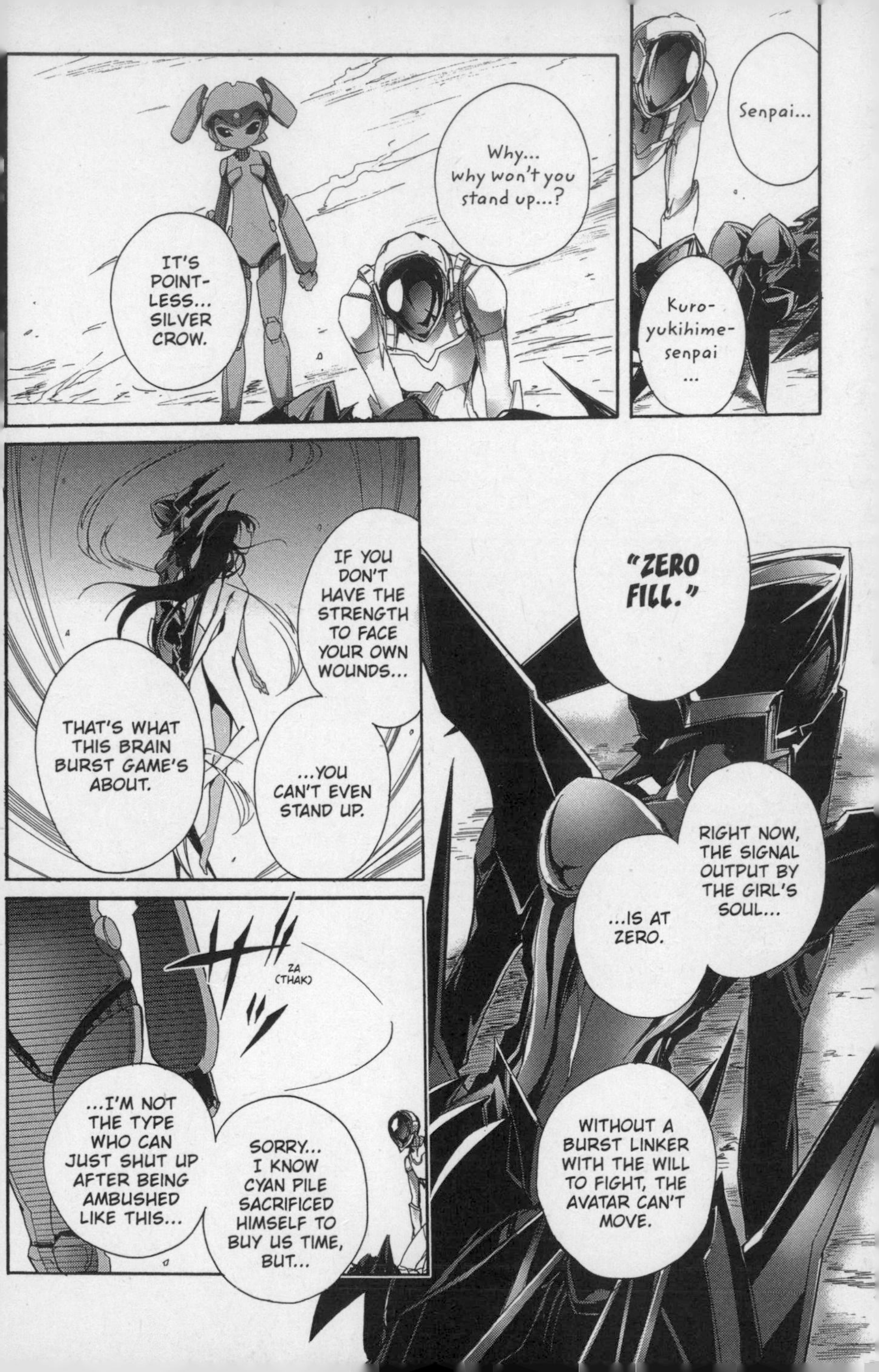
Senpai...
Kuro-yukihime-senpai...
Why... why won't you stand up...?
IT'S POINT-LESS... SILVER CROW.
"ZERO FILL."
RIGHT NOW, THE SIGNAL OUTPUT BY THE GIRL'S SOUL...
...IS AT ZERO.
WITHOUT A BURST LINKER WITH THE WILL TO FIGHT, THE AVATAR CAN'T MOVE.
IF YOU DON'T HAVE THE STRENGTH TO FACE YOUR OWN WOUNDS...
...YOU CAN'T EVEN STAND UP.
THAT'S WHAT THIS BRAIN BURST GAME'S ABOUT.
ZA (THAK)
SORRY... I KNOW CYAN PILE SACRIFICED HIMSELF TO BUY US TIME, BUT...
...I'M NOT THE TYPE WHO CAN JUST SHUT UP AFTER BEING AMBUSHED LIKE THIS...

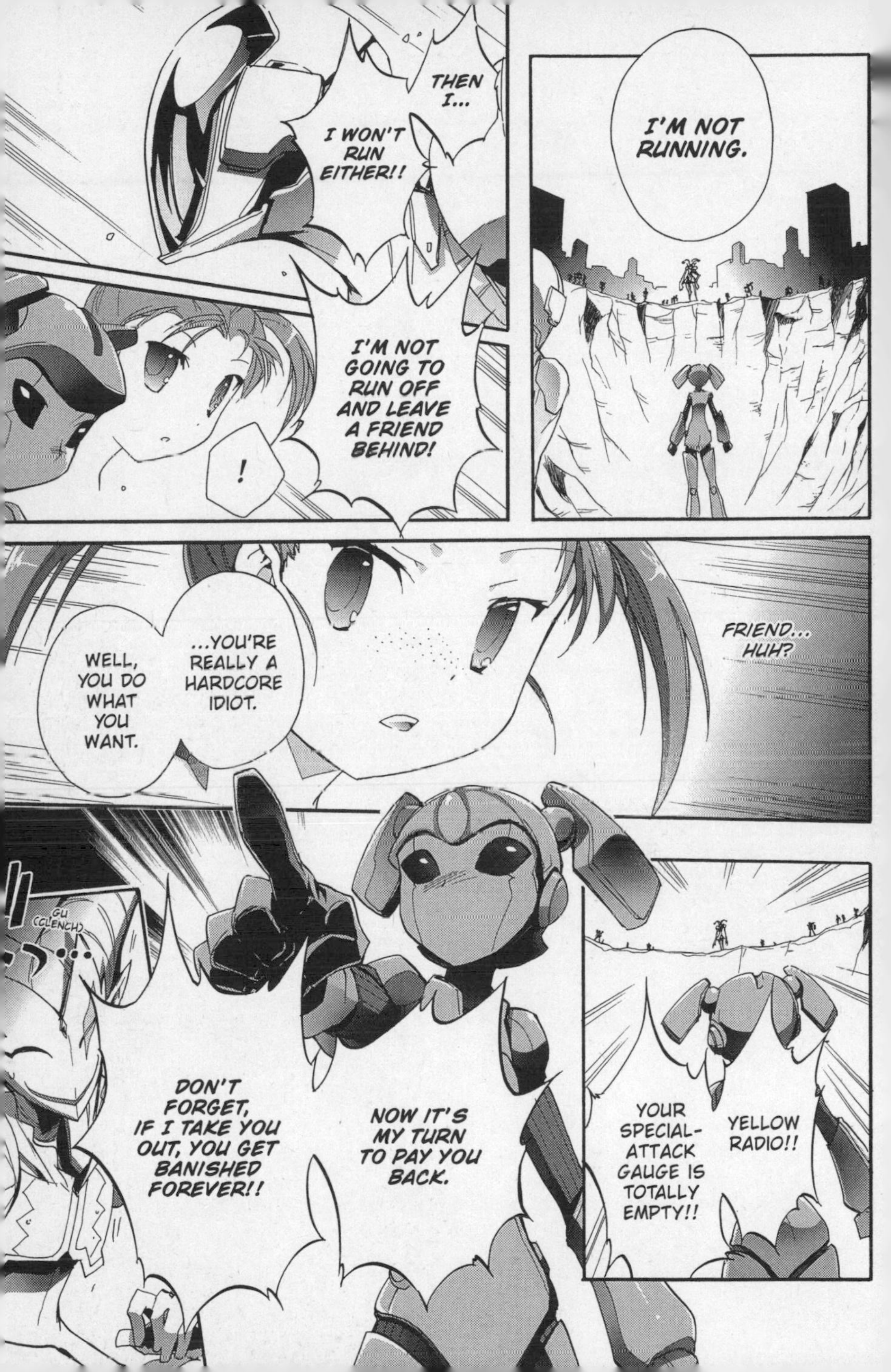
I'M NOT RUNNING.
THEN I...
I WON'T RUN EITHER!!
I'M NOT GOING TO RUN OFF AND LEAVE A FRIEND BEHIND!
!
FRIEND... HUH?
...YOU'RE REALLY A HARDCORE IDIOT.
WELL, YOU DO WHAT YOU WANT.
YELLOW RADIO!!
YOUR SPECIAL-ATTACK GAUGE IS TOTALLY EMPTY!!
NOW IT'S MY TURN TO PAY YOU BACK.
DON'T FORGET, IF I TAKE YOU OUT, YOU GET BANISHED FOREVER!!
GU (CLENCH)

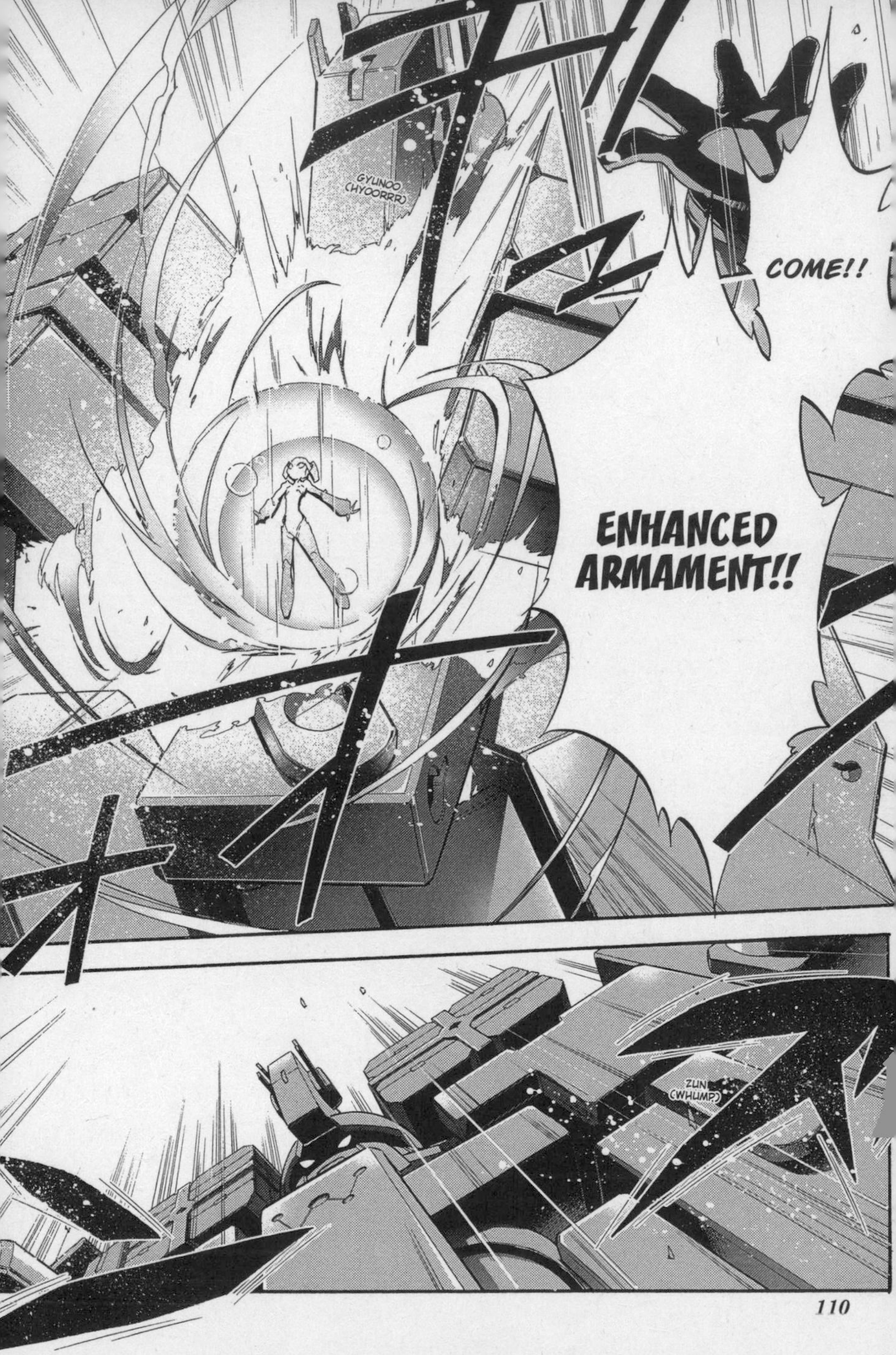
COME!!
GYUNOO
(HYOORRR)
ENHANCED ARMAMENT!!
ZUN
(WHUMP)

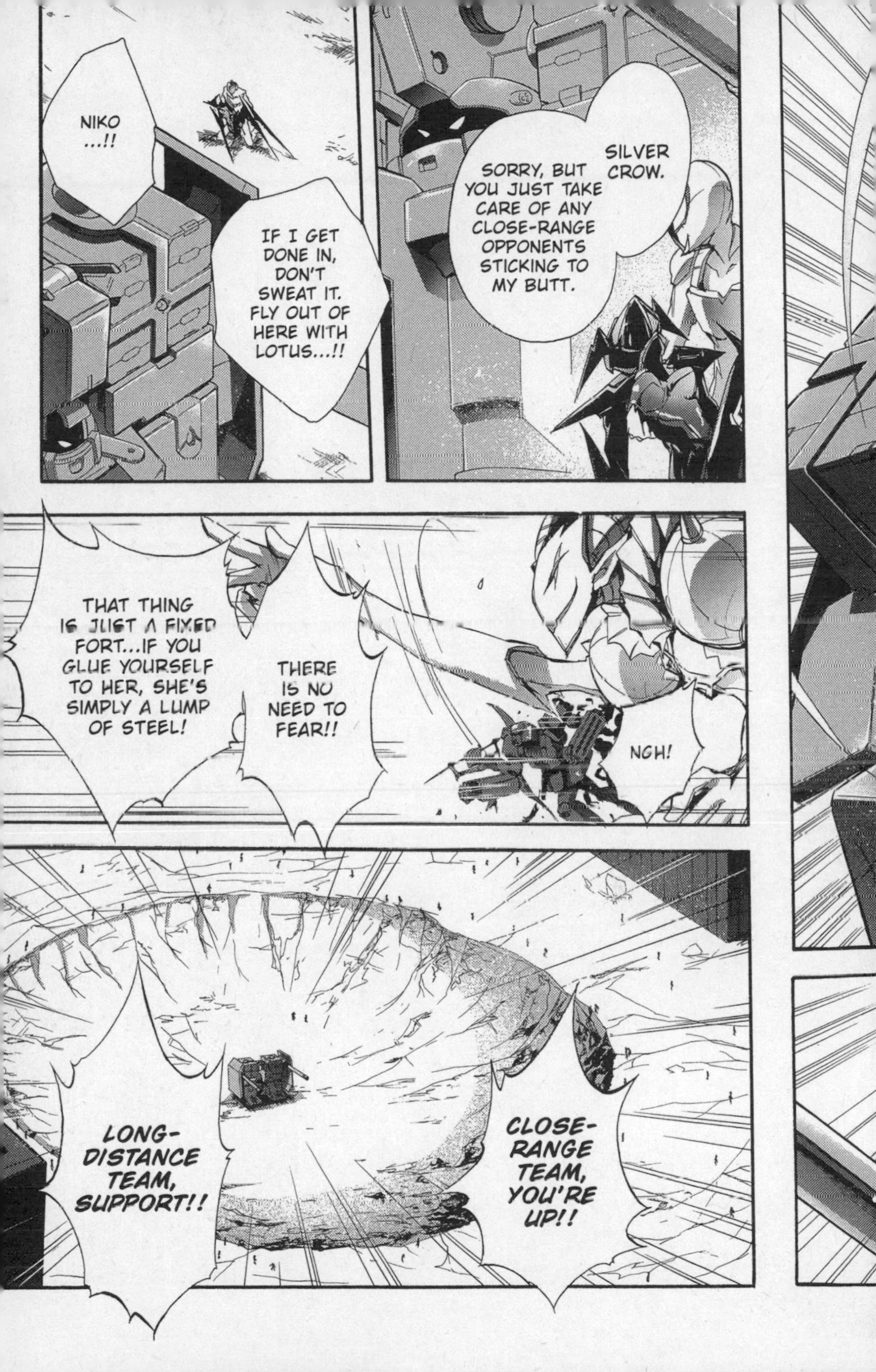
SILVER CROW.
SORRY, BUT YOU JUST TAKE CARE OF ANY CLOSE-RANGE OPPONENTS STICKING TO MY BUTT.
IF I GET DONE IN, DON'T SWEAT IT. FLY OUT OF HERE WITH LOTUS...!!
NIKO ...!!
NGH!
THERE IS NO NEED TO FEAR!!
THAT THING IS JUST A FIXED FORT...IF YOU GLUE YOURSELF TO HER, SHE'S SIMPLY A LUMP OF STEEL!
CLOSE-RANGE TEAM, YOU'RE UP!!
LONG-DISTANCE TEAM, SUPPORT!!

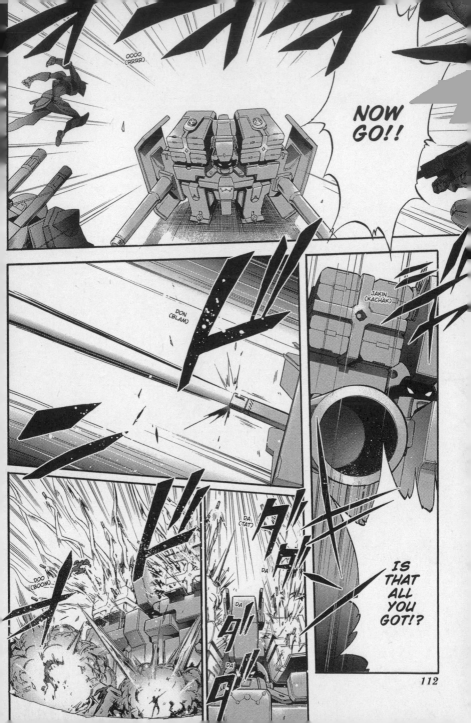

OOOO
(RRRRR)

NOW
GO!!

DON
(BLAM)

JAKIN
(KACHAK)

DA
(TAT)

DA

POO
(BOOM)

DA

IS
THAT
ALL
YOU
GOT!?

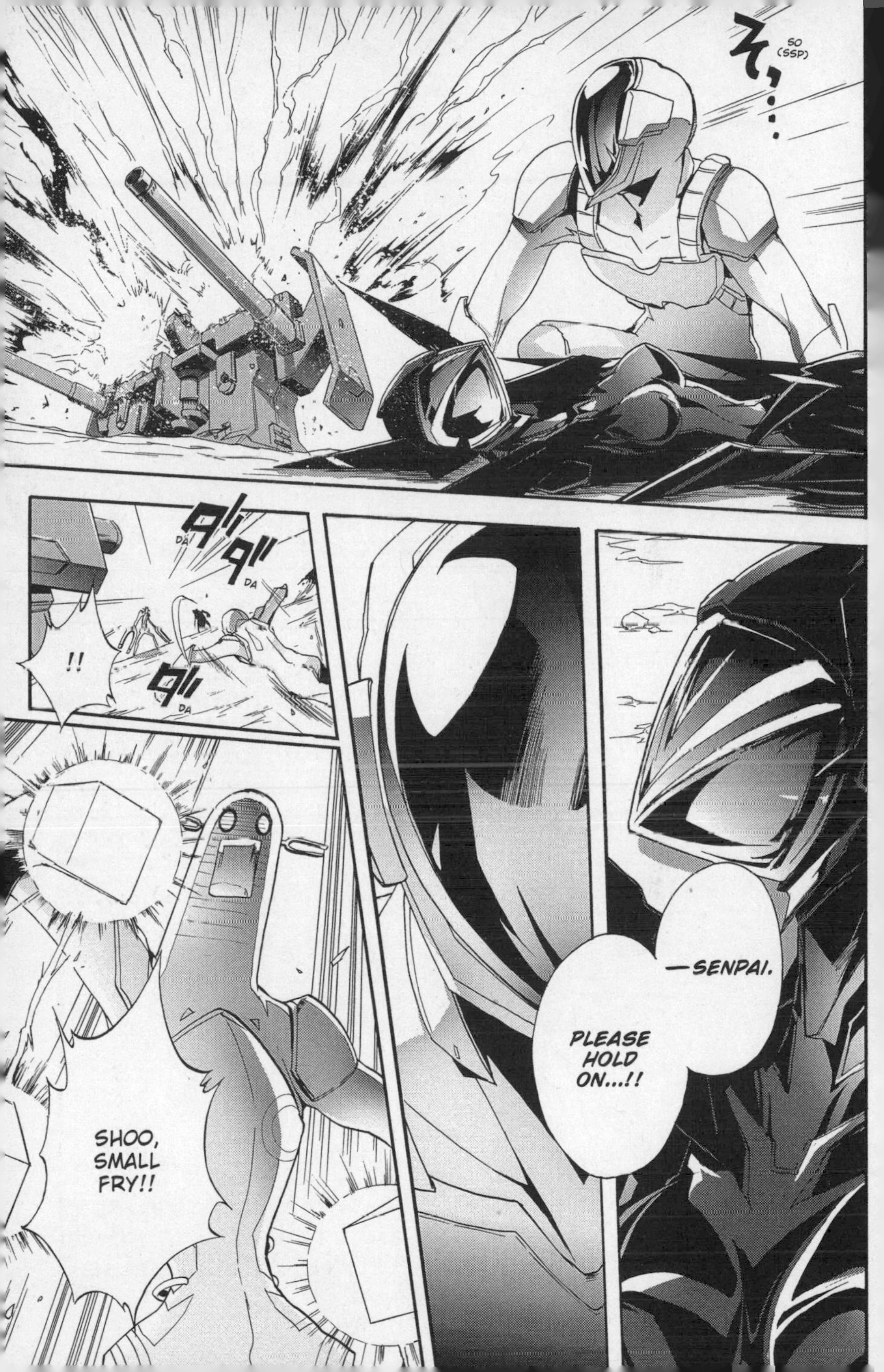
SO (SSP)
—SENPAI.
PLEASE HOLD ON...!!
DA
DA
DA
!!
SHOO, SMALL FRY!!

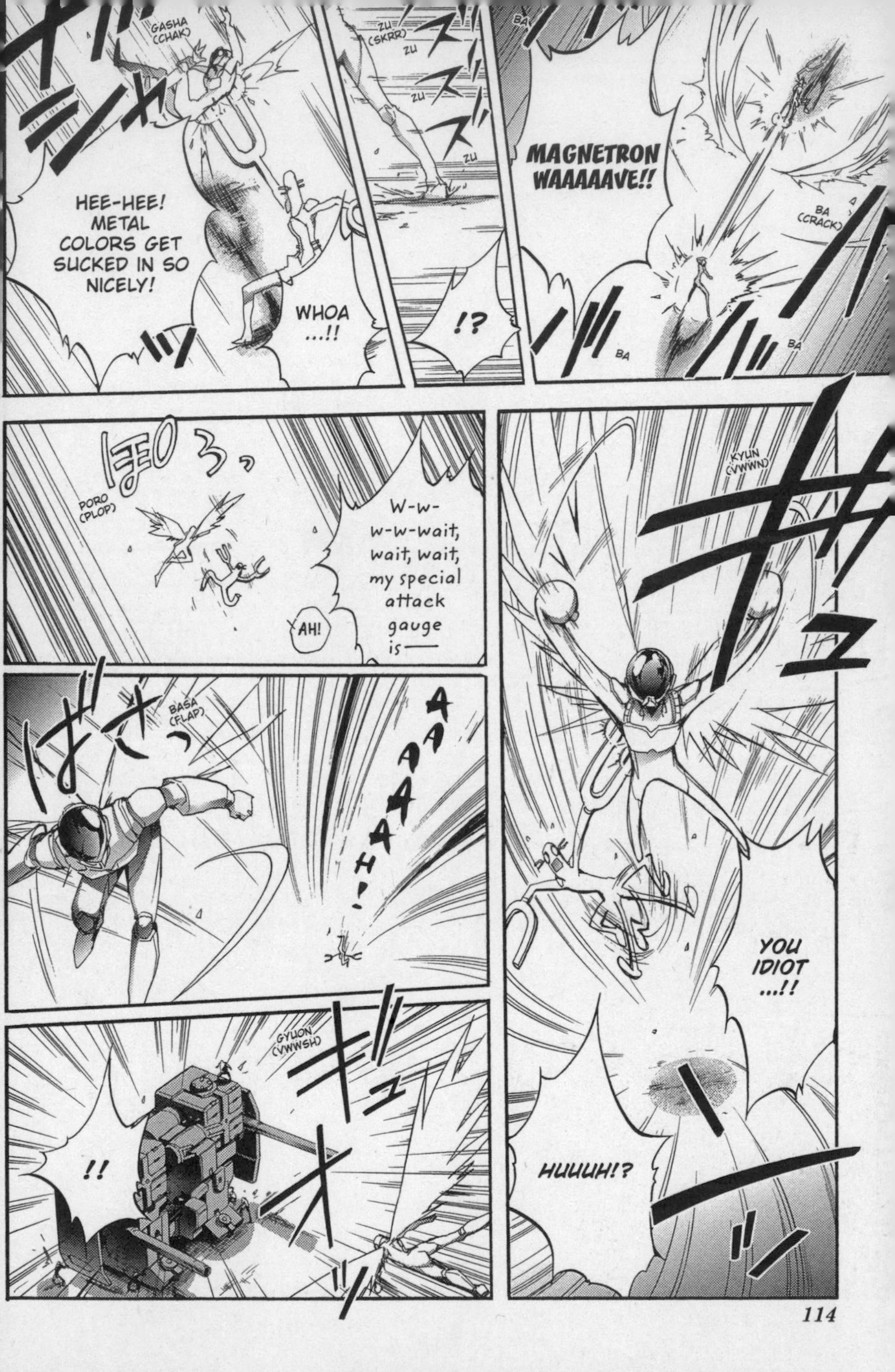
BA
MAGNETRON WAAAAAVE!!
BA (CRACK)
BA
BA
ZU (SKRR)
ZU
ZU
ZU
!?
GASHA (CHAK)
HEE-HEE! METAL COLORS GET SUCKED IN SO NICELY!
WHOA ...!!
KYUN (VWWN)
YOU IDIOT ...!!
HUUUH!?
PORO (PLOP)
W-w-w-w-wait, wait, wait, my special attack gauge is—
AH!
BASA (FLAP)
AAAAAAH!
GYUON (VWWSH)
!!

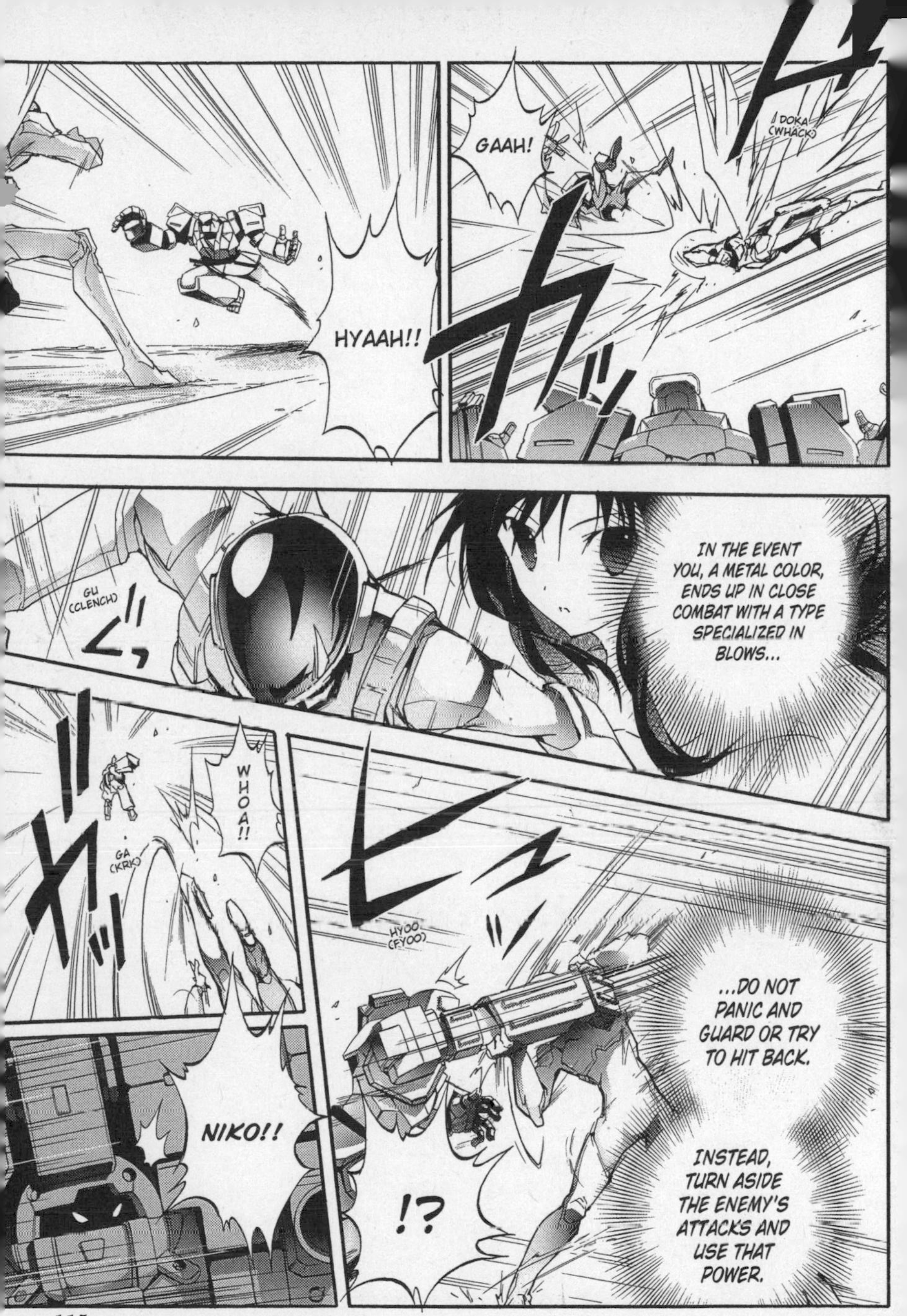
DOKA
(WHACK)
GAAH!
HYAAH!!
IN THE EVENT YOU, A METAL COLOR, ENDS UP IN CLOSE COMBAT WITH A TYPE SPECIALIZED IN BLOWS...
GU
(CLENCH)
...DO NOT PANIC AND GUARD OR TRY TO HIT BACK.
HYOO
(FYOO)
!?
INSTEAD, TURN ASIDE THE ENEMY'S ATTACKS AND USE THAT POWER.
WHOA!!
GA
(KRK)
NIKO!!

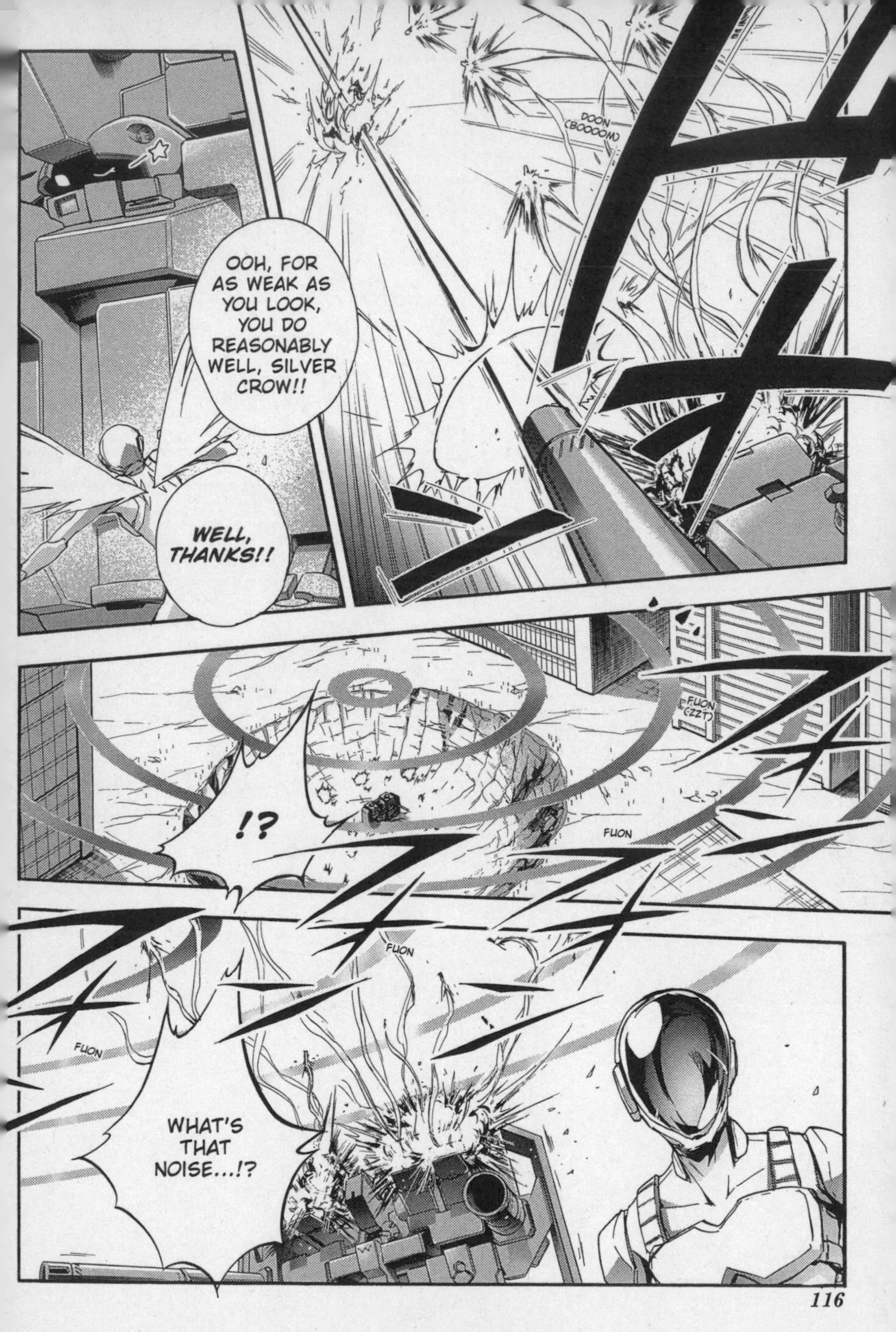
DOON (BOOOOM)
OOH, FOR AS WEAK AS YOU LOOK, YOU DO REASONABLY WELL, SILVER CROW!!
WELL, THANKS!!
FUON (ZZT)
!?
FUON
FUON
FUON
WHAT'S THAT NOISE...!?

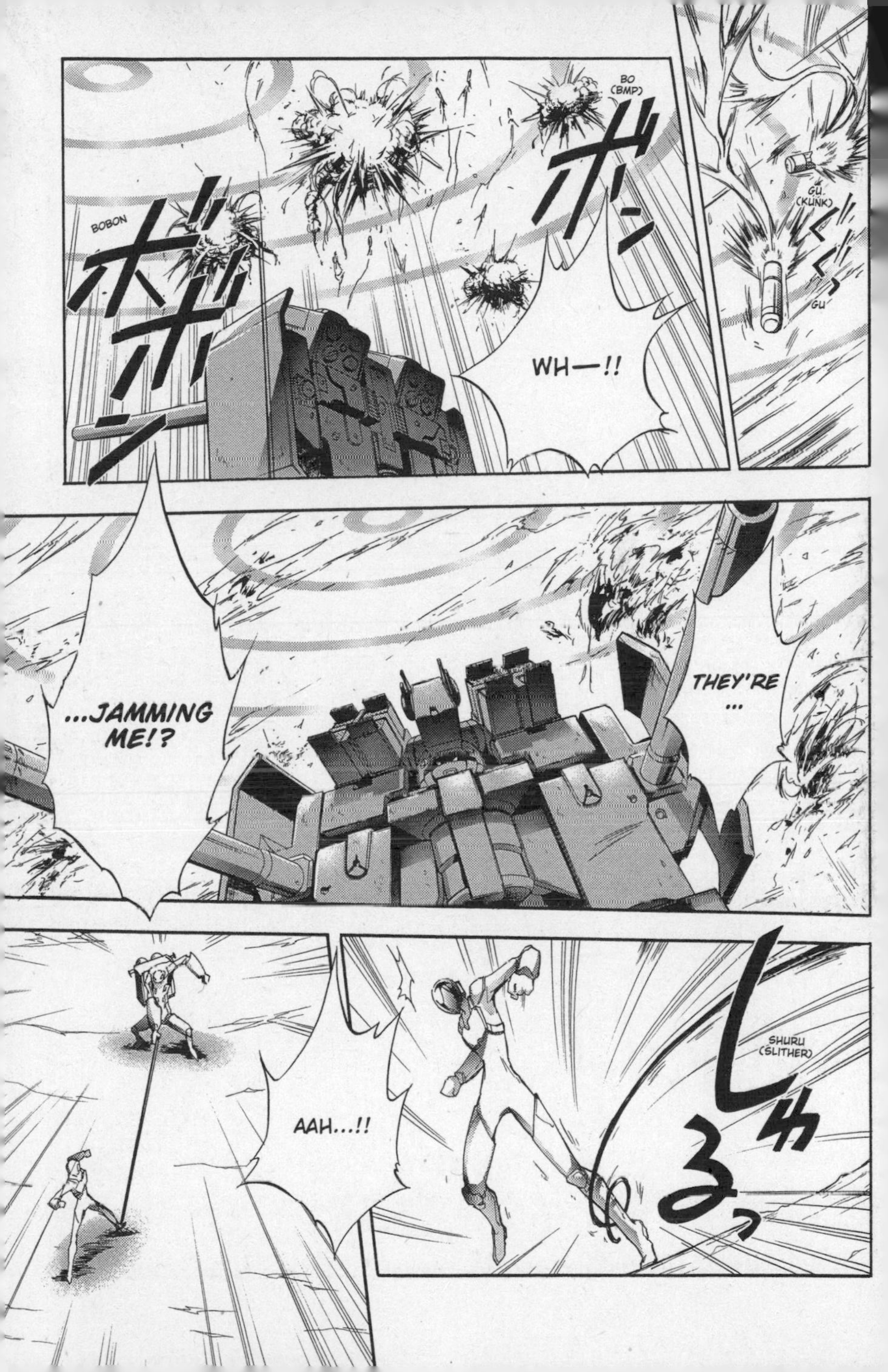
GU (KUNK)
GU
BO (BMP)
BOBON
WH—!!
THEY'RE ...
...JAMMING ME!?
SHURU (SLITHER)
AAH...!!

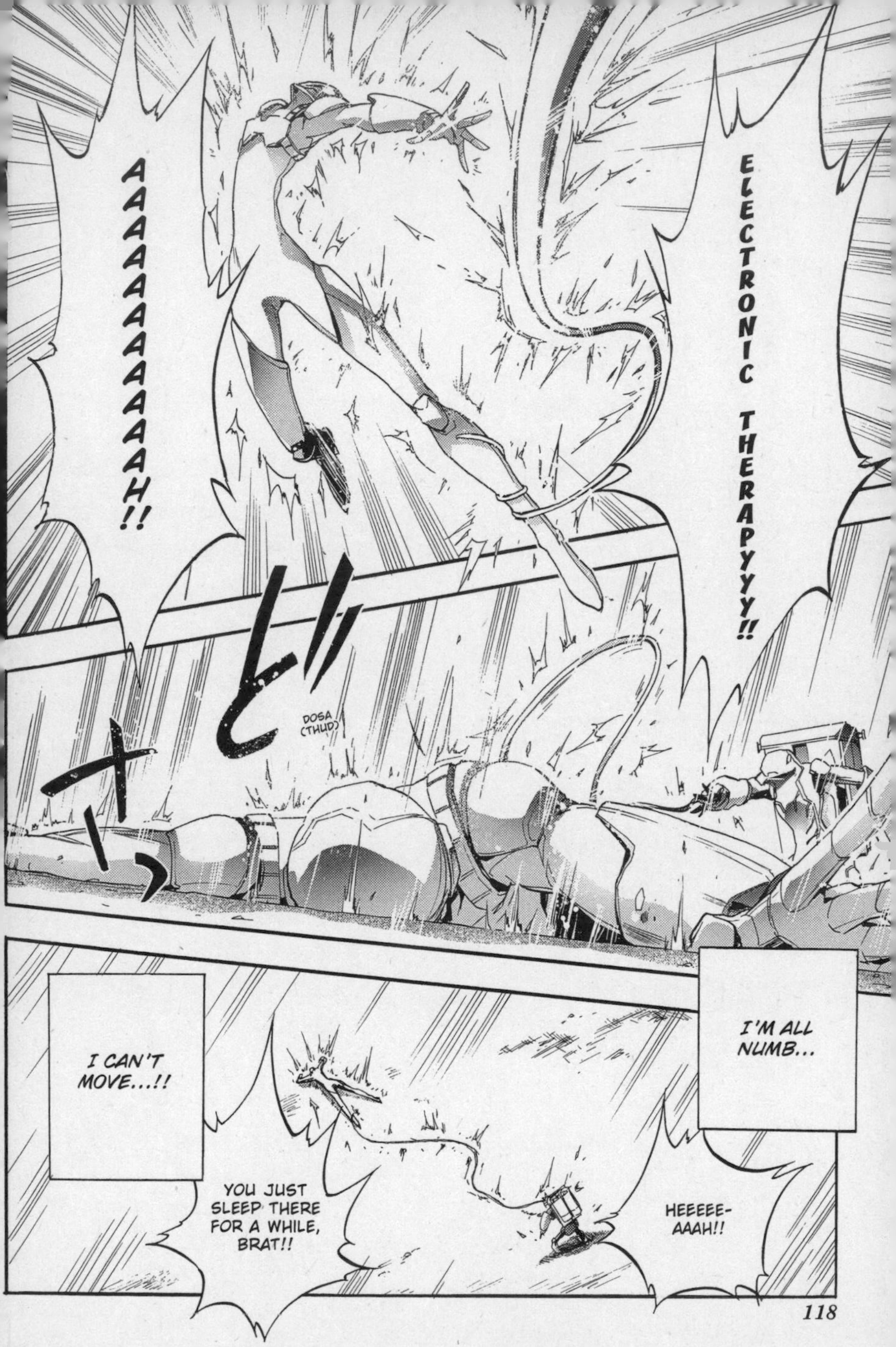
ELECTRONIC THERAPYYY!!
AAAAAAAAAAAH!!
ドサッ
DOSA (THUD)
I'M ALL NUMB...
HEEEEE-AAAH!!
YOU JUST SLEEP THERE FOR A WHILE, BRAT!!
I CAN'T MOVE...!!

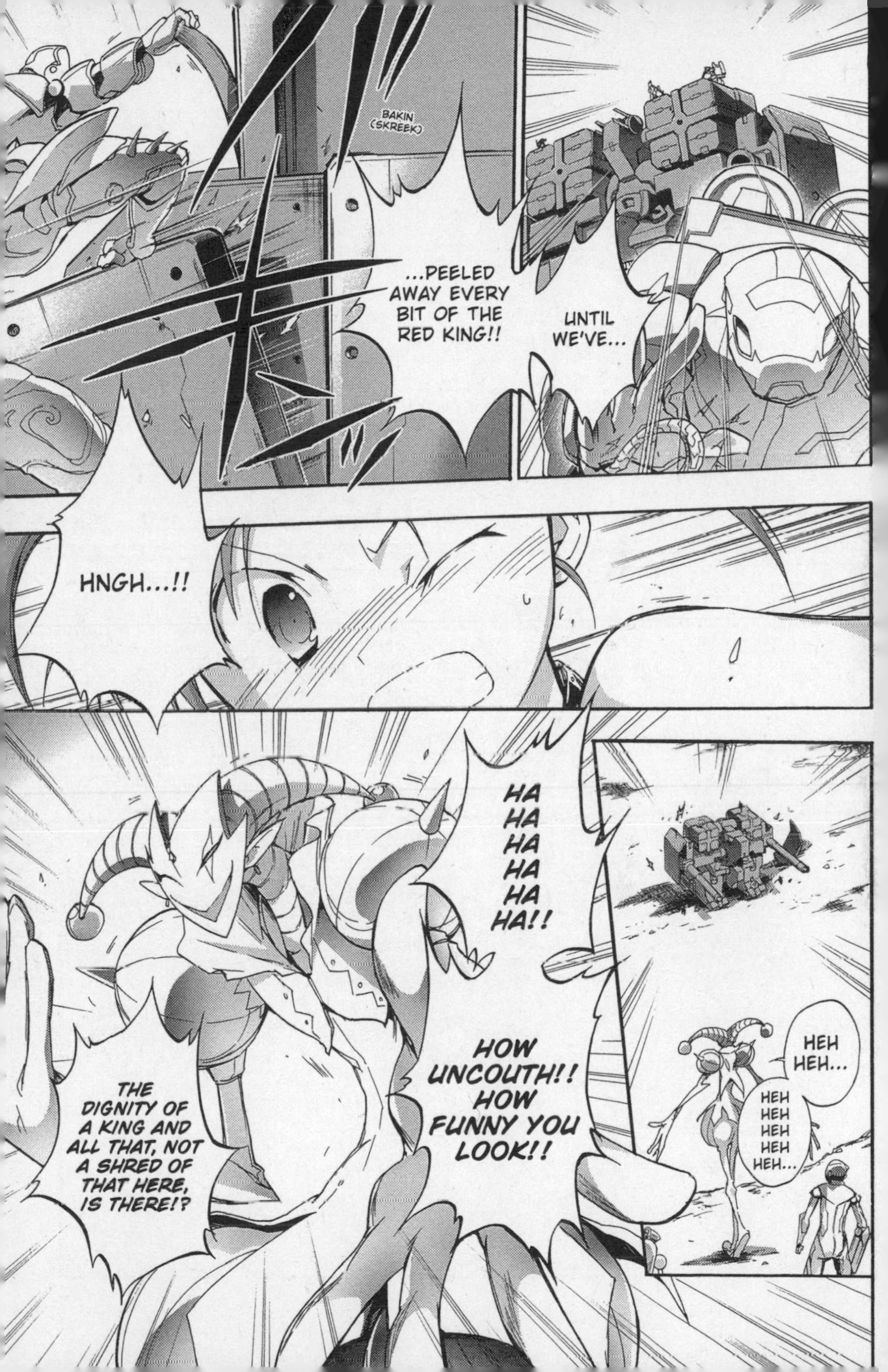
UNTIL WE'VE...
...PEELED AWAY EVERY BIT OF THE RED KING!!
BAKIN (SKREEK)
HNGH...!!
HEH HEH...
HEH HEH HEH HEH HEH...
HA HA HA HA HA HA!!
HOW UNCOUTH!! HOW FUNNY YOU LOOK!!
THE DIGNITY OF A KING AND ALL THAT, NOT A SHRED OF THAT HERE, IS THERE!?

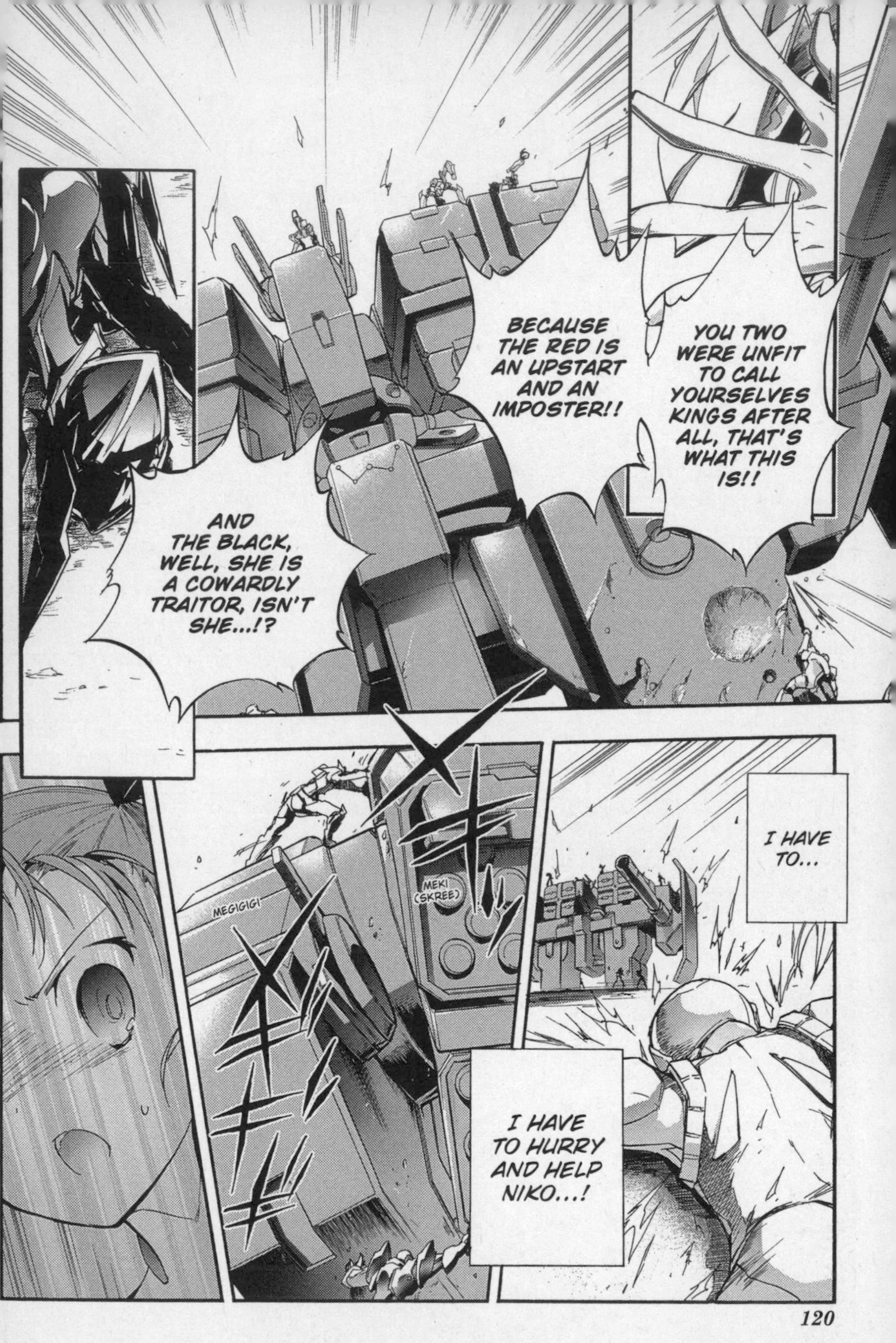
YOU TWO WERE UNFIT TO CALL YOURSELVES KINGS AFTER ALL, THAT'S WHAT THIS IS!!
BECAUSE THE RED IS AN UPSTART AND AN IMPOSTER!!
AND THE BLACK, WELL, SHE IS A COWARDLY TRAITOR, ISN'T SHE...!?
I HAVE TO...
I HAVE TO HURRY AND HELP NIKO...!
MEKI (SKREE)
MEGIGIGI

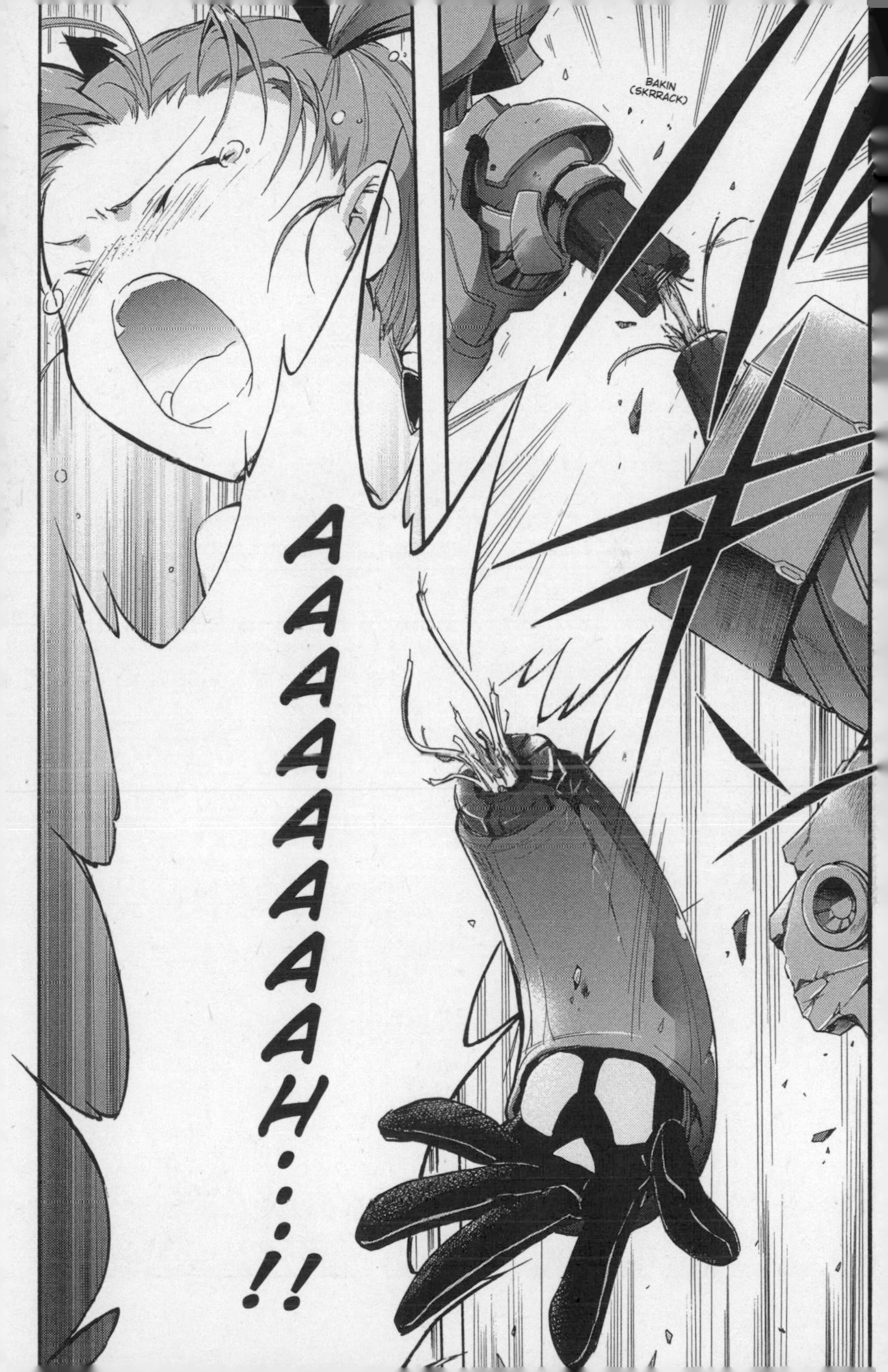
BAKIN
(SKRRACK)
AAAAAAAAAH...!!

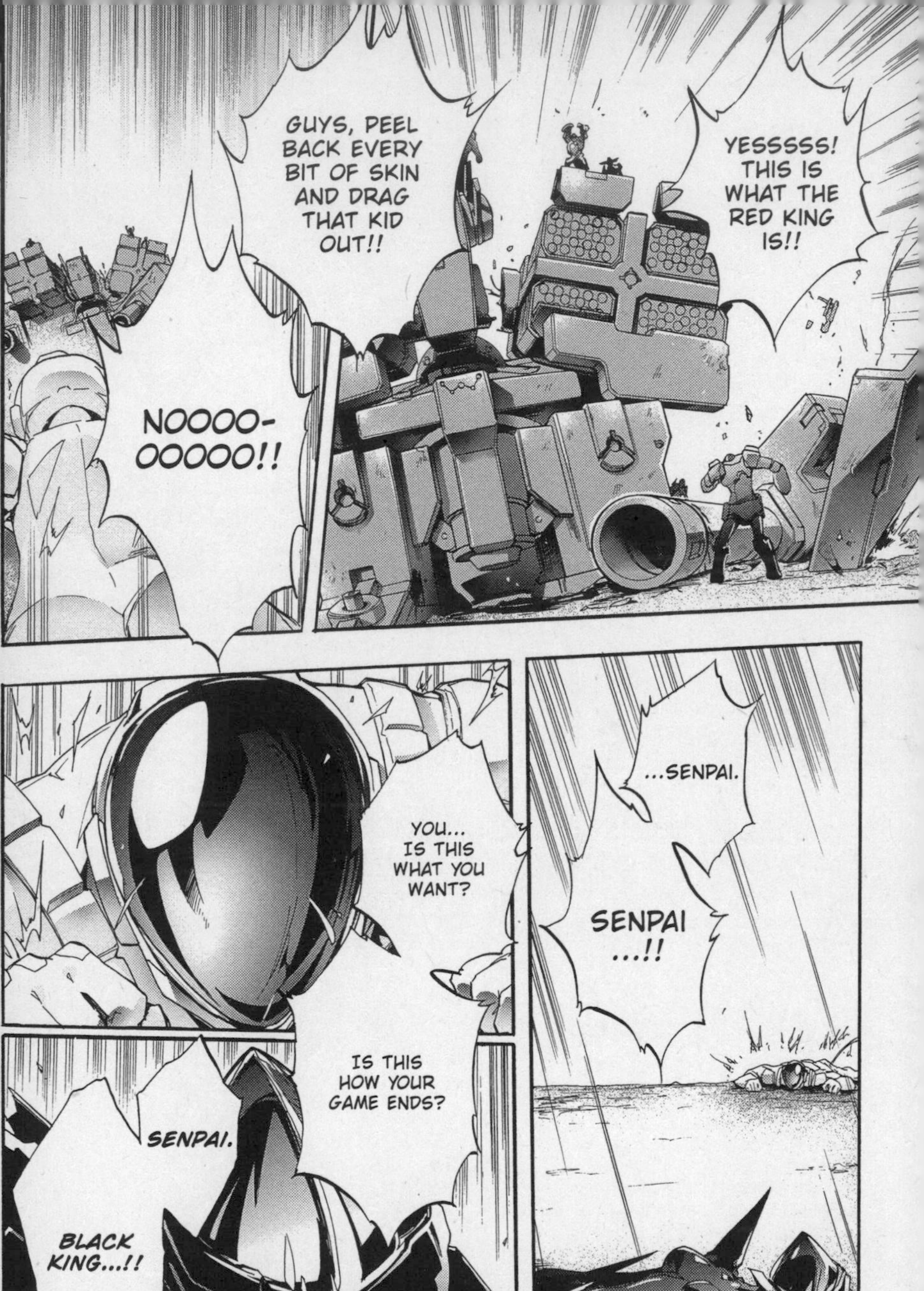
YESSSSS! THIS IS WHAT THE RED KING IS!!
GUYS, PEEL BACK EVERY BIT OF SKIN AND DRAG THAT KID OUT!!
NOOOO-OOOOO!!
...SENPAI.
SENPAI ...!!
YOU... IS THIS WHAT YOU WANT?
IS THIS HOW YOUR GAME ENDS?
SENPAI.
BLACK KING...!!

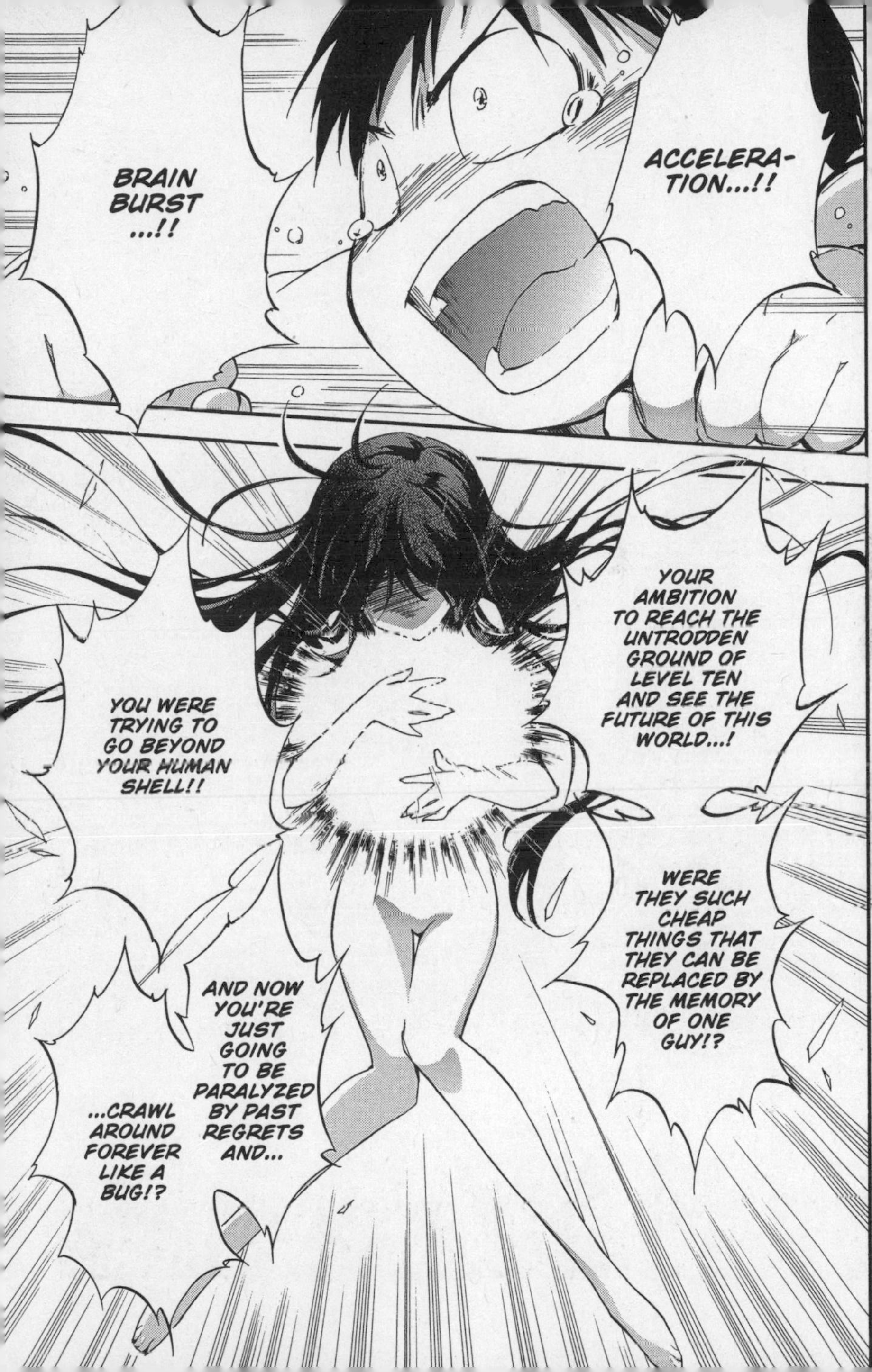
ACCELERA-TION...!!
BRAIN BURST...!!
YOUR AMBITION TO REACH THE UNTRODDEN GROUND OF LEVEL TEN AND SEE THE FUTURE OF THIS WORLD...!
YOU WERE TRYING TO GO BEYOND YOUR HUMAN SHELL!!
WERE THEY SUCH CHEAP THINGS THAT THEY CAN BE REPLACED BY THE MEMORY OF ONE GUY!?
AND NOW YOU'RE JUST GOING TO BE PARALYZED BY PAST REGRETS AND...
...CRAWL AROUND FOREVER LIKE A BUG!?

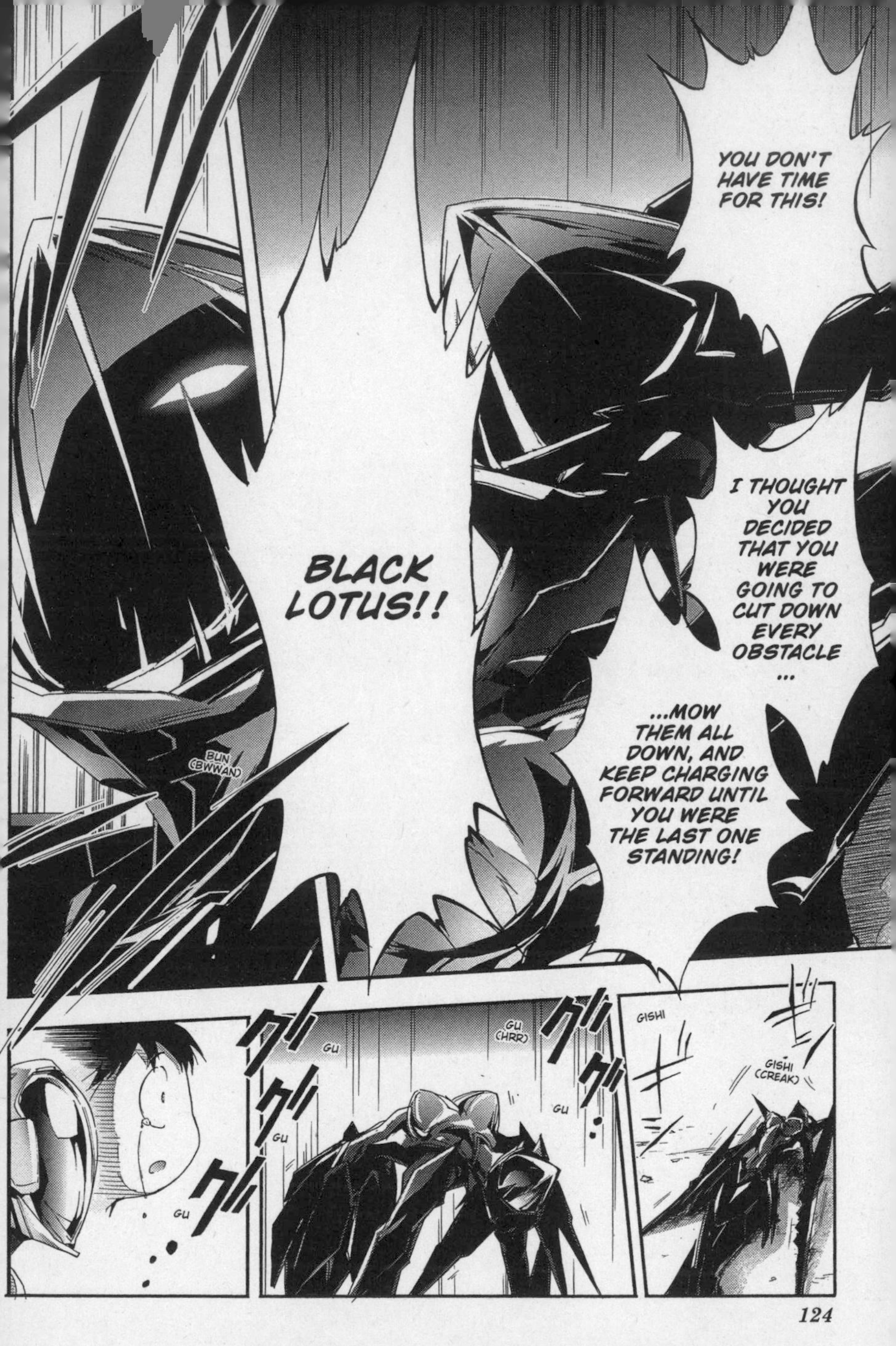
YOU DON'T HAVE TIME FOR THIS!
I THOUGHT YOU DECIDED THAT YOU WERE GOING TO CUT DOWN EVERY OBSTACLE ...
...MOW THEM ALL DOWN, AND KEEP CHARGING FORWARD UNTIL YOU WERE THE LAST ONE STANDING!
BLACK LOTUS!!
BUN (BWWAN)
GISHI
GISHI (CREAK)
GU (HRR)
GU
GU
GU
GU

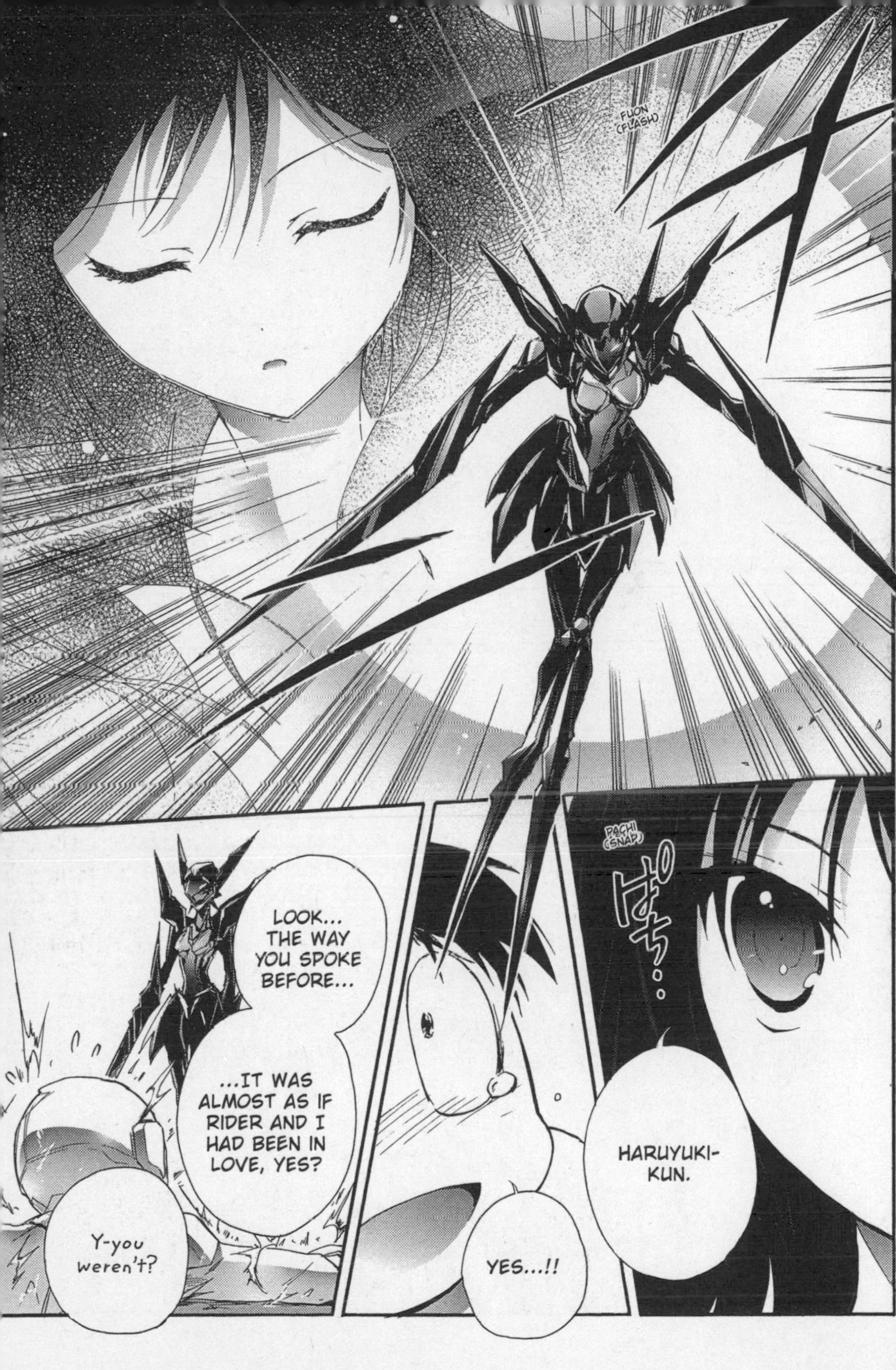
FUON (FLASH)
PACHI (SNAP)
ぱち…
HARUYUKI-KUN.
YES...!!
LOOK... THE WAY YOU SPOKE BEFORE...
...IT WAS ALMOST AS IF RIDER AND I HAD BEEN IN LOVE, YES?
Y-you weren't?

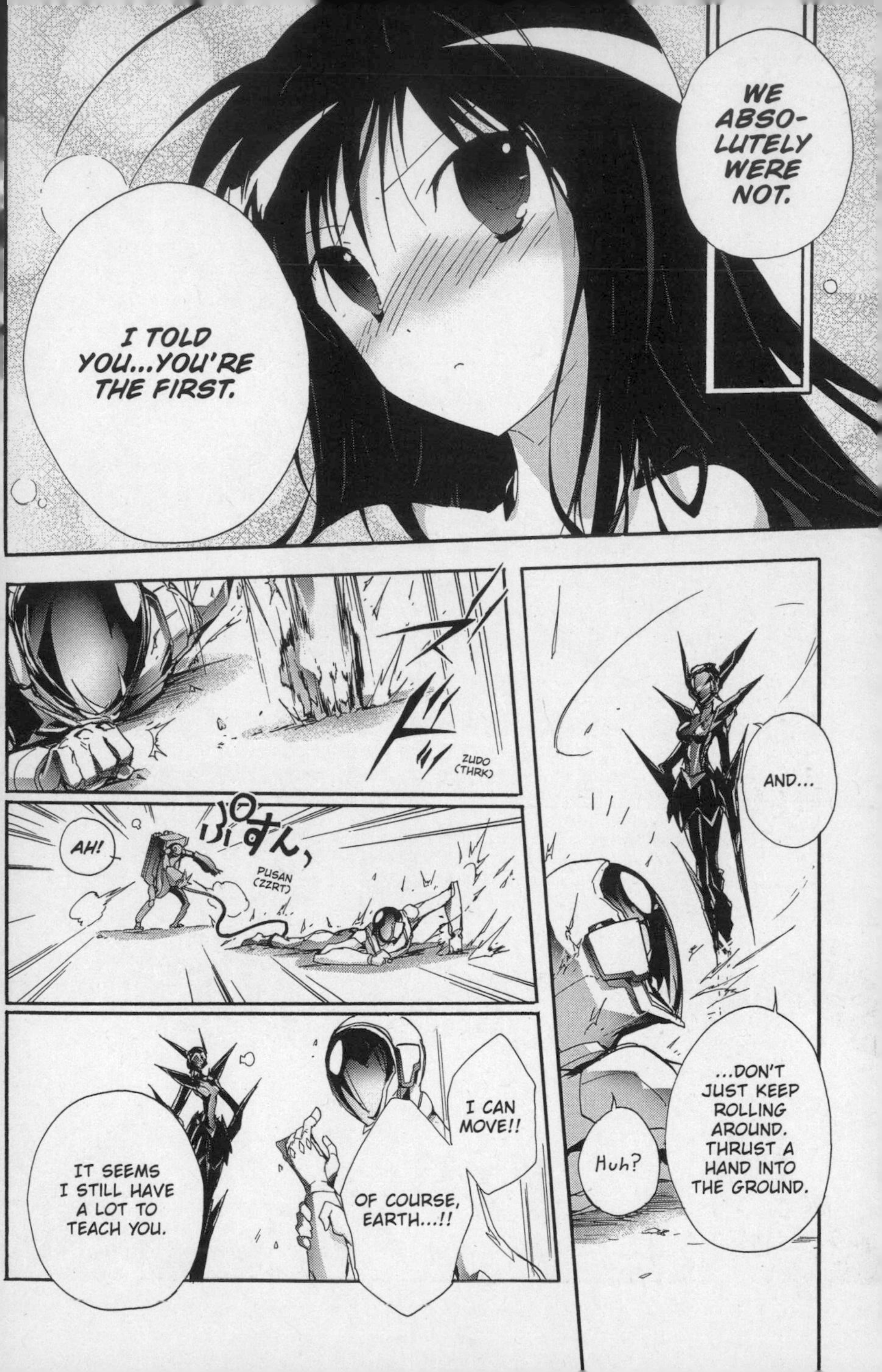
WE ABSO-LUTELY WERE NOT.
I TOLD YOU...YOU'RE THE FIRST.
AND...
...DON'T JUST KEEP ROLLING AROUND. THRUST A HAND INTO THE GROUND.
Huh?
ZUDO (THRK)
ぷすん,
PUSAN (ZZRT)
AH!
I CAN MOVE!!
OF COURSE, EARTH...!!
IT SEEMS I STILL HAVE A LOT TO TEACH YOU.

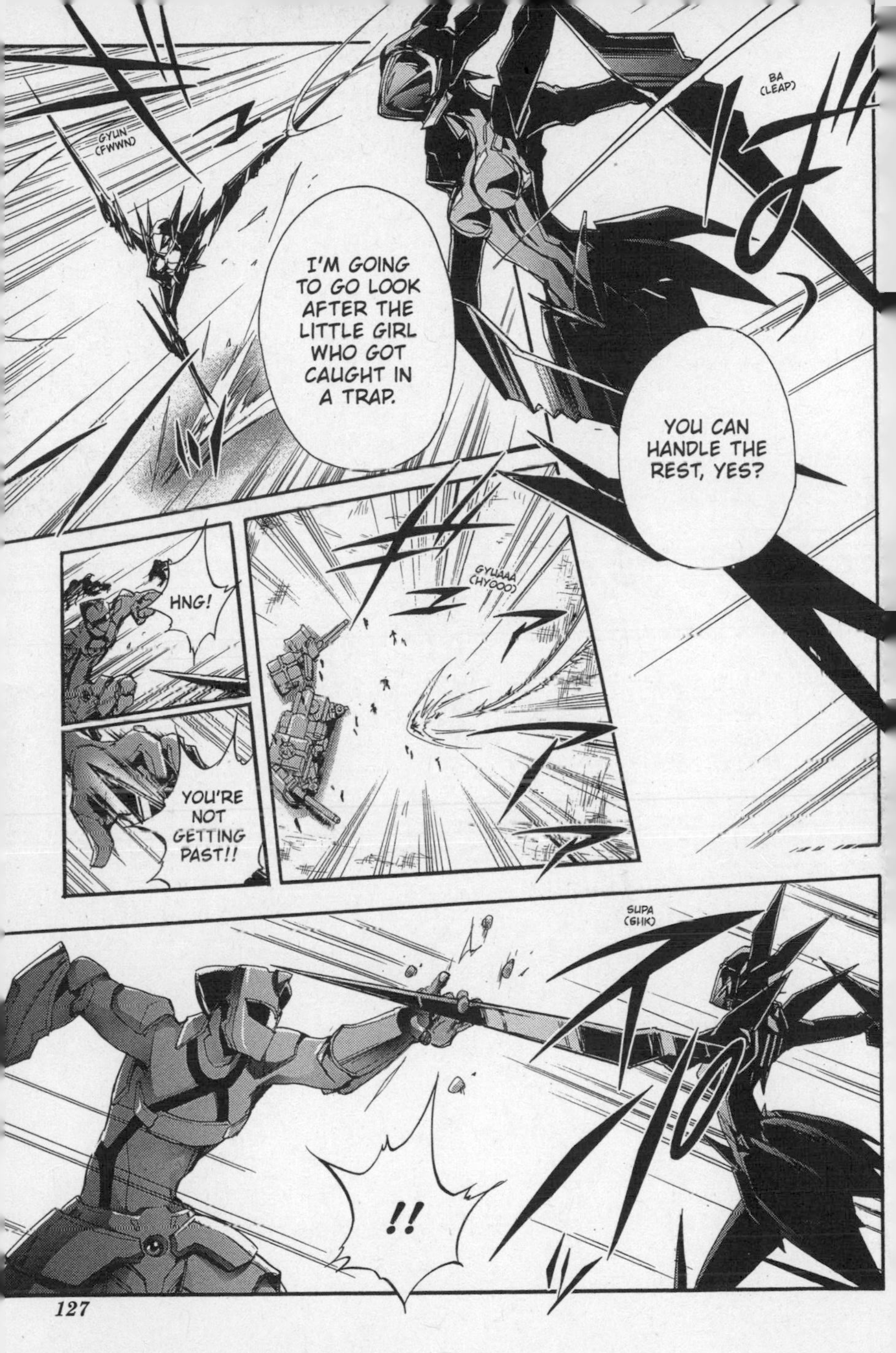
BA
(LEAP)
I'M GOING TO GO LOOK AFTER THE LITTLE GIRL WHO GOT CAUGHT IN A TRAP.
YOU CAN HANDLE THE REST, YES?
GYUN
(FWWN)
GYUAAA
(HYOOO)
HNG!
YOU'RE NOT GETTING PAST!!
SUPA
(SHK)
!!

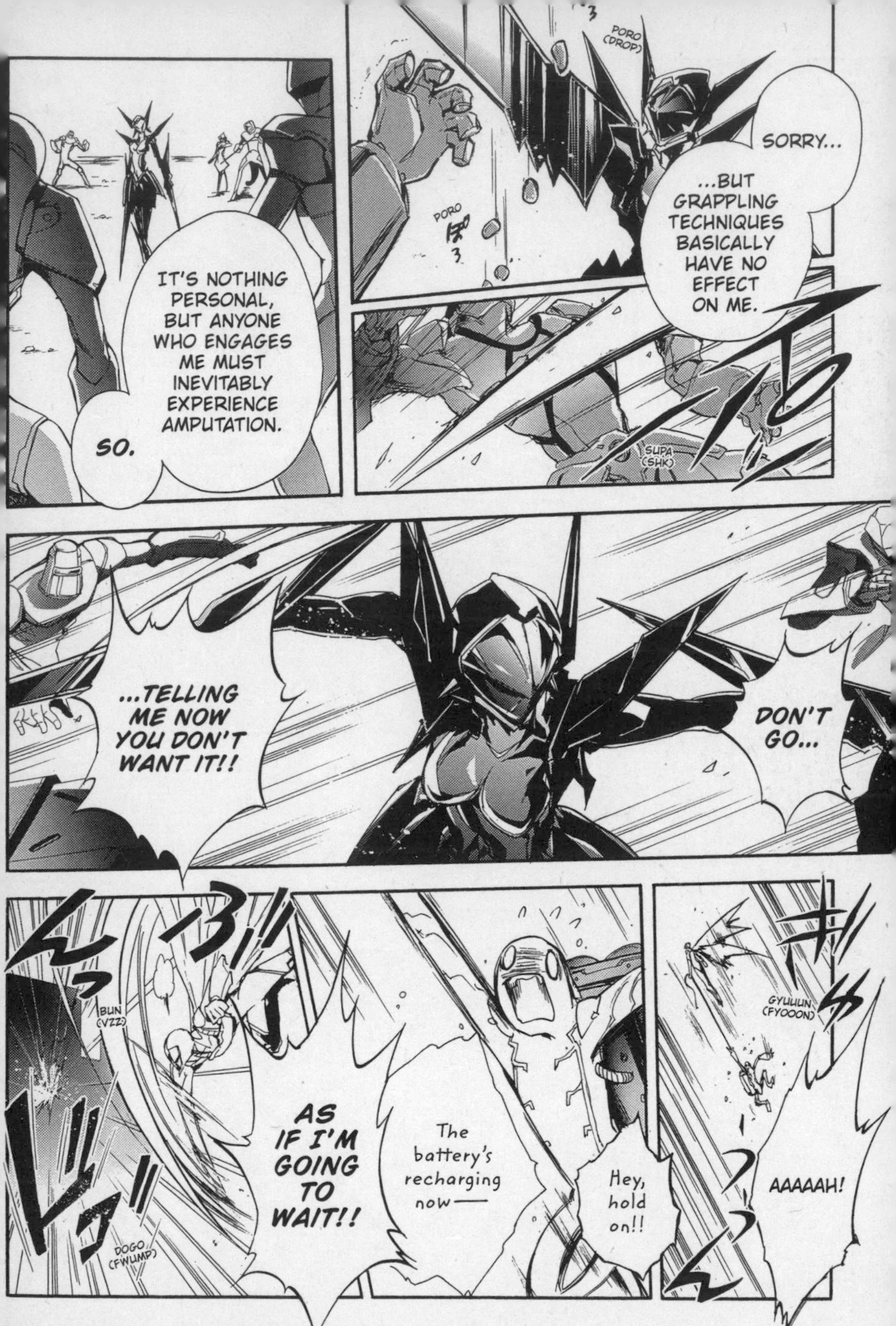
PORO (DROP)
SORRY...
...BUT GRAPPLING TECHNIQUES BASICALLY HAVE NO EFFECT ON ME.
PORO
SUPA (SHK)
IT'S NOTHING PERSONAL, BUT ANYONE WHO ENGAGES ME MUST INEVITABLY EXPERIENCE AMPUTATION.
SO.
DON'T GO...
...TELLING ME NOW YOU DON'T WANT IT!!
GYUUUN (FYOOON)
AAAAAH!
Hey, hold on!!
The battery's recharging now—
AS IF I'M GOING TO WAIT!!
BUN (VZZ)
DOGO (FWUMP)

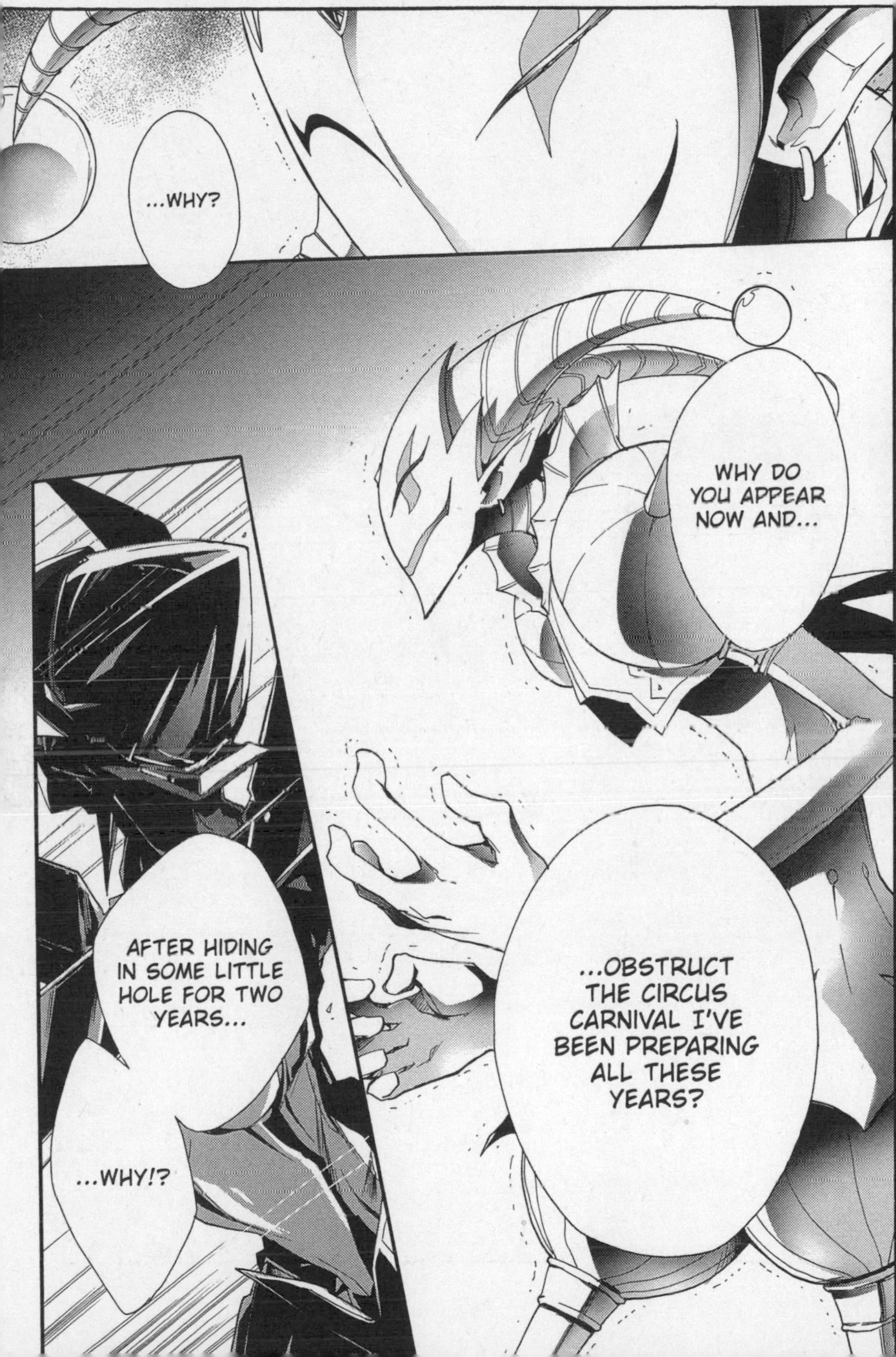
...WHY?
WHY DO YOU APPEAR NOW AND...
...OBSTRUCT THE CIRCUS CARNIVAL I'VE BEEN PREPARING ALL THESE YEARS?
AFTER HIDING IN SOME LITTLE HOLE FOR TWO YEARS...
...WHY!?

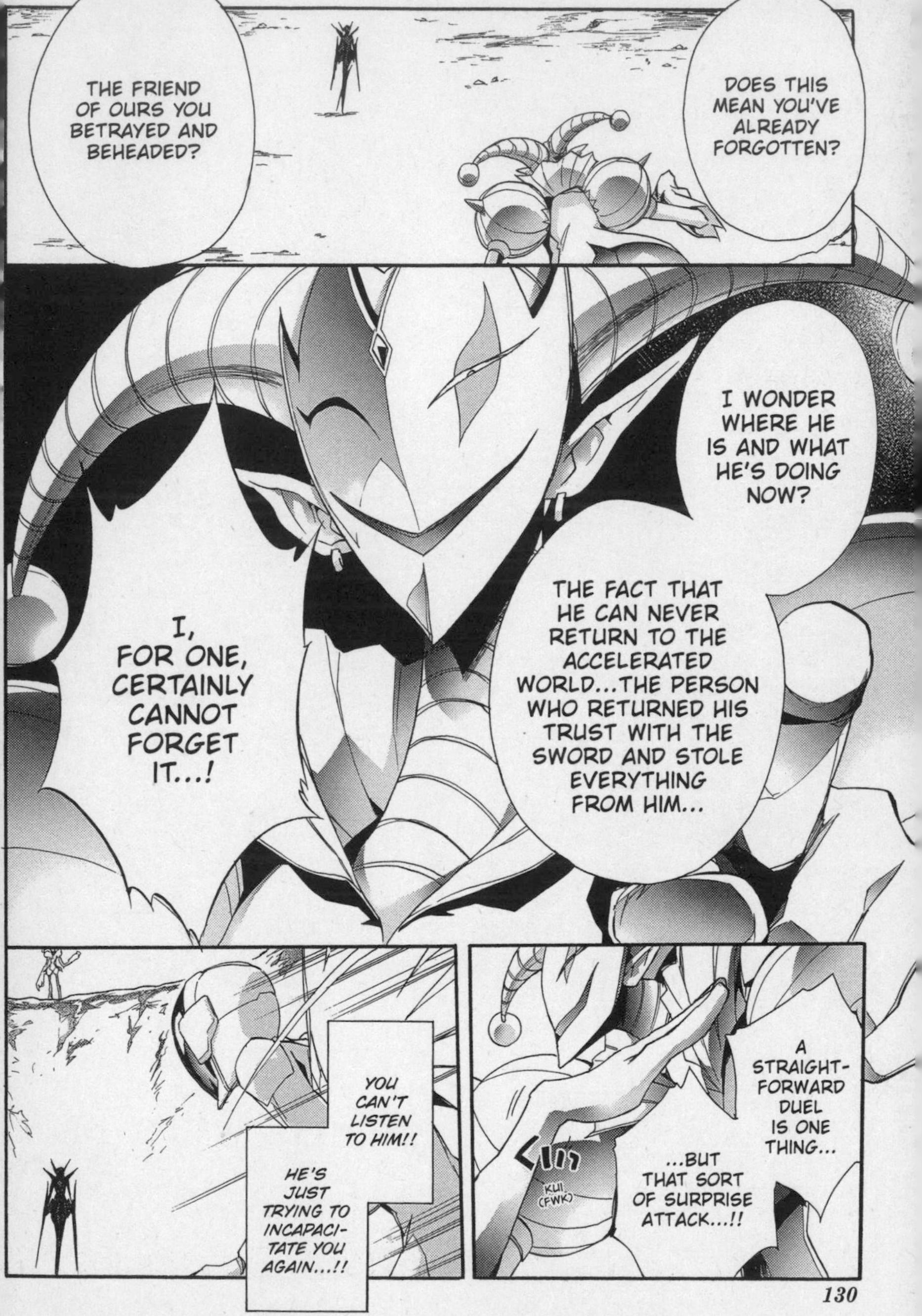
DOES THIS MEAN YOU'VE ALREADY FORGOTTEN?
THE FRIEND OF OURS YOU BETRAYED AND BEHEADED?
I WONDER WHERE HE IS AND WHAT HE'S DOING NOW?
THE FACT THAT HE CAN NEVER RETURN TO THE ACCELERATED WORLD...THE PERSON WHO RETURNED HIS TRUST WITH THE SWORD AND STOLE EVERYTHING FROM HIM...
I, FOR ONE, CERTAINLY CANNOT FORGET IT...!
A STRAIGHT-FORWARD DUEL IS ONE THING...
...BUT THAT SORT OF SURPRISE ATTACK...!!
KUI (FWK)
YOU CAN'T LISTEN TO HIM!!
HE'S JUST TRYING TO INCAPACITATE YOU AGAIN...!!

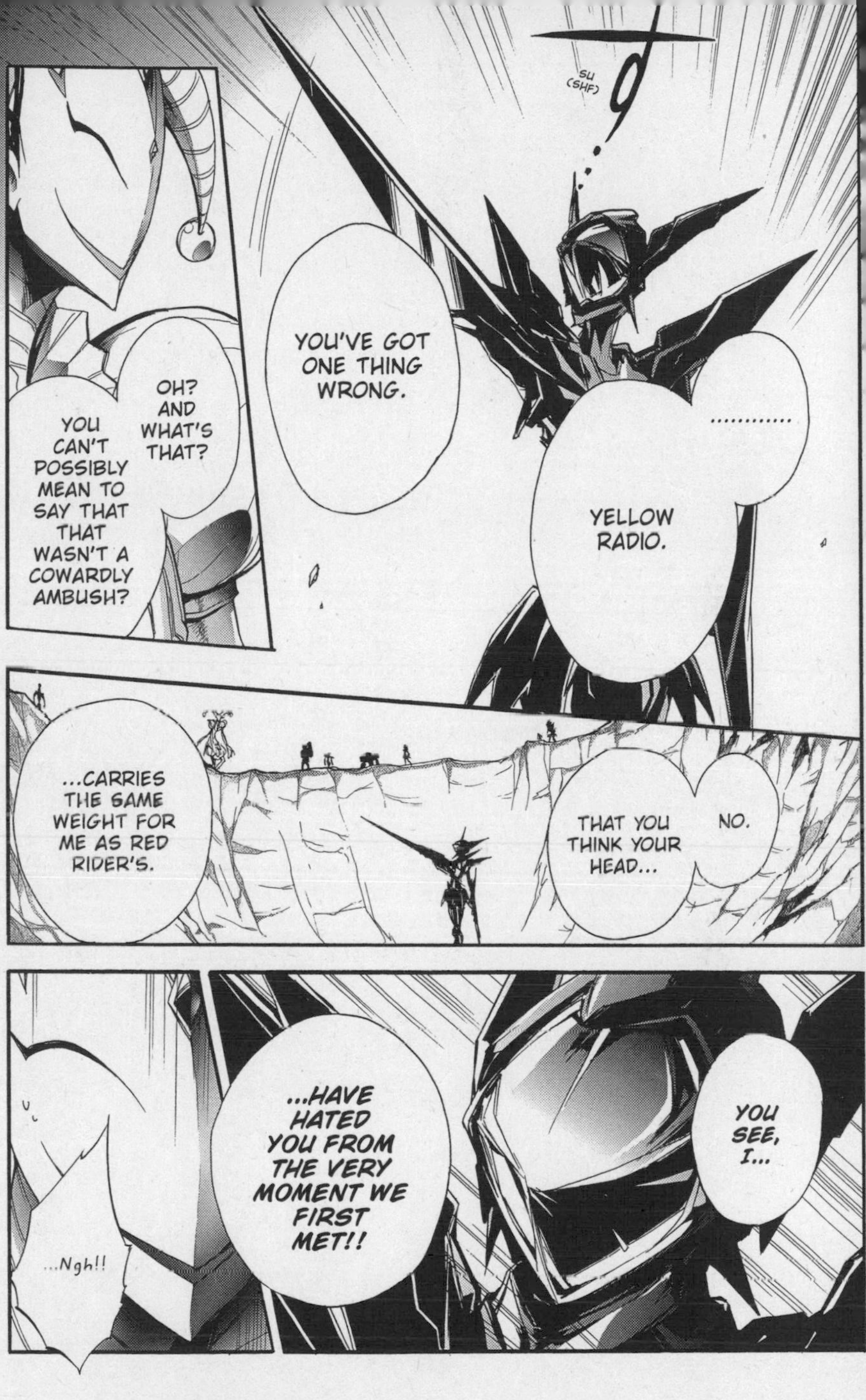
SU (SHF)
....
YELLOW RADIO.
YOU'VE GOT ONE THING WRONG.
OH? AND WHAT'S THAT?
YOU CAN'T POSSIBLY MEAN TO SAY THAT THAT WASN'T A COWARDLY AMBUSH?
NO.
THAT YOU THINK YOUR HEAD...
...CARRIES THE SAME WEIGHT FOR ME AS RED RIDER'S.
YOU SEE, I...
...HAVE HATED YOU FROM THE VERY MOMENT WE FIRST MET!!
...Ngh!!

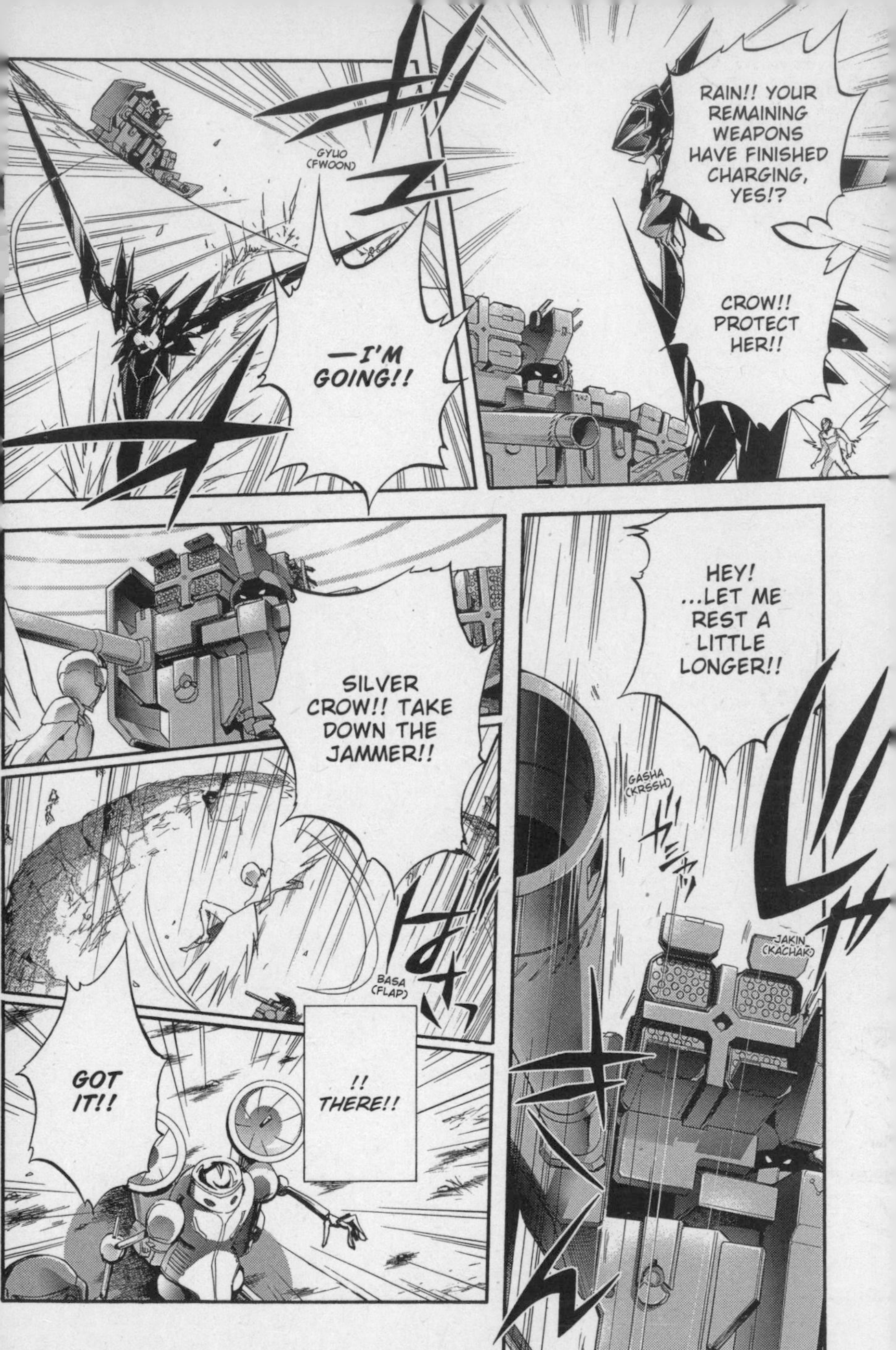
RAIN!! YOUR REMAINING WEAPONS HAVE FINISHED CHARGING, YES!?
CROW!! PROTECT HER!!
GYUO (FWOON)
—I'M GOING!!
HEY! ...LET ME REST A LITTLE LONGER!!
GASHA (KRSSH)
JAKIN (KACHAK)
SILVER CROW!! TAKE DOWN THE JAMMER!!
BASA (FLAP)
!! THERE!!
GOT IT!!

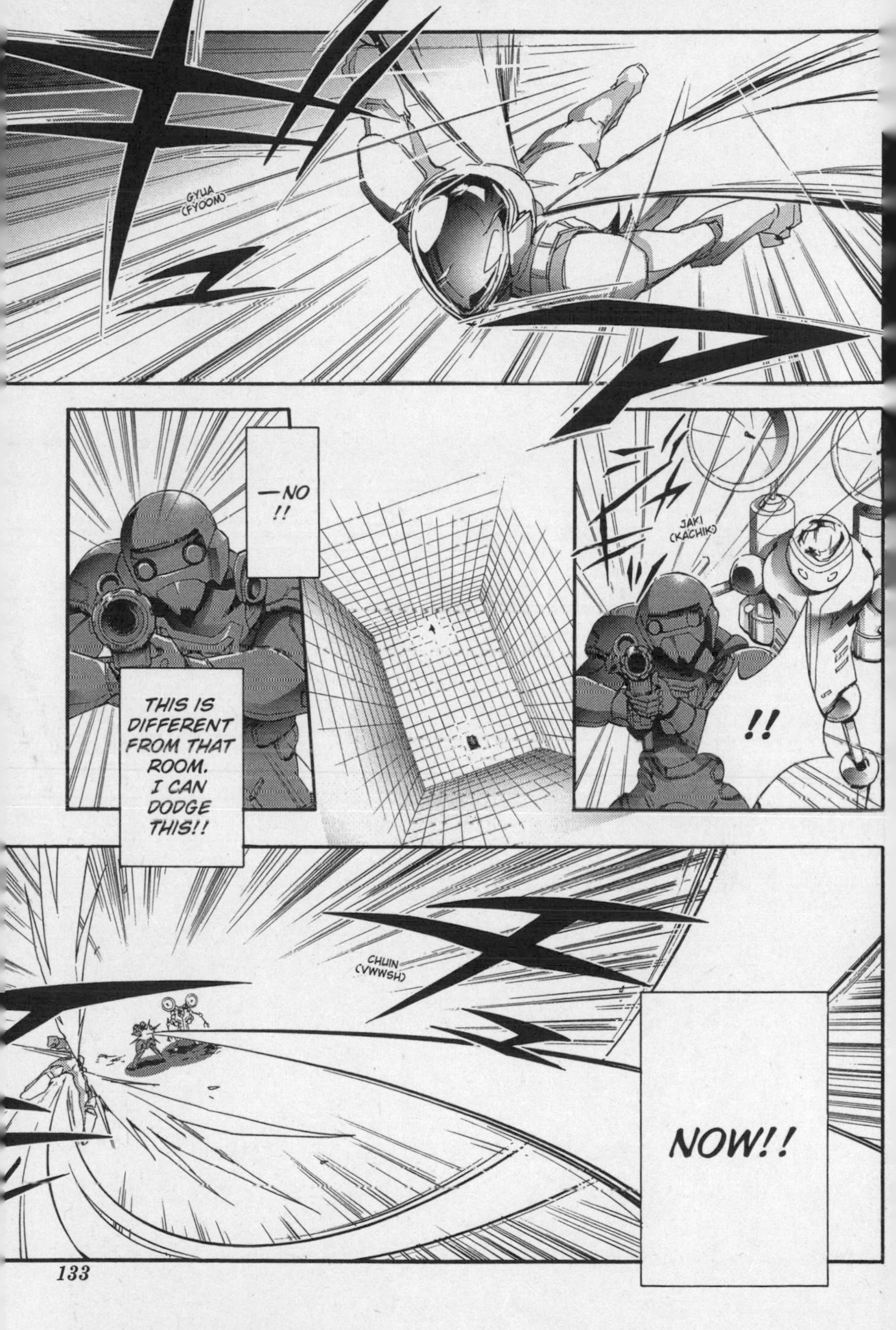
GYUA (FYOOM)
JAKI (KACHIK)
!!
—NO !!
THIS IS DIFFERENT FROM THAT ROOM. I CAN DODGE THIS!!
CHUIN (VWWSH)
NOW!!

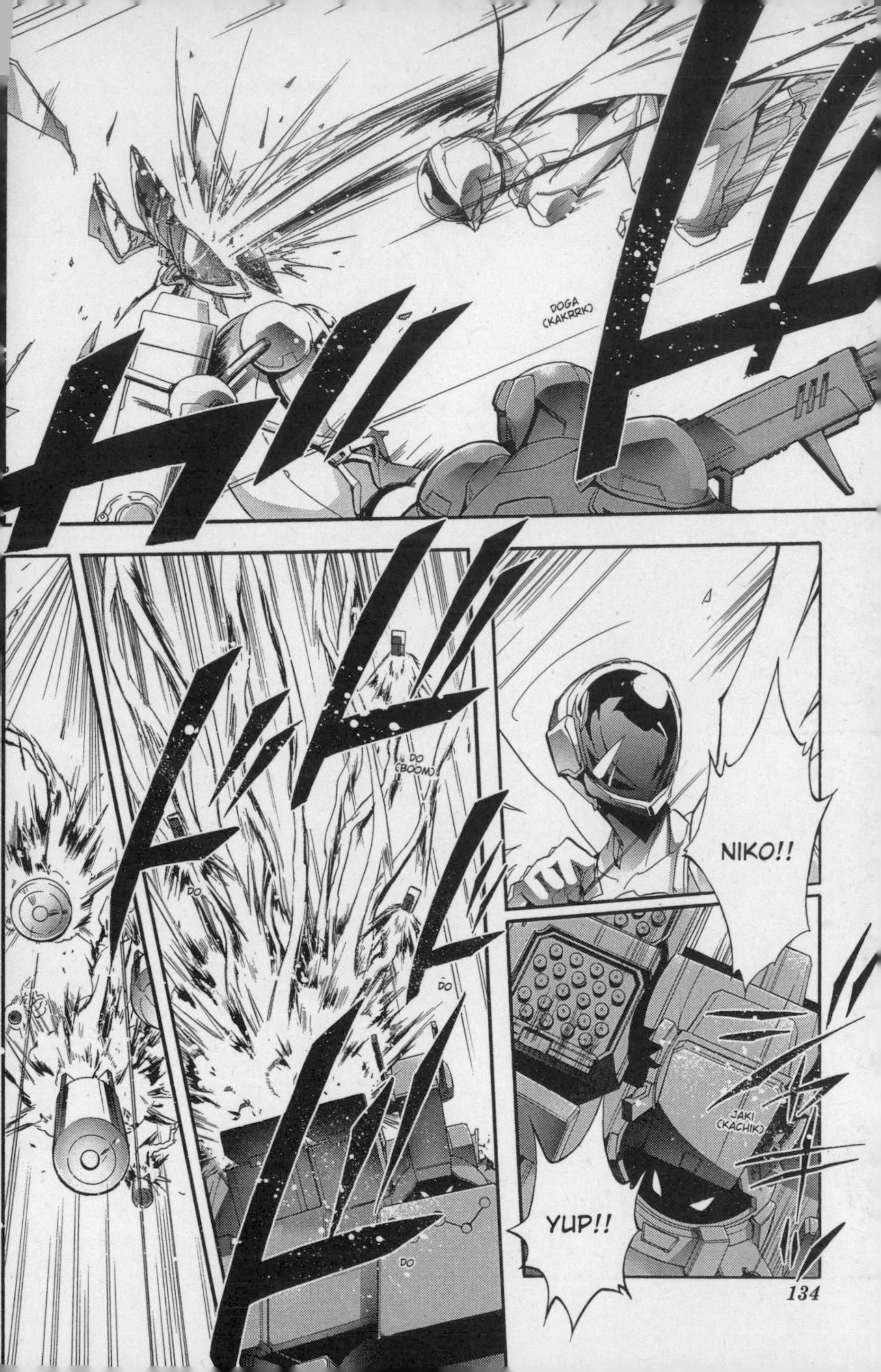
DOGA
(KAKRRK)
NIKO!!
JAKI
(KACHIK)
YUP!!
DO
(BOOM)
DO
DO
DO

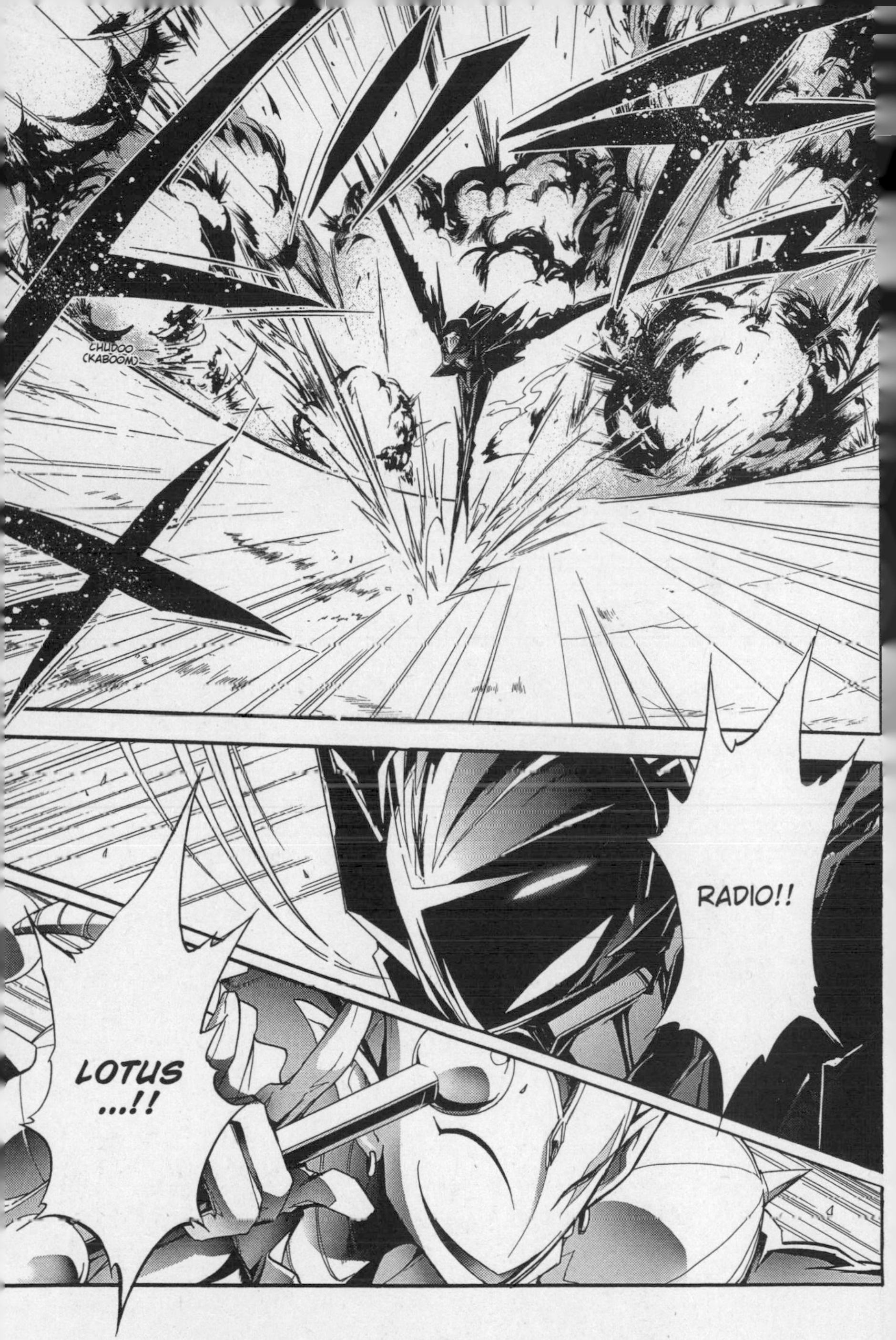
CHUDOO (KABOOM)
RADIO!!
LOTUS ...!!

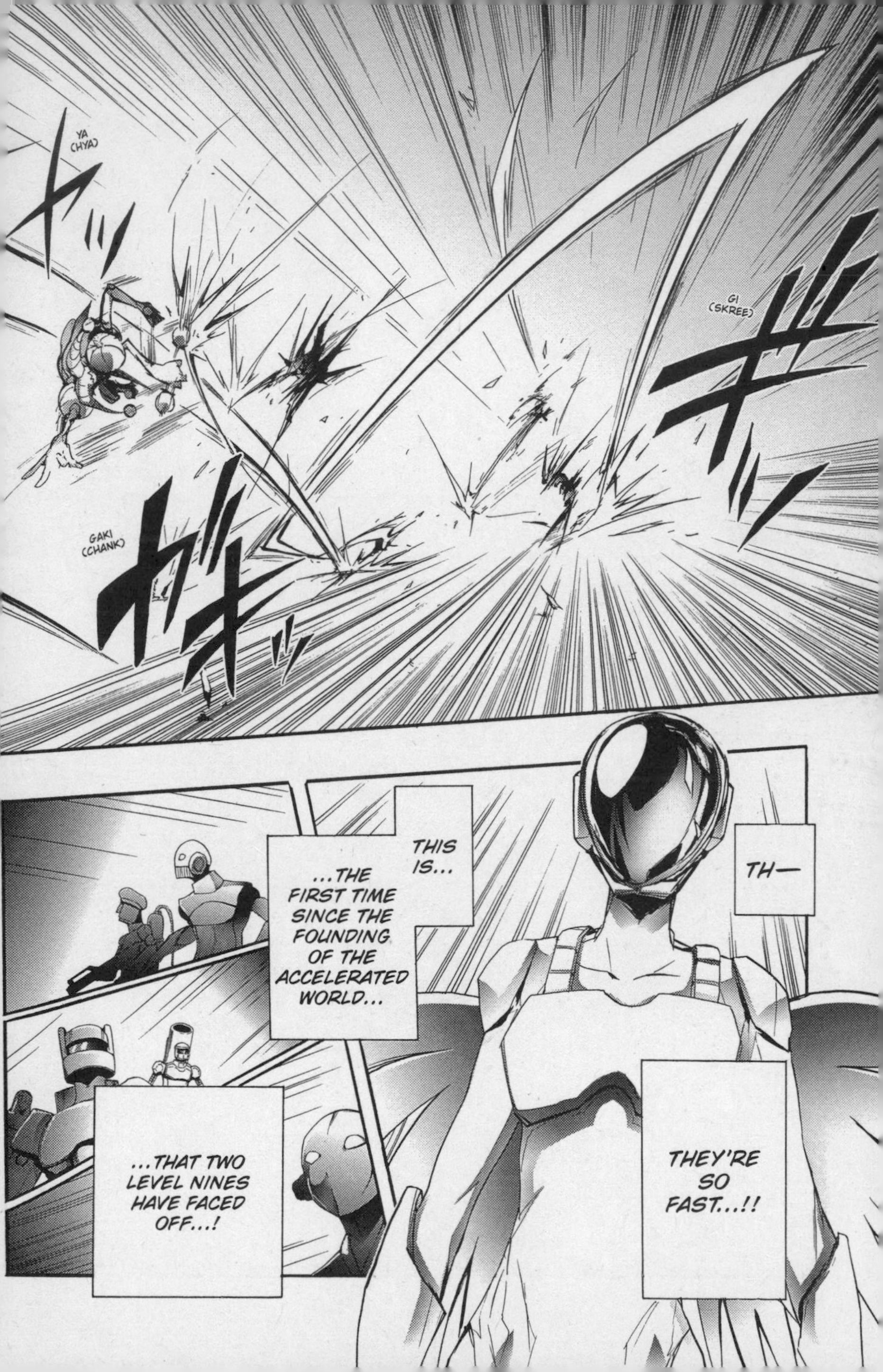
GI (SKREE)
YA (HYA)
GAKI (CHANK)
TH—
THIS IS...
...THE FIRST TIME SINCE THE FOUNDING OF THE ACCELERATED WORLD...
THEY'RE SO FAST...!!
...THAT TWO LEVEL NINES HAVE FACED OFF...!

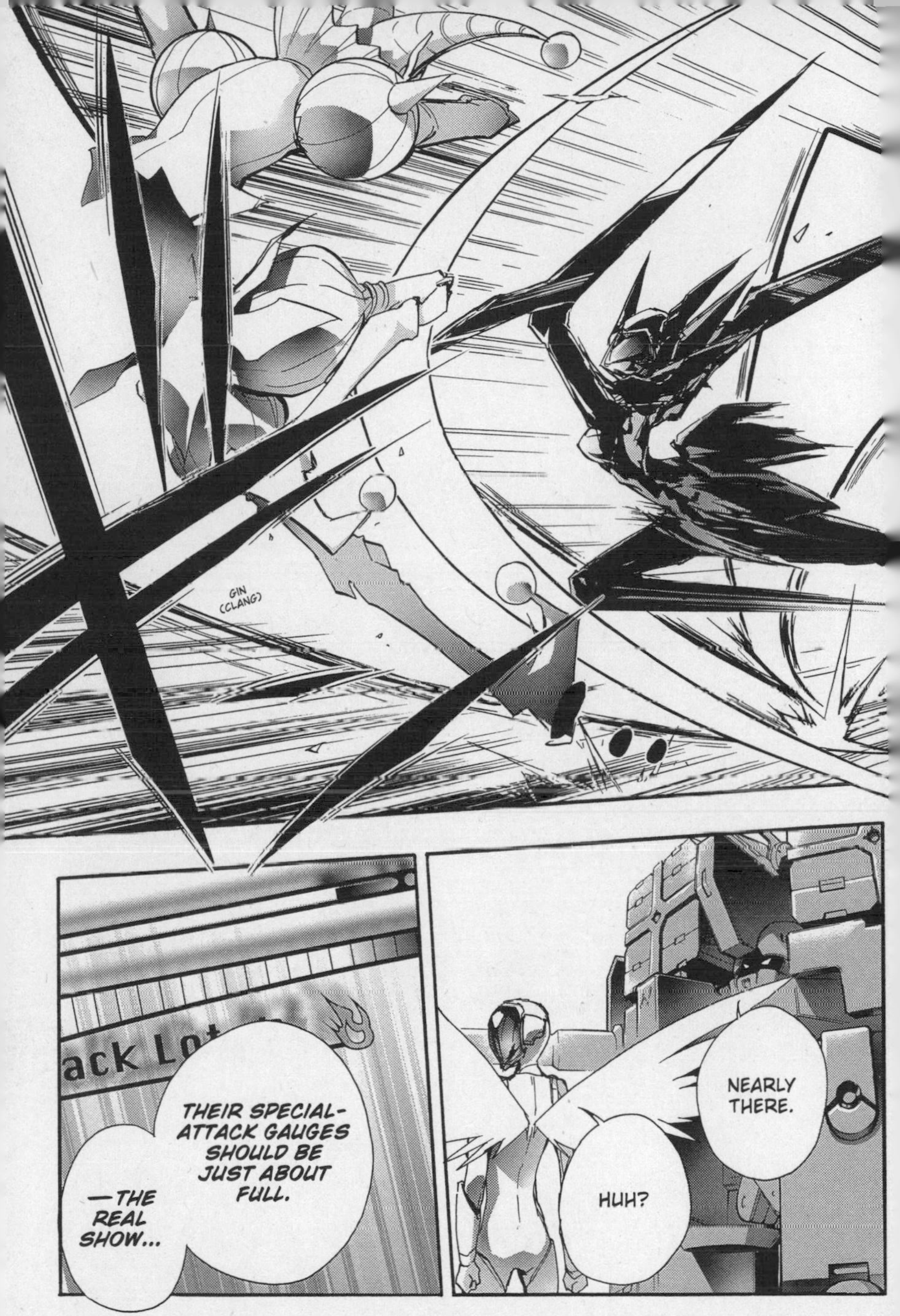
GIN (CLANG)
NEARLY THERE.
HUH?
THEIR SPECIAL-ATTACK GAUGES SHOULD BE JUST ABOUT FULL.
—THE REAL SHOW...

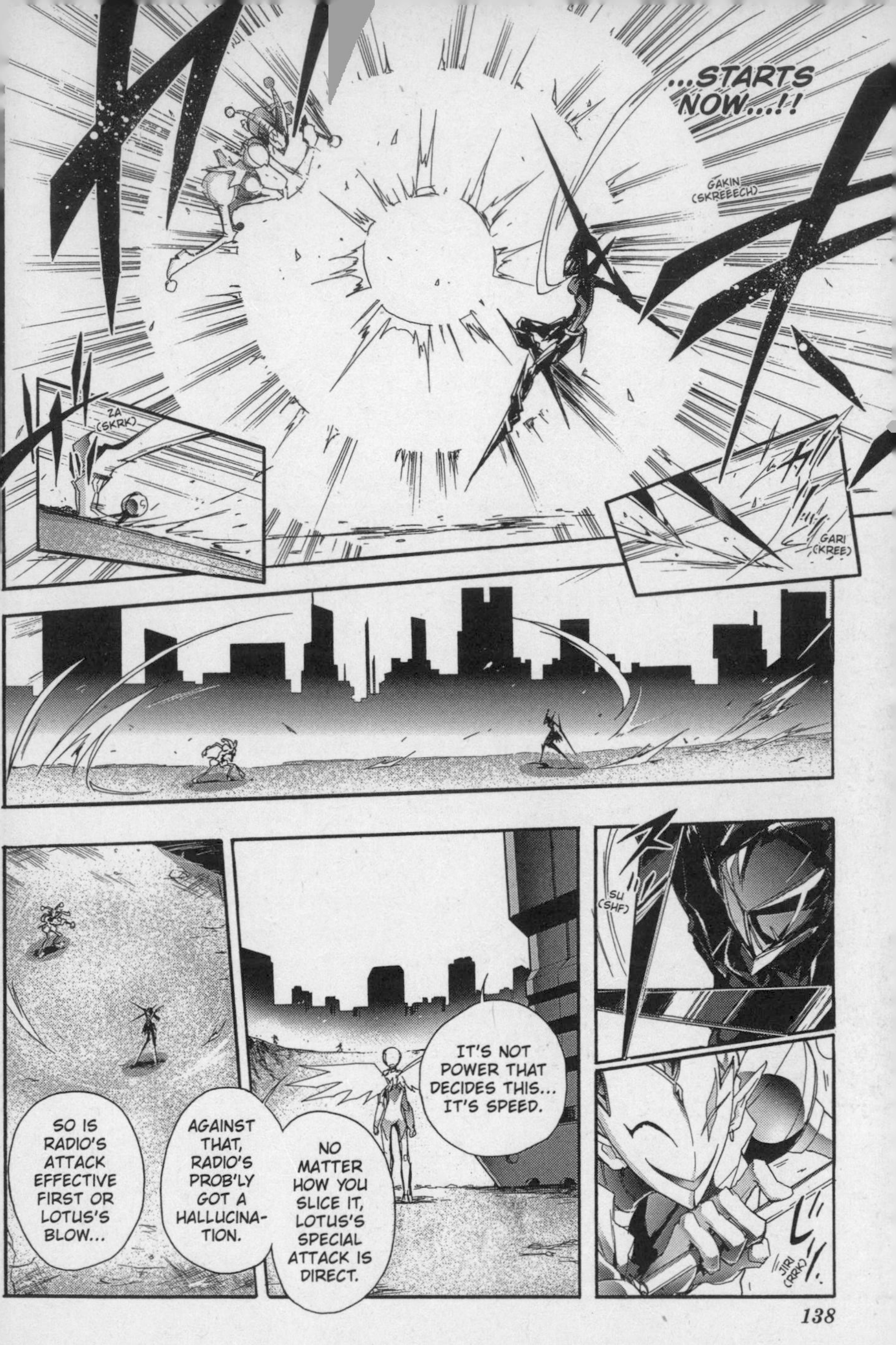
...STARTS NOW...!!
GAKIN (SKREEECH)
GARI (KREE)
ZA (SKRK)
SU (SHF)
JIRI (RRK)
IT'S NOT POWER THAT DECIDES THIS... IT'S SPEED.
NO MATTER HOW YOU SLICE IT, LOTUS'S SPECIAL ATTACK IS DIRECT.
AGAINST THAT, RADIO'S PROB'LY GOT A HALLUCINATION.
SO IS RADIO'S ATTACK EFFECTIVE FIRST OR LOTUS'S BLOW...

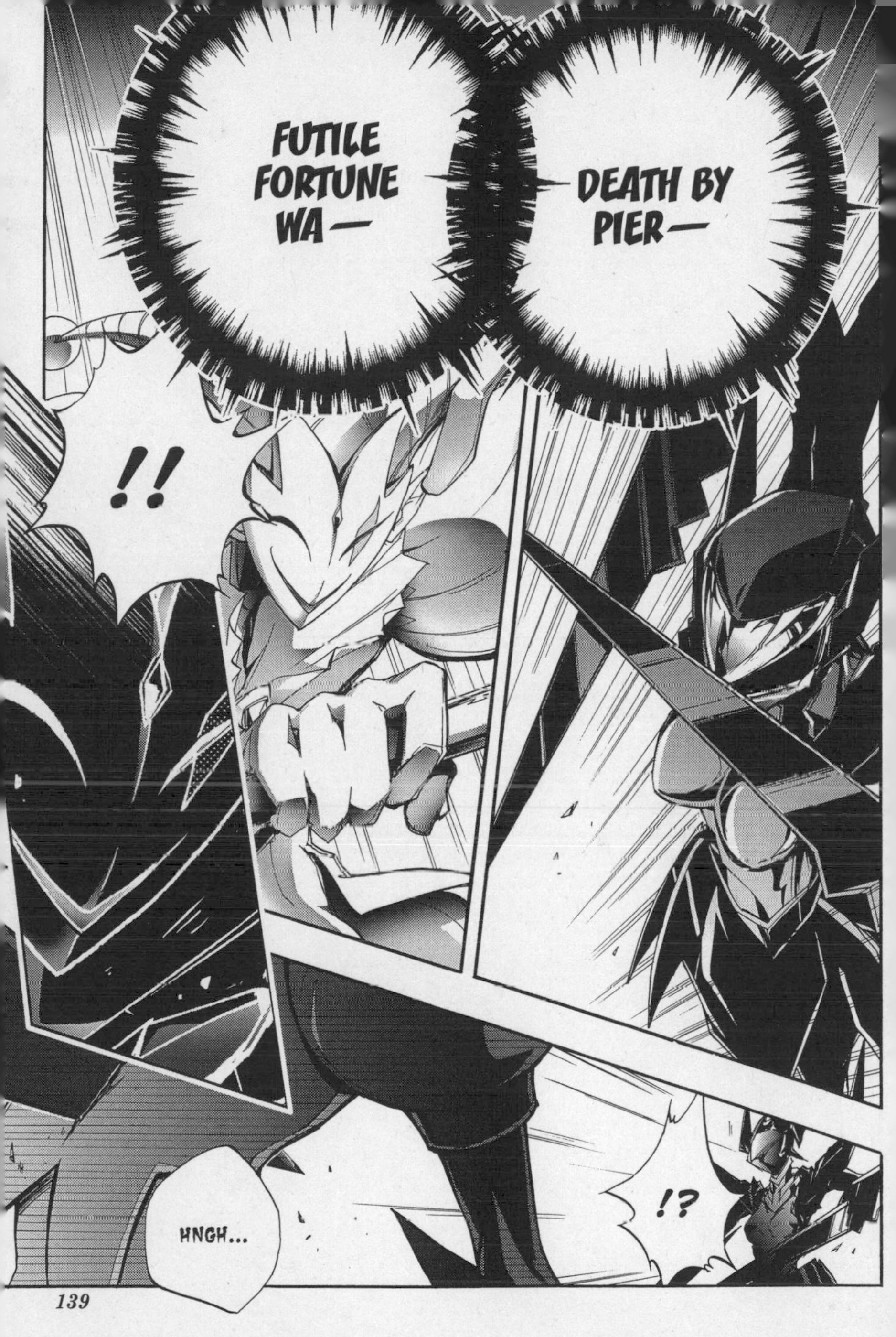
DEATH BY PIER—
FUTILE FORTUNE WA—
!!
!?
HNGH...

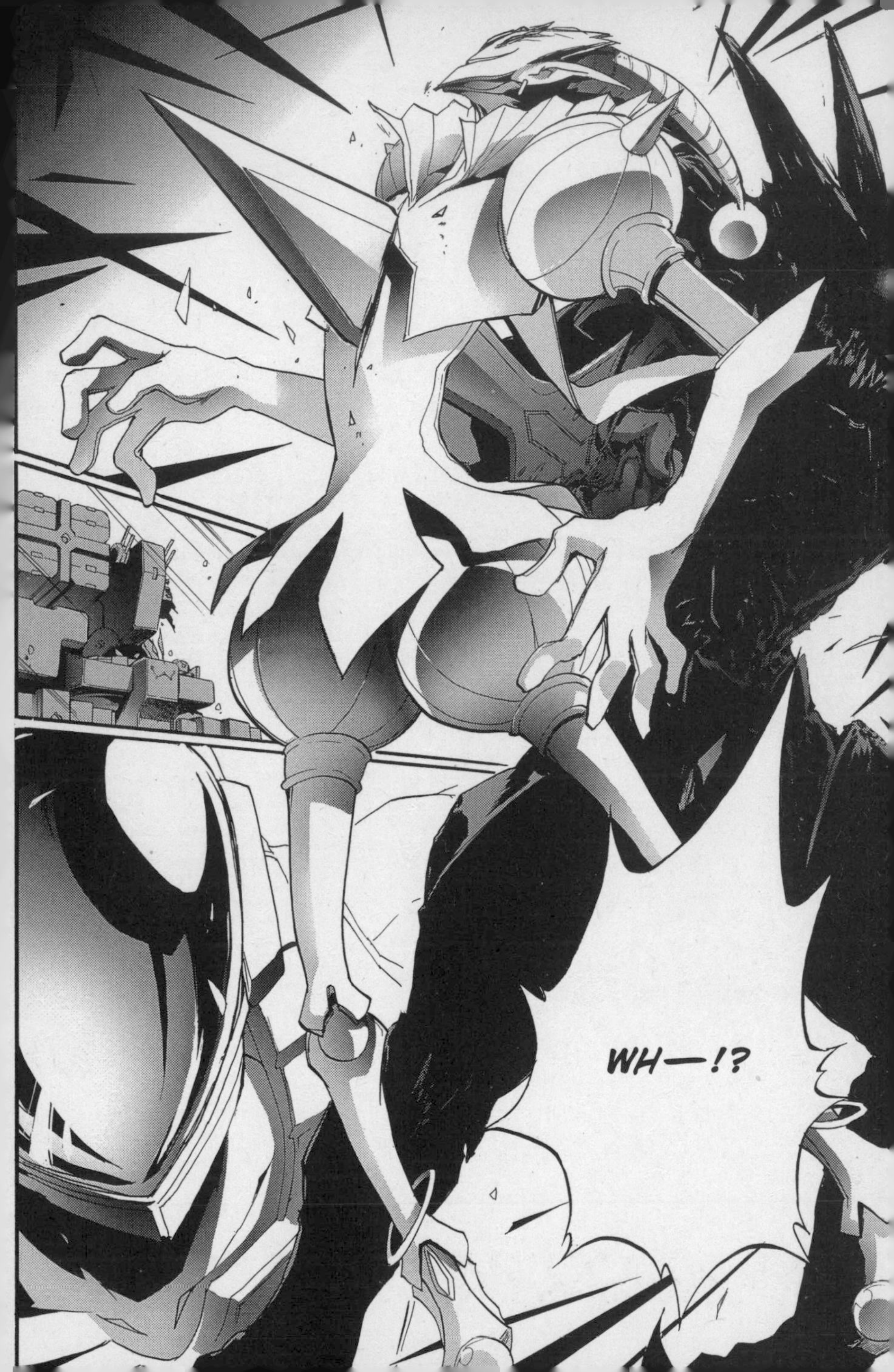
WH—!?

▶▶▶ ACCEL·WORLD

CHAPTER #16

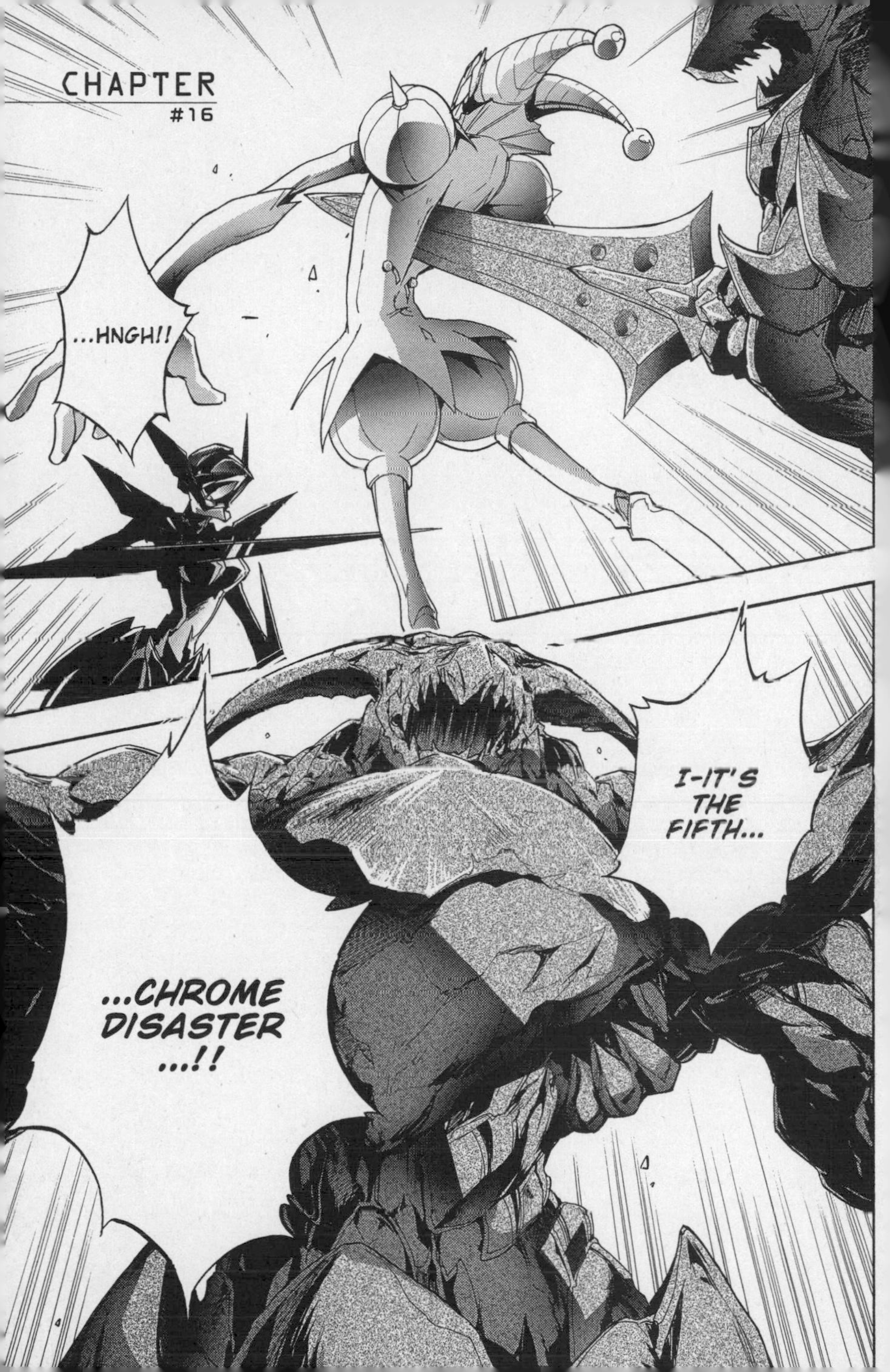
...HNGH!!
I-IT'S THE FIFTH...
...CHROME DISASTER ...!!

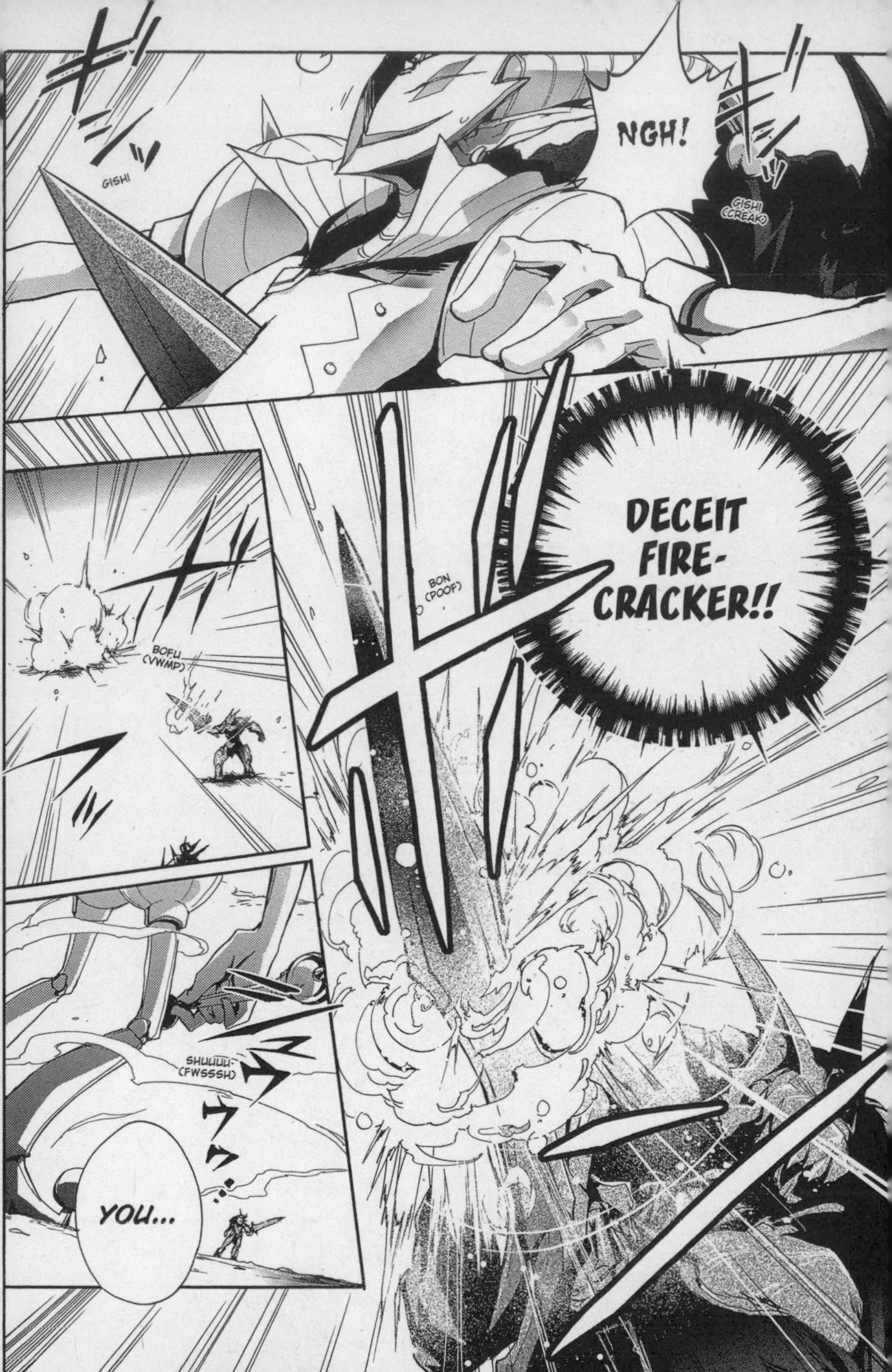
NGH!
GISHI (CREAK)
GISHI
DECEIT FIRE-CRACKER!!
BON (POOF)
BOFU (VWMP)
SHUUUU (FWSSSH)
YOU...

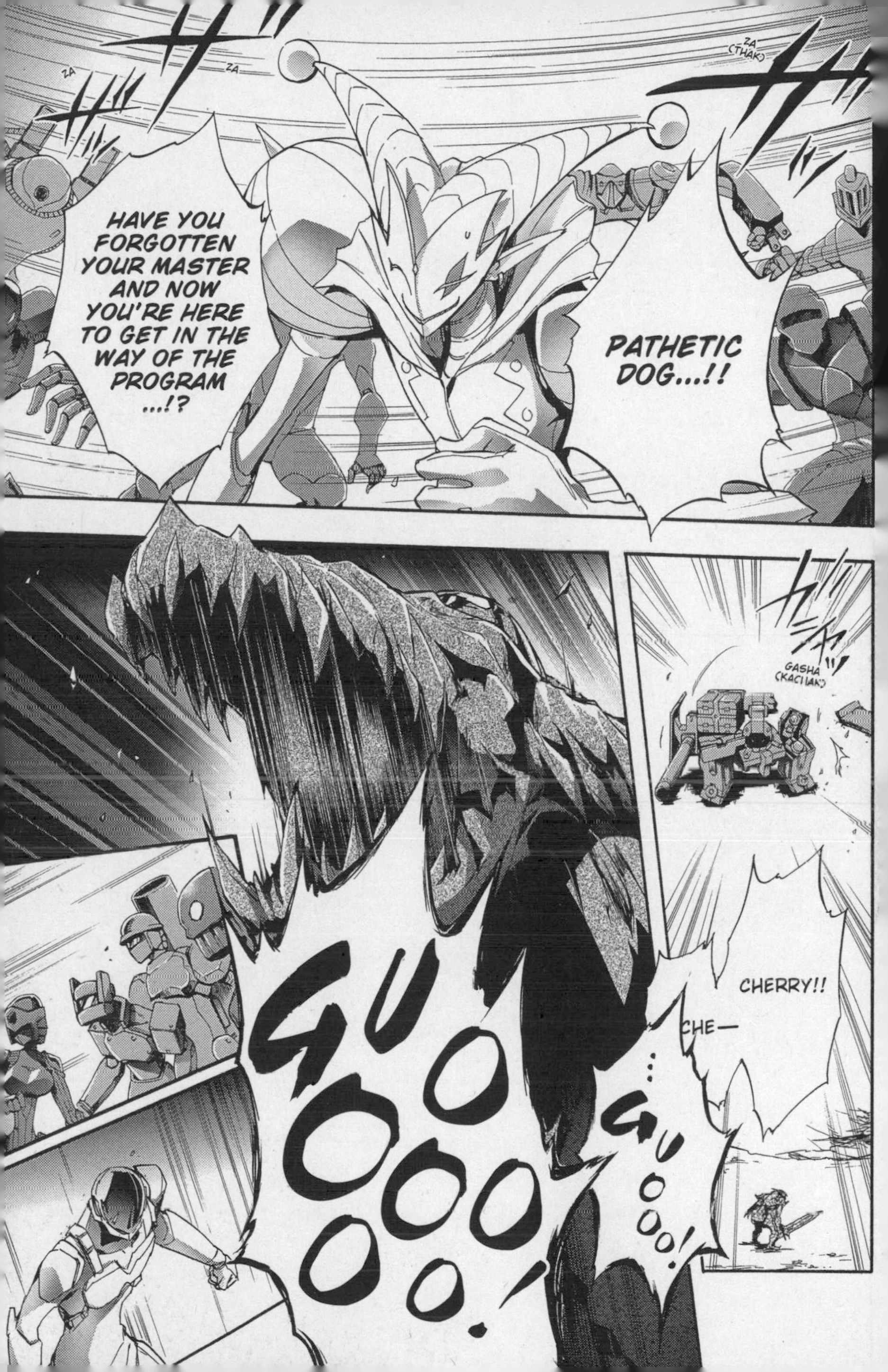
ZA (THAK)
ZA
ZA
HAVE YOU FORGOTTEN YOUR MASTER AND NOW YOU'RE HERE TO GET IN THE WAY OF THE PROGRAM ...!?
PATHETIC DOG...!!
GASHA (KACHAK)
CHERRY!!
CHE—
...GUOOOO!
GUOOOOOO!

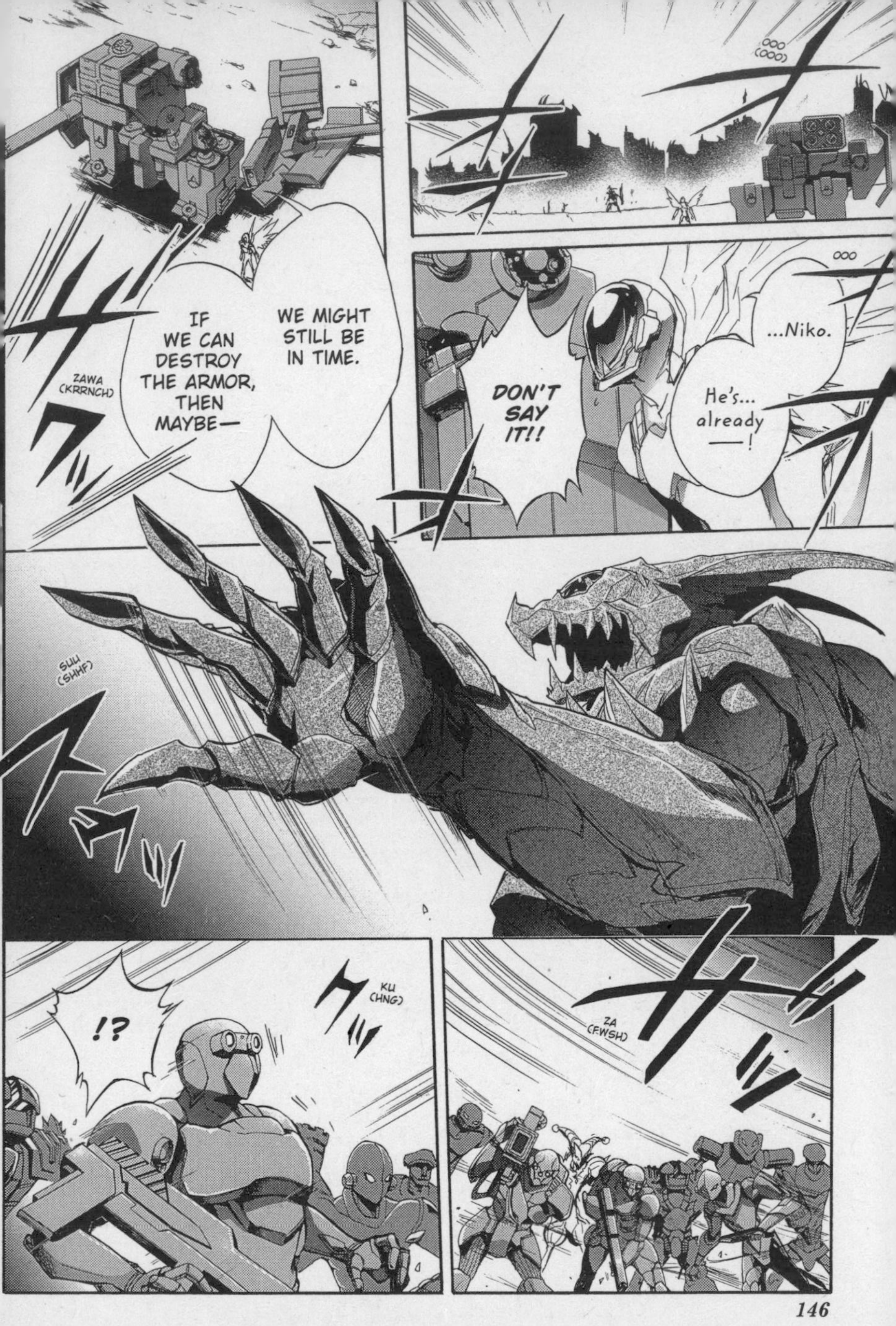
OOO
(OOO)
OOO
...Niko.
He's... already —!
DON'T SAY IT!!
WE MIGHT STILL BE IN TIME.
IF WE CAN DESTROY THE ARMOR, THEN MAYBE—
ZAWA
(KRRNCH)
SUU
(SHHF)
ZA
(FWSH)
KU
(HNG)
!?

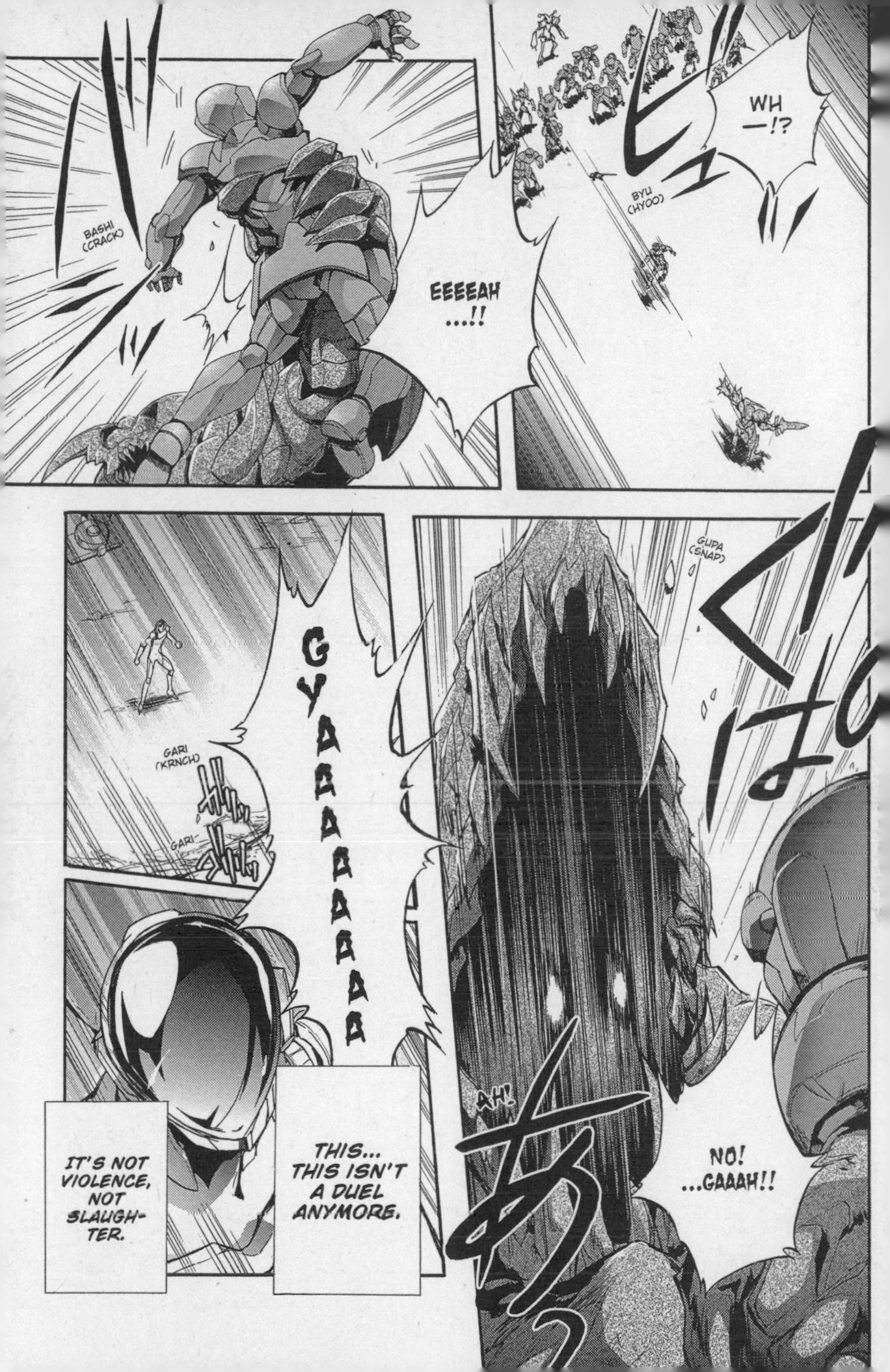
WH—!?
BYU (HYOO)
EEEEAH ....!!
BASHI (CRACK)
GUPA (SNAP)
NO! ...GAAAH!!
AH!
GARI (KRNCH)
GARI
GYAAAAAAAA
THIS... THIS ISN'T A DUEL ANYMORE.
IT'S NOT VIOLENCE, NOT SLAUGHTER.

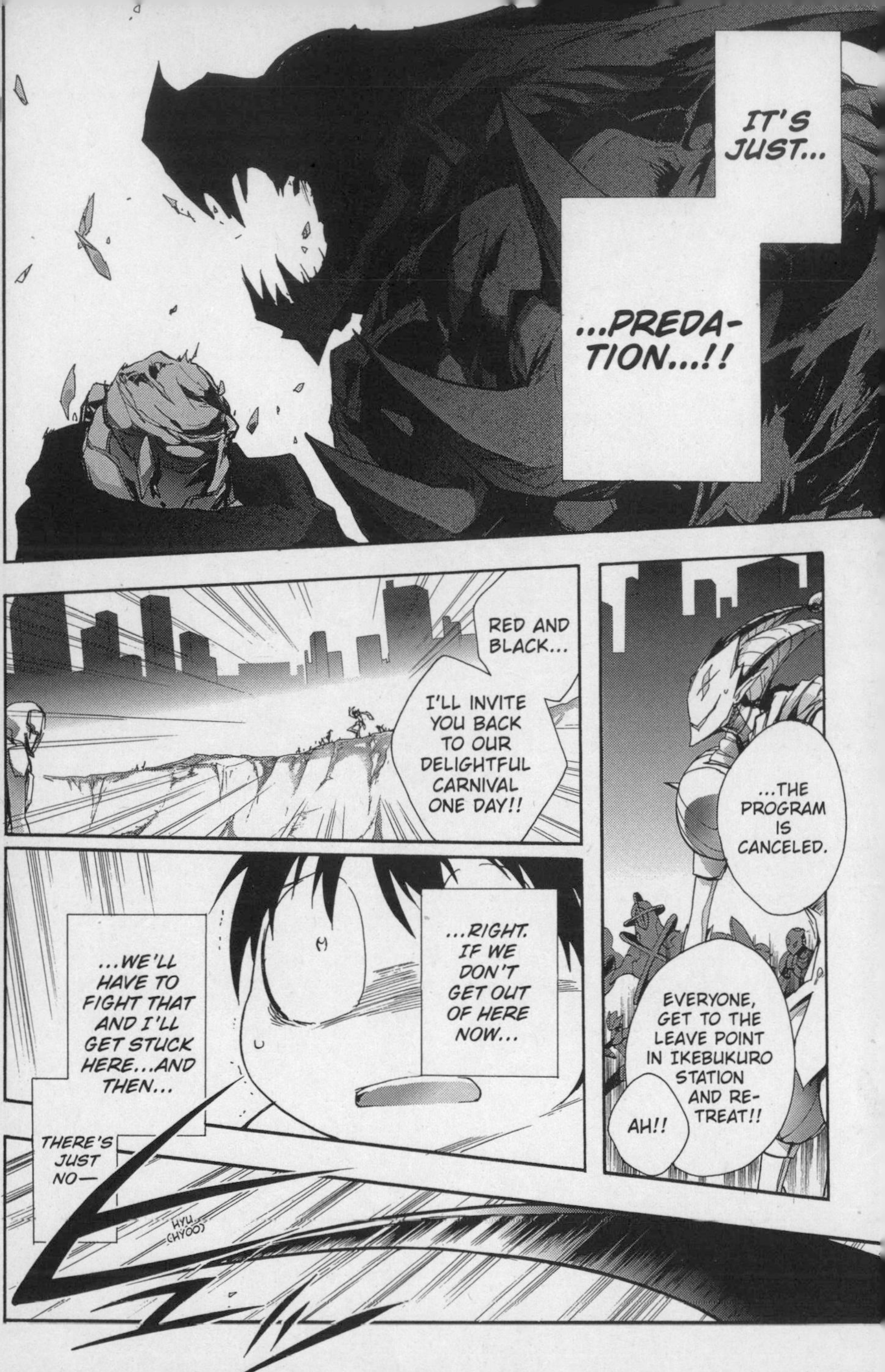
IT'S JUST...
...PREDATION...!!
...THE PROGRAM IS CANCELED.
EVERYONE, GET TO THE LEAVE POINT IN IKEBUKURO STATION AND RE-TREAT!!
AH!!
RED AND BLACK...
I'LL INVITE YOU BACK TO OUR DELIGHTFUL CARNIVAL ONE DAY!!
...RIGHT. IF WE DON'T GET OUT OF HERE NOW...
...WE'LL HAVE TO FIGHT THAT AND I'LL GET STUCK HERE...AND THEN...
THERE'S JUST NO—
HYU (HYOO)

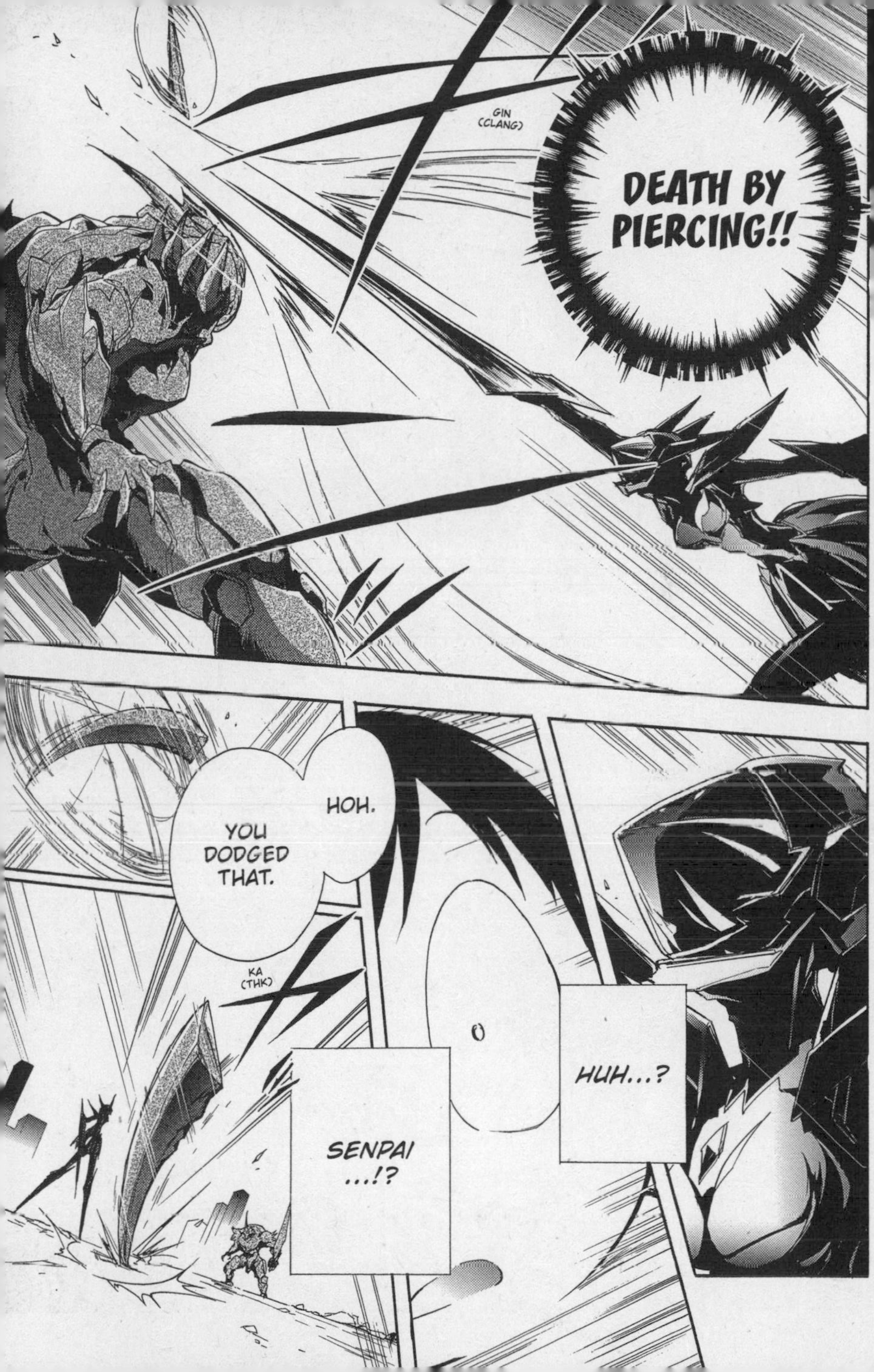
DEATH BY PIERCING!!
GIN (CLANG)
HUH...?
HOH.
YOU DODGED THAT.
SENPAI ...!?
KA (THK)

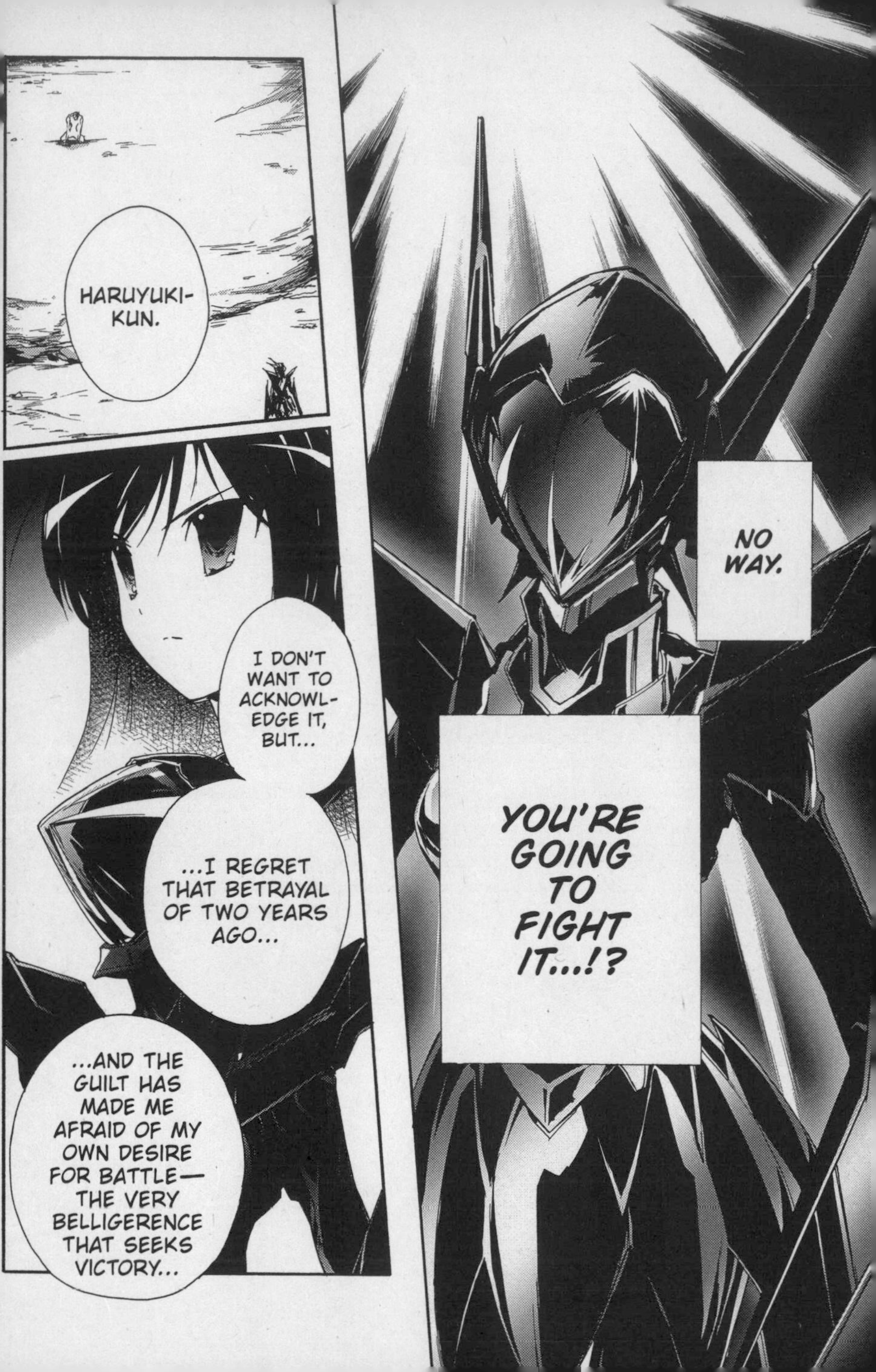
NO WAY.
YOU'RE GOING TO FIGHT IT...!?
HARUYUKI-KUN.
I DON'T WANT TO ACKNOWLEDGE IT, BUT...
...I REGRET THAT BETRAYAL OF TWO YEARS AGO...
...AND THE GUILT HAS MADE ME AFRAID OF MY OWN DESIRE FOR BATTLE—THE VERY BELLIGERENCE THAT SEEKS VICTORY...

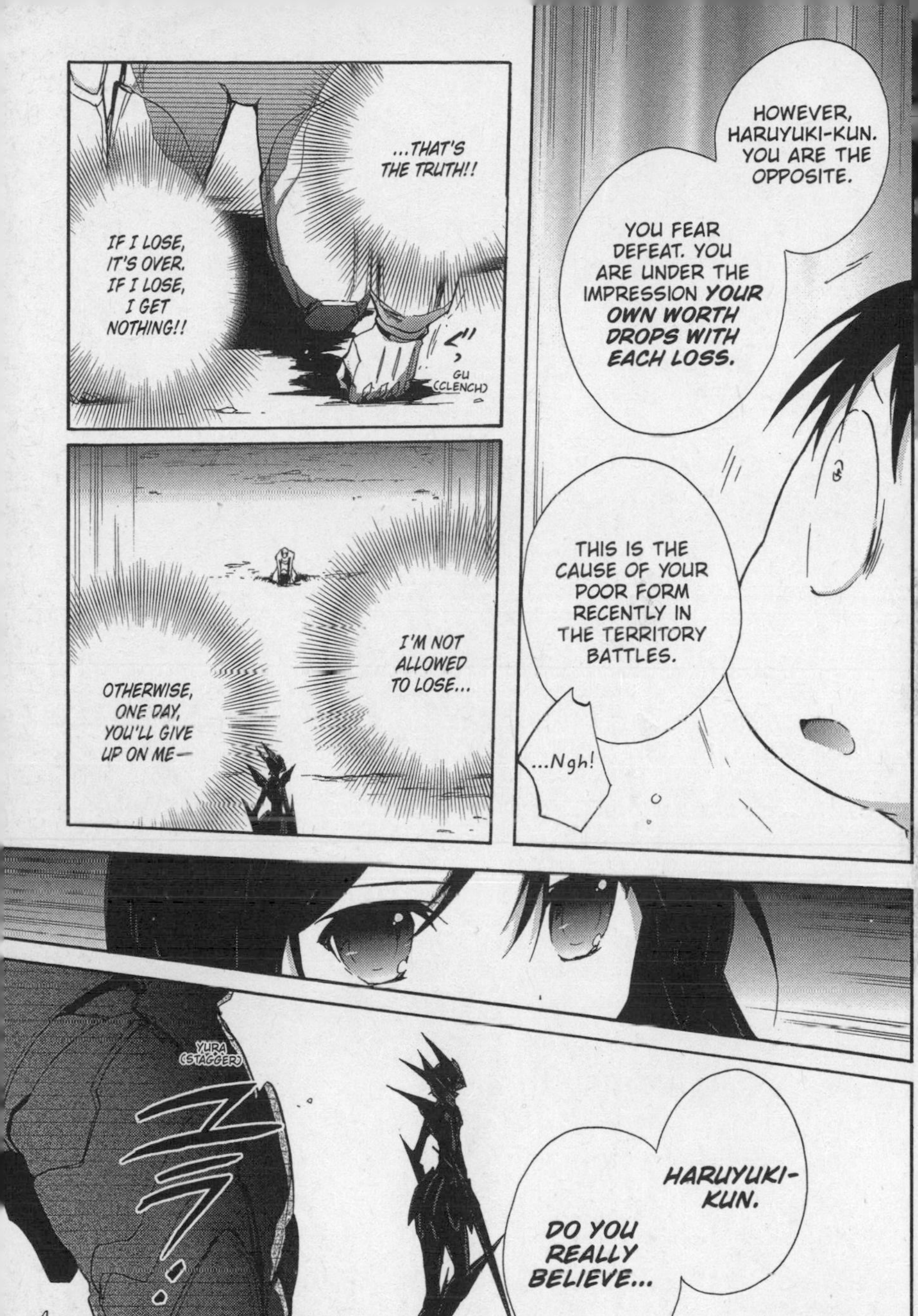
HOWEVER, HARUYUKI-KUN. YOU ARE THE OPPOSITE.
YOU FEAR DEFEAT. YOU ARE UNDER THE IMPRESSION YOUR OWN WORTH DROPS WITH EACH LOSS.
THIS IS THE CAUSE OF YOUR POOR FORM RECENTLY IN THE TERRITORY BATTLES.
...Ngh!
...THAT'S THE TRUTH!!
IF I LOSE, IT'S OVER. IF I LOSE, I GET NOTHING!!
GU (CLENCH)
I'M NOT ALLOWED TO LOSE...
OTHERWISE, ONE DAY, YOU'LL GIVE UP ON ME—
HARUYUKI-KUN.
DO YOU REALLY BELIEVE...
YURA (STAGGER)

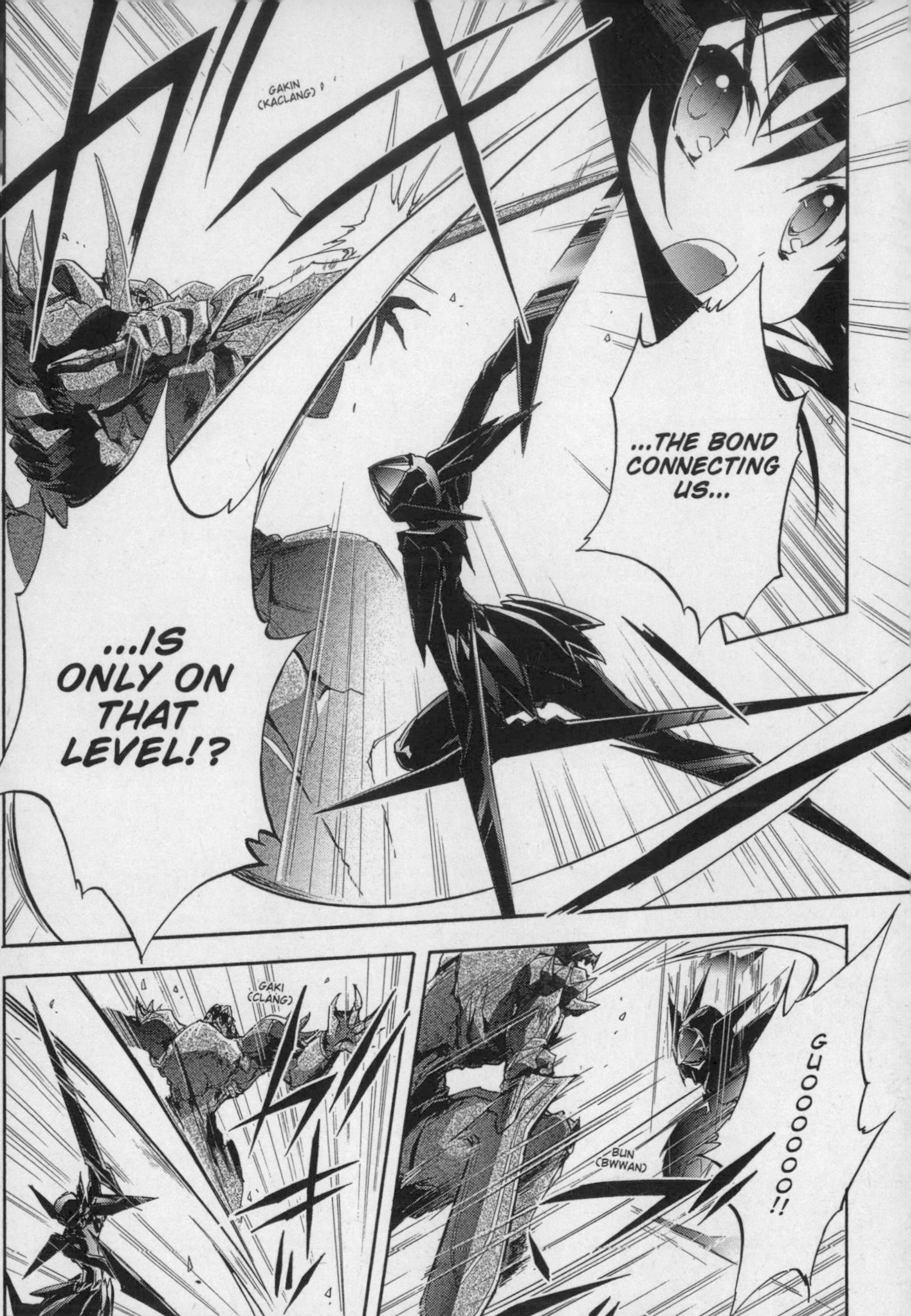
GAKIN (KACLANG)
...THE BOND CONNECTING US...
...IS ONLY ON THAT LEVEL!?
GUOOOOOOO!!
BUN (BWWAN)
GAKI (CLANG)

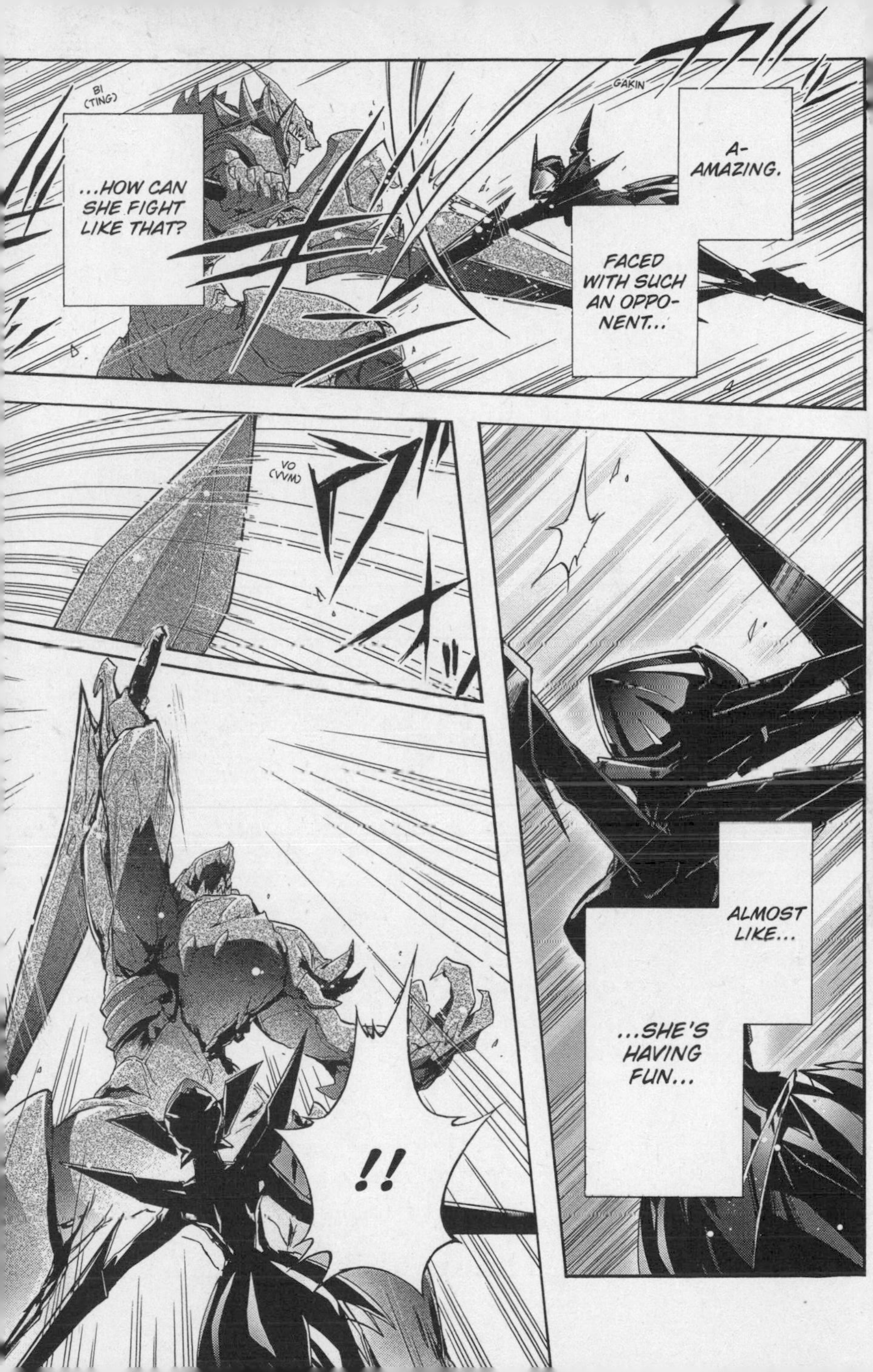
GAKIN
A-AMAZING.
FACED WITH SUCH AN OPPONENT...
BI (TING)
...HOW CAN SHE FIGHT LIKE THAT?
ALMOST LIKE...
...SHE'S HAVING FUN...
VO (VVM)
!!

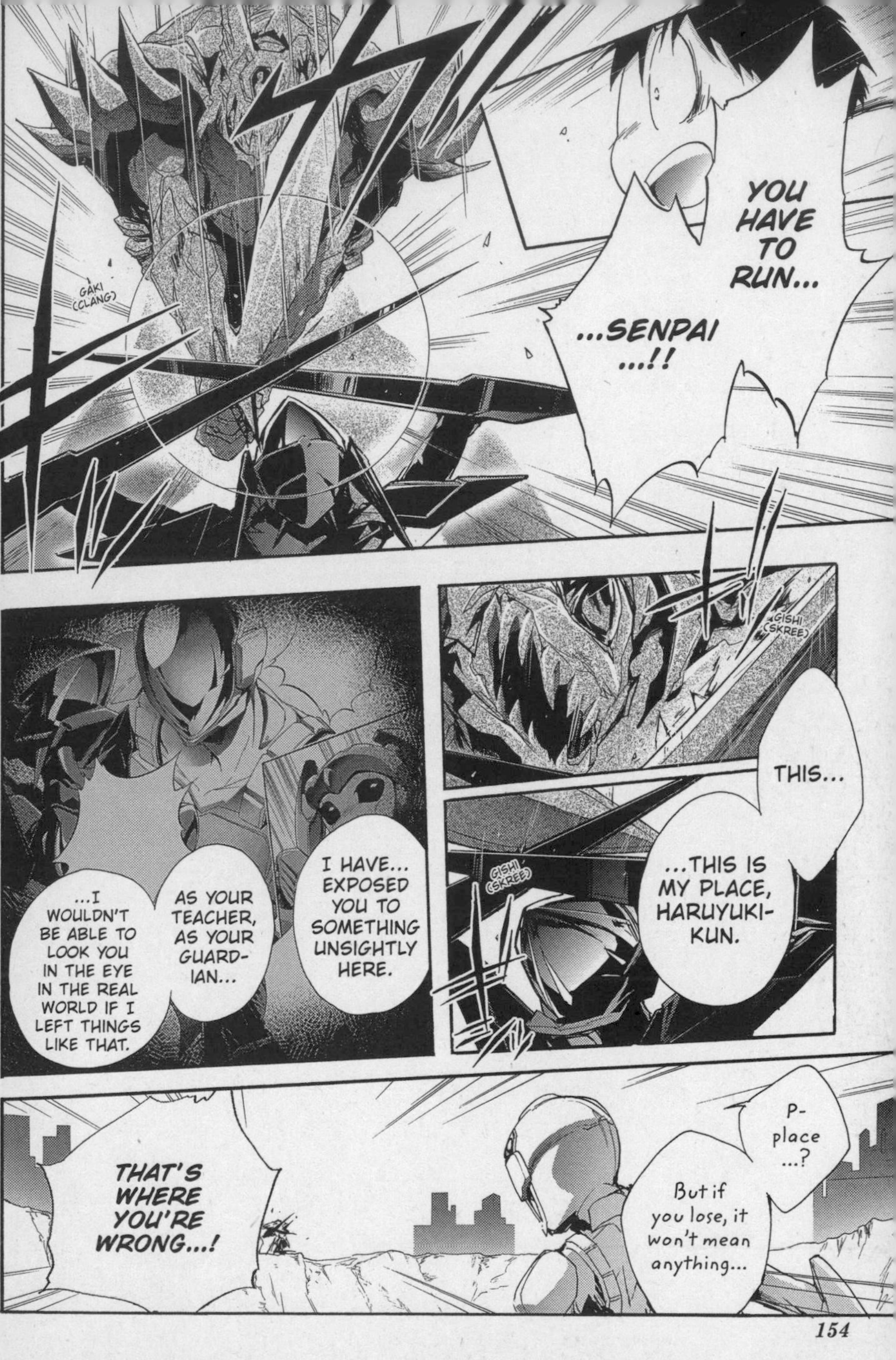
YOU HAVE TO RUN...
...SENPAI ...!!
GAKI (CLANG)
GISHI (SKREE)
THIS...
...THIS IS MY PLACE, HARUYUKI-KUN.
GISHI (SKREE)
I HAVE... EXPOSED YOU TO SOMETHING UNSIGHTLY HERE.
AS YOUR TEACHER, AS YOUR GUARDIAN...
...I WOULDN'T BE ABLE TO LOOK YOU IN THE EYE IN THE REAL WORLD IF I LEFT THINGS LIKE THAT.
P-place ...?
But if you lose, it won't mean anything...
THAT'S WHERE YOU'RE WRONG...!

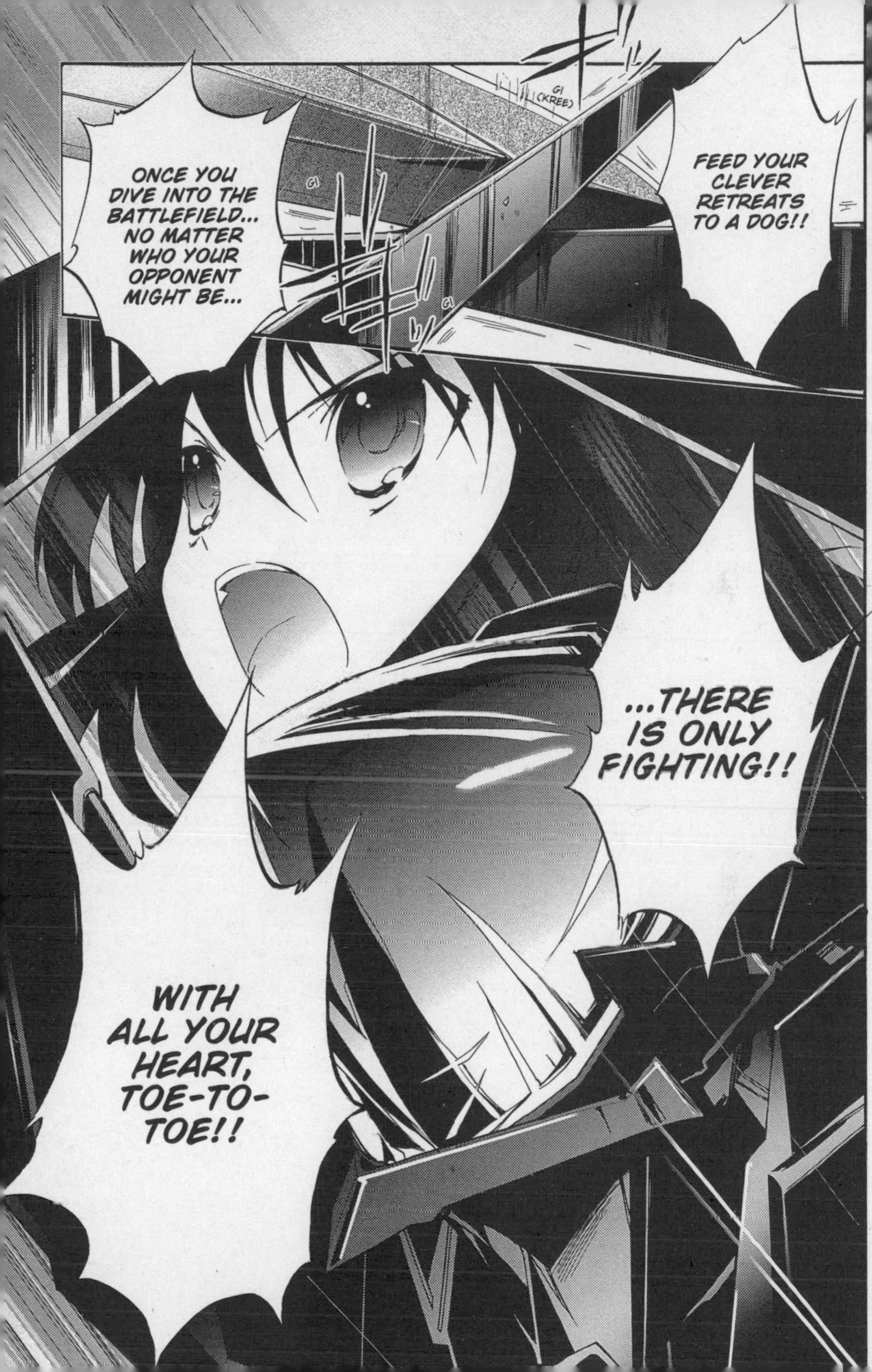
FEED YOUR CLEVER RETREATS TO A DOG!!
GI (KREE)
GI
GI
ONCE YOU DIVE INTO THE BATTLEFIELD... NO MATTER WHO YOUR OPPONENT MIGHT BE...
...THERE IS ONLY FIGHTING!!
WITH ALL YOUR HEART, TOE-TO-TOE!!

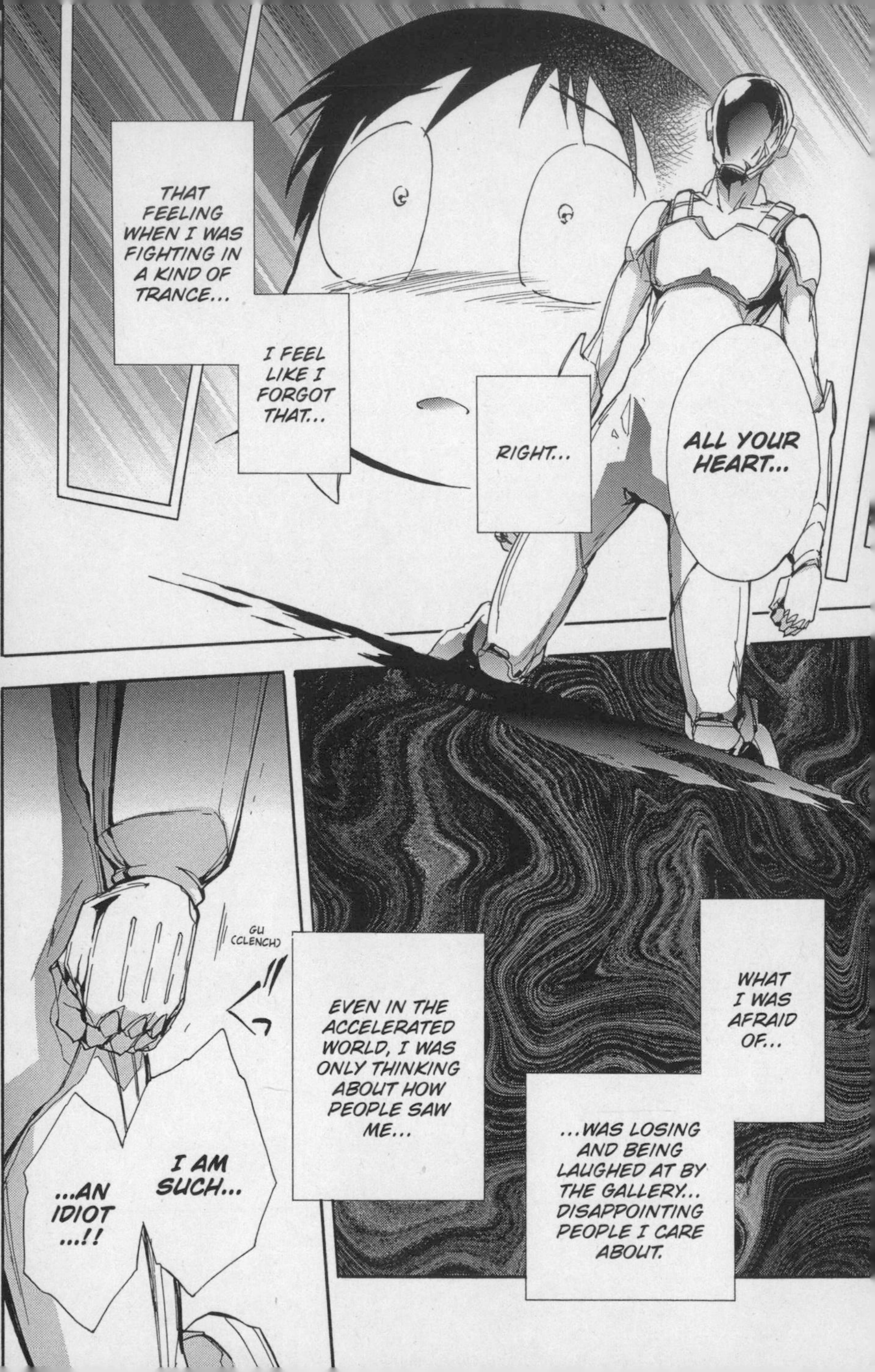
ALL YOUR HEART...
RIGHT...
THAT FEELING WHEN I WAS FIGHTING IN A KIND OF TRANCE...
I FEEL LIKE I FORGOT THAT...
WHAT I WAS AFRAID OF...
...WAS LOSING AND BEING LAUGHED AT BY THE GALLERY... DISAPPOINTING PEOPLE I CARE ABOUT.
EVEN IN THE ACCELERATED WORLD, I WAS ONLY THINKING ABOUT HOW PEOPLE SAW ME...
GU (CLENCH)
I AM SUCH...
...AN IDIOT...!!

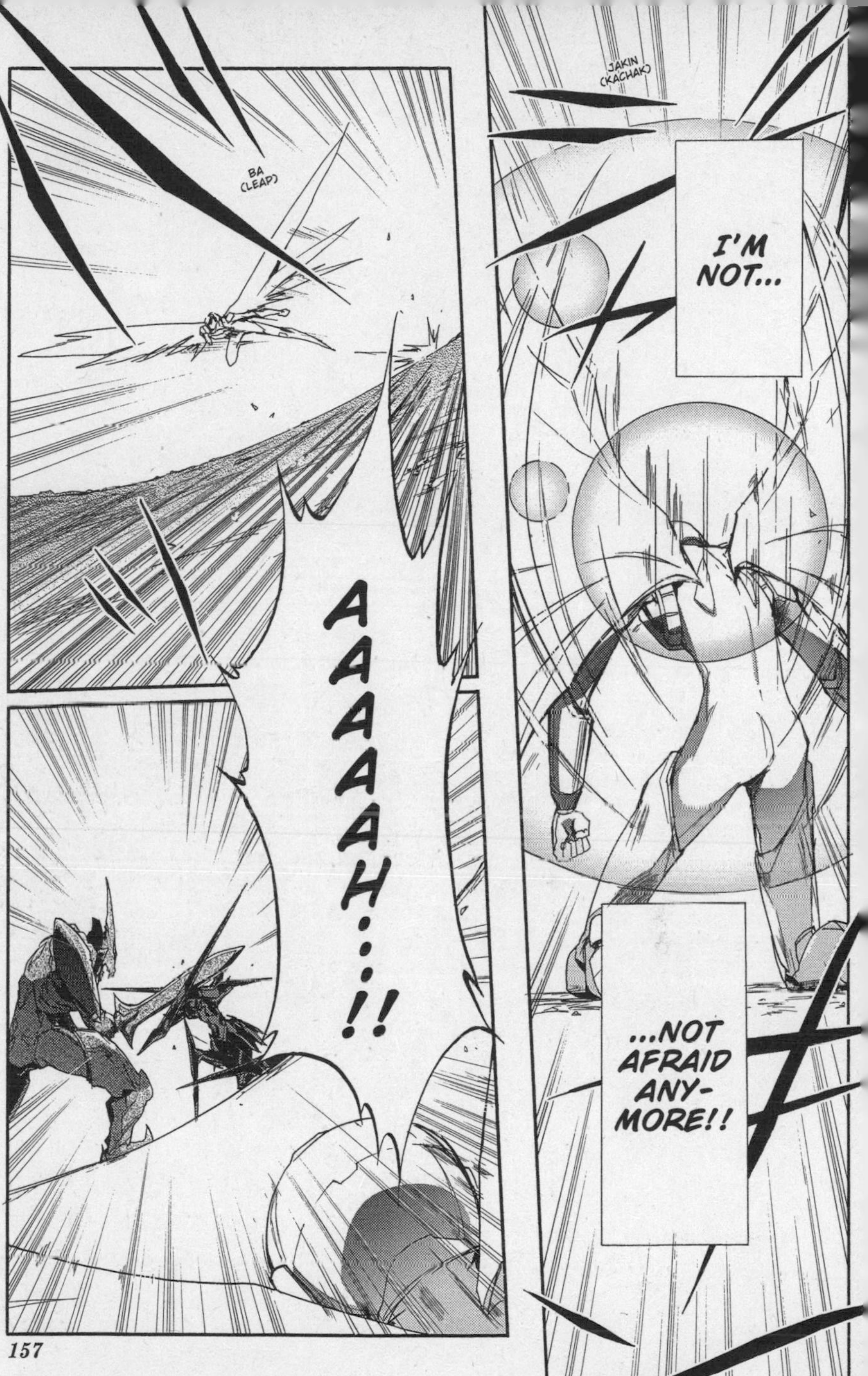
JAKIN (KACHAK)
I'M NOT...
...NOT AFRAID ANY-MORE!!
BA (LEAP)
AAAAAH...!!

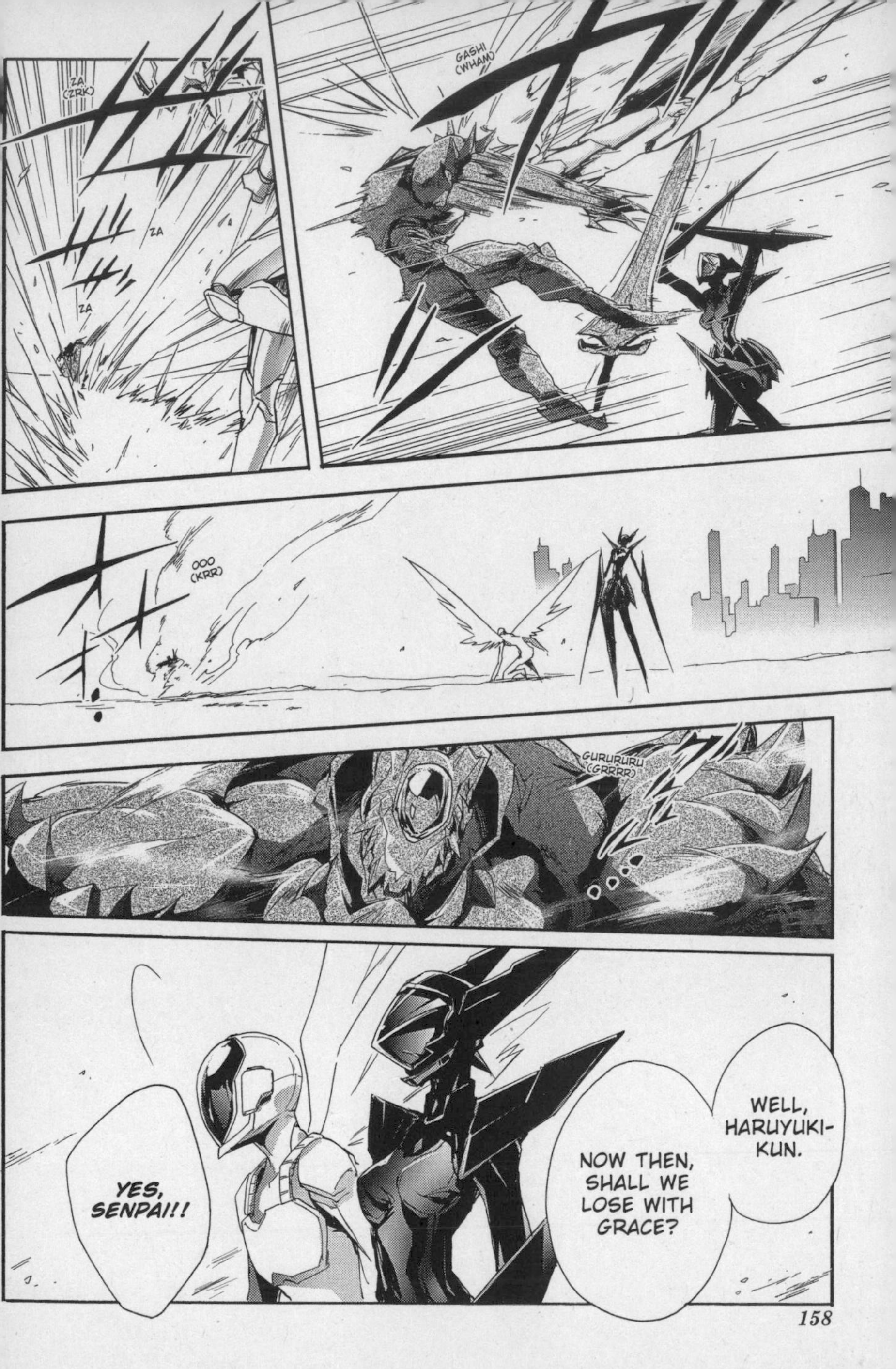
GASHI (WHAN)
ZA (ZRK)
ZA
ZA
OOO (KRR)
GURURURU (GRRRR)
WELL, HARUYUKI-KUN.
NOW THEN, SHALL WE LOSE WITH GRACE?
YES, SENPAI!!

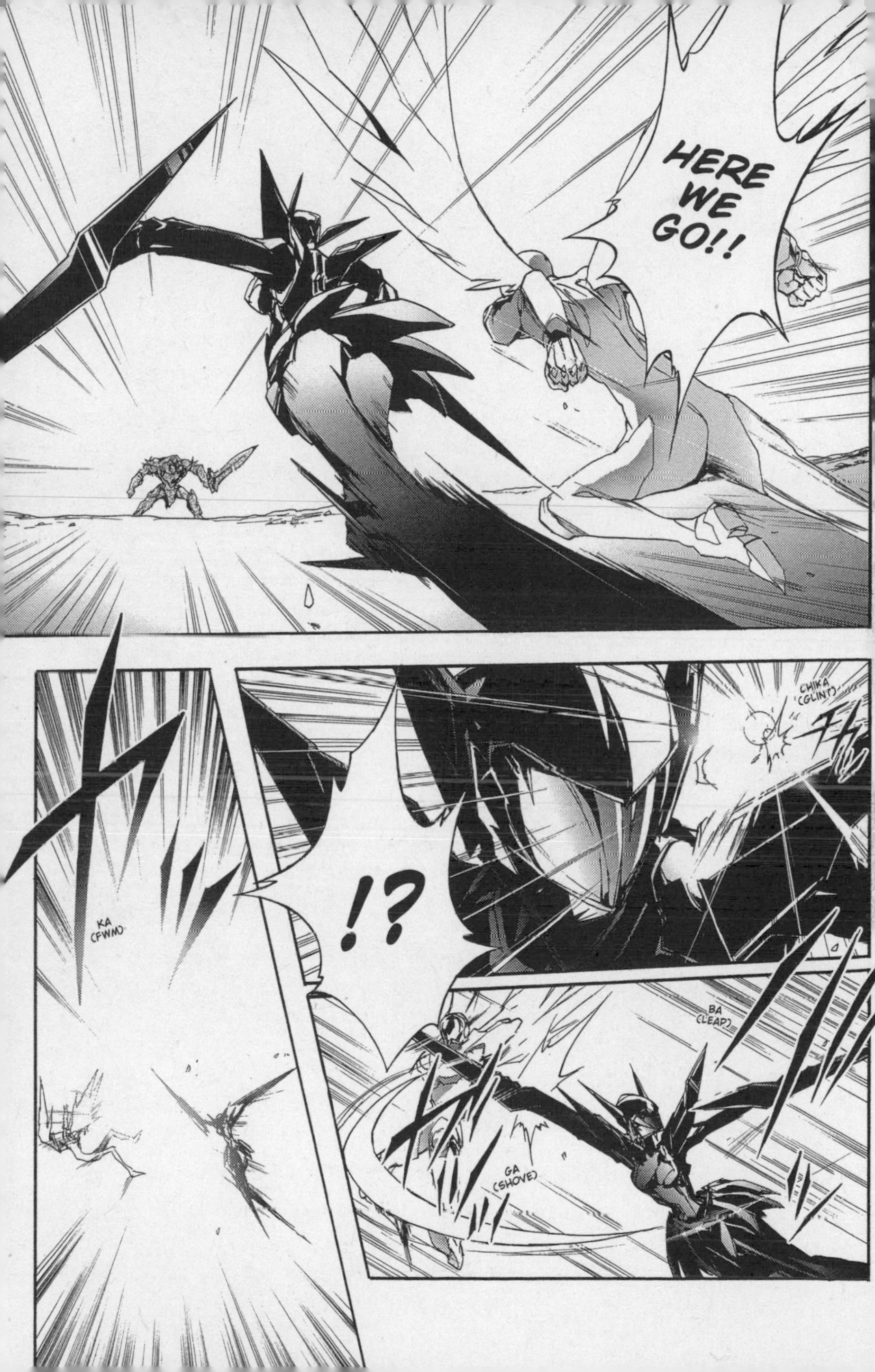
HERE WE GO!!
CHIKA (GLINT)
!?
BA (LEAP)
GA (SHOVE)
KA (FWM)

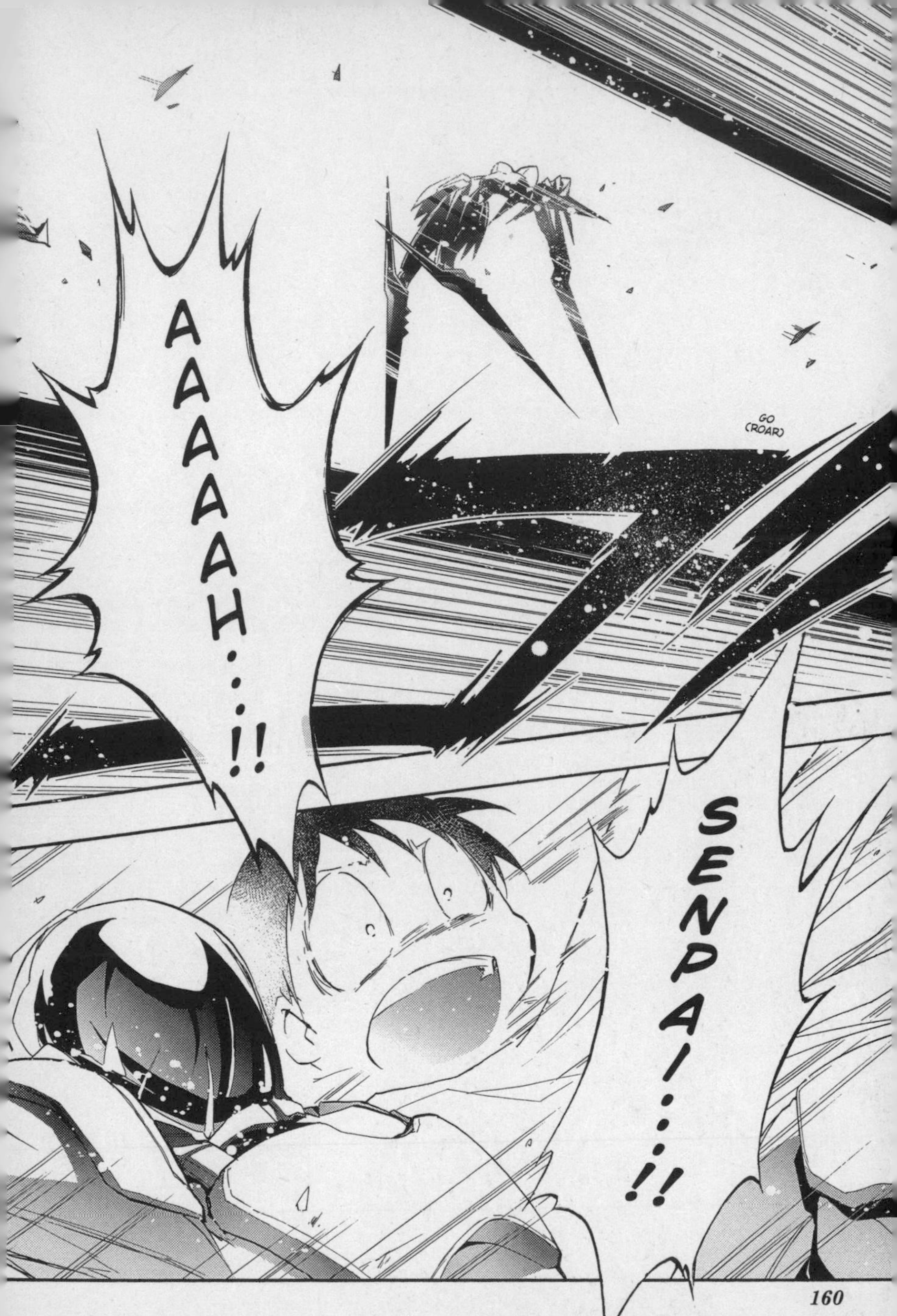
GO (ROAR)
AAAAAAH...!!
SENPAI...!!

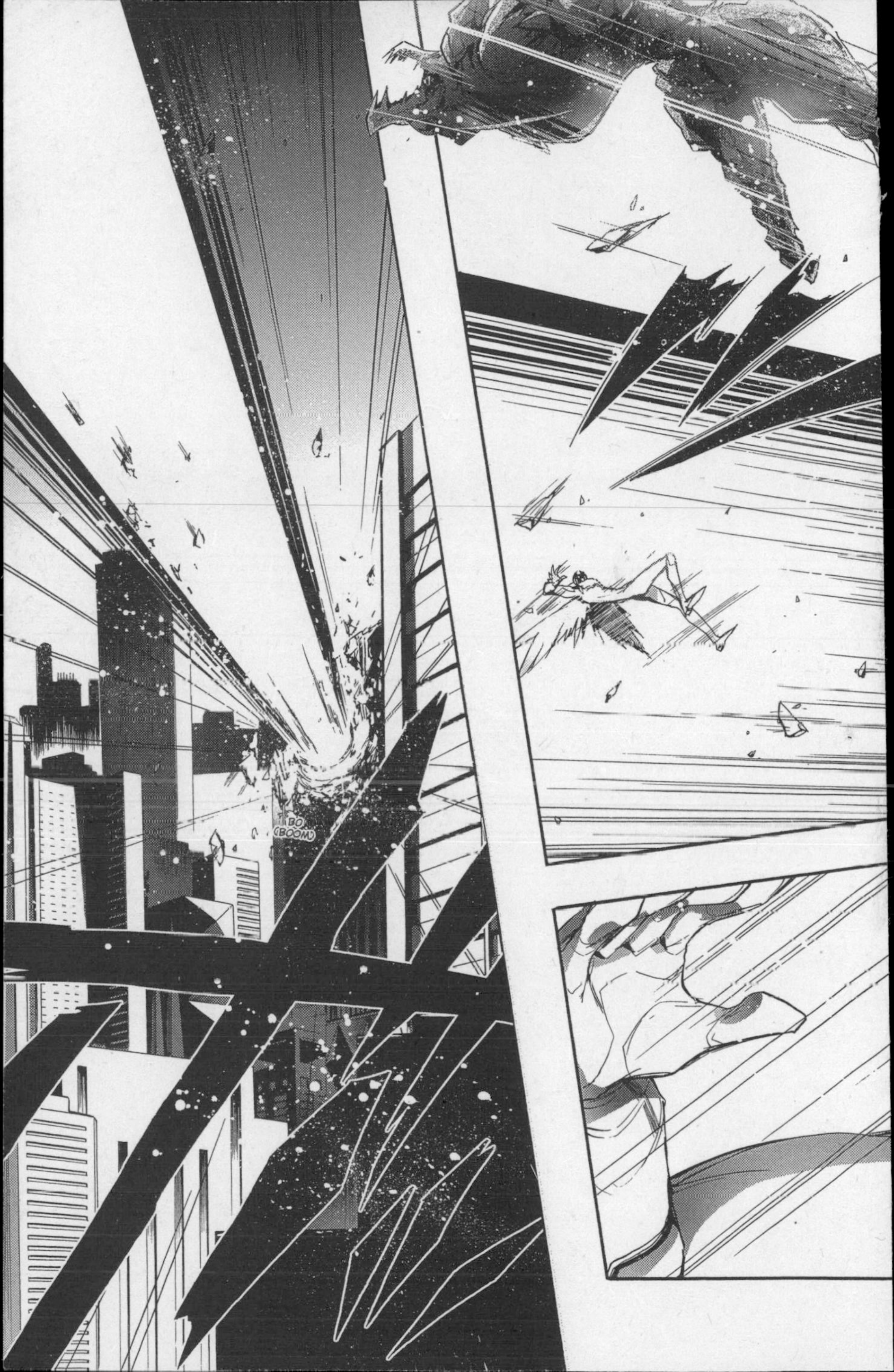
BO
(BOOM)

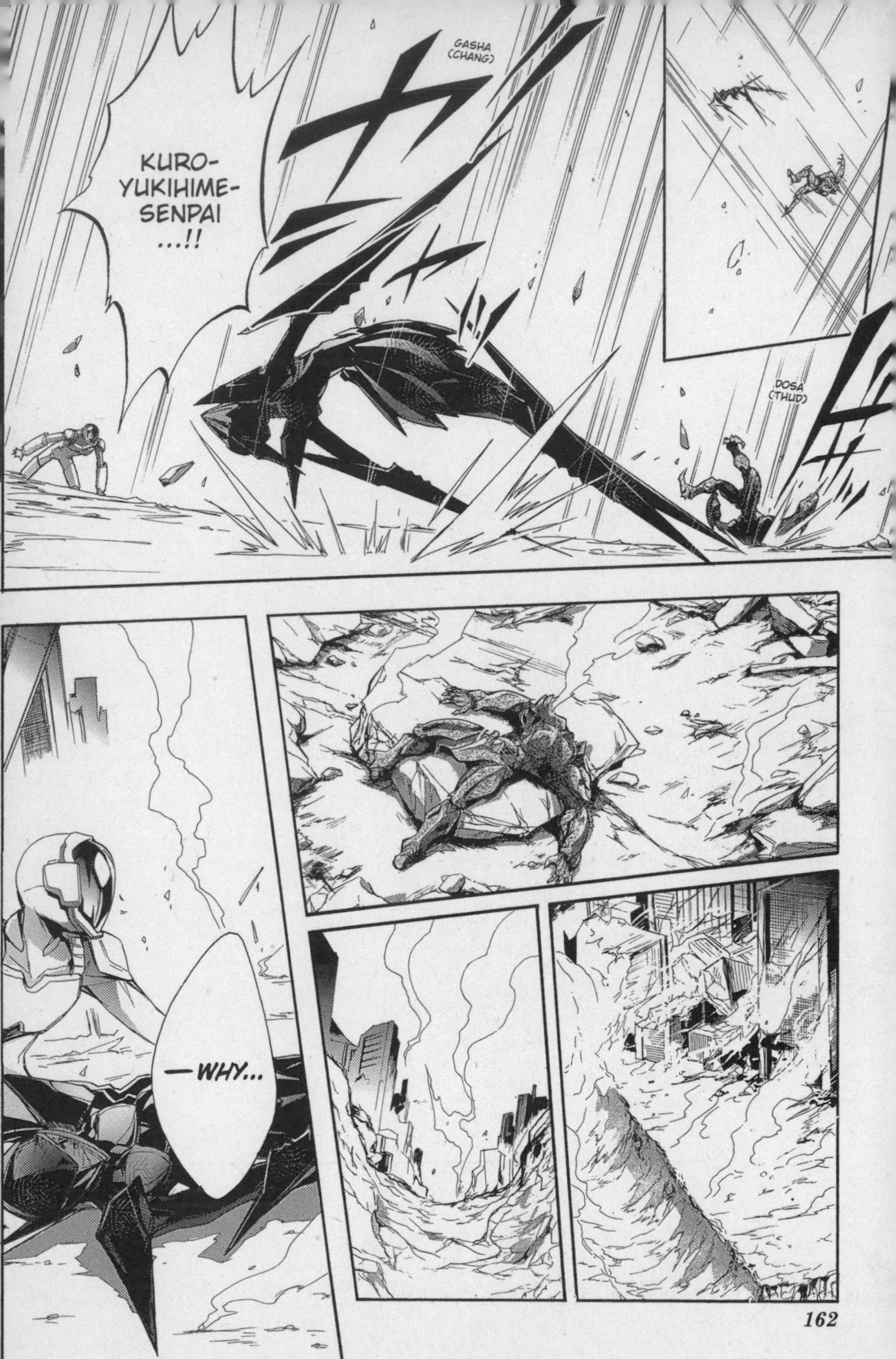
GASHA (CHANG)
DOSA (THUD)
KURO-YUKIHIME-SENPAI ...!!
—WHY...

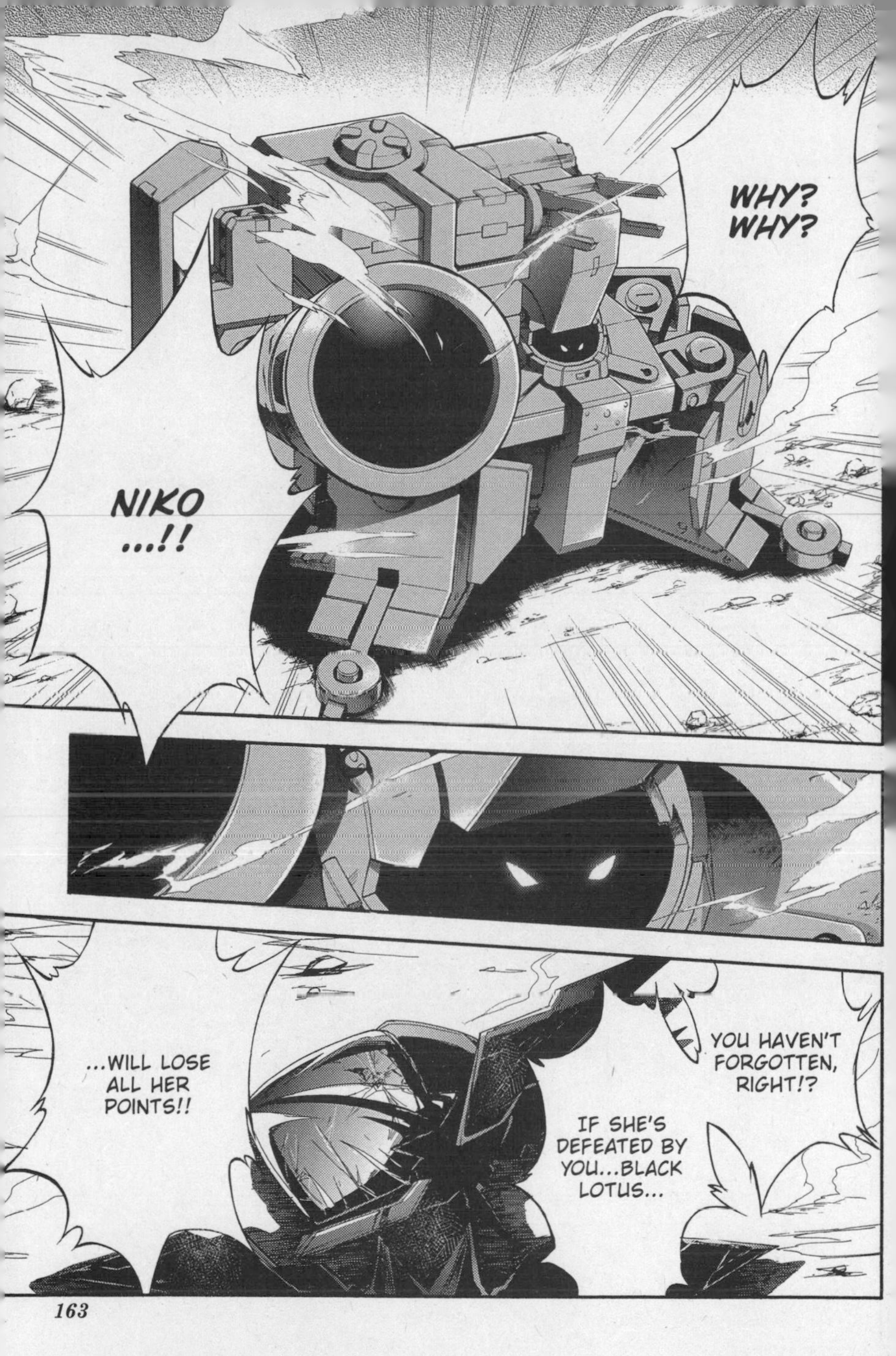
WHY? WHY?
NIKO ...!!
YOU HAVEN'T FORGOTTEN, RIGHT!?
IF SHE'S DEFEATED BY YOU...BLACK LOTUS...
...WILL LOSE ALL HER POINTS!!

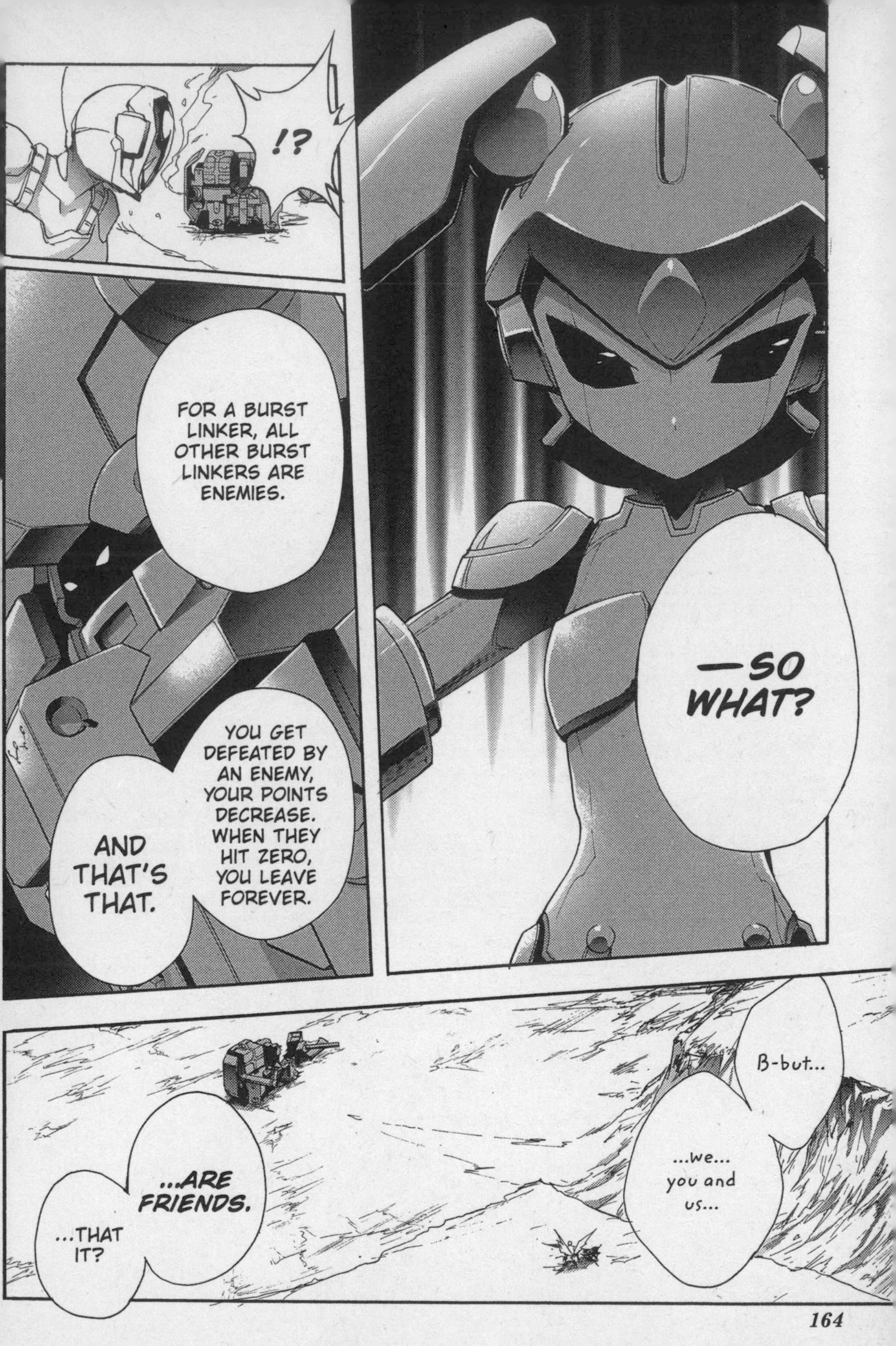
—SO WHAT?
!?
FOR A BURST LINKER, ALL OTHER BURST LINKERS ARE ENEMIES.
YOU GET DEFEATED BY AN ENEMY, YOUR POINTS DECREASE. WHEN THEY HIT ZERO, YOU LEAVE FOREVER.
AND THAT'S THAT.
B-but...
...we... you and us...
...ARE FRIENDS.
...THAT IT?

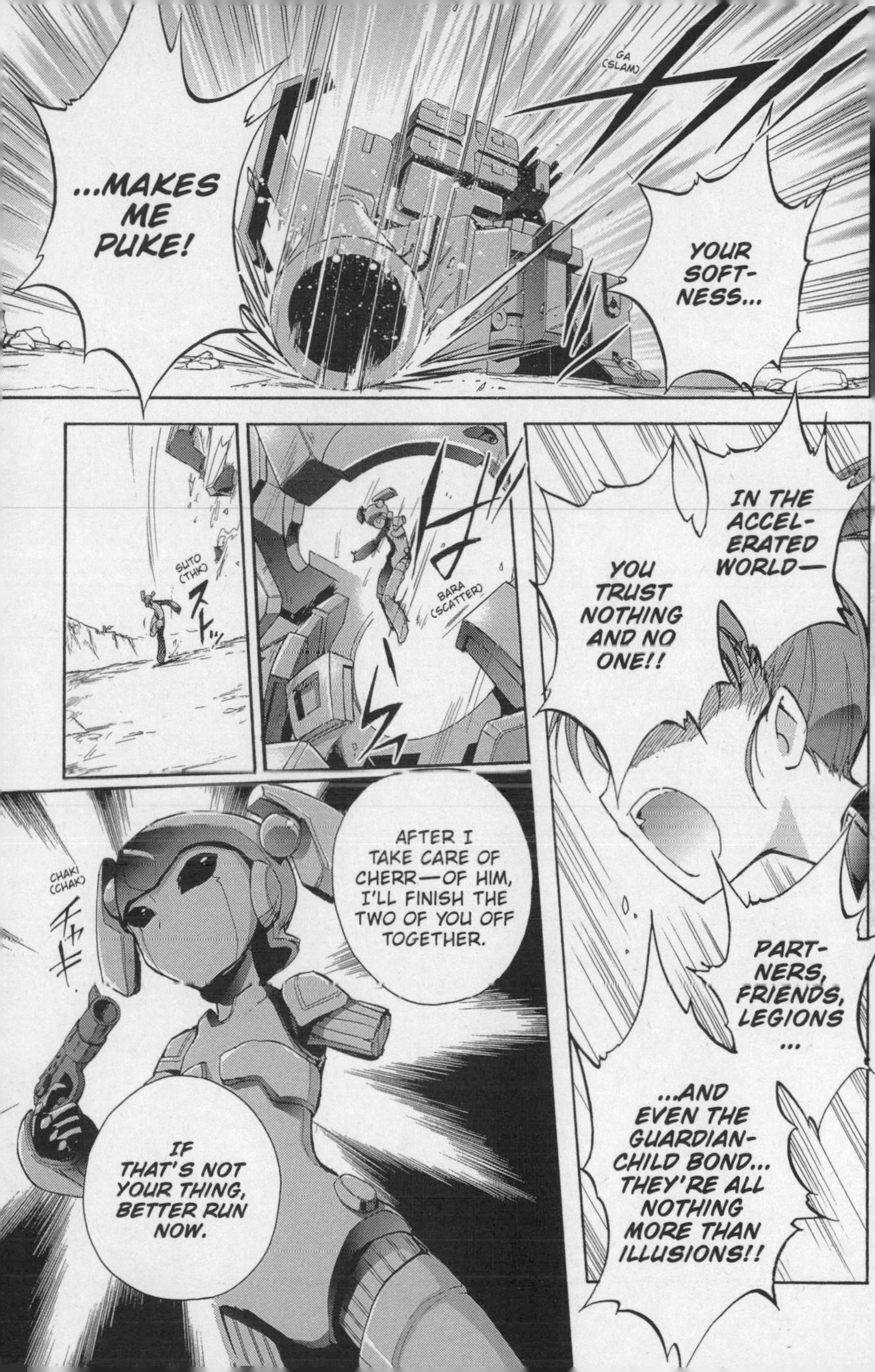
GA (SLAM)
YOUR SOFT-NESS...
...MAKES ME PUKE!
IN THE ACCEL-ERATED WORLD—
YOU TRUST NOTHING AND NO ONE!!
PART-NERS, FRIENDS, LEGIONS...
...AND EVEN THE GUARDIAN-CHILD BOND... THEY'RE ALL NOTHING MORE THAN ILLUSIONS!!
BARA (SCATTER)
SUTO (THK)
AFTER I TAKE CARE OF CHERR—OF HIM, I'LL FINISH THE TWO OF YOU OFF TOGETHER.
CHAKI (CHAK)
IF THAT'S NOT YOUR THING, BETTER RUN NOW.

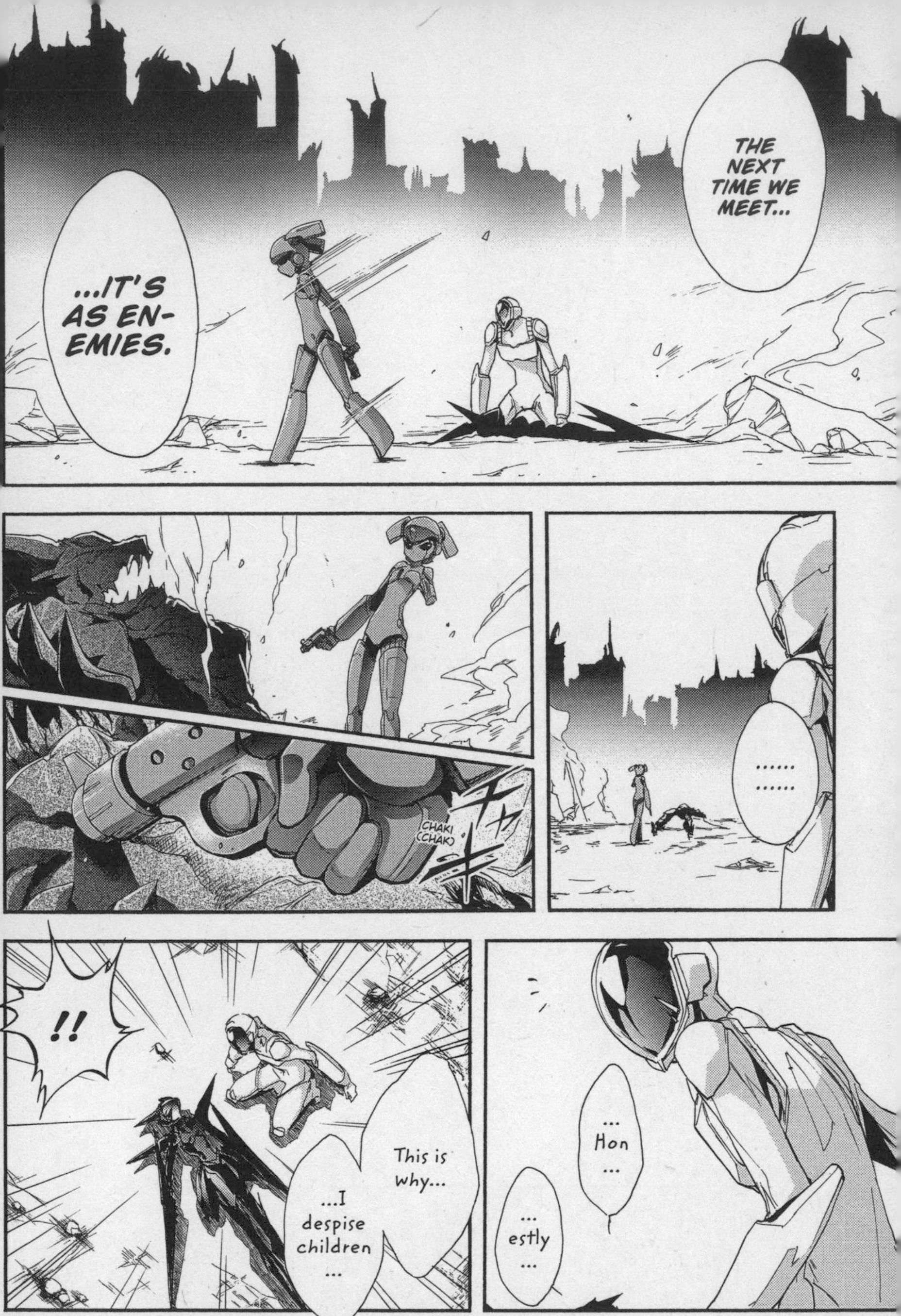
THE NEXT TIME WE MEET...
...IT'S AS EN-EMIES.
......
......
CHAKI (CHAK)
... Hon ...
... estly ...
!!
This is why...
...I despise children ...

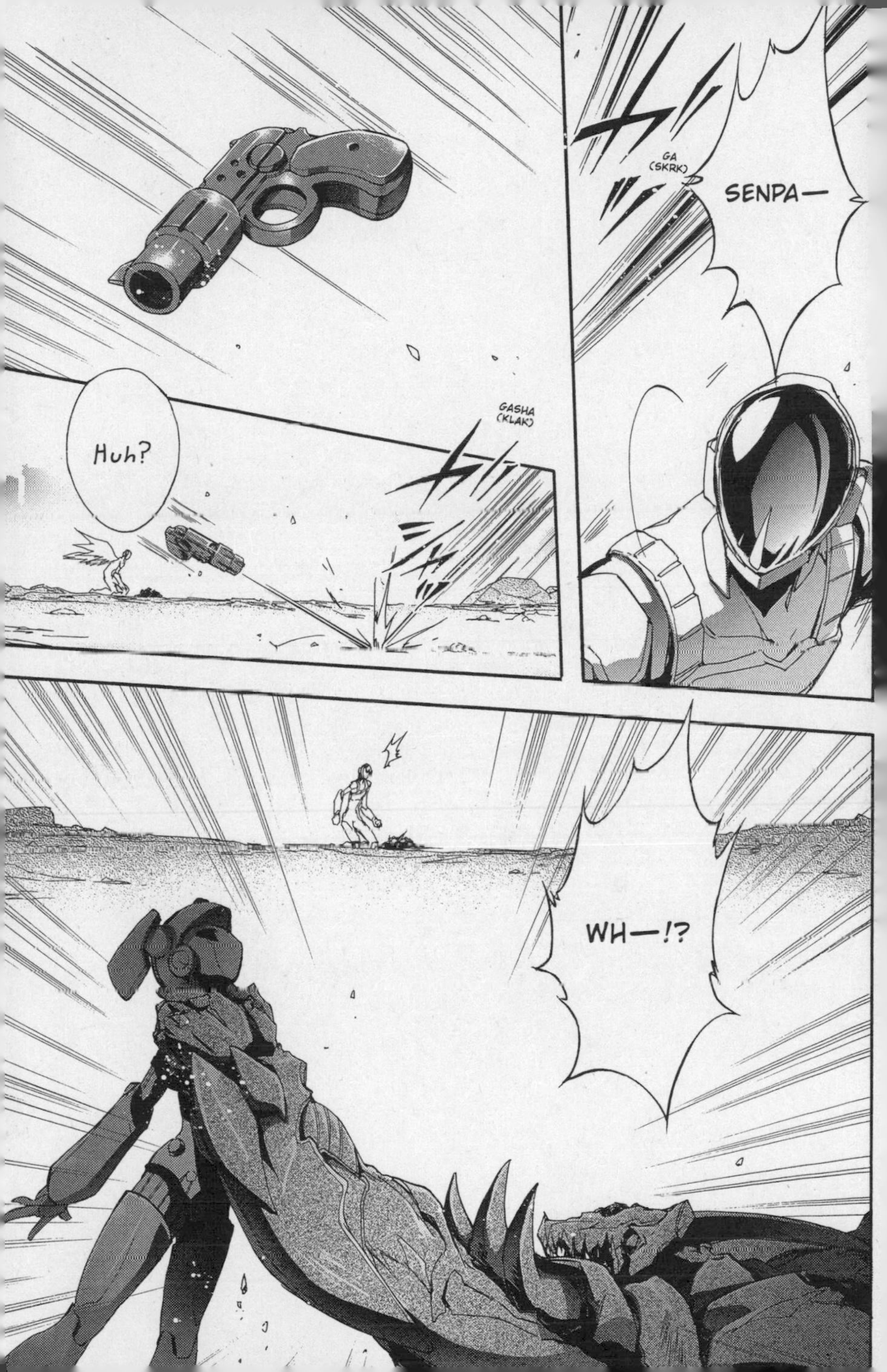
GA (SKRK)
SENPA—
GASHA (KLAK)
Huh?
WH—!?

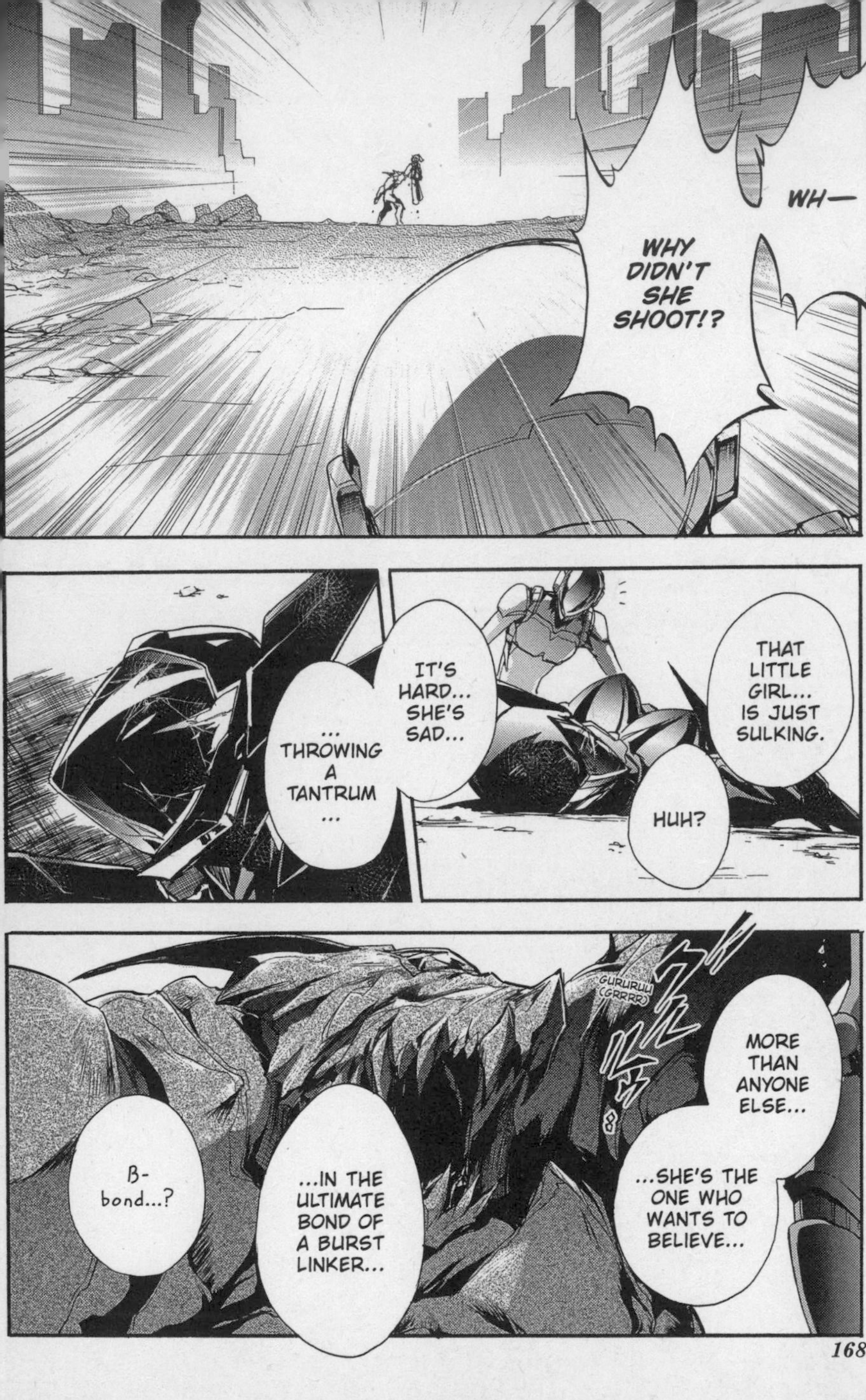
WH—
WHY DIDN'T SHE SHOOT!?
THAT LITTLE GIRL... IS JUST SULKING.
HUH?
IT'S HARD... SHE'S SAD...
... THROWING A TANTRUM ...
GURURUU (GRRRR)
MORE THAN ANYONE ELSE...
...SHE'S THE ONE WHO WANTS TO BELIEVE...
...IN THE ULTIMATE BOND OF A BURST LINKER...
B-bond...?

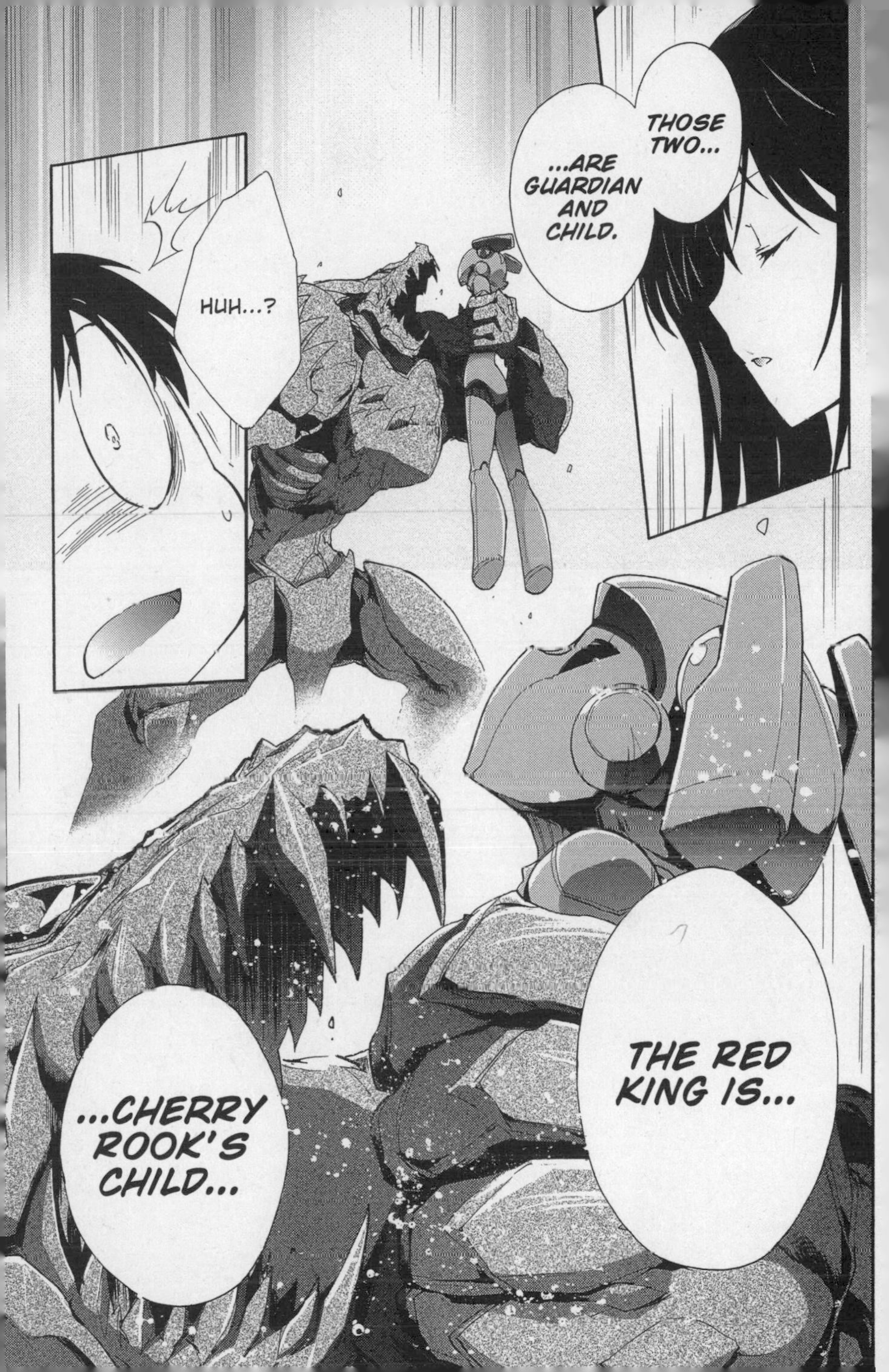
THOSE TWO...
...ARE GUARDIAN AND CHILD.
HUH...?
THE RED KING IS...
...CHERRY ROOK'S CHILD...

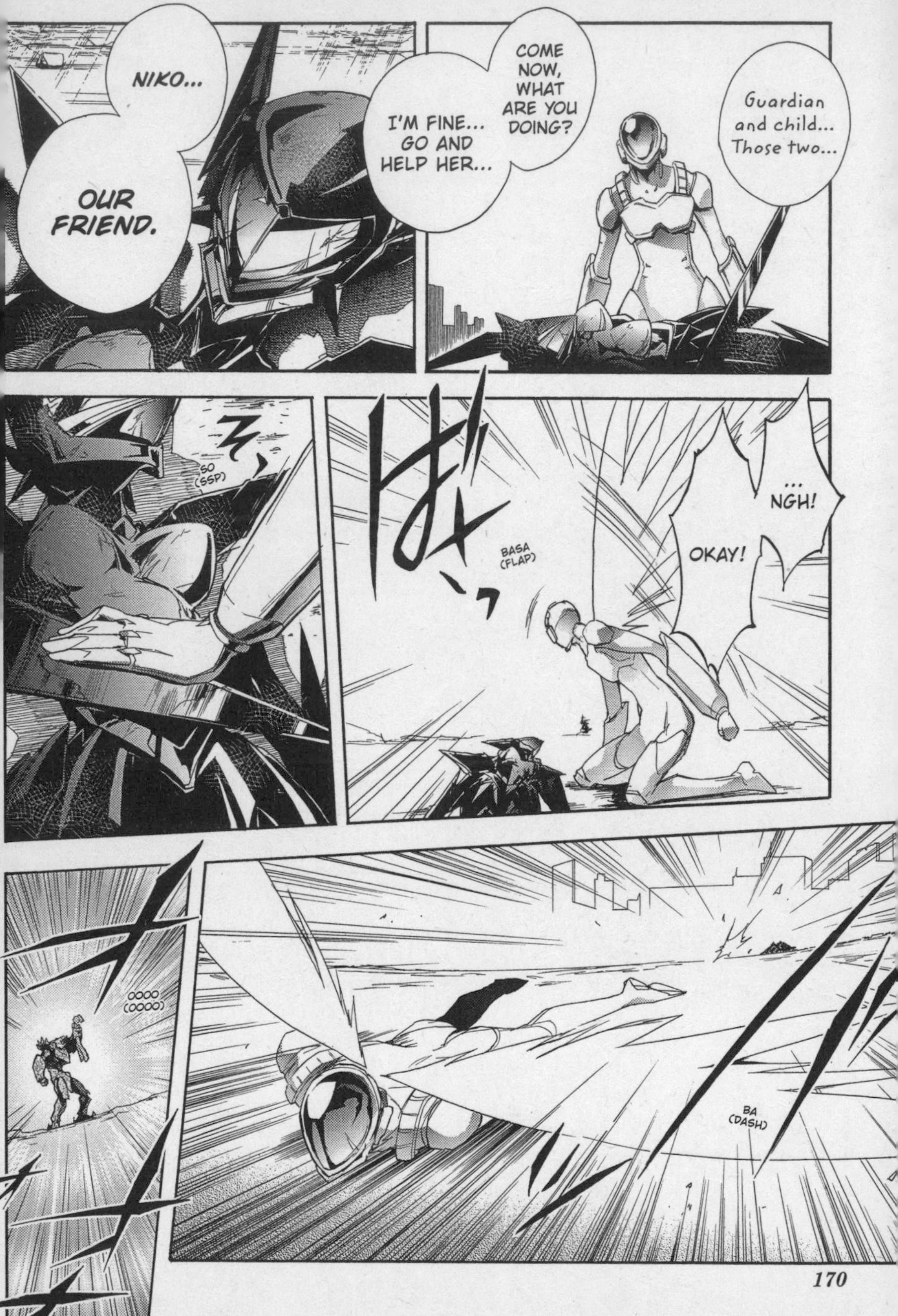
Guardian and child... Those two...
COME NOW, WHAT ARE YOU DOING?
I'M FINE... GO AND HELP HER...
NIKO...
OUR FRIEND.
...NGH!
OKAY!
BASA (FLAP)
SO (SSP)
BA (DASH)
OOOO (OOOO)

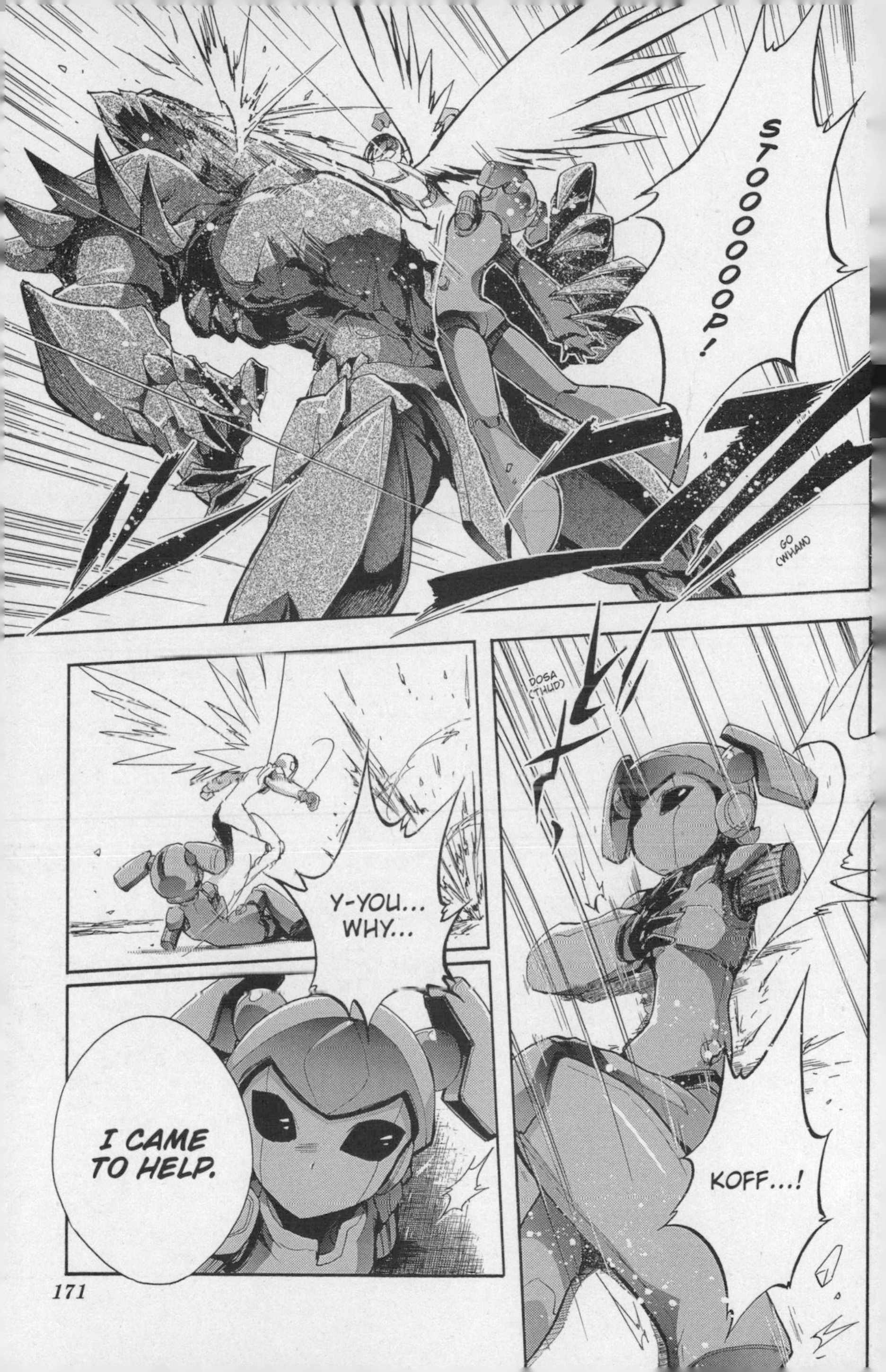
STOOOOOOOP!
GO (WHAM)
DOSA (THUD)
KOFF...!
Y-YOU... WHY...
I CAME TO HELP.

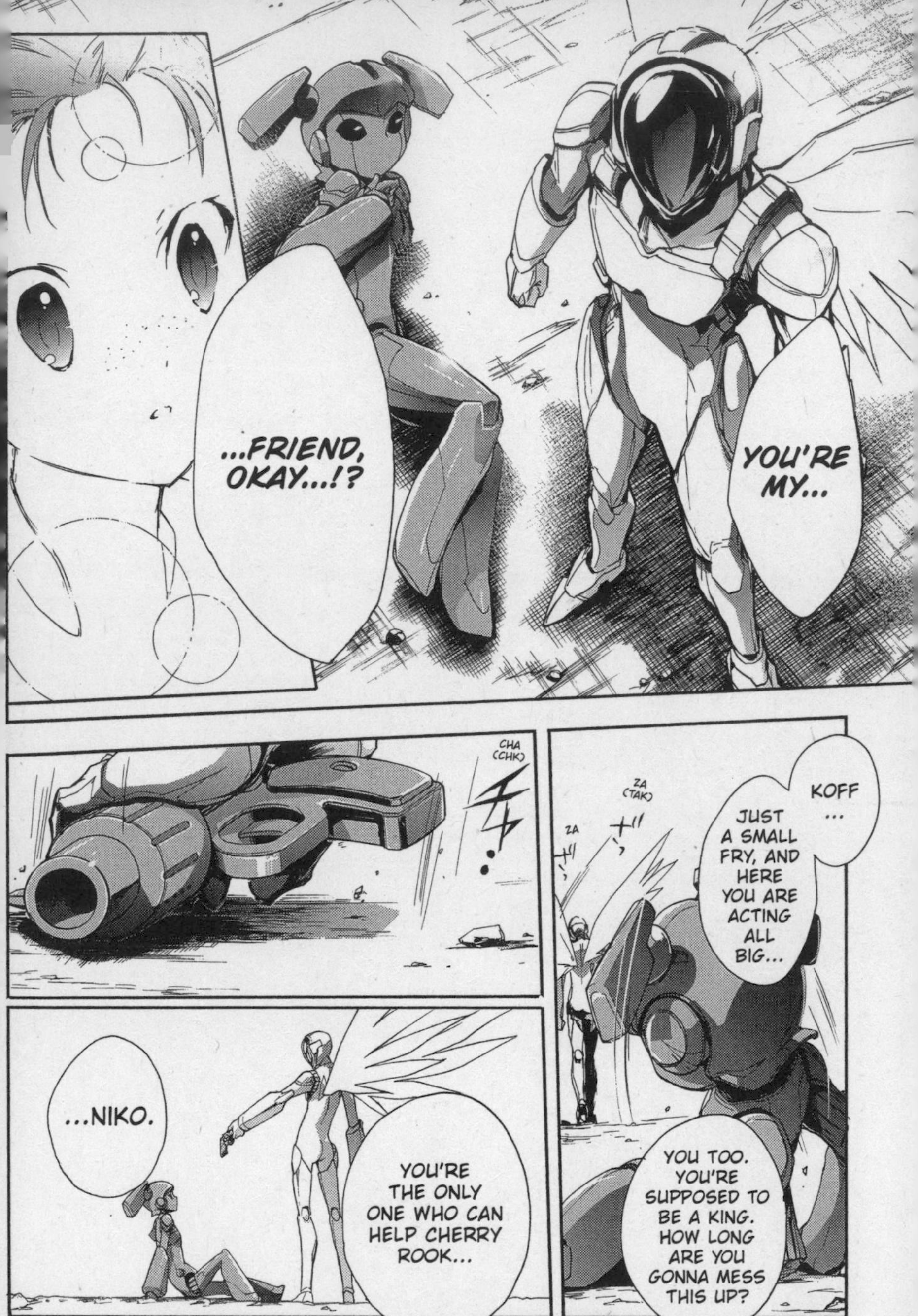
YOU'RE MY...
...FRIEND, OKAY...!?
ZA (TAK)
ZA
KOFF ...
JUST A SMALL FRY, AND HERE YOU ARE ACTING ALL BIG...
YOU TOO. YOU'RE SUPPOSED TO BE A KING. HOW LONG ARE YOU GONNA MESS THIS UP?
CHA (CHK)
...NIKO.
YOU'RE THE ONLY ONE WHO CAN HELP CHERRY ROOK...

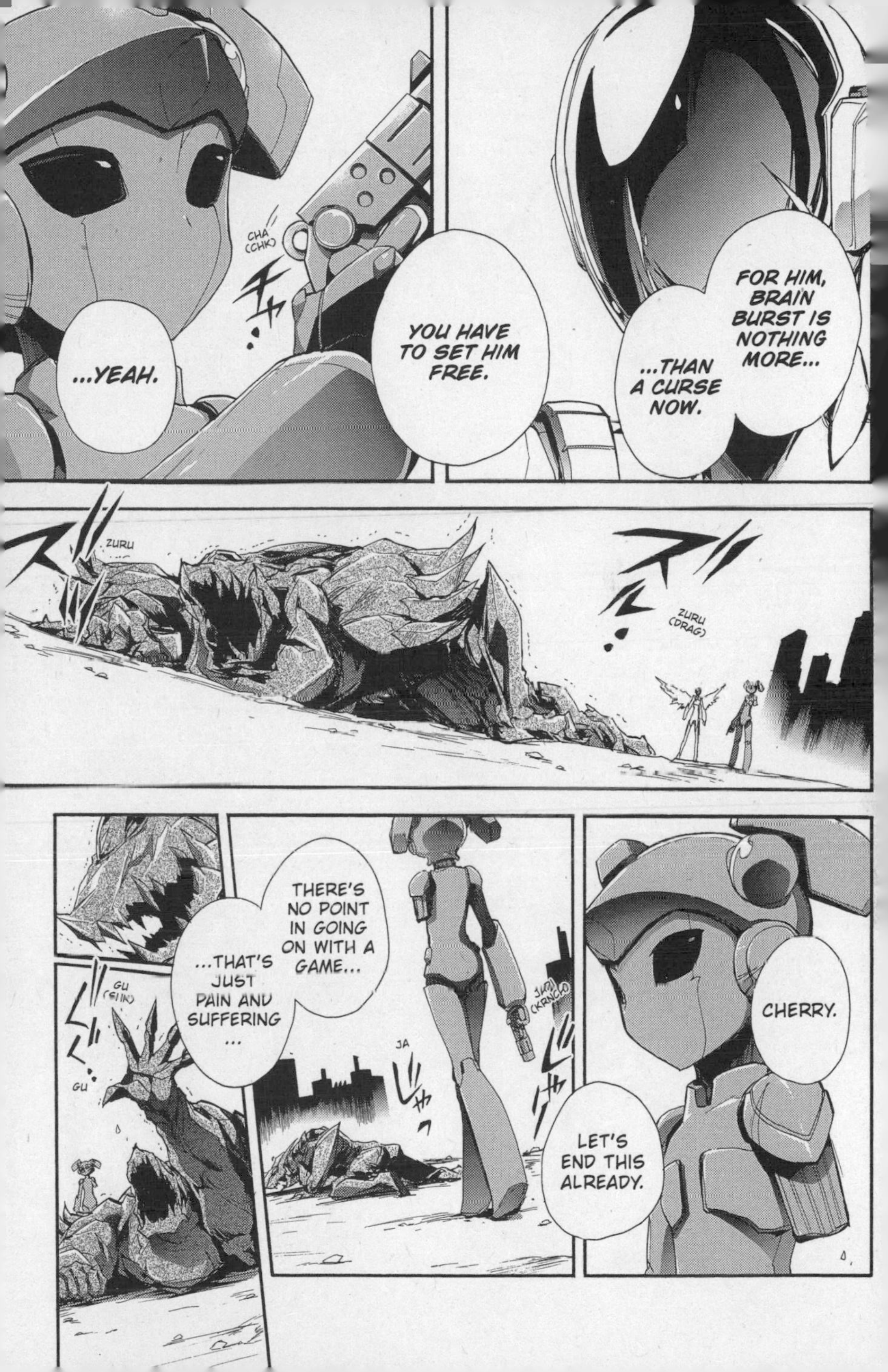
FOR HIM, BRAIN BURST IS NOTHING MORE...
...THAN A CURSE NOW.
YOU HAVE TO SET HIM FREE.
CHA (CHK)
...YEAH.
ZURU (DRAG)
ZURU
CHERRY.
LET'S END THIS ALREADY.
JAKI (KRNCH)
JA
THERE'S NO POINT IN GOING ON WITH A GAME...
...THAT'S JUST PAIN AND SUFFERING ...
GU
GU

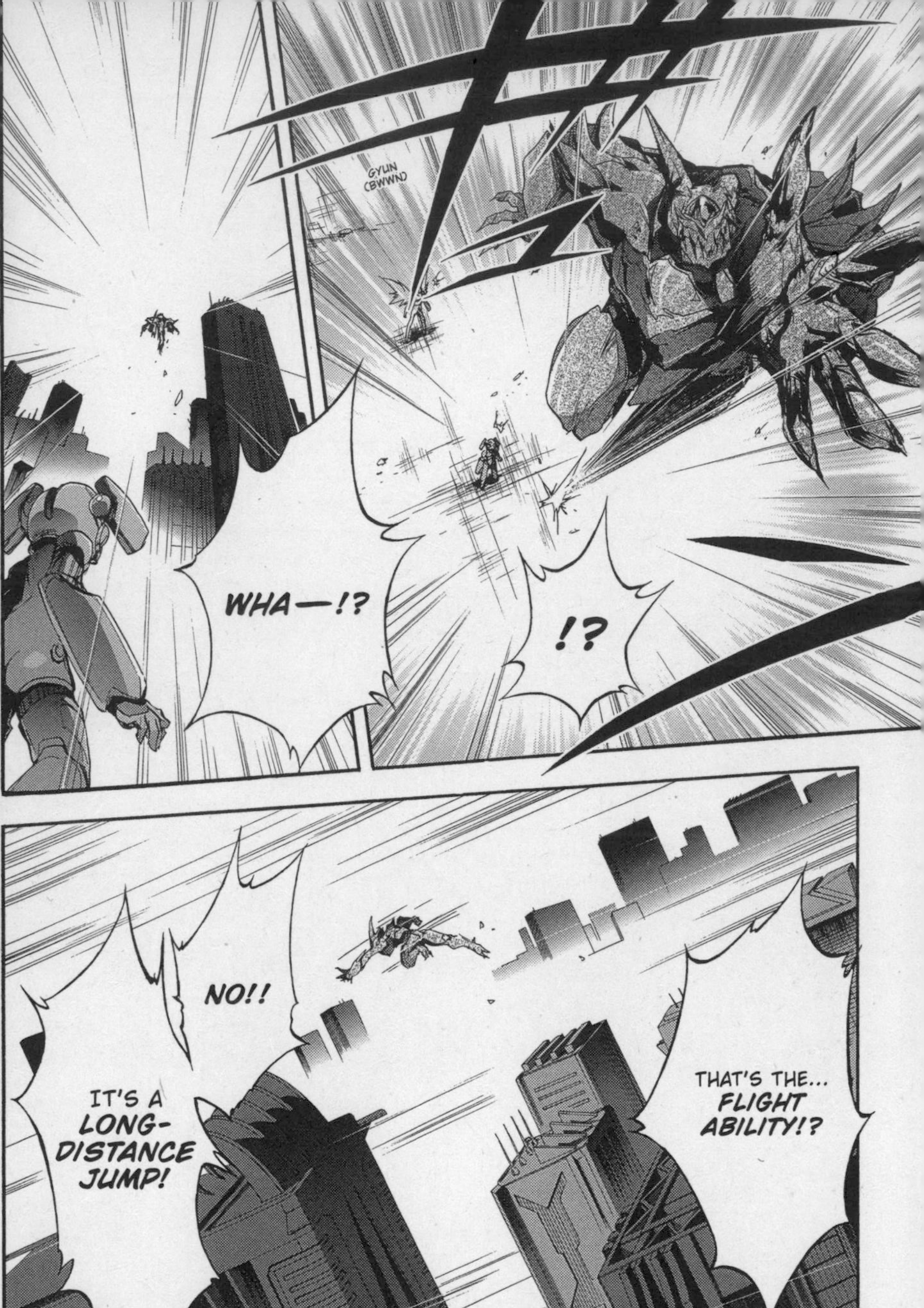
GYUN (BWWN)
!?
WHA—!?
THAT'S THE... FLIGHT ABILITY!?
NO!!
IT'S A LONG-DISTANCE JUMP!

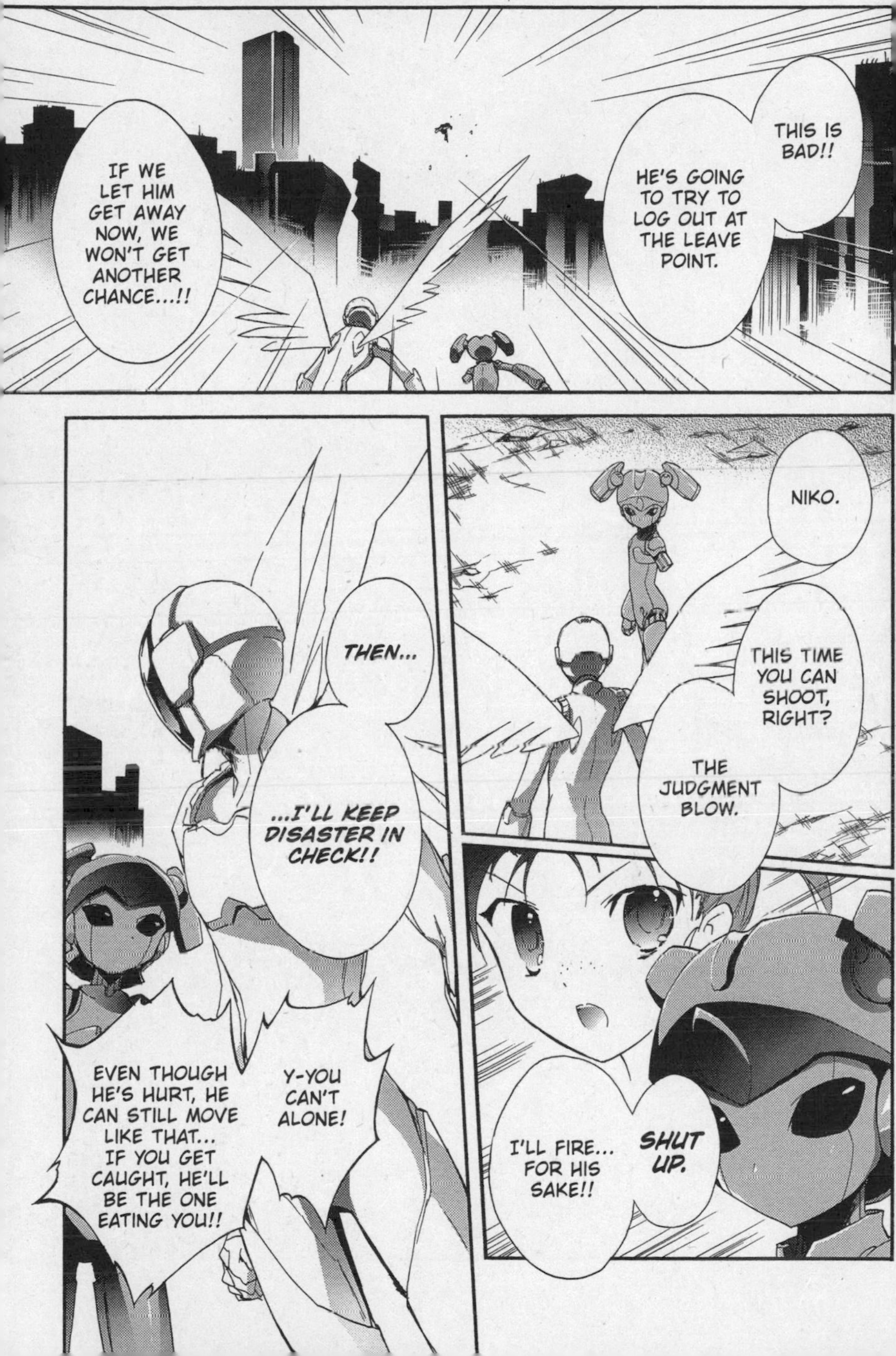
THIS IS BAD!!
HE'S GOING TO TRY TO LOG OUT AT THE LEAVE POINT.
IF WE LET HIM GET AWAY NOW, WE WON'T GET ANOTHER CHANCE...!!
NIKO.
THIS TIME YOU CAN SHOOT, RIGHT?
THE JUDGMENT BLOW.
SHUT UP.
I'LL FIRE... FOR HIS SAKE!!
THEN...
...I'LL KEEP DISASTER IN CHECK!!
Y-YOU CAN'T ALONE!
EVEN THOUGH HE'S HURT, HE CAN STILL MOVE LIKE THAT... IF YOU GET CAUGHT, HE'LL BE THE ONE EATING YOU!!

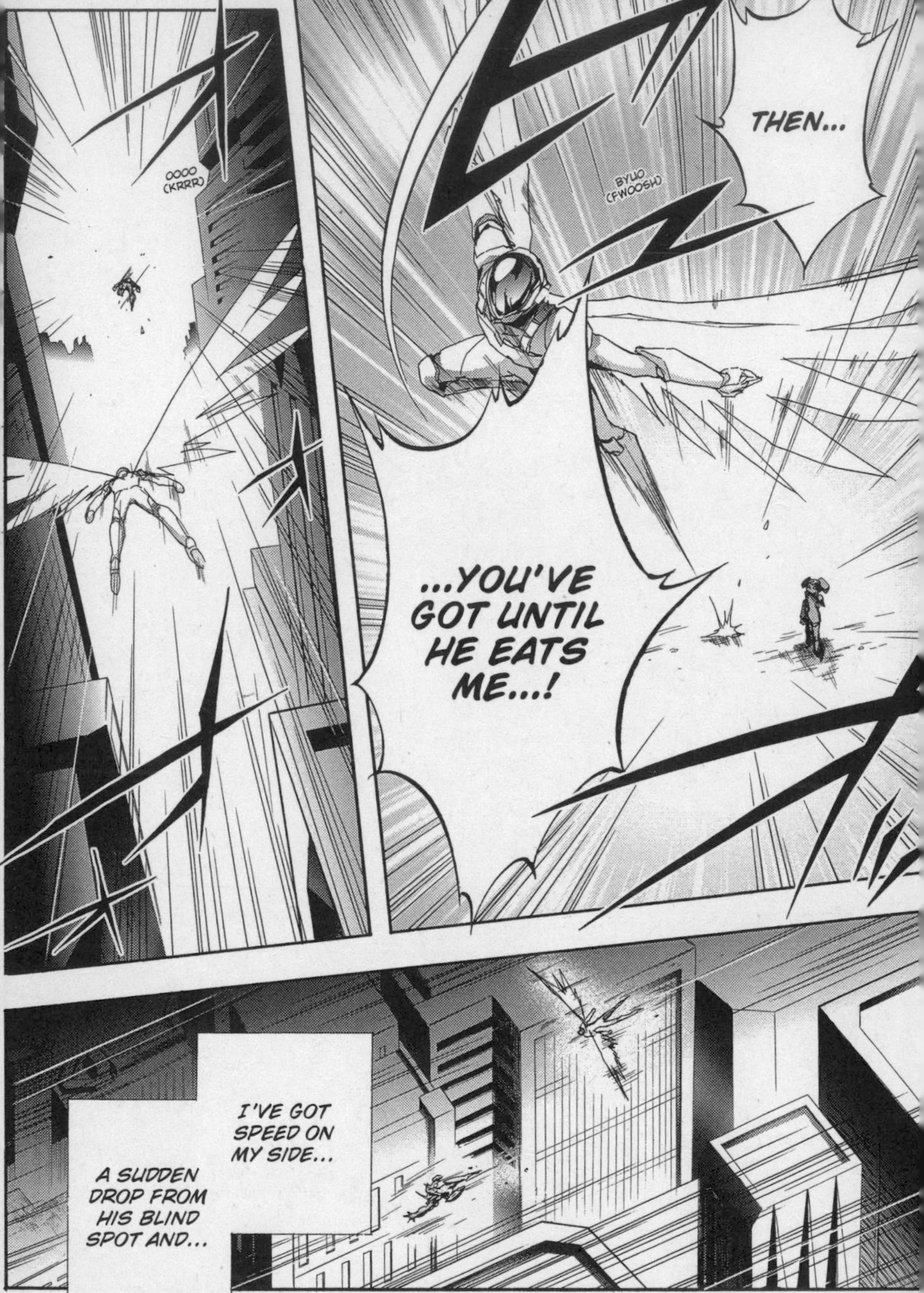
THEN...
BYUO (FWOOSH)
...YOU'VE GOT UNTIL HE EATS ME...!
OOOO (KRRR)
I'VE GOT SPEED ON MY SIDE...
A SUDDEN DROP FROM HIS BLIND SPOT AND...

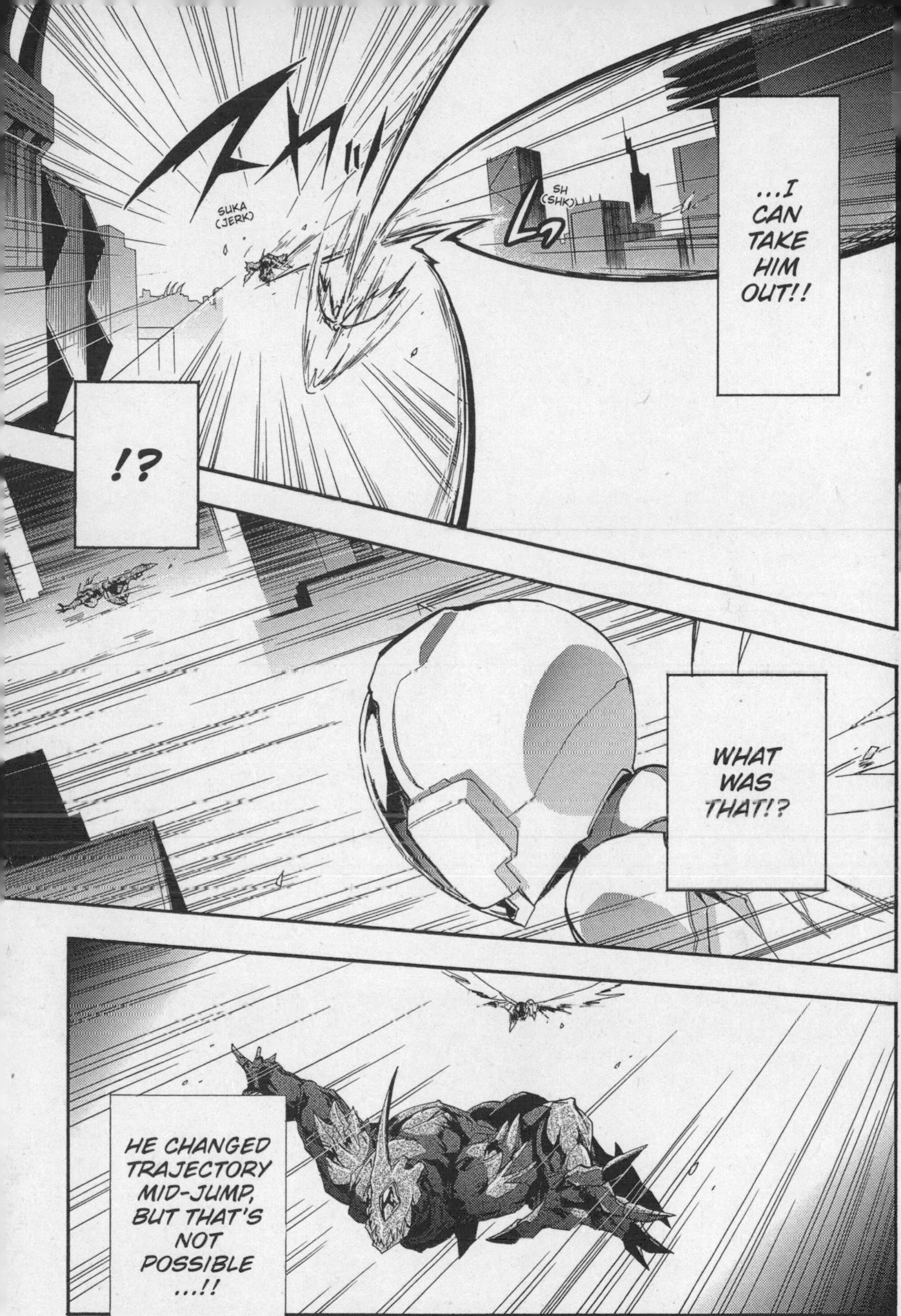
...I CAN TAKE HIM OUT!!
SH (SHK)
SUKA (JERK)
!?
WHAT WAS THAT!?
HE CHANGED TRAJECTORY MID-JUMP, BUT THAT'S NOT POSSIBLE ...!!

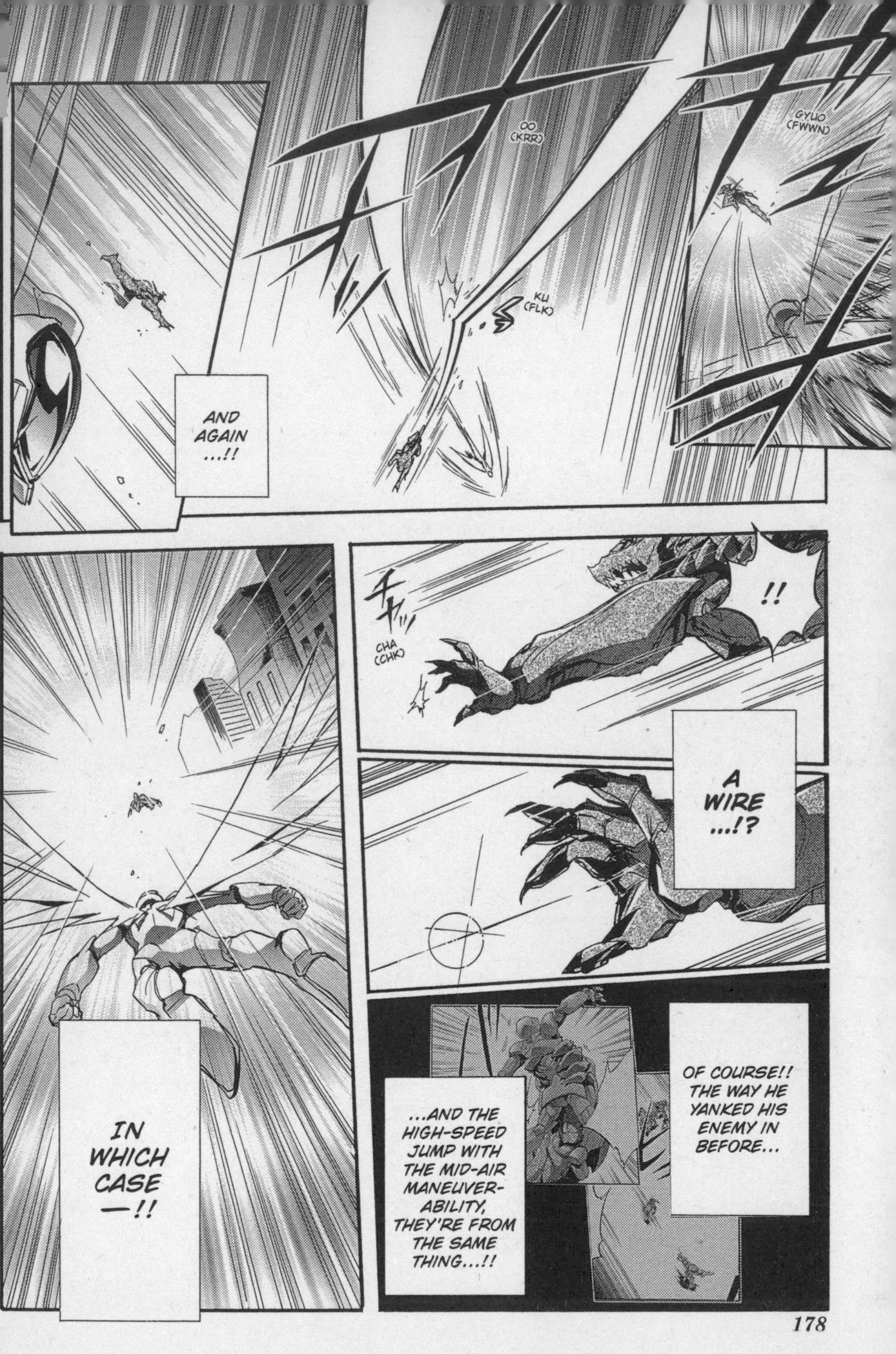

GYUO (FWWN)
OO (KRR)
KU (FLK)
AND AGAIN ...!!
!!
CHA (CHK)
A WIRE ...!?
OF COURSE!! THE WAY HE YANKED HIS ENEMY IN BEFORE...
...AND THE HIGH-SPEED JUMP WITH THE MID-AIR MANEUVER-ABILITY, THEY'RE FROM THE SAME THING...!!
IN WHICH CASE —!!

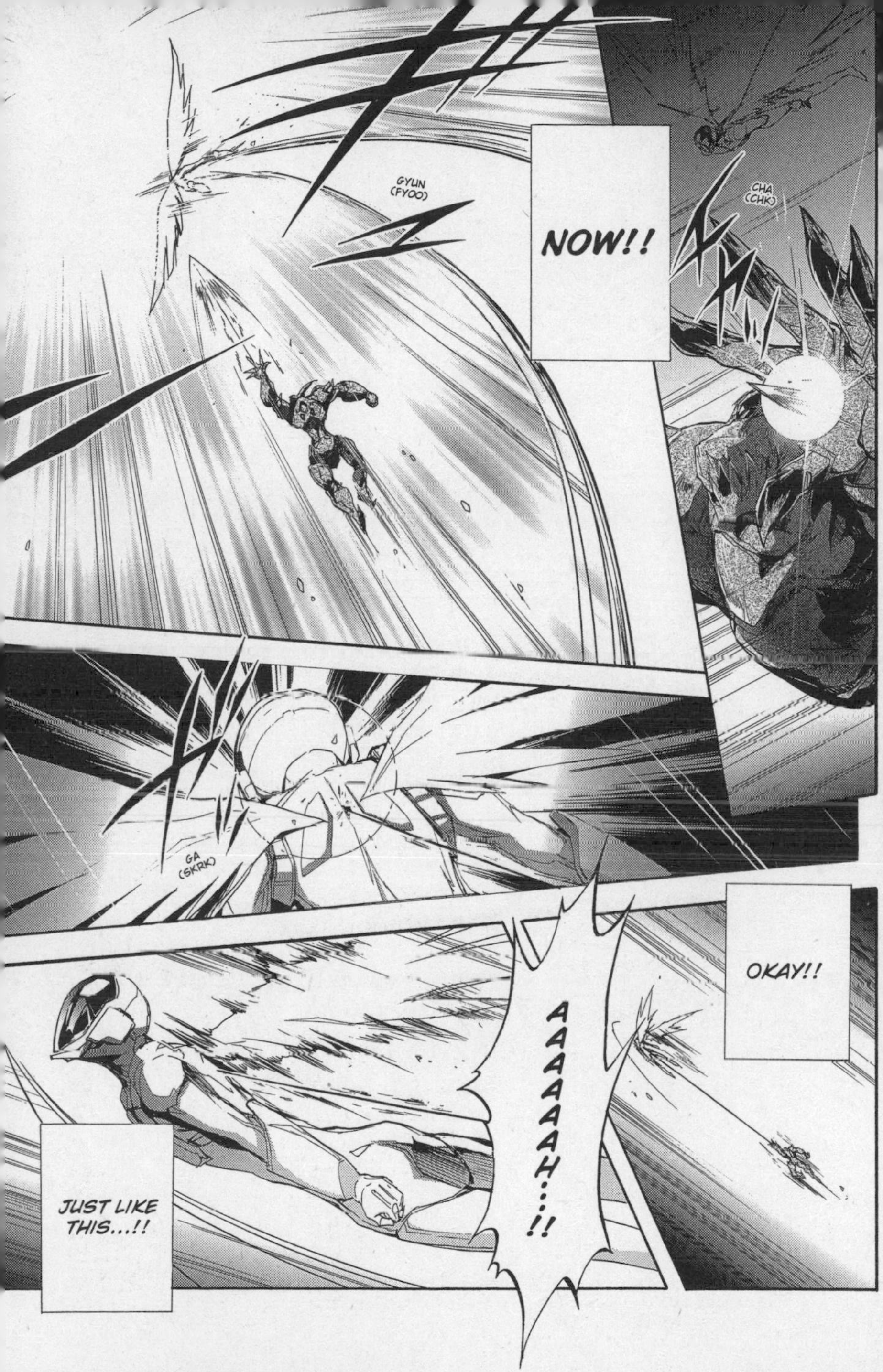
CHA
(CHK)
NOW!!
GYUN
(FYOO)
GA
(SKRK)
OKAY!!
AAAAAAAH...!!
JUST LIKE
THIS...!!

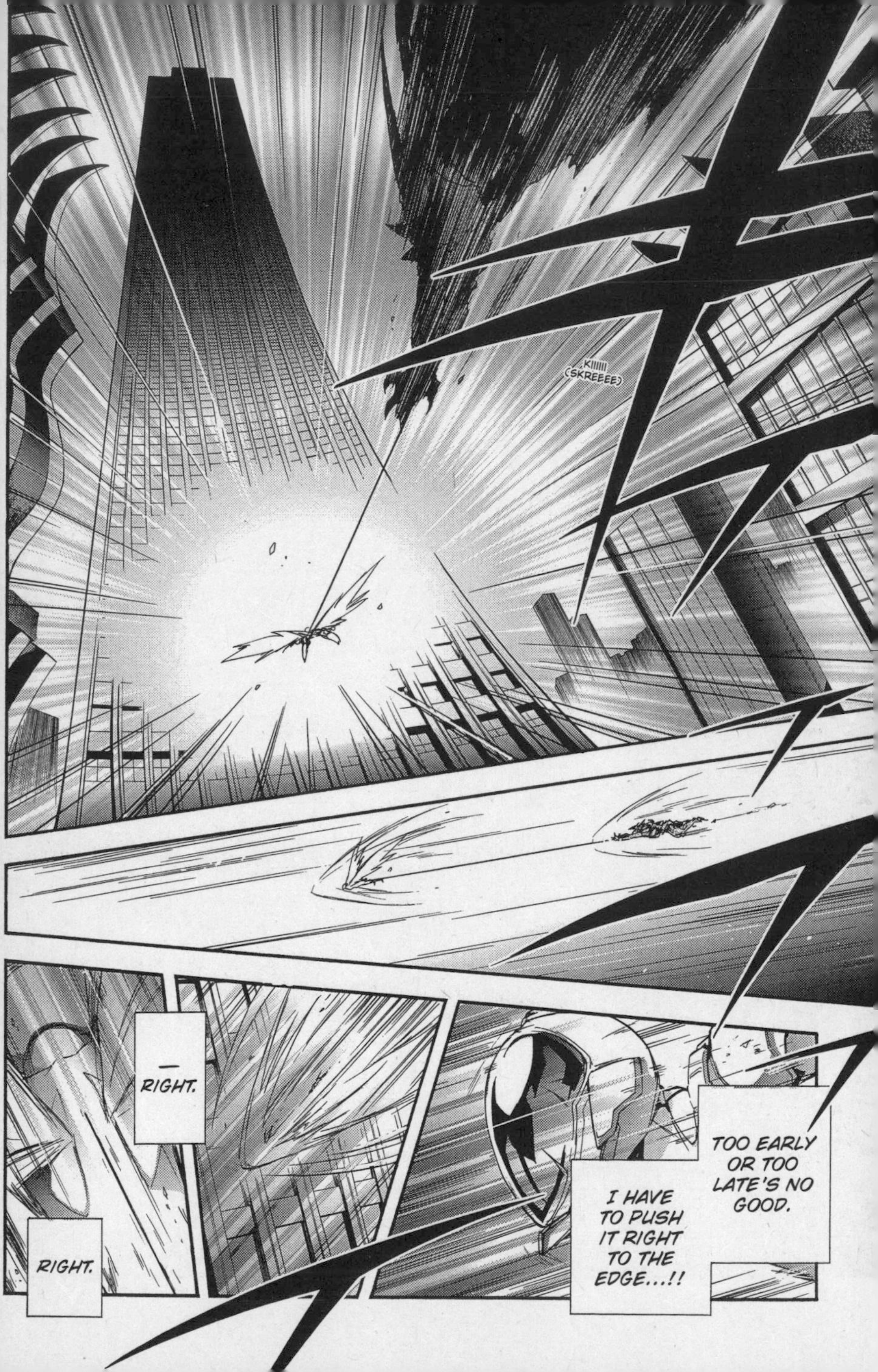
KIIIII
(SKREEEE)
TOO EARLY OR TOO LATE'S NO GOOD.
I HAVE TO PUSH IT RIGHT TO THE EDGE...!!
—RIGHT.
RIGHT.

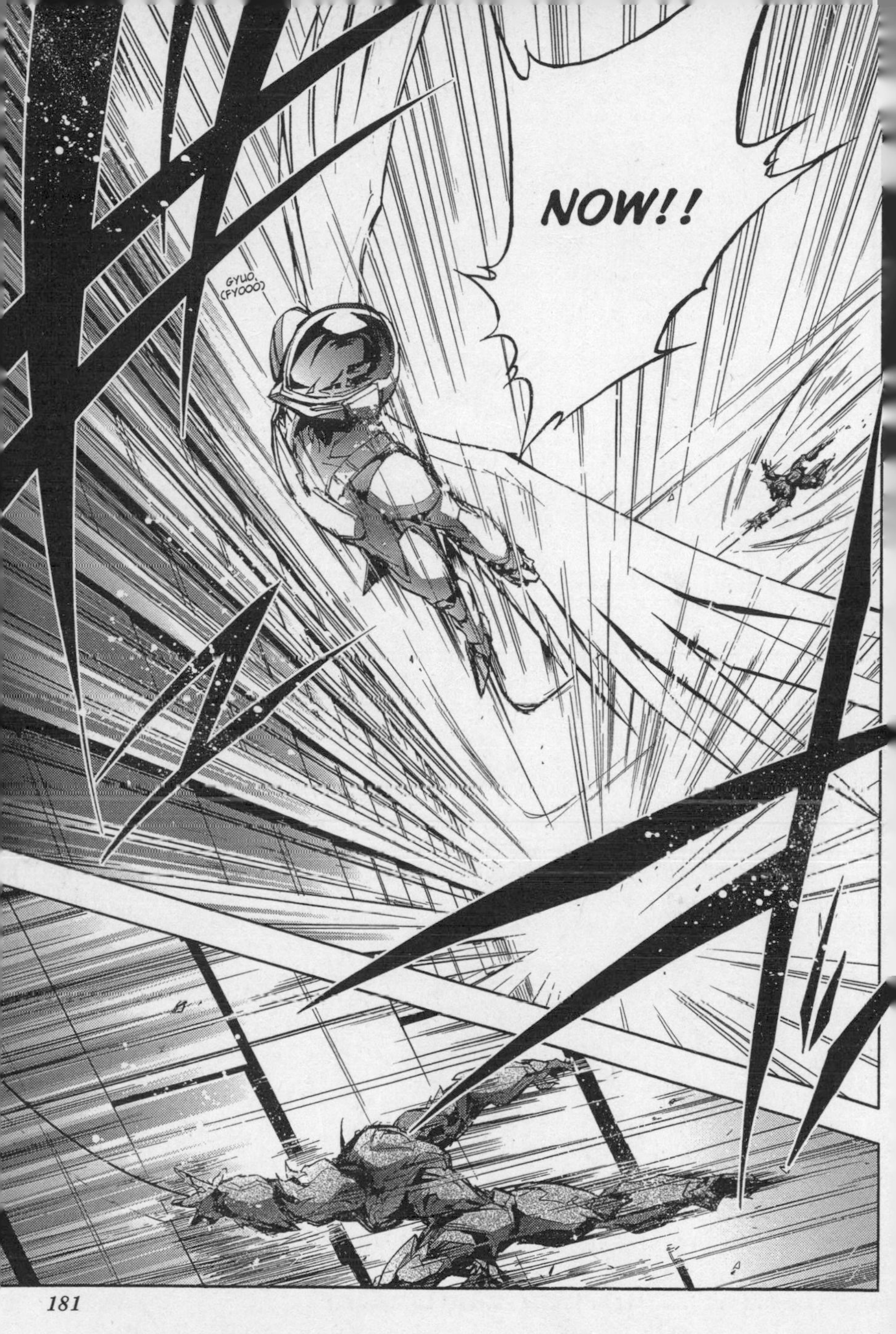
NOW!!
GYUO
(FYOOO)

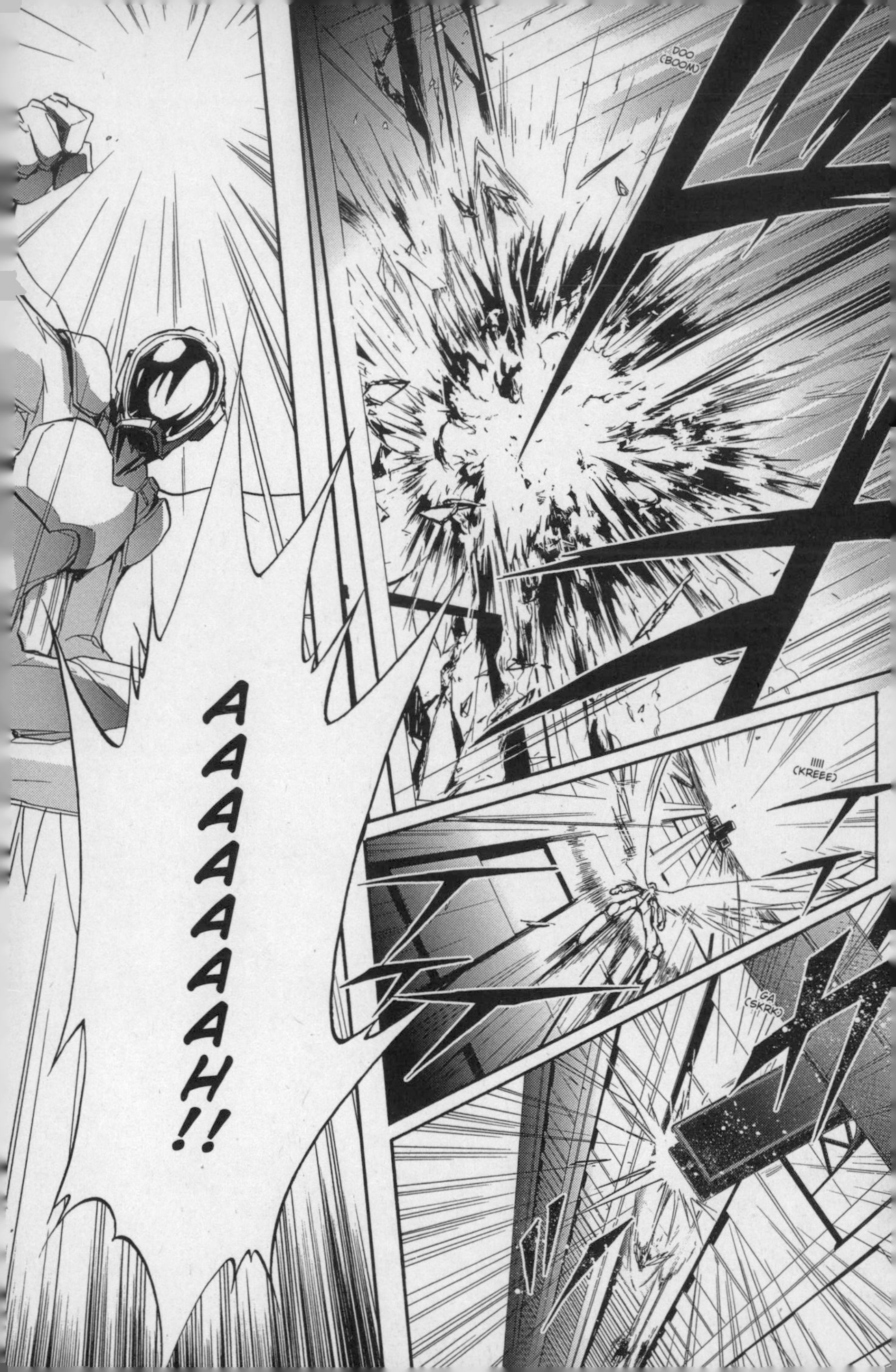
DOO
(BOOM)
IIII
(KREEE)
GA
(SKRK)
AAAAAAAH!!

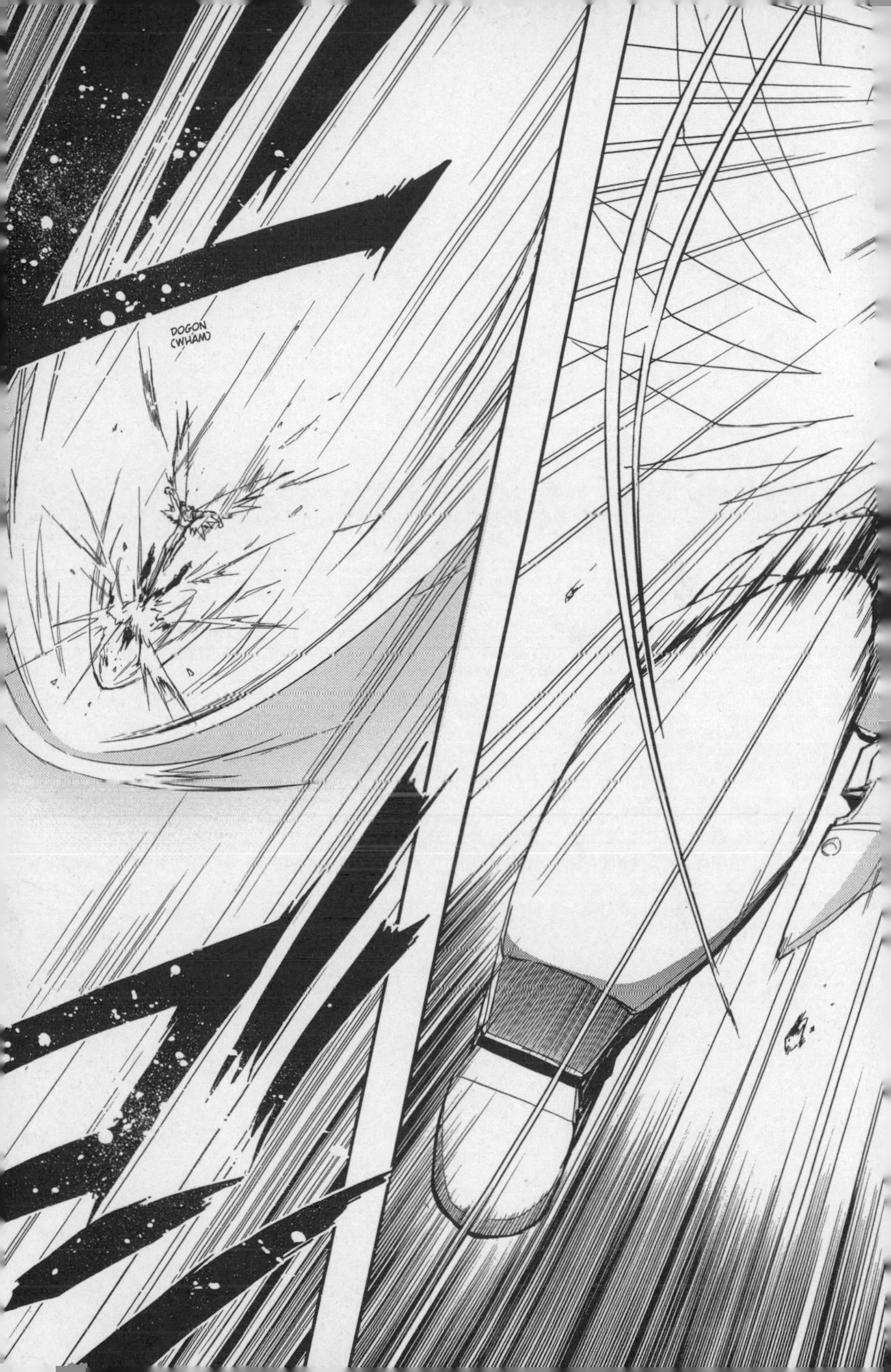
DOGON
(WHAM)

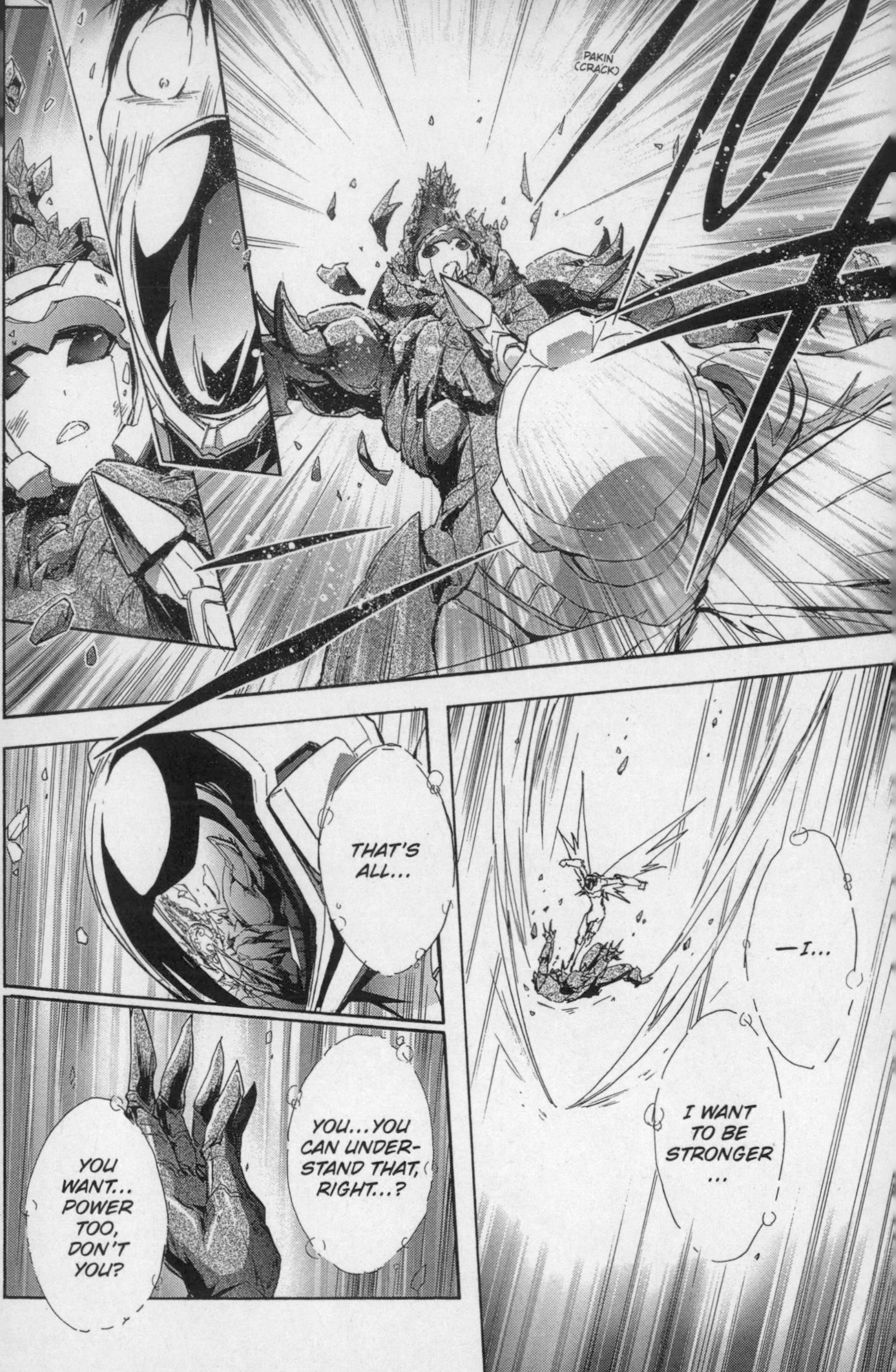
PAKIN (CRACK)
—I...
I WANT TO BE STRONGER ...
THAT'S ALL...
YOU...YOU CAN UNDERSTAND THAT, RIGHT...?
YOU WANT... POWER TOO, DON'T YOU?

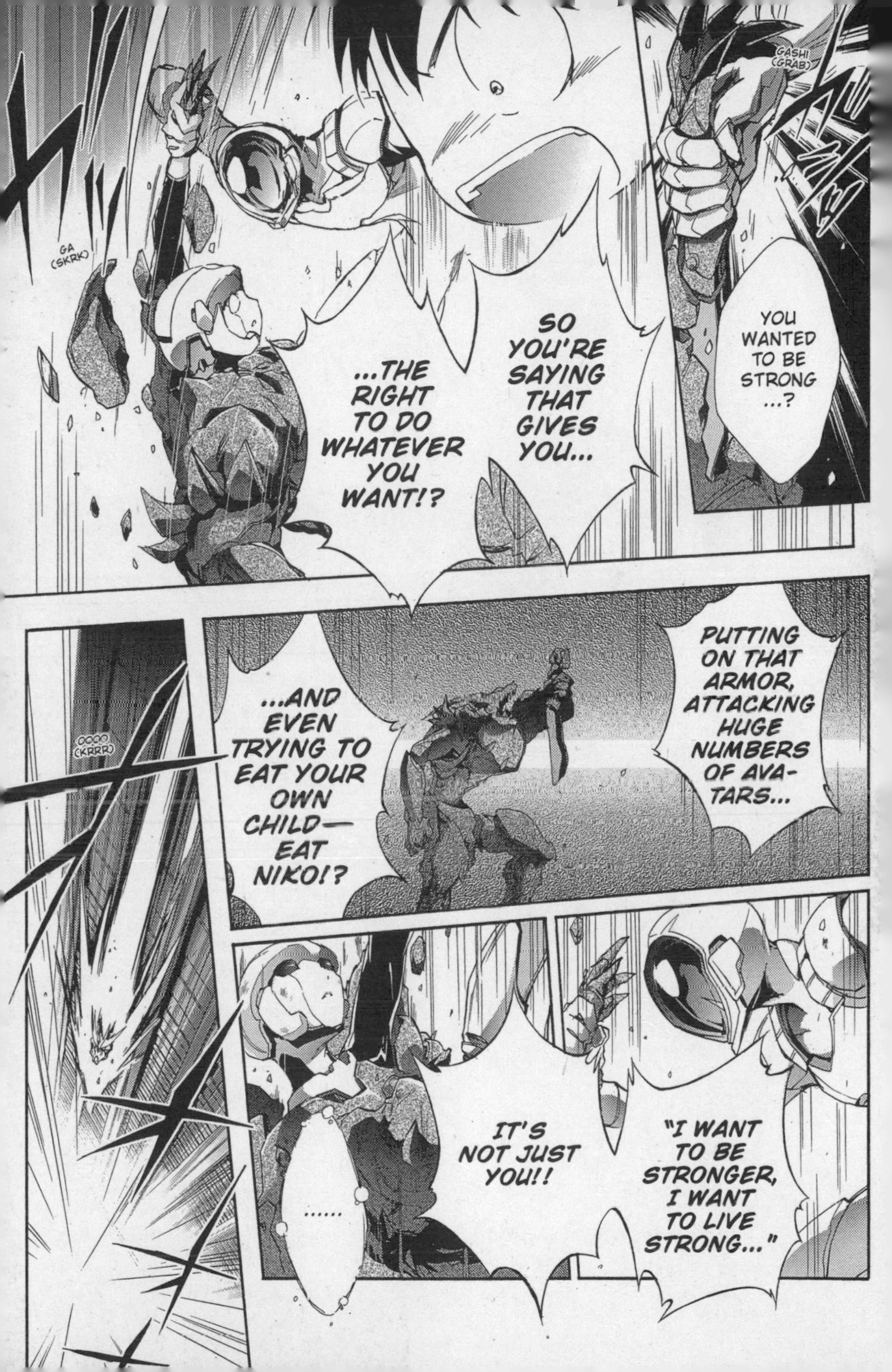
GASHI (GRAB)
YOU WANTED TO BE STRONG...?
SO YOU'RE SAYING THAT GIVES YOU...
...THE RIGHT TO DO WHATEVER YOU WANT!?
GA (SKRK)
PUTTING ON THAT ARMOR, ATTACKING HUGE NUMBERS OF AVA-TARS...
...AND EVEN TRYING TO EAT YOUR OWN CHILD— EAT NIKO!?
(KRRR)
"I WANT TO BE STRONGER, I WANT TO LIVE STRONG..."
IT'S NOT JUST YOU!!
......

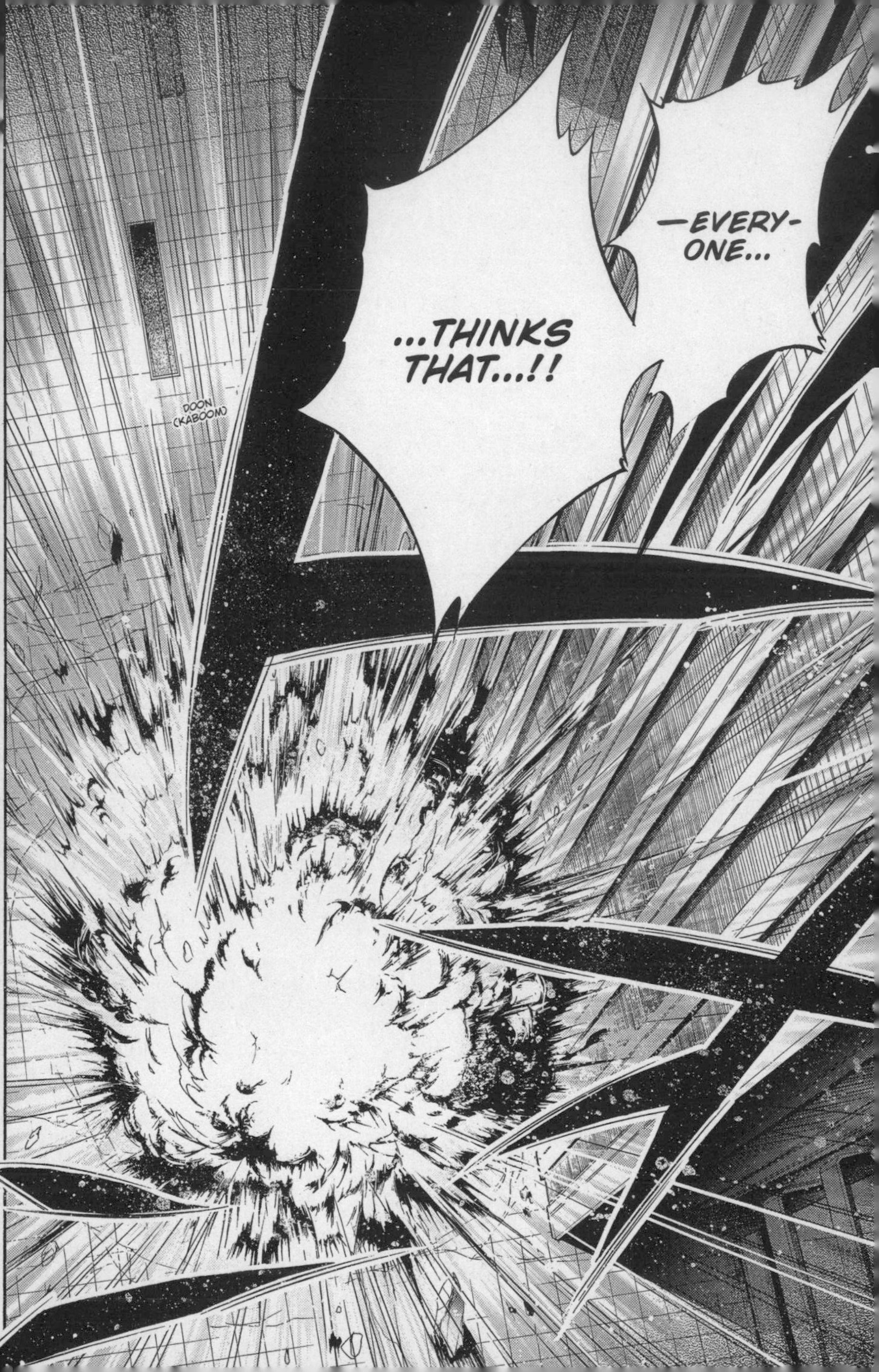
—EVERY-ONE...
...THINKS THAT...!!
DOON (KABOOM)

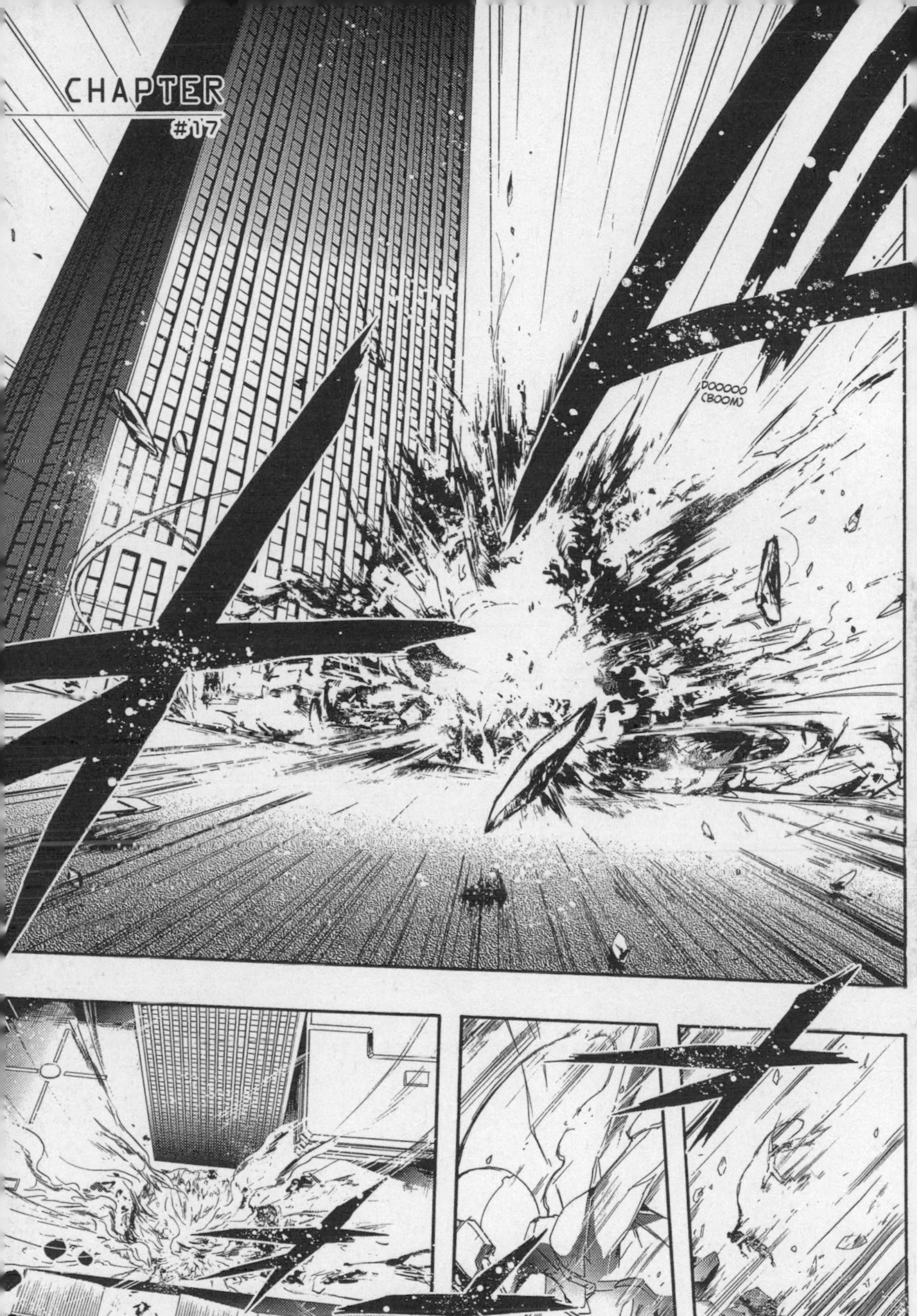
CHAPTER
#17
DOOOOO
(BOOM)

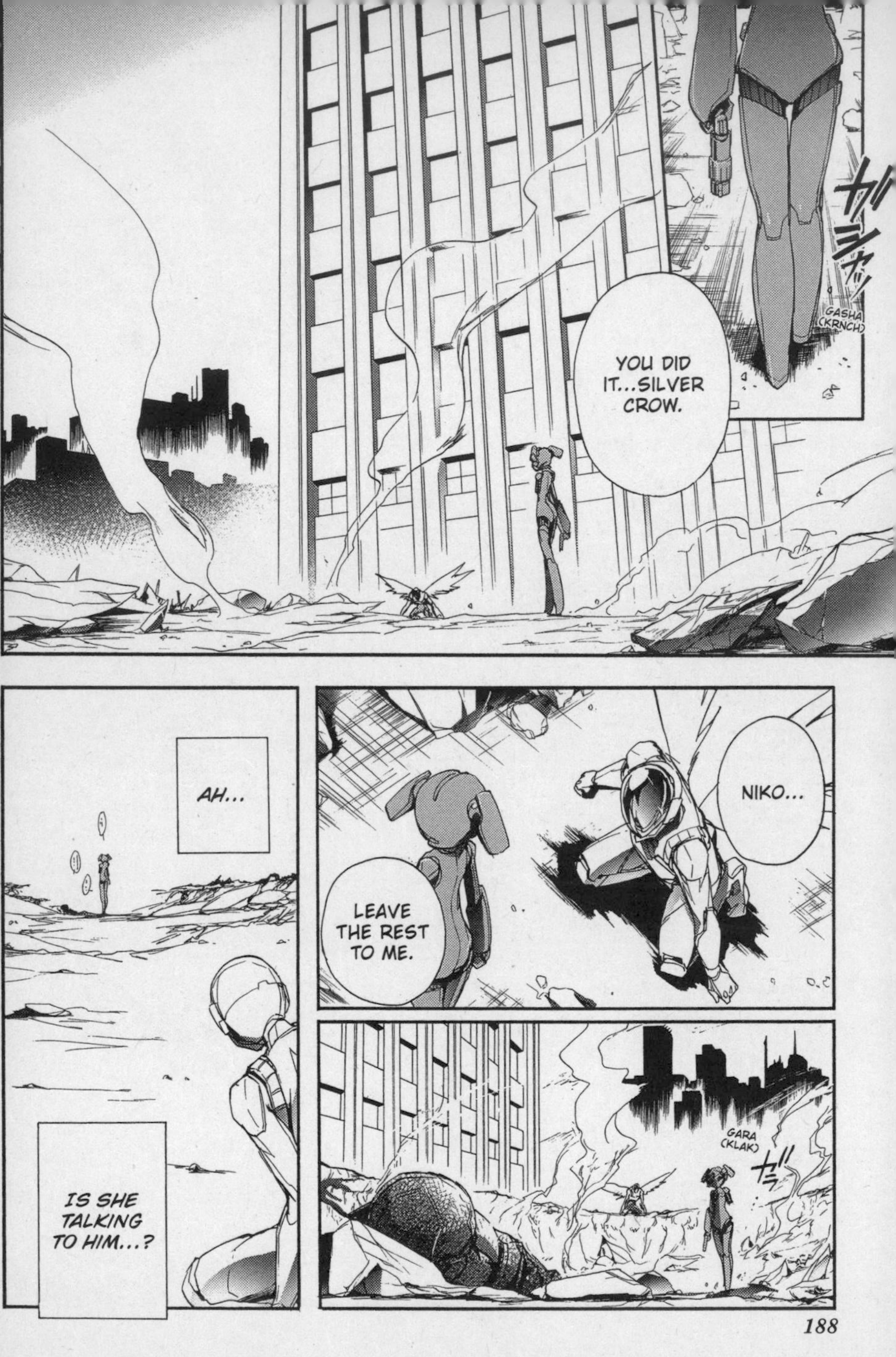
GASHA (KRNCH)
YOU DID IT...SILVER CROW.
NIKO...
LEAVE THE REST TO ME.
GARA (KLAK)
AH...
IS SHE TALKING TO HIM...?

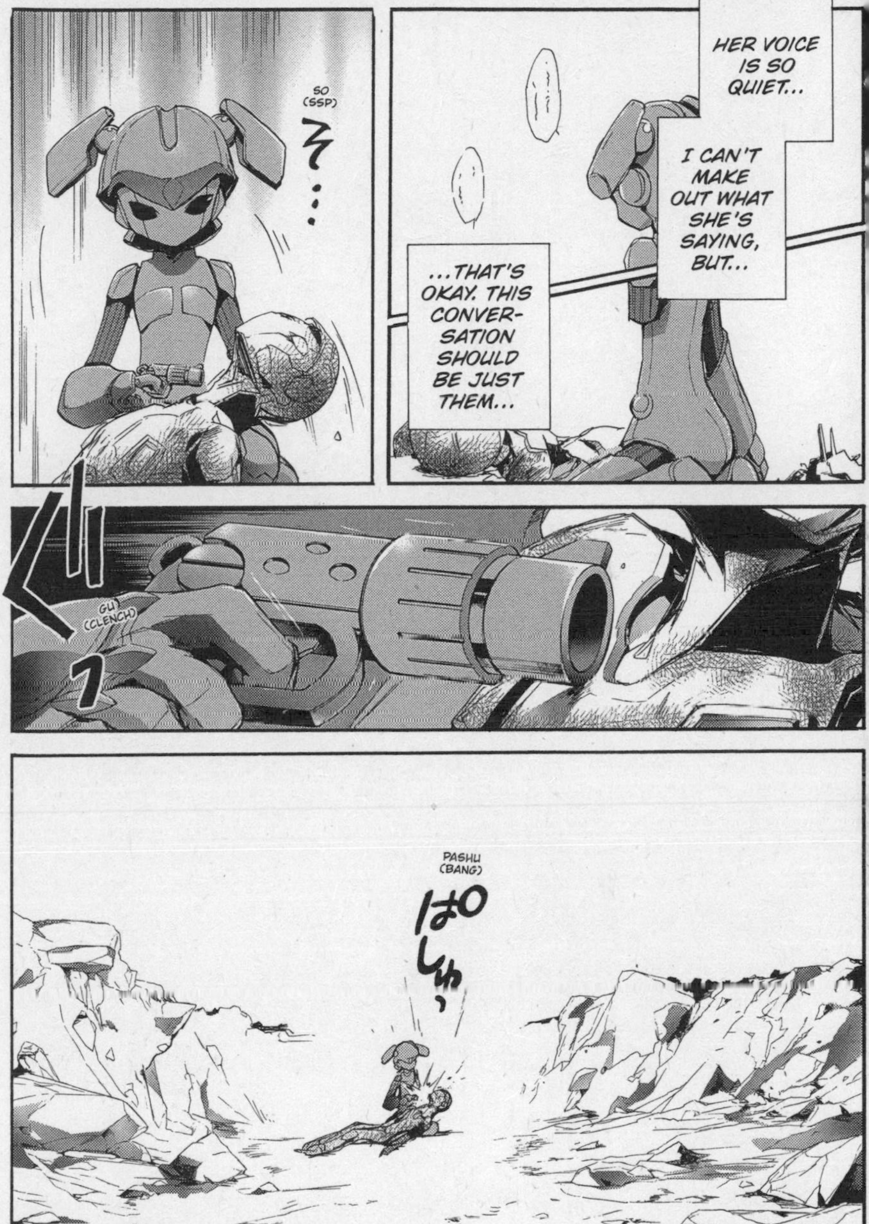
HER VOICE IS SO QUIET...
I CAN'T MAKE OUT WHAT SHE'S SAYING, BUT...
...THAT'S OKAY. THIS CONVER-SATION SHOULD BE JUST THEM...
SO (SSP)
GU (CLENCH)
PASHU (BANG)

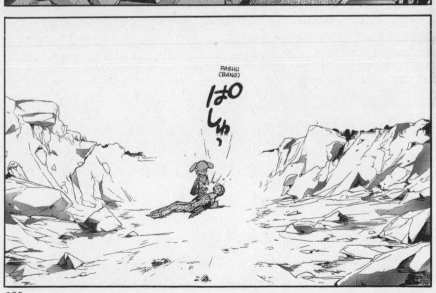

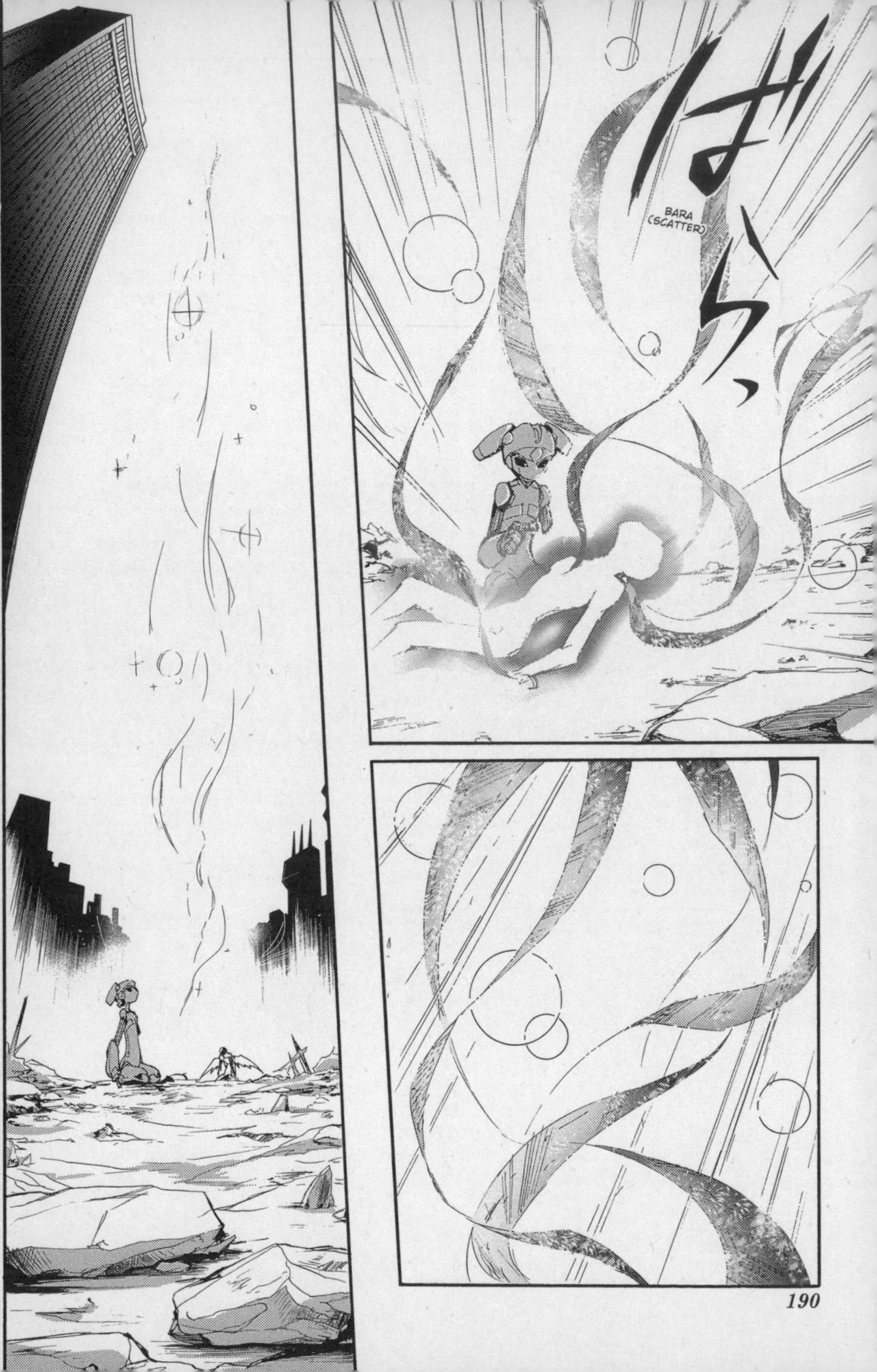
ばらっ
BARA (SCATTER)

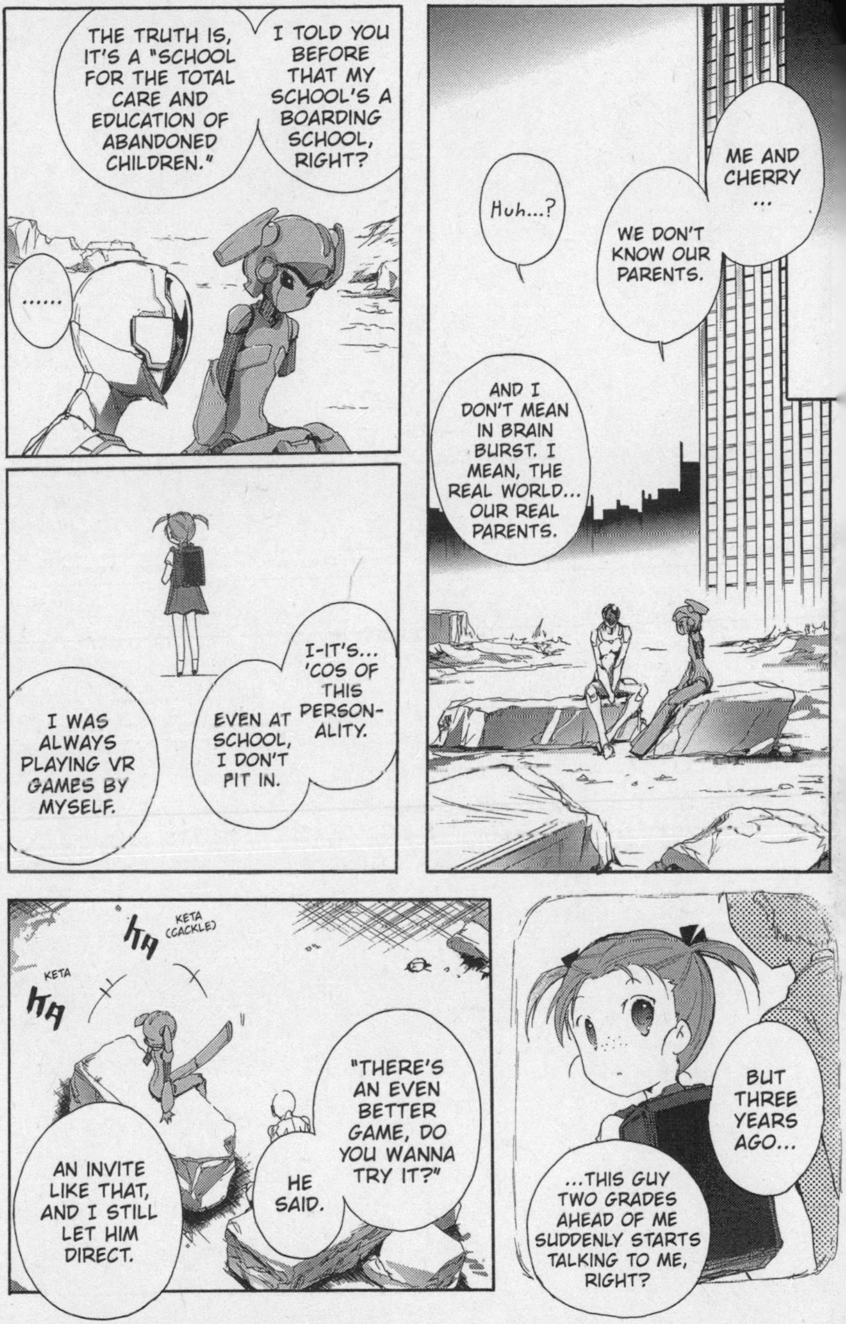
ME AND CHERRY ...
WE DON'T KNOW OUR PARENTS.
Huh...?
AND I DON'T MEAN IN BRAIN BURST. I MEAN, THE REAL WORLD... OUR REAL PARENTS.
I TOLD YOU BEFORE THAT MY SCHOOL'S A BOARDING SCHOOL, RIGHT?
THE TRUTH IS, IT'S A "SCHOOL FOR THE TOTAL CARE AND EDUCATION OF ABANDONED CHILDREN."
......
I-IT'S... 'COS OF THIS PERSON-ALITY.
EVEN AT SCHOOL, I DON'T FIT IN.
I WAS ALWAYS PLAYING VR GAMES BY MYSELF.
BUT THREE YEARS AGO...
...THIS GUY TWO GRADES AHEAD OF ME SUDDENLY STARTS TALKING TO ME, RIGHT?
KA KETA (CACKLE)
KA KETA
"THERE'S AN EVEN BETTER GAME, DO YOU WANNA TRY IT?"
HE SAID.
AN INVITE LIKE THAT, AND I STILL LET HIM DIRECT.

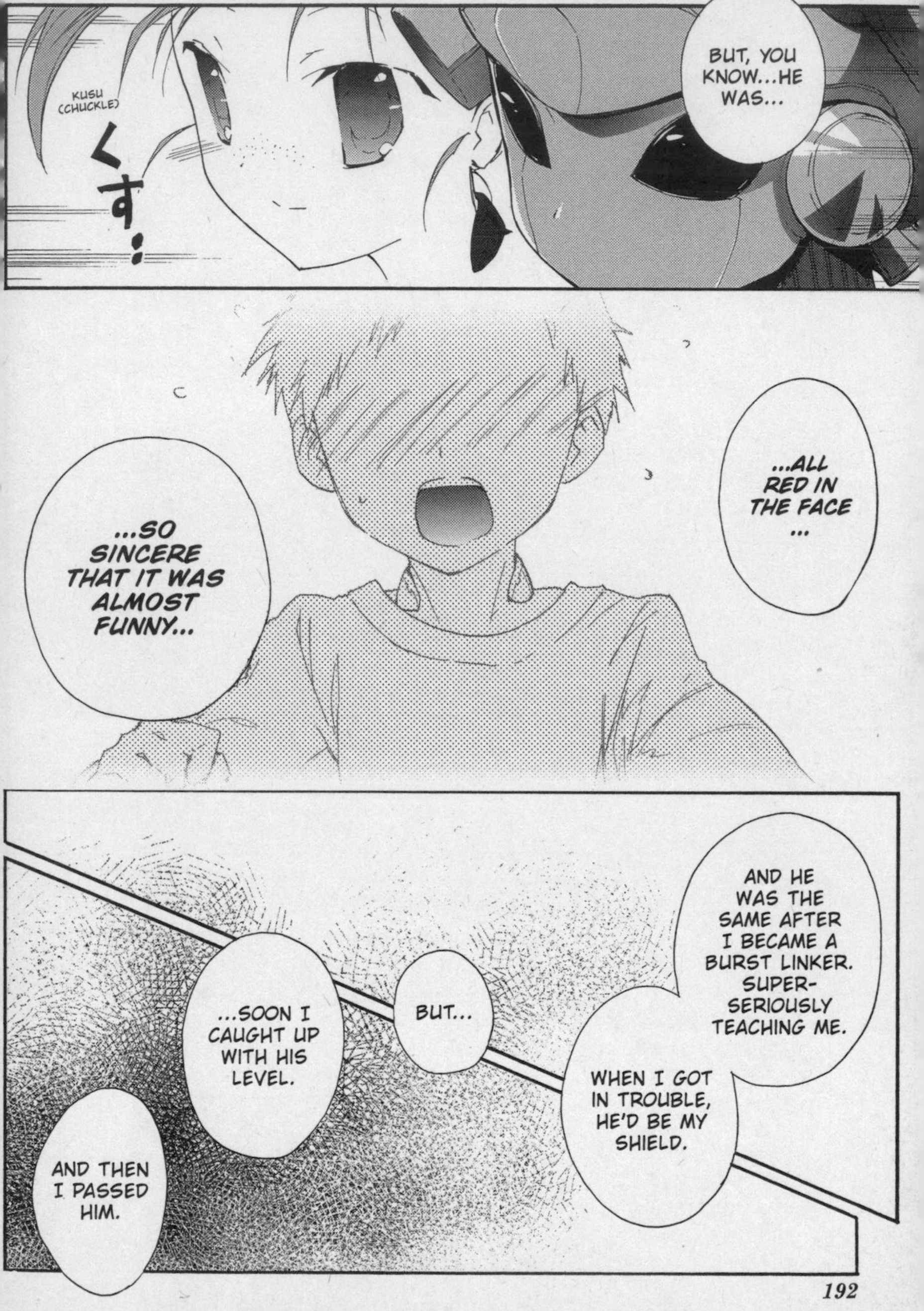
BUT, YOU KNOW...HE WAS...
KUSU (CHUCKLE)
くすっ
...ALL RED IN THE FACE...
...SO SINCERE THAT IT WAS ALMOST FUNNY...
AND HE WAS THE SAME AFTER I BECAME A BURST LINKER. SUPER-SERIOUSLY TEACHING ME.
WHEN I GOT IN TROUBLE, HE'D BE MY SHIELD.
BUT...
...SOON I CAUGHT UP WITH HIS LEVEL.
AND THEN I PASSED HIM.

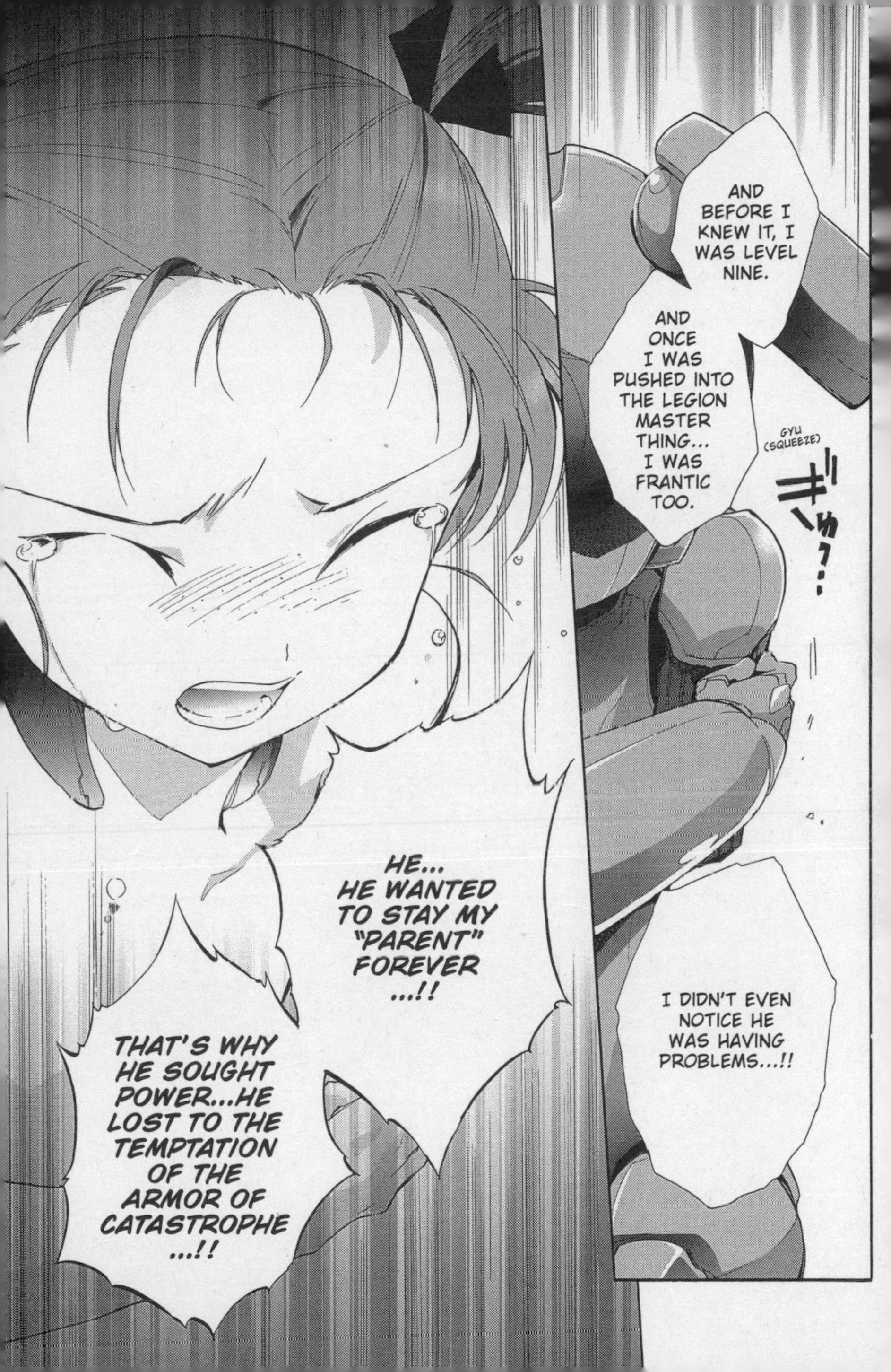
AND BEFORE I KNEW IT, I WAS LEVEL NINE.
AND ONCE I WAS PUSHED INTO THE LEGION MASTER THING... I WAS FRANTIC TOO.
GYU (SQUEEZE)
I DIDN'T EVEN NOTICE HE WAS HAVING PROBLEMS...!!
HE... HE WANTED TO STAY MY "PARENT" FOREVER ...!!
THAT'S WHY HE SOUGHT POWER...HE LOST TO THE TEMPTATION OF THE ARMOR OF CATASTROPHE ...!!

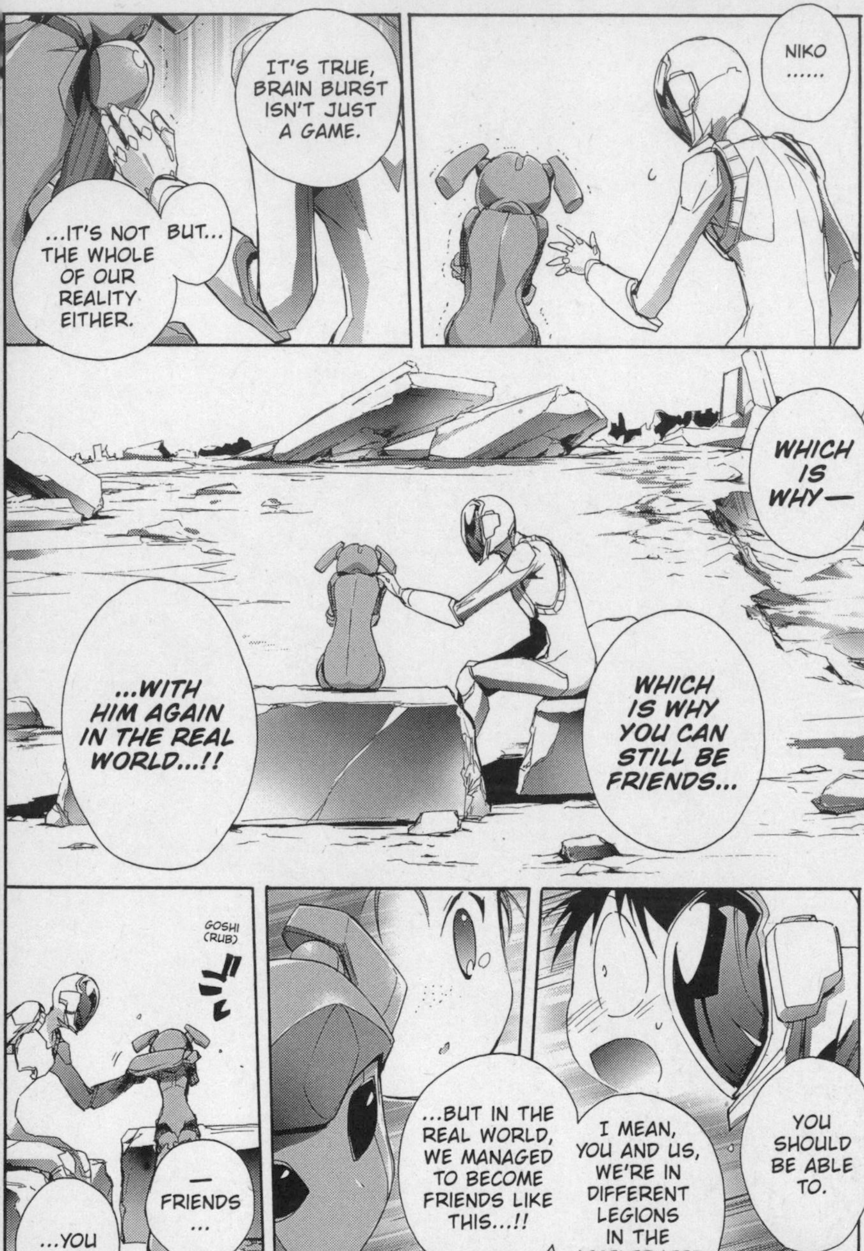
NIKO ......
IT'S TRUE, BRAIN BURST ISN'T JUST A GAME.
BUT...
...IT'S NOT THE WHOLE OF OUR REALITY EITHER.
WHICH IS WHY—
WHICH IS WHY YOU CAN STILL BE FRIENDS...
...WITH HIM AGAIN IN THE REAL WORLD...!!
YOU SHOULD BE ABLE TO.
I MEAN, YOU AND US, WE'RE IN DIFFERENT LEGIONS IN THE ACCELERATED WORLD...
...BUT IN THE REAL WORLD, WE MANAGED TO BECOME FRIENDS LIKE THIS...!!
GOSHI (RUB)
— FRIENDS ...
...YOU SAY?

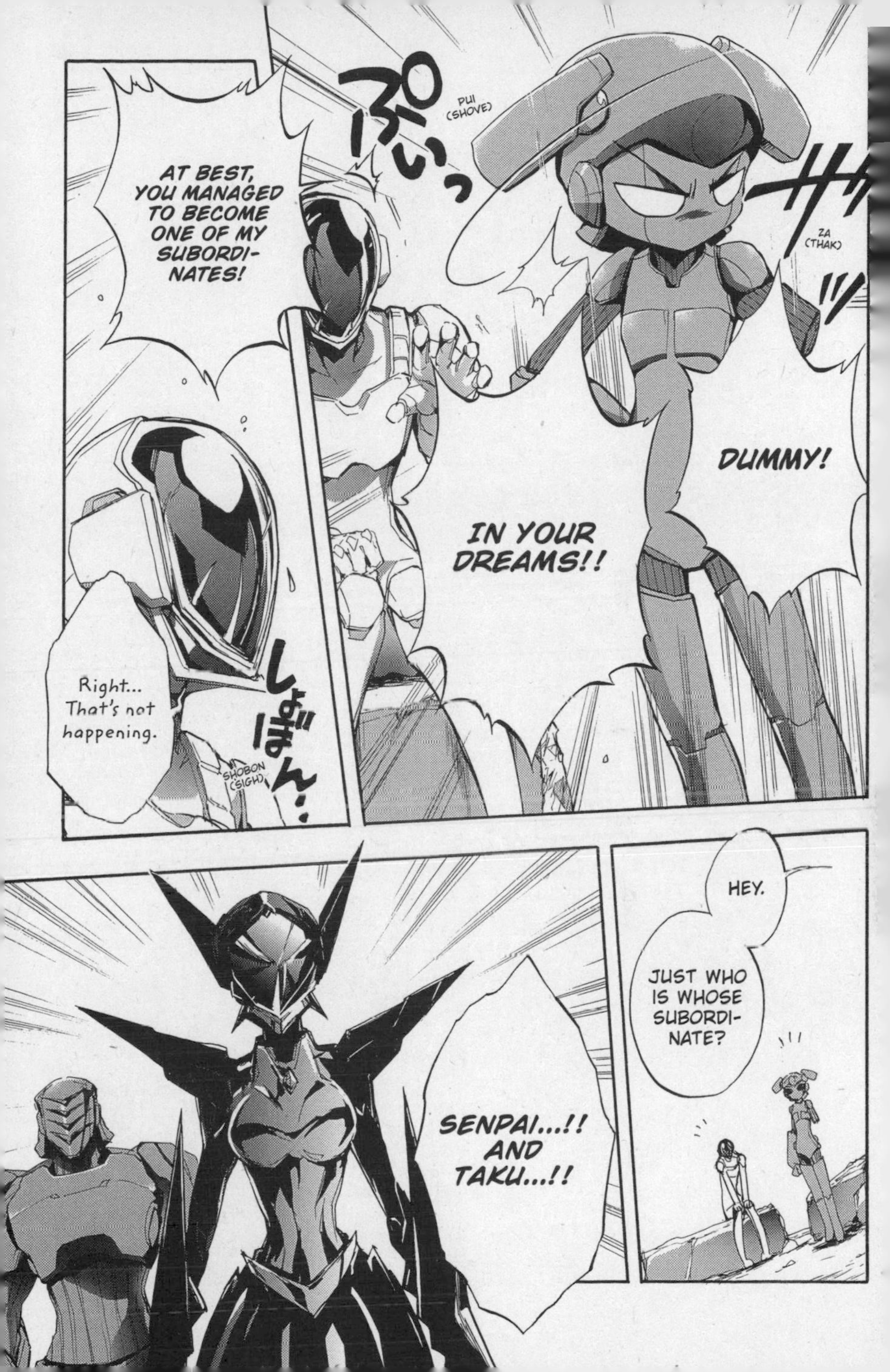
AT BEST, YOU MANAGED TO BECOME ONE OF MY SUBORDINATES!
ぷいっ
PUI (SHOVE)
ザッ
ZA (THAK)
DUMMY!
IN YOUR DREAMS!!
Right... That's not happening.
しょぼん
SHOBON (SIGH)
HEY.
JUST WHO IS WHOSE SUBORDINATE?
SENPAI...!! AND TAKU...!!

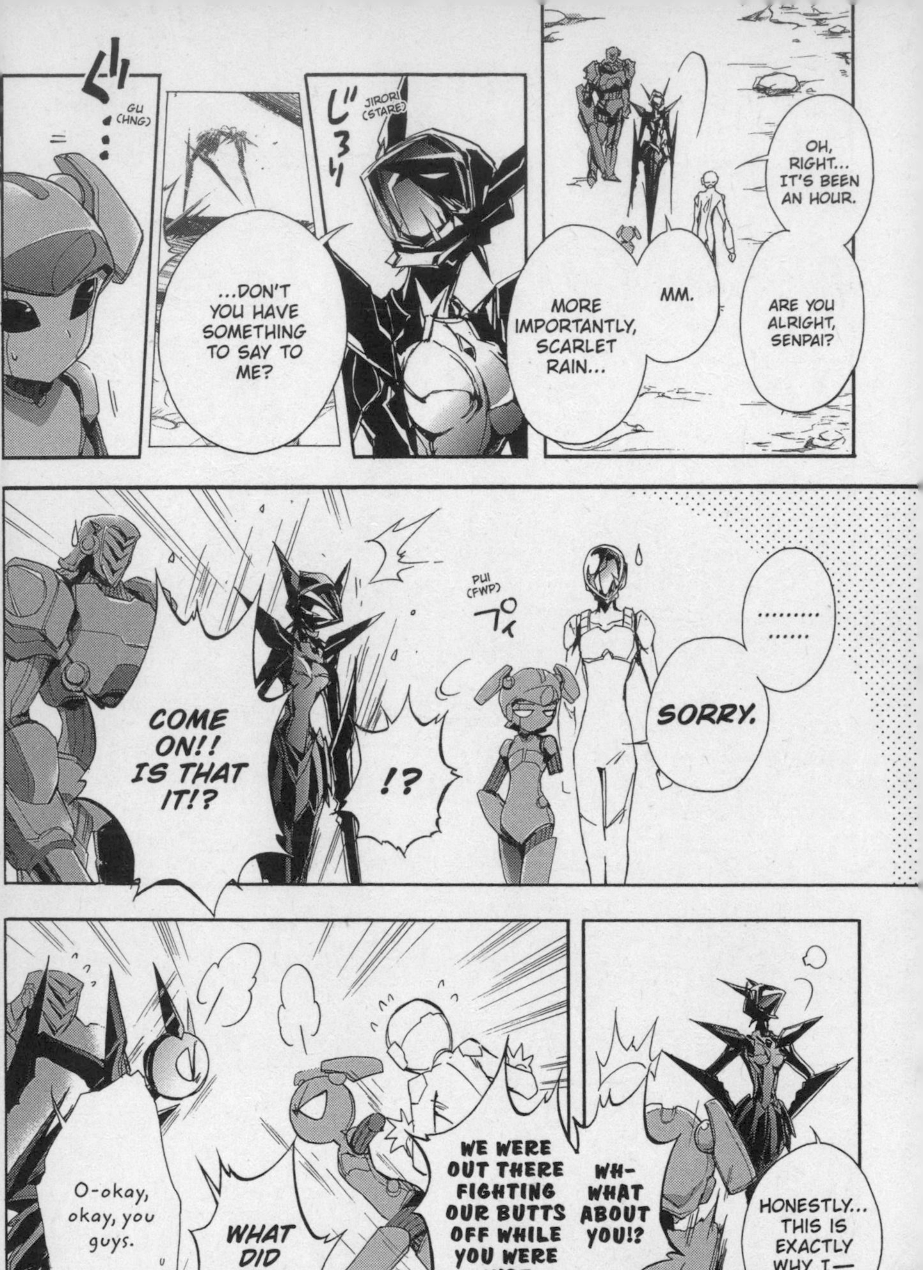
OH, RIGHT... IT'S BEEN AN HOUR.
ARE YOU ALRIGHT, SENPAI?
MM.
MORE IMPORTANTLY, SCARLET RAIN...
JIRORI (STARE)
...DON'T YOU HAVE SOMETHING TO SAY TO ME?
GU (HNG)
....
......
SORRY.
PUI (FWP)
!?
COME ON!! IS THAT IT!?
HONESTLY... THIS IS EXACTLY WHY I—
WH- WHAT ABOUT YOU!?
WE WERE OUT THERE FIGHTING OUR BUTTS OFF WHILE YOU WERE JUST TAKING A NAP!!
WHAT DID YOU SAY!?
O-okay, okay, you guys.

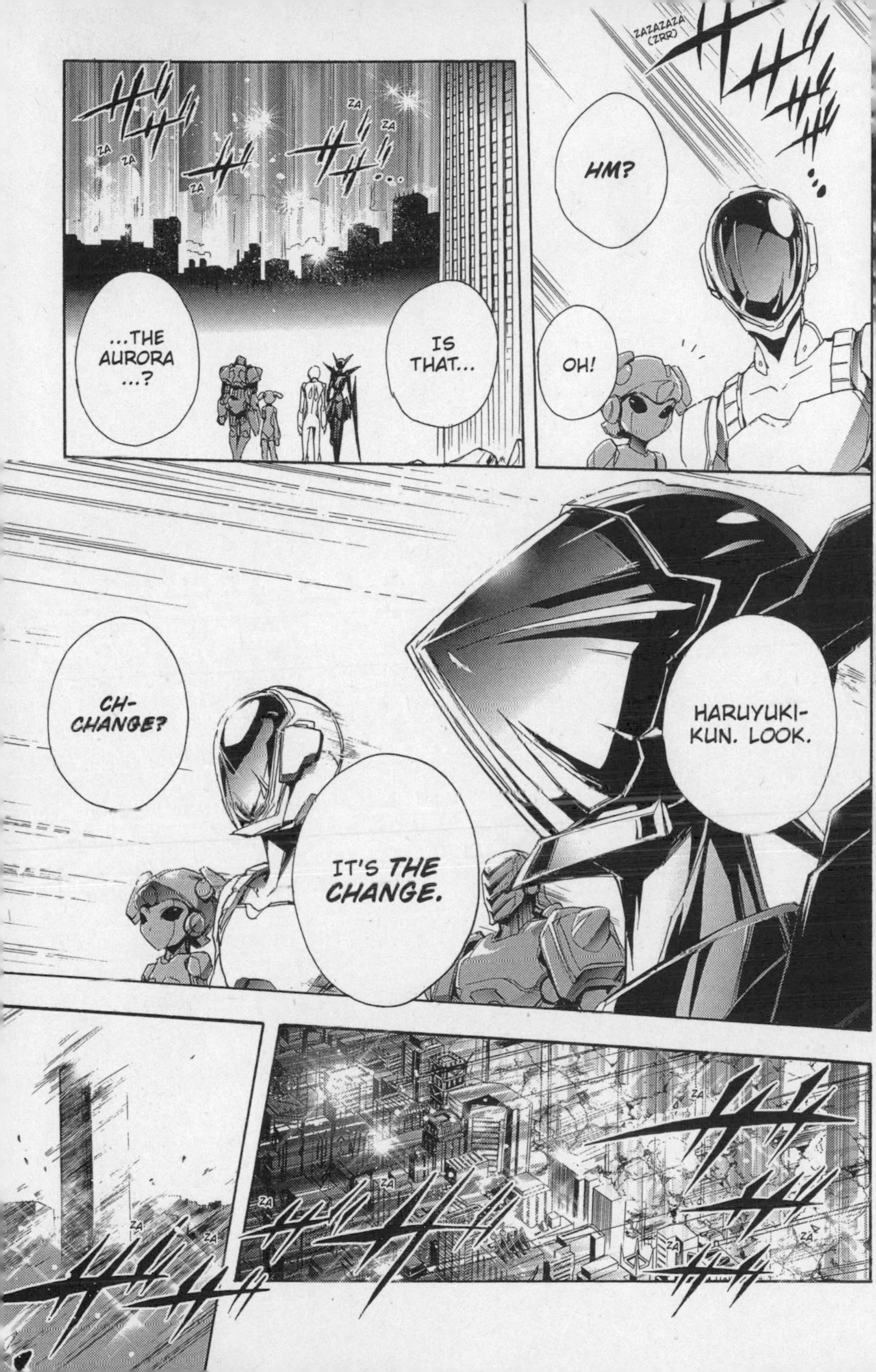
ZAZAZAZA (ZRR)
HM?
OH!
ZA
ZA
ZA
ZA
ZA
IS THAT...
...THE AURORA ...?
HARUYUKI-KUN. LOOK.
IT'S *THE* CHANGE.
CH-CHANGE?
ZA
ZA
ZA
ZA
ZA
ZA
ZA

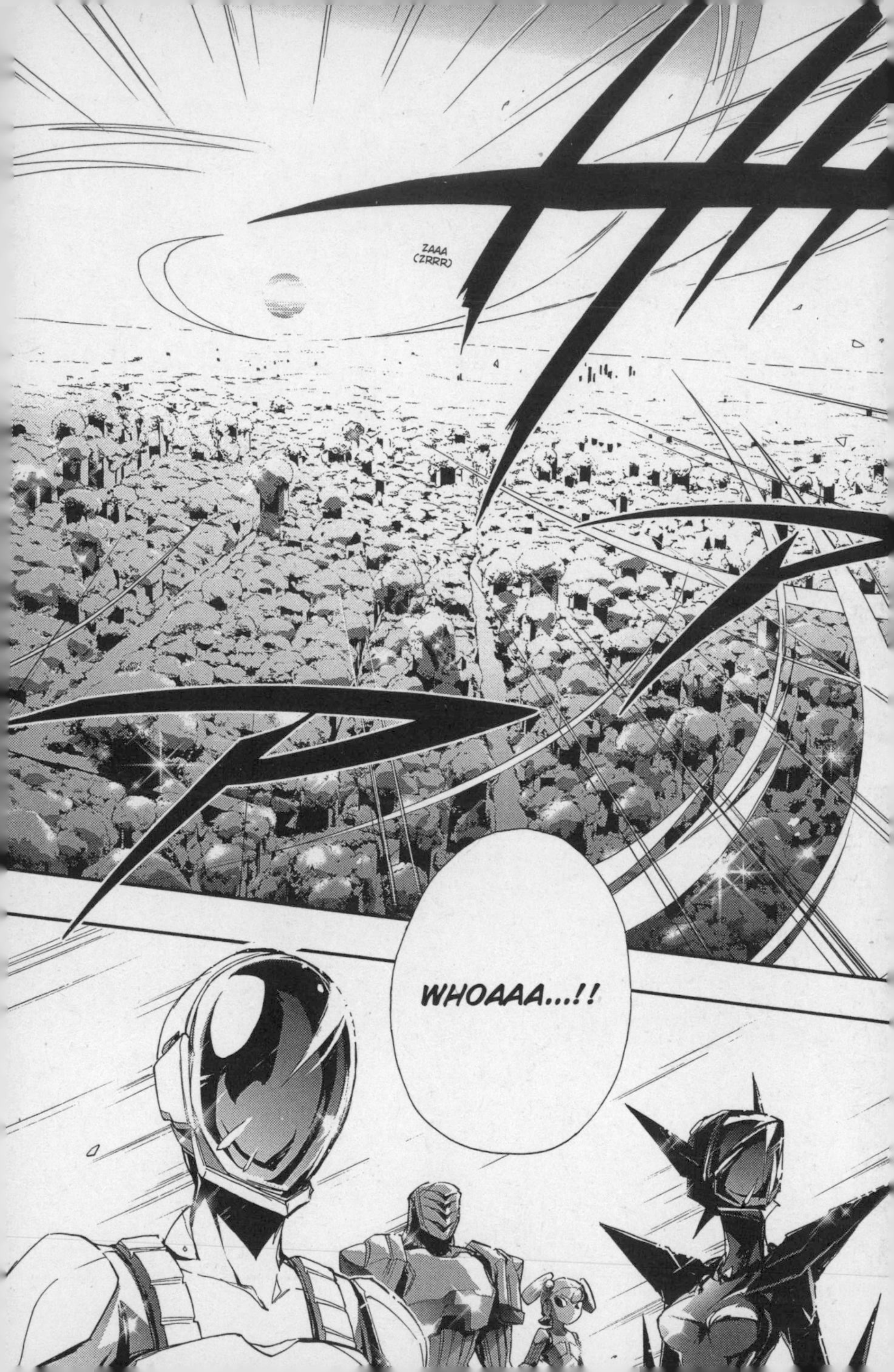
ZAAA
(ZRRR)
WHOAAA...!!

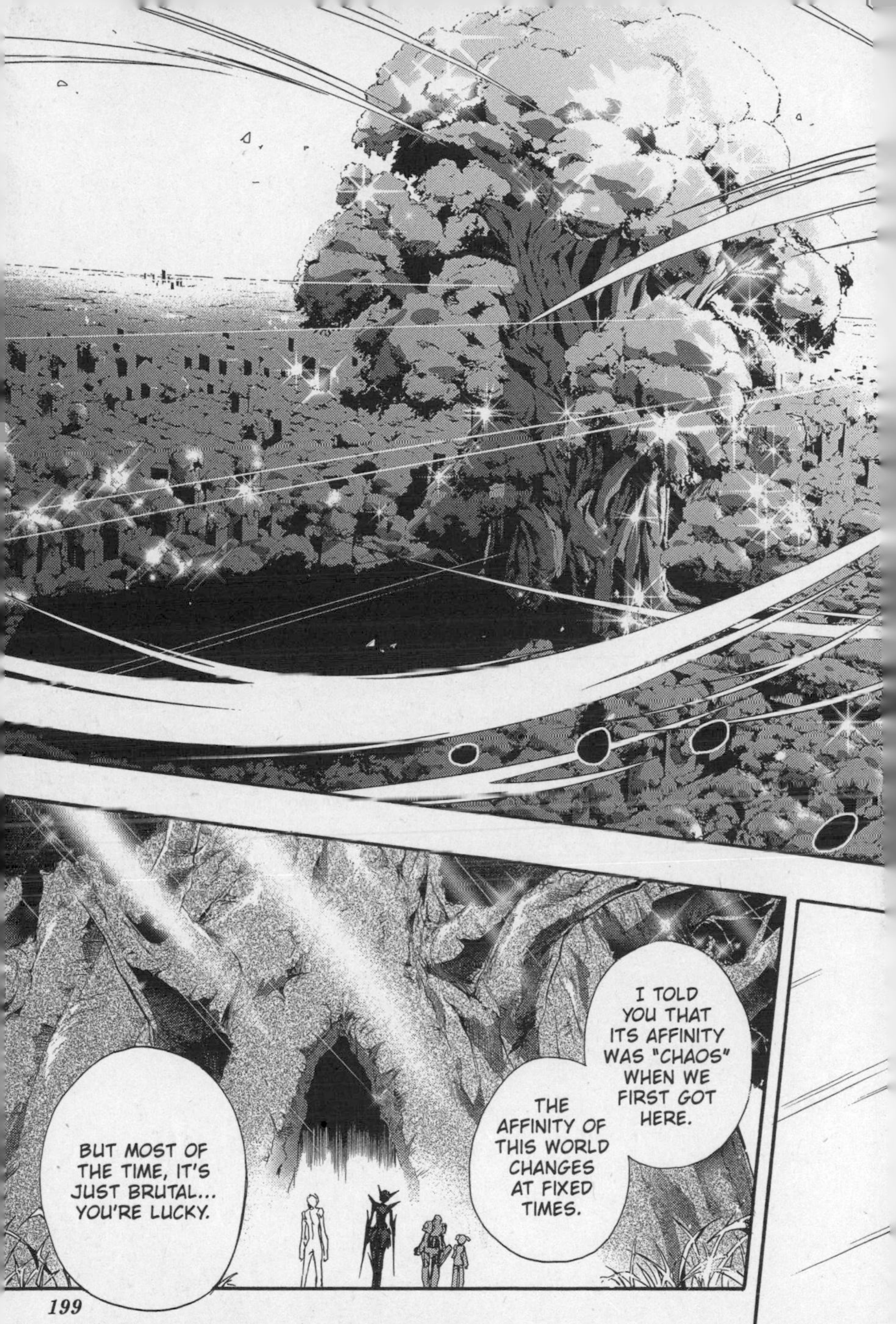
I TOLD YOU THAT ITS AFFINITY WAS "CHAOS" WHEN WE FIRST GOT HERE.
THE AFFINITY OF THIS WORLD CHANGES AT FIXED TIMES.
BUT MOST OF THE TIME, IT'S JUST BRUTAL... YOU'RE LUCKY.

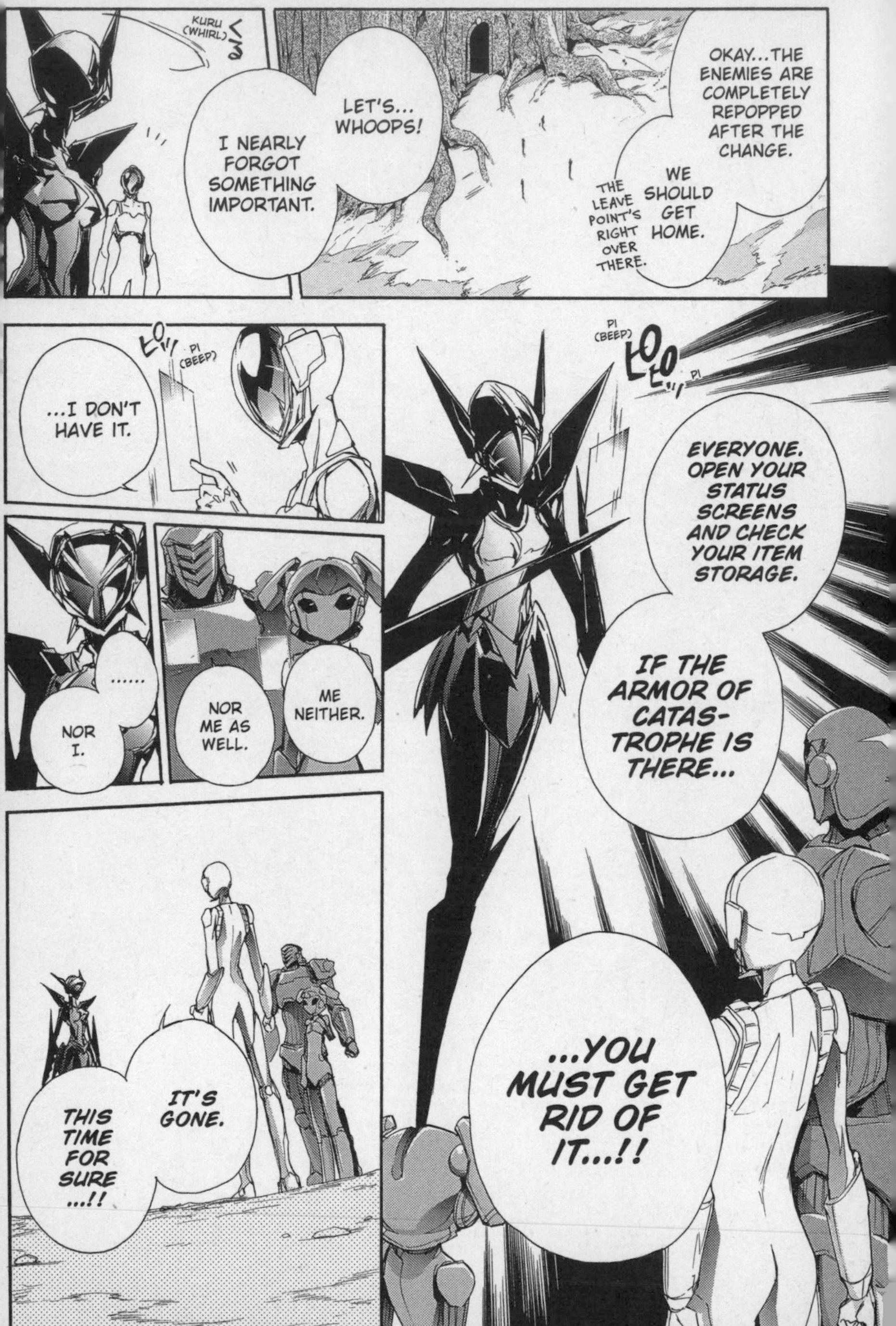
OKAY...THE ENEMIES ARE COMPLETELY REPOPPED AFTER THE CHANGE.
WE SHOULD GET HOME.
THE LEAVE POINT'S RIGHT OVER THERE.
KURU (WHIRL)
LET'S... WHOOPS!
I NEARLY FORGOT SOMETHING IMPORTANT.
PI (BEEP)
PI
EVERYONE. OPEN YOUR STATUS SCREENS AND CHECK YOUR ITEM STORAGE.
IF THE ARMOR OF CATAS-TROPHE IS THERE...
...YOU MUST GET RID OF IT...!!
PI (BEEP)
...I DON'T HAVE IT.
ME NEITHER.
NOR ME AS WELL.
......
NOR I.
IT'S GONE.
THIS TIME FOR SURE...!!

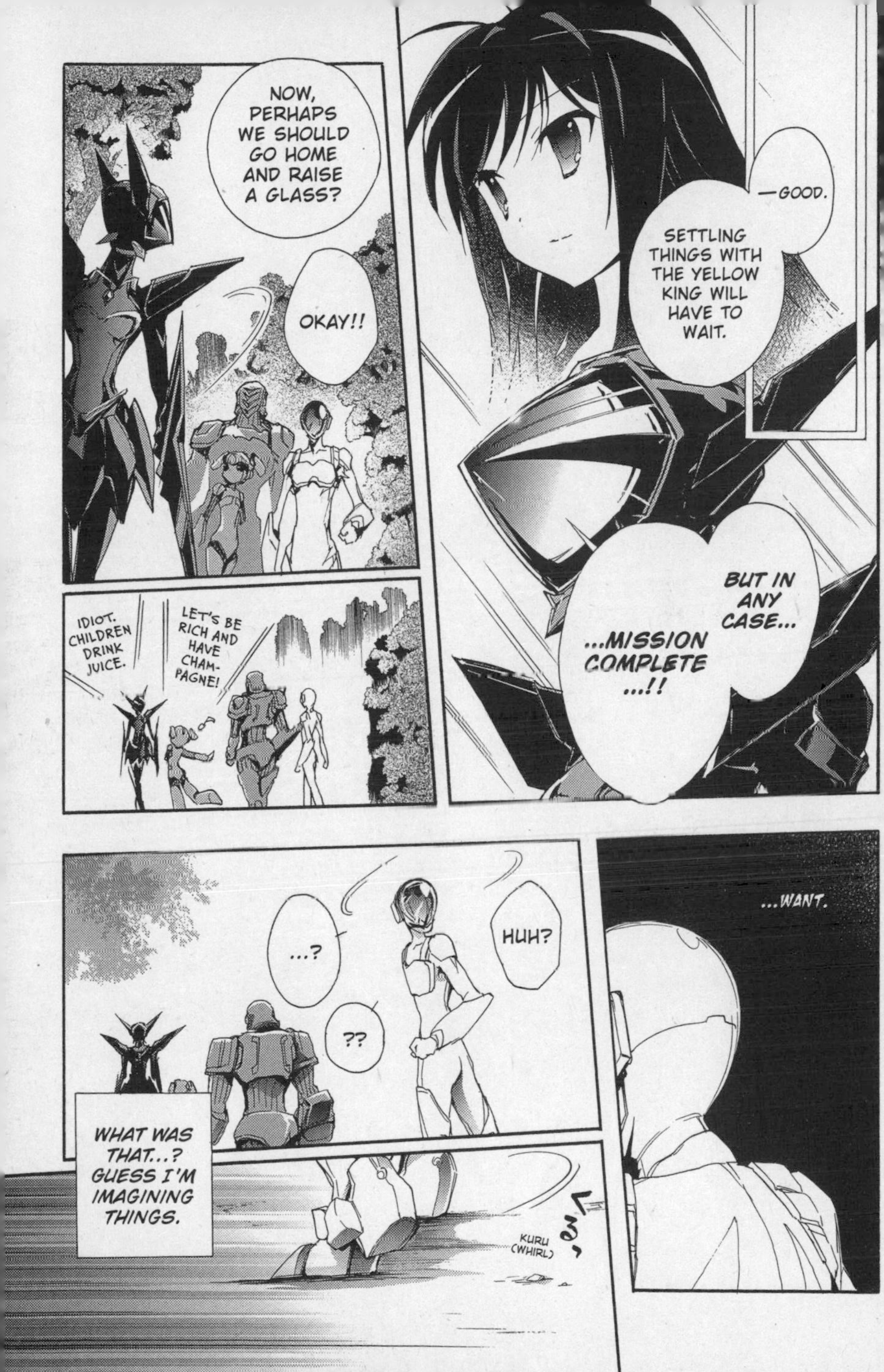
—GOOD.
SETTLING THINGS WITH THE YELLOW KING WILL HAVE TO WAIT.
BUT IN ANY CASE...
...MISSION COMPLETE ...!!
NOW, PERHAPS WE SHOULD GO HOME AND RAISE A GLASS?
OKAY!!
LET'S BE RICH AND HAVE CHAMPAGNE!
IDIOT. CHILDREN DRINK JUICE.
...WANT.
HUH?
...?
??
WHAT WAS THAT...? GUESS I'M IMAGINING THINGS.
KURU (WHIRL)

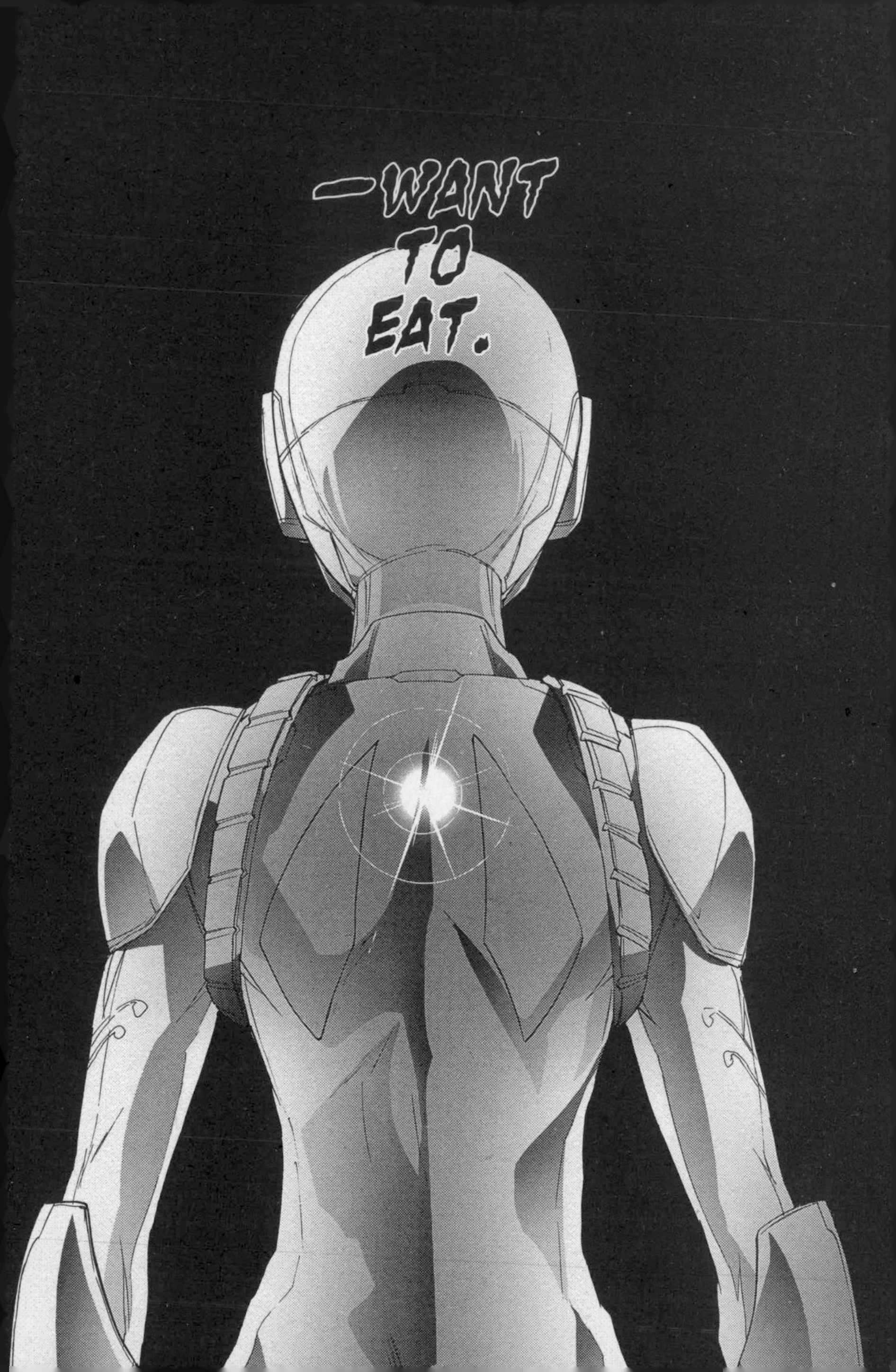
—WANT TO EAT.

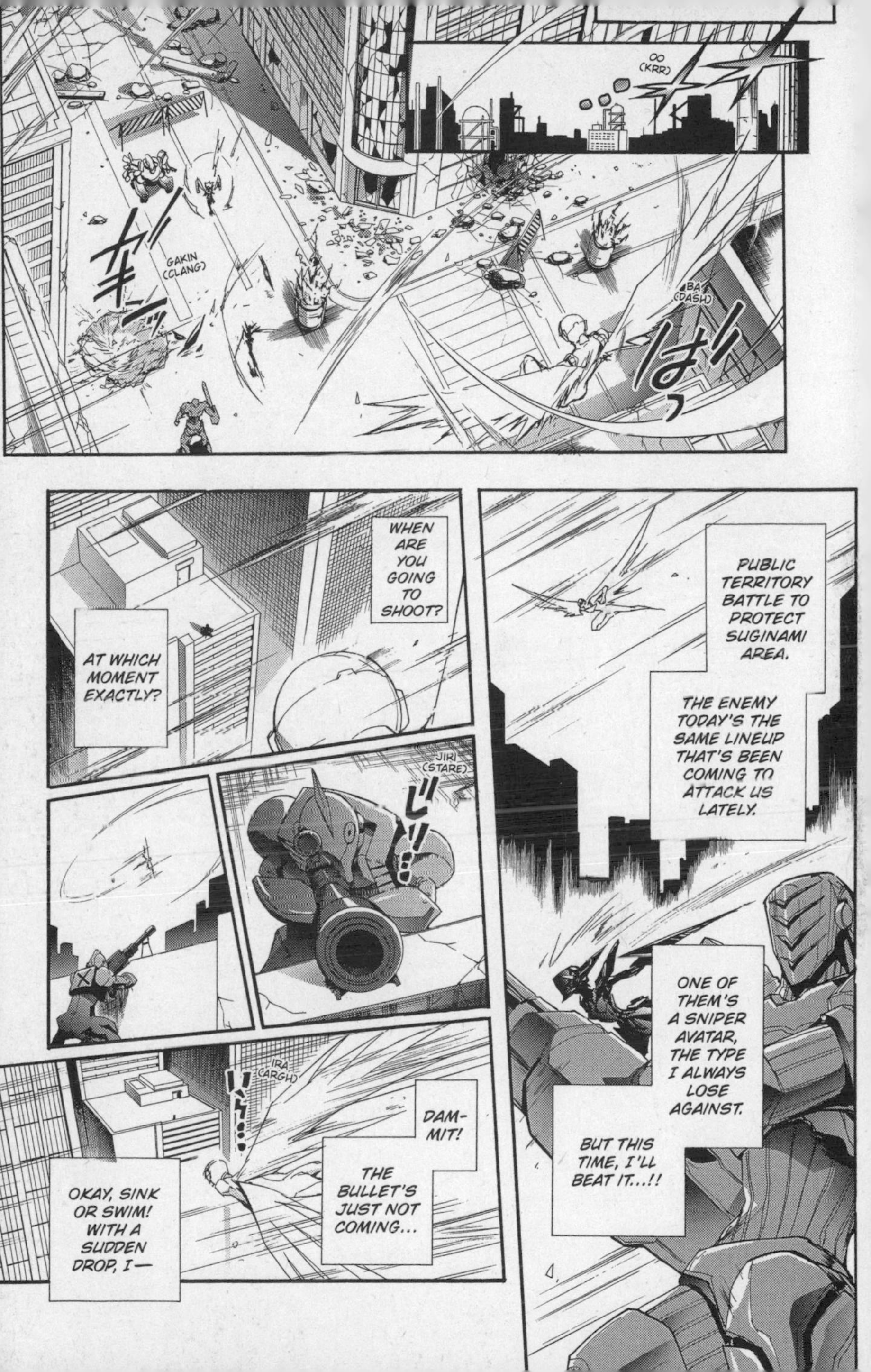
(KRR)
BA (DASH)
GAKIN (CLANG)
PUBLIC TERRITORY BATTLE TO PROTECT SUGINAMI AREA.
THE ENEMY TODAY'S THE SAME LINEUP THAT'S BEEN COMING TO ATTACK US LATELY.
ONE OF THEM'S A SNIPER AVATAR, THE TYPE I ALWAYS LOSE AGAINST.
BUT THIS TIME, I'LL BEAT IT...!!
WHEN ARE YOU GOING TO SHOOT?
AT WHICH MOMENT EXACTLY?
JIRI (STARE)
IRA (ARGH)
DAM-MIT!
THE BULLET'S JUST NOT COMING...
OKAY, SINK OR SWIM! WITH A SUDDEN DROP, I—

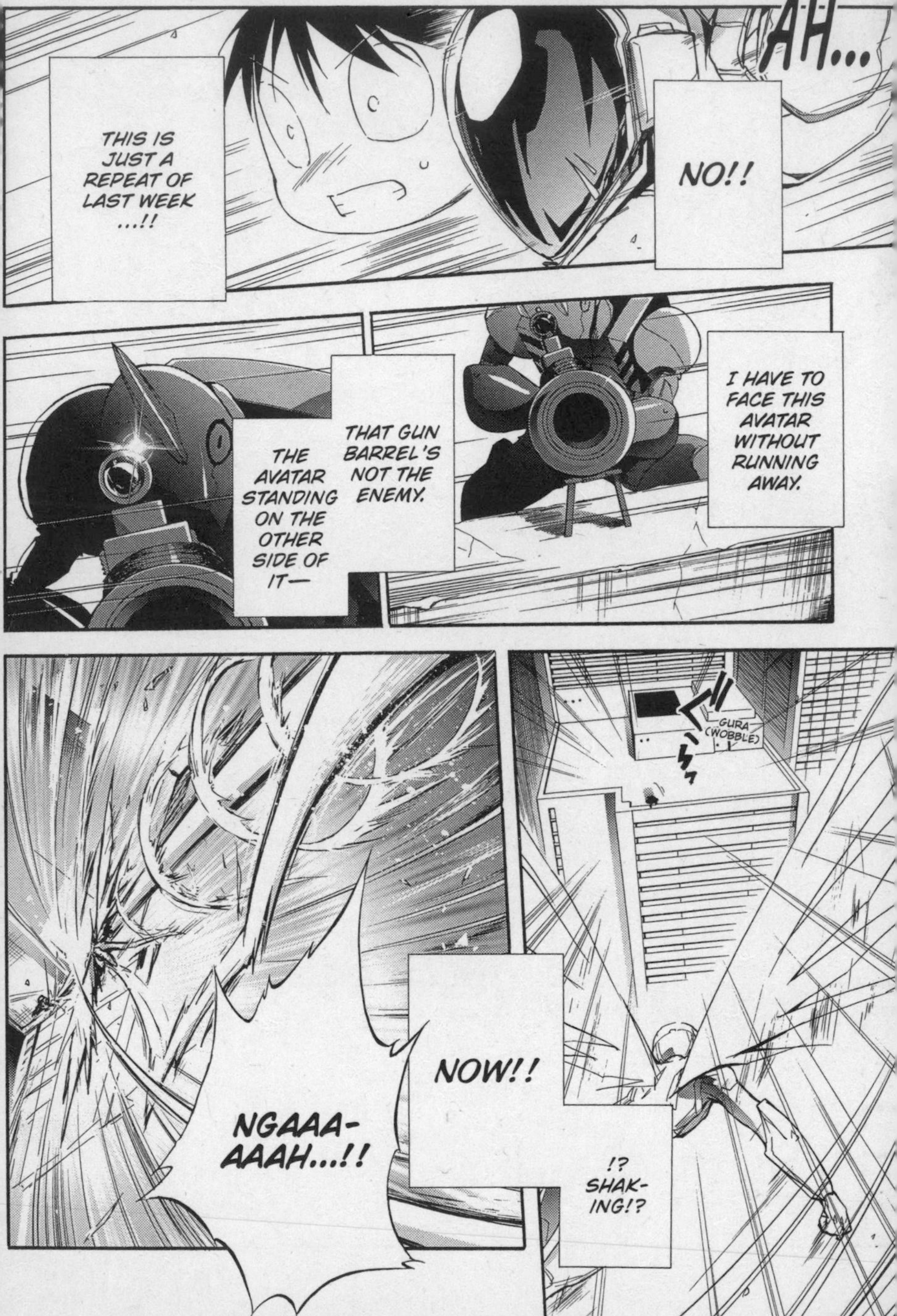

AH...
NO!!
THIS IS JUST A REPEAT OF LAST WEEK ...!!
I HAVE TO FACE THIS AVATAR WITHOUT RUNNING AWAY.
THAT GUN BARREL'S NOT THE ENEMY.
THE AVATAR STANDING ON THE OTHER SIDE OF IT—
GURA (WOBBLE)
NOW!!
!? SHAK-ING!?
NGAAA-AAAH...!!

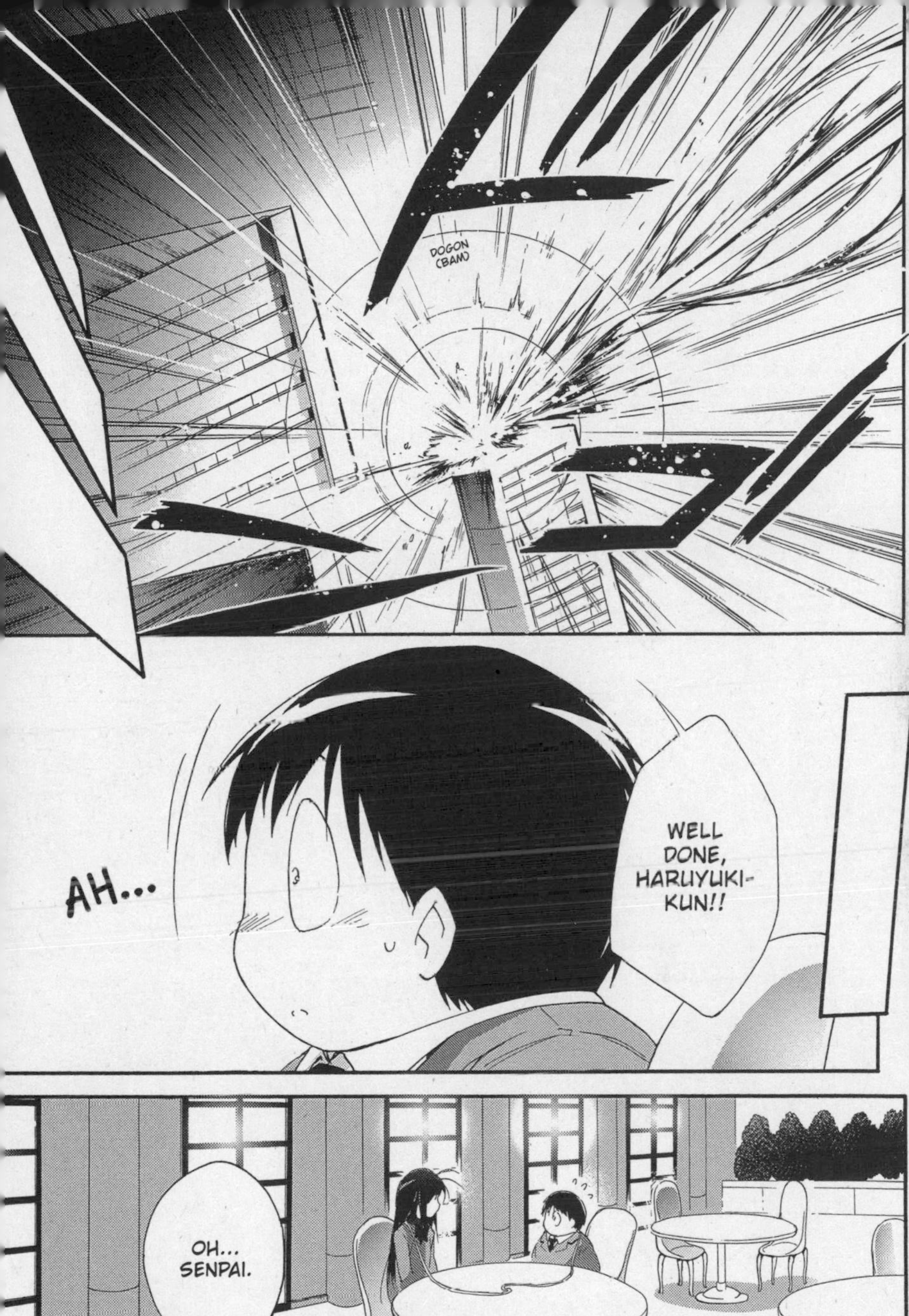
DOGON (BAM)
WELL DONE, HARUYUKI-KUN!!
AH...
OH... SENPAI.

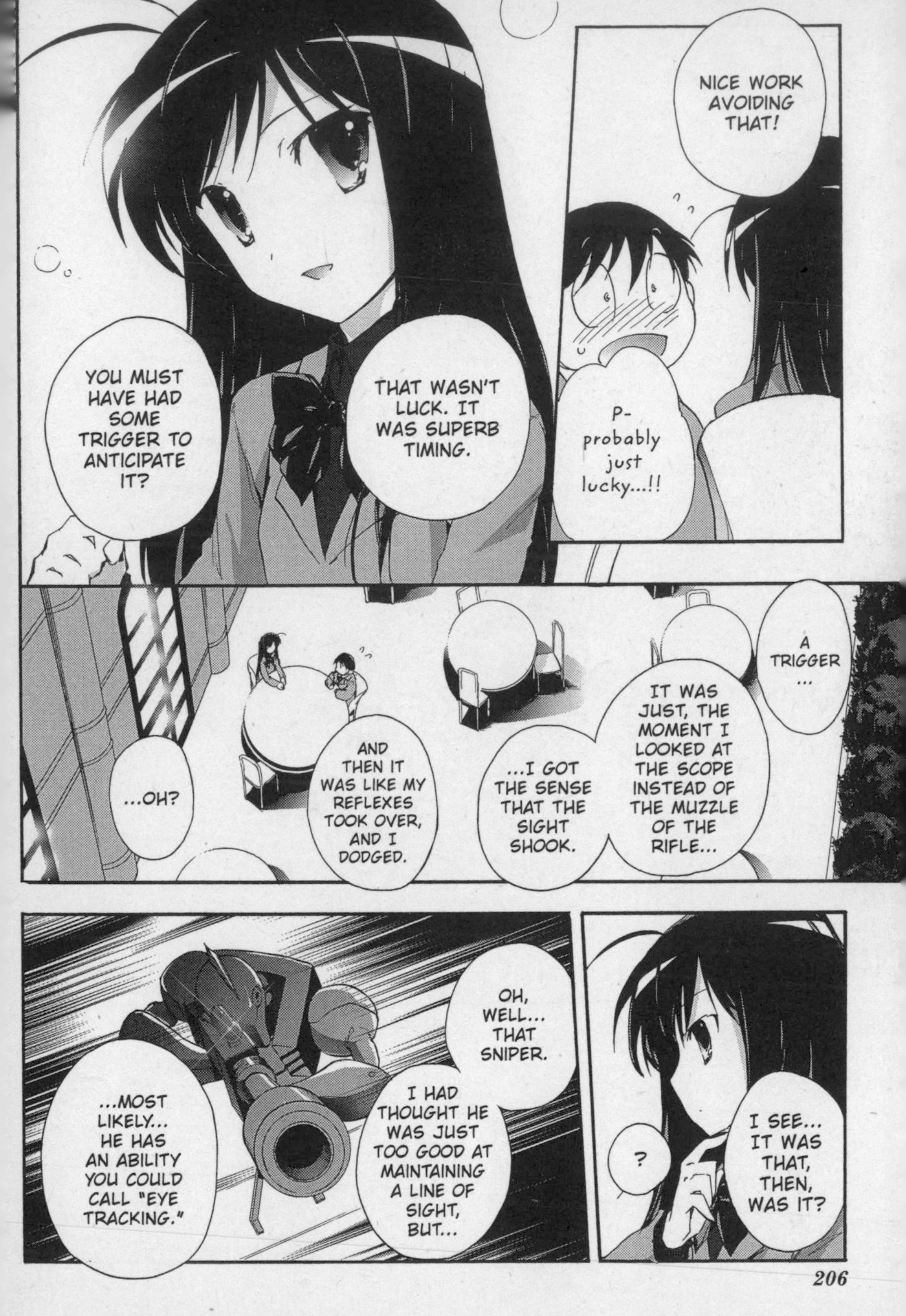
NICE WORK AVOIDING THAT!
P-probably just lucky...!!
THAT WASN'T LUCK. IT WAS SUPERB TIMING.
YOU MUST HAVE HAD SOME TRIGGER TO ANTICIPATE IT?
A TRIGGER...
IT WAS JUST, THE MOMENT I LOOKED AT THE SCOPE INSTEAD OF THE MUZZLE OF THE RIFLE...
...I GOT THE SENSE THAT THE SIGHT SHOOK.
AND THEN IT WAS LIKE MY REFLEXES TOOK OVER, AND I DODGED.
...OH?
I SEE... IT WAS THAT, THEN, WAS IT?
?
OH, WELL... THAT SNIPER.
I HAD THOUGHT HE WAS JUST TOO GOOD AT MAINTAINING A LINE OF SIGHT, BUT...
...MOST LIKELY... HE HAS AN ABILITY YOU COULD CALL "EYE TRACKING."

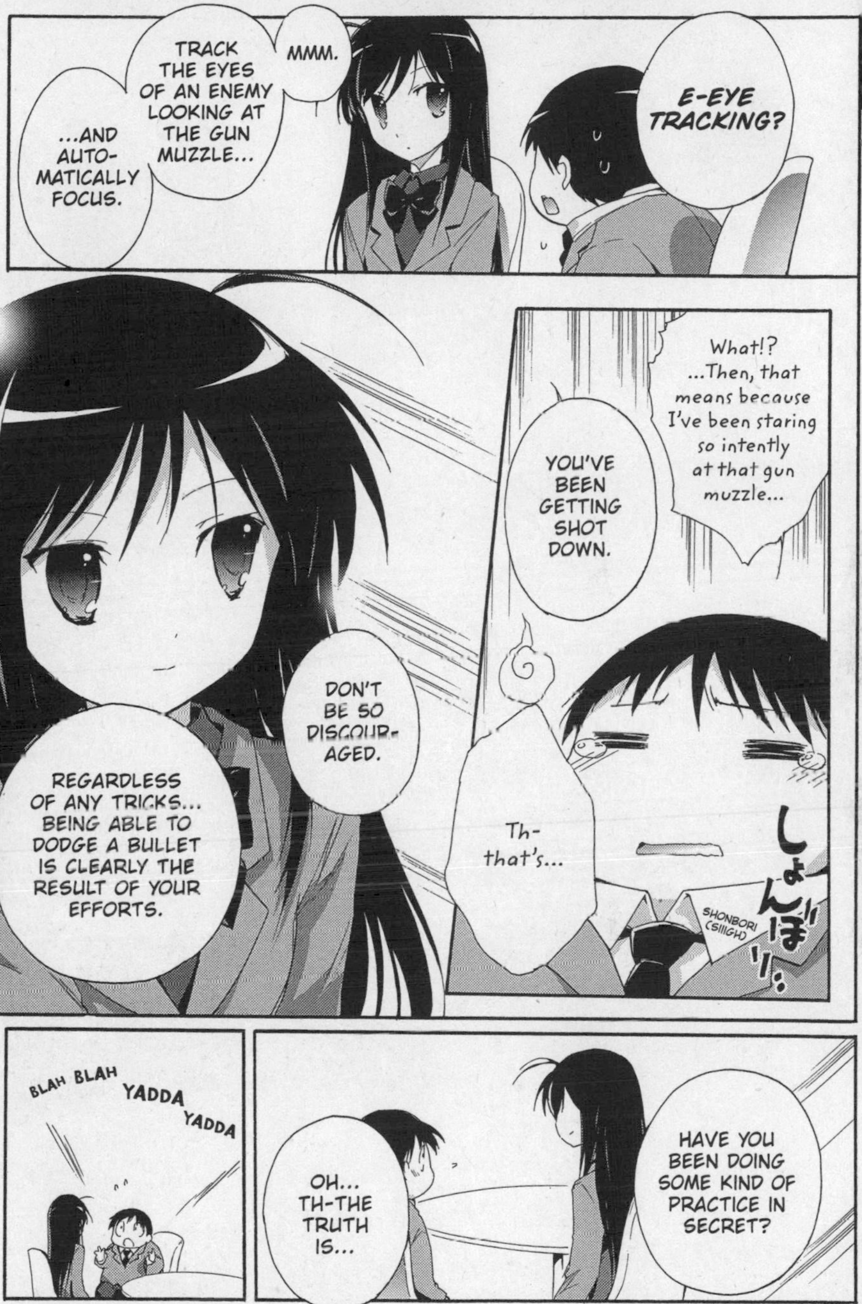
E-EYE TRACKING?
MMM.
TRACK THE EYES OF AN ENEMY LOOKING AT THE GUN MUZZLE...
...AND AUTOMATICALLY FOCUS.
What!? ...Then, that means because I've been staring so intently at that gun muzzle...
YOU'VE BEEN GETTING SHOT DOWN.
Th- that's...
しょんぼ
SHONBORI (SIIIGH)
DON'T BE SO DISCOURAGED.
REGARDLESS OF ANY TRICKS... BEING ABLE TO DODGE A BULLET IS CLEARLY THE RESULT OF YOUR EFFORTS.
HAVE YOU BEEN DOING SOME KIND OF PRACTICE IN SECRET?
OH... TH-THE TRUTH IS...
BLAH BLAH YADDA YADDA

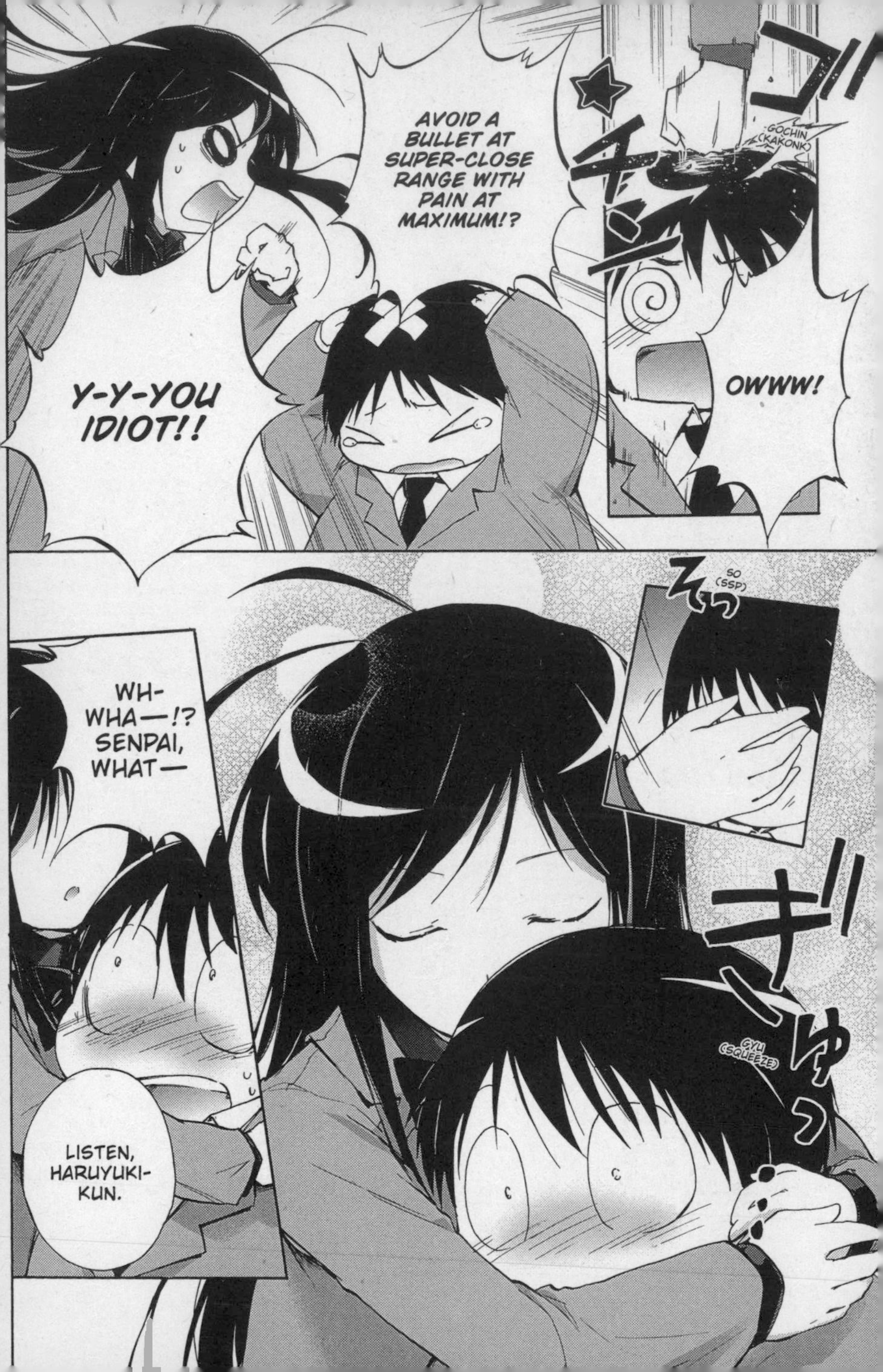
GOCHIN (KAKONK)
OWWW!
AVOID A BULLET AT SUPER-CLOSE RANGE WITH PAIN AT MAXIMUM!?
Y-Y-YOU IDIOT!!
SO (SSP)
GYU (SQUEEZE)
WH- WHA—!? SENPAI, WHAT—
LISTEN, HARUYUKI-KUN.

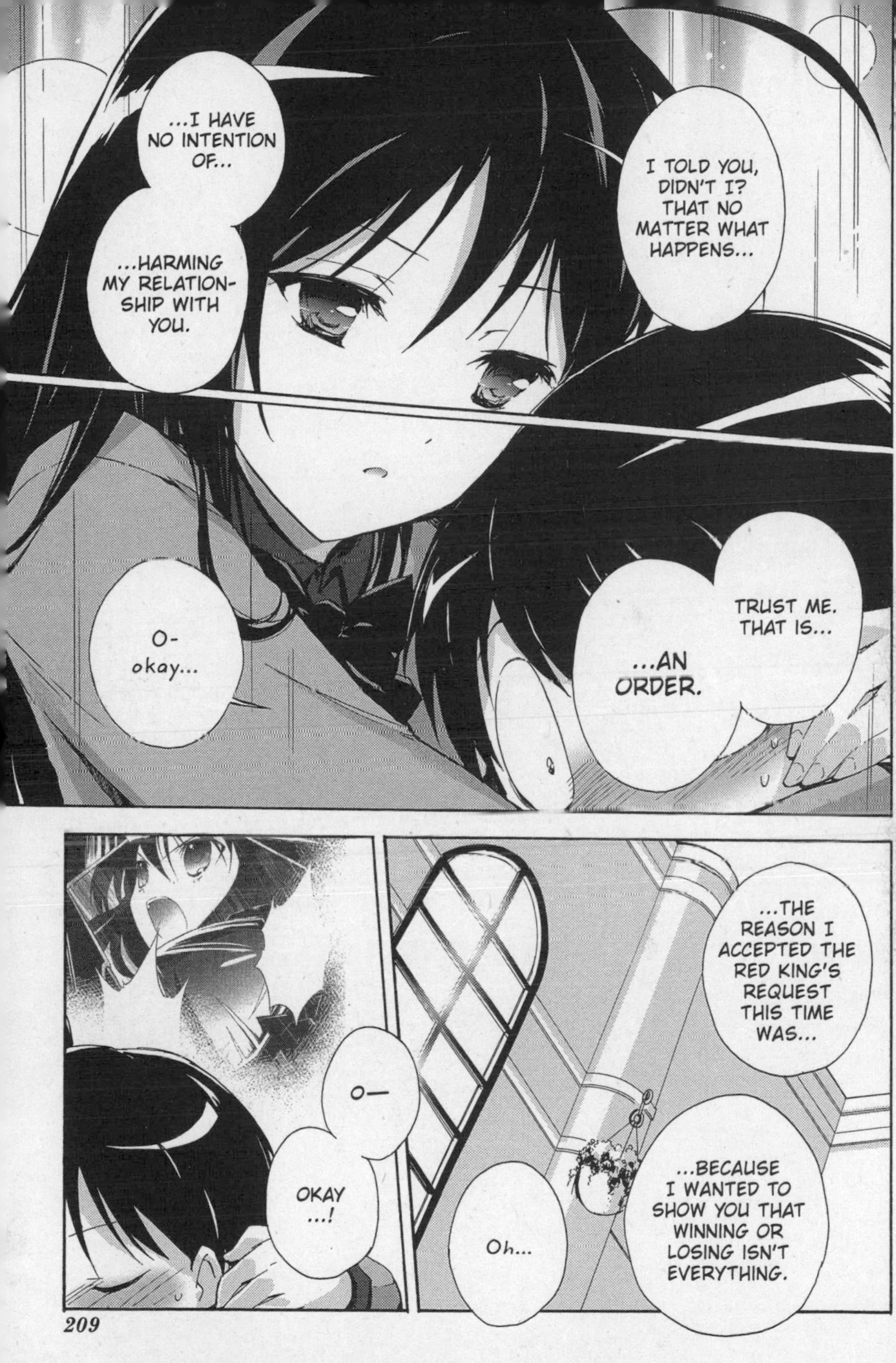
I TOLD YOU, DIDN'T I? THAT NO MATTER WHAT HAPPENS...
...I HAVE NO INTENTION OF...
...HARMING MY RELATION-SHIP WITH YOU.
TRUST ME. THAT IS...
...AN ORDER.
O- okay...
...THE REASON I ACCEPTED THE RED KING'S REQUEST THIS TIME WAS...
...BECAUSE I WANTED TO SHOW YOU THAT WINNING OR LOSING ISN'T EVERYTHING.
Oh...
O—
OKAY ...!

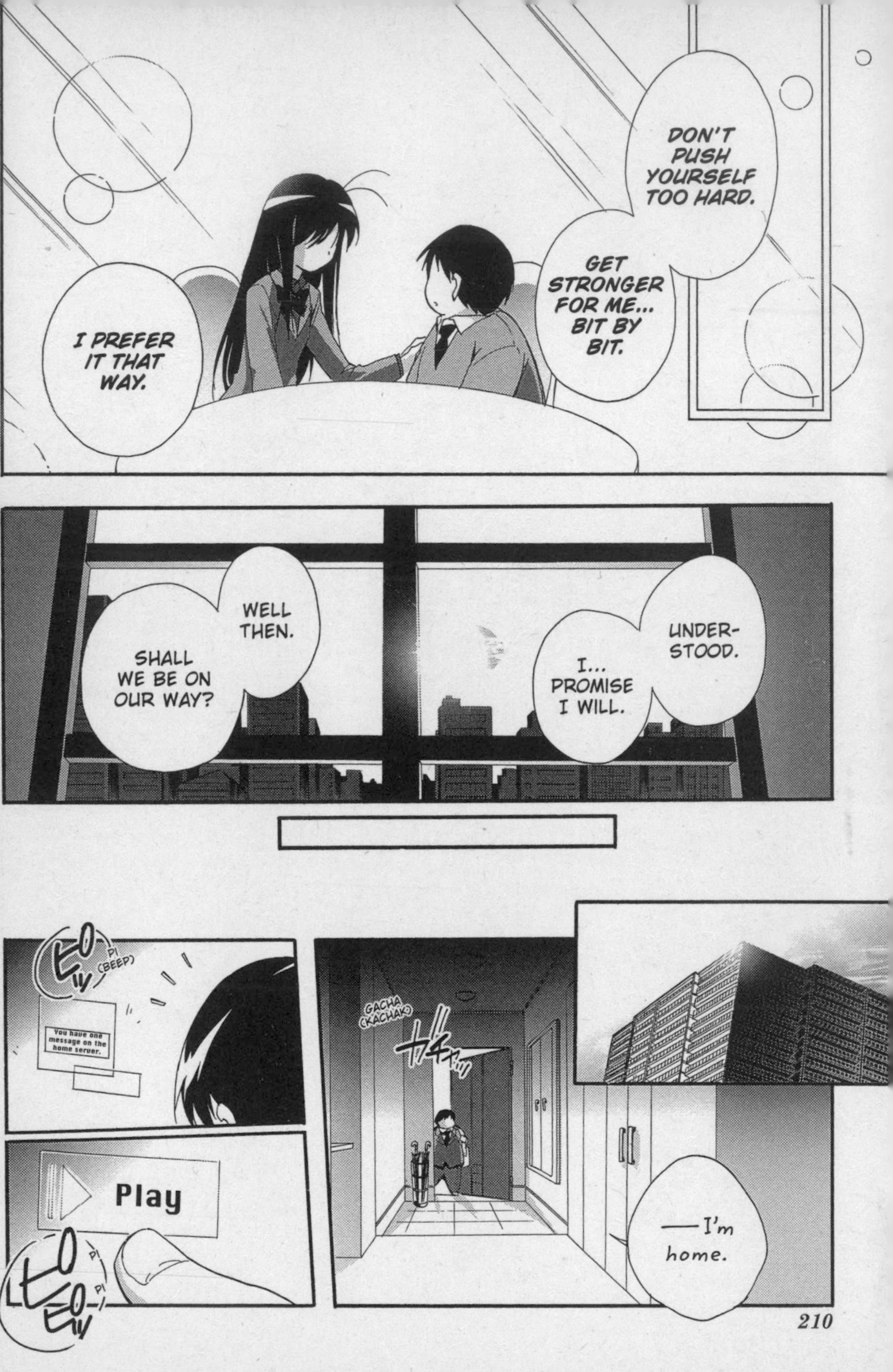
DON'T PUSH YOURSELF TOO HARD.
GET STRONGER FOR ME... BIT BY BIT.
I PREFER IT THAT WAY.
UNDER-STOOD.
I... PROMISE I WILL.
WELL THEN.
SHALL WE BE ON OUR WAY?
GACHA (KACHAK)
—I'm home.
PI (BEEP)
You have one message on the home server.
Play
PI
PI

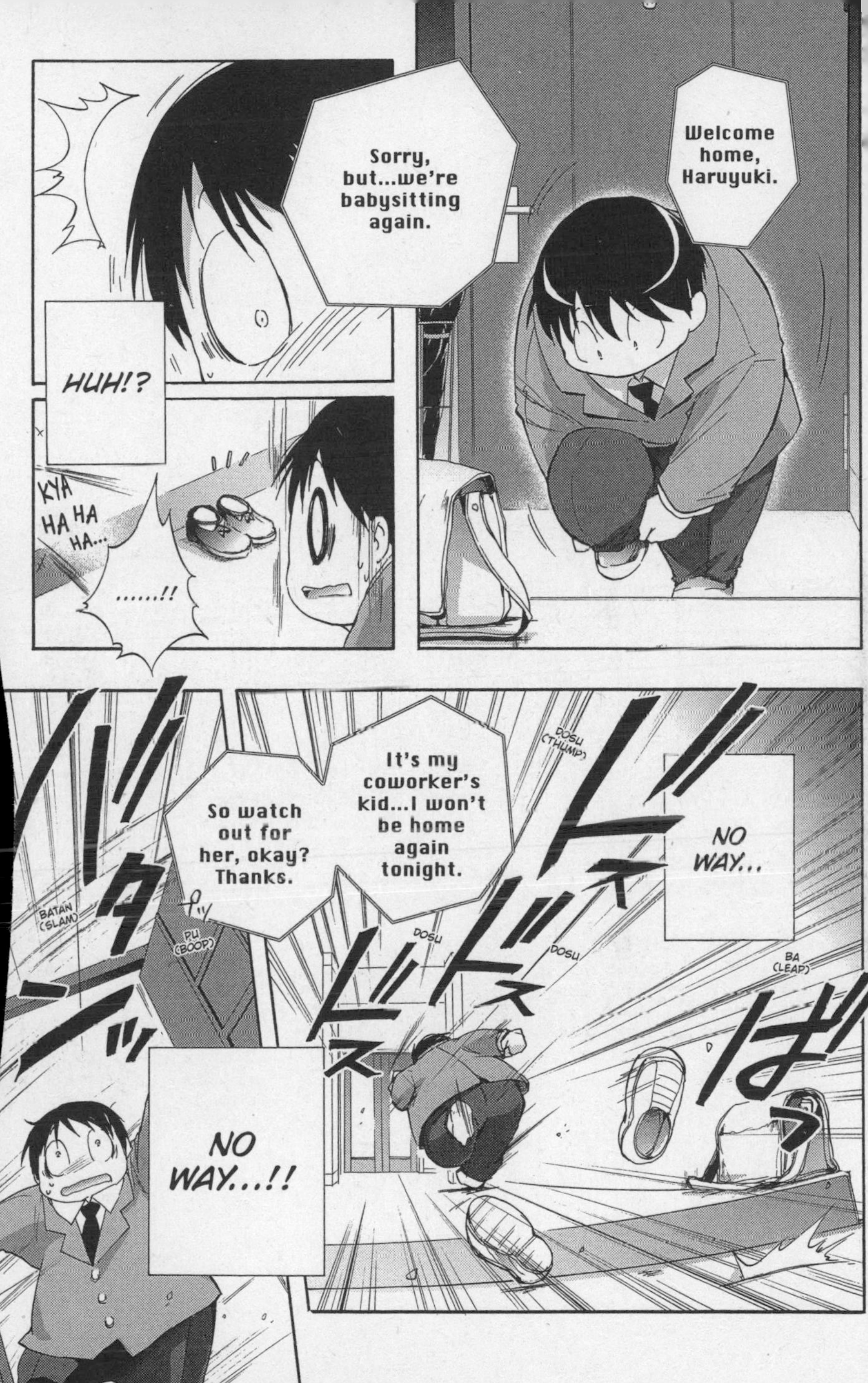
Welcome home, Haruyuki.
Sorry, but...we're babysitting again.
HUH!?
KYA HA HA HA...
......!!
DOSU (THUMP)
NO WAY...
BA (LEAP)
DOSU
DOSU
It's my coworker's kid...I won't be home again tonight.
So watch out for her, okay? Thanks.
PU (BOOP)
BATAN (SLAM)
NO WAY...!!

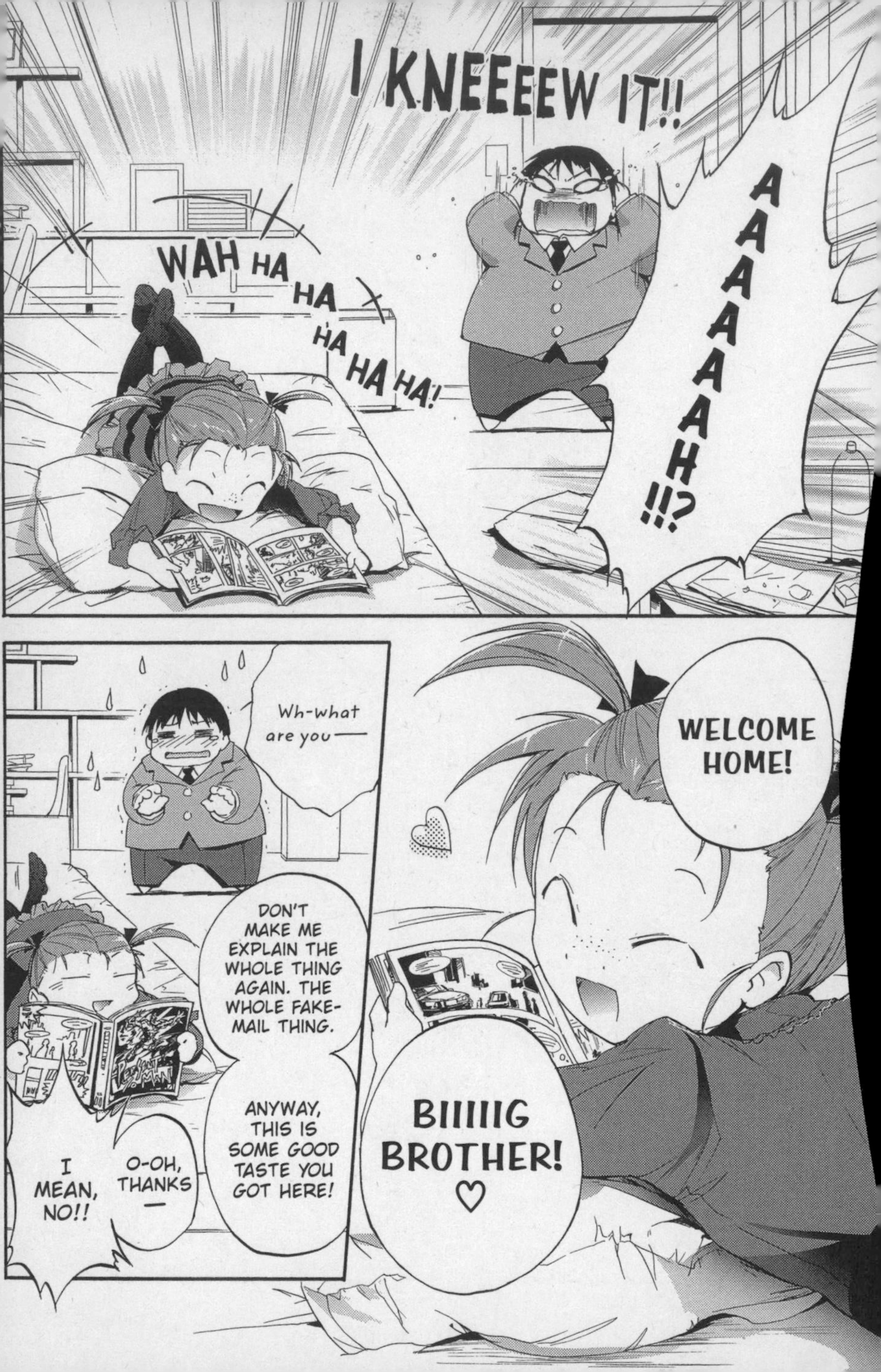
I KNEEEEW IT!!
AAAAAAH!!?
WAH HA HA HA HA HA!
WELCOME HOME!
BIIIIIG BROTHER! ♡
Wh-what are you—
DON'T MAKE ME EXPLAIN THE WHOLE THING AGAIN. THE WHOLE FAKE-MAIL THING.
ANYWAY, THIS IS SOME GOOD TASTE YOU GOT HERE!
O-OH, THANKS—
I MEAN, NO!!

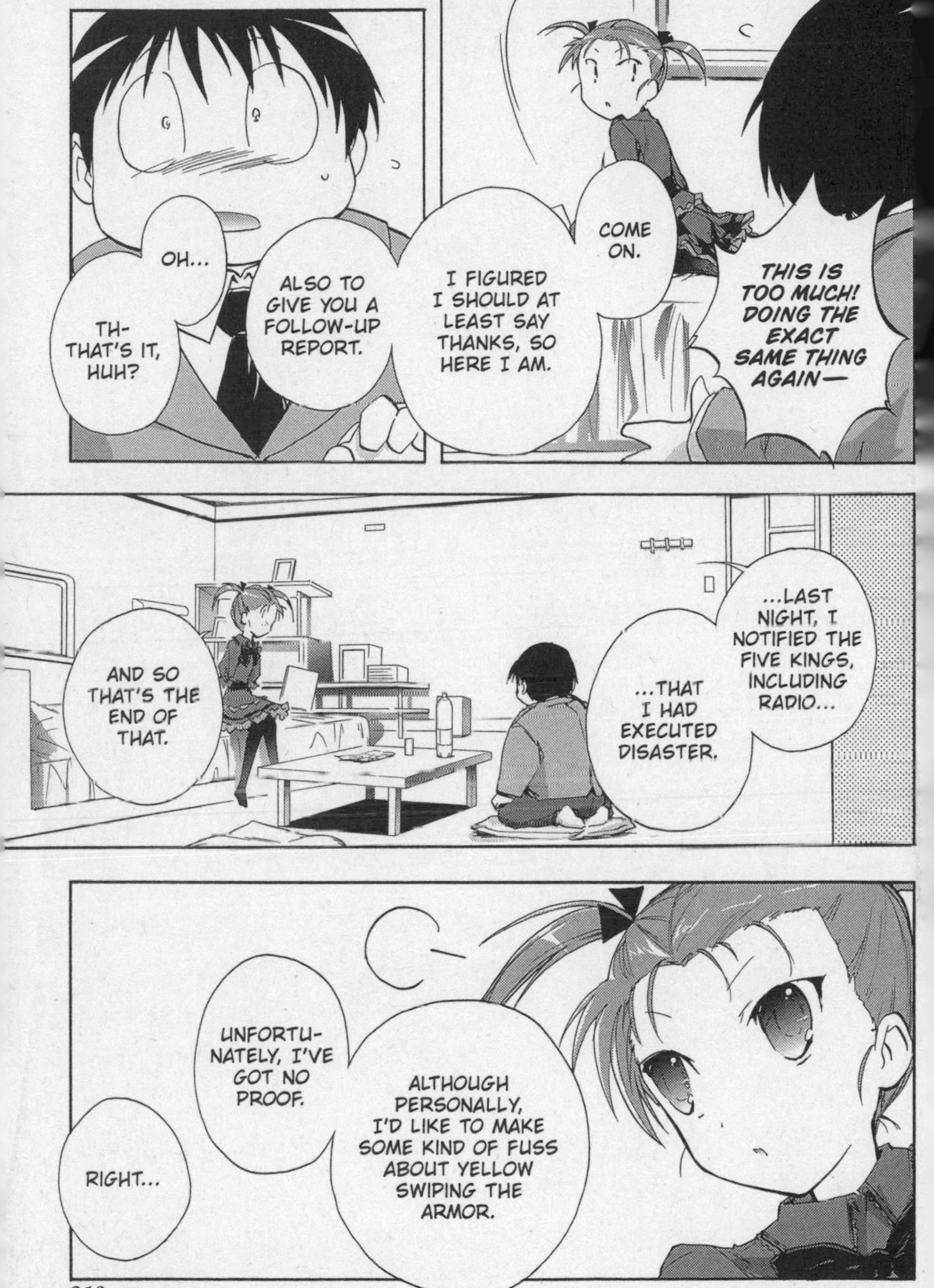
THIS IS TOO MUCH! DOING THE EXACT SAME THING AGAIN—
COME ON.
I FIGURED I SHOULD AT LEAST SAY THANKS, SO HERE I AM.
ALSO TO GIVE YOU A FOLLOW-UP REPORT.
OH...
TH- THAT'S IT, HUH?
...LAST NIGHT, I NOTIFIED THE FIVE KINGS, INCLUDING RADIO...
...THAT I HAD EXECUTED DISASTER.
AND SO THAT'S THE END OF THAT.
ALTHOUGH PERSONALLY, I'D LIKE TO MAKE SOME KIND OF FUSS ABOUT YELLOW SWIPING THE ARMOR.
UNFORTU- NATELY, I'VE GOT NO PROOF.
RIGHT...

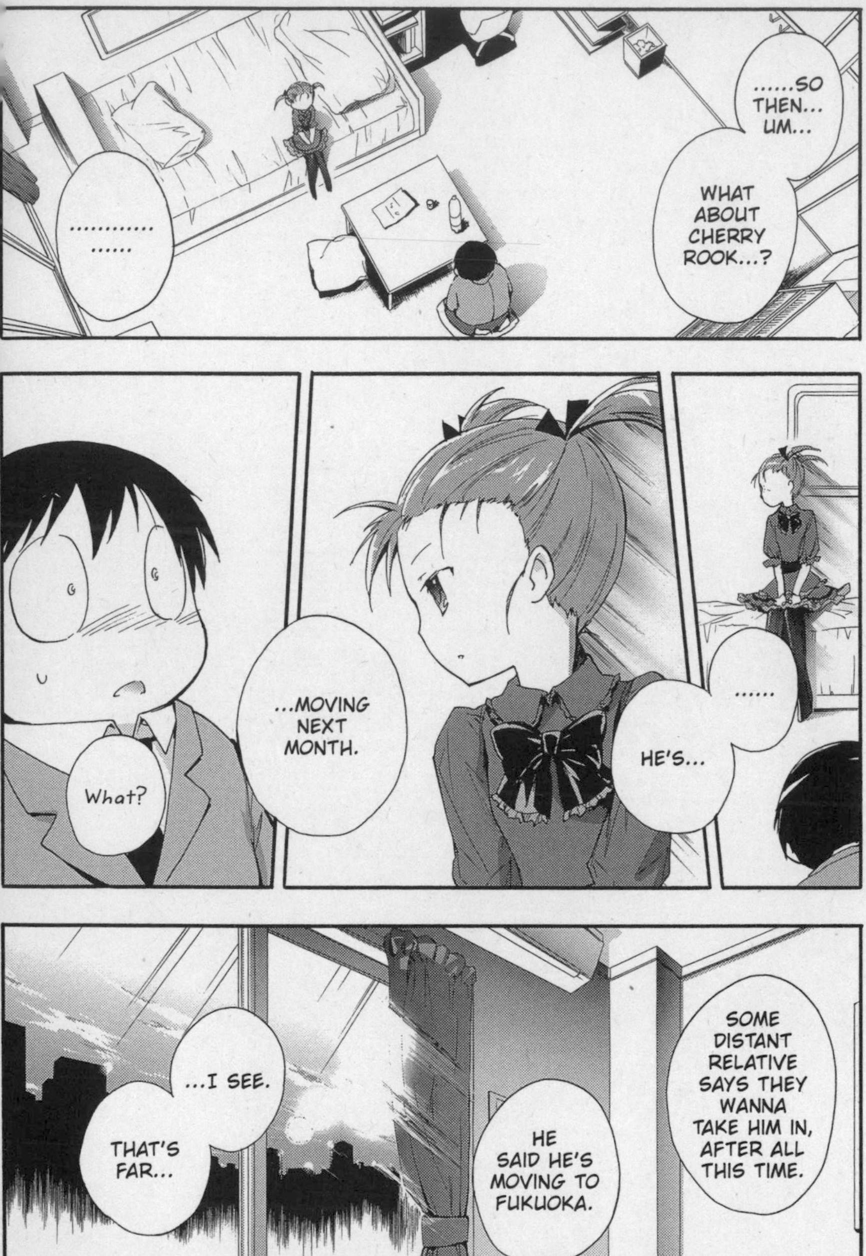
......SO THEN... UM...
WHAT ABOUT CHERRY ROOK...?
....
......
HE'S...
...MOVING NEXT MONTH.
What?
SOME DISTANT RELATIVE SAYS THEY WANNA TAKE HIM IN, AFTER ALL THIS TIME.
HE SAID HE'S MOVING TO FUKUOKA.
...I SEE.
THAT'S FAR...

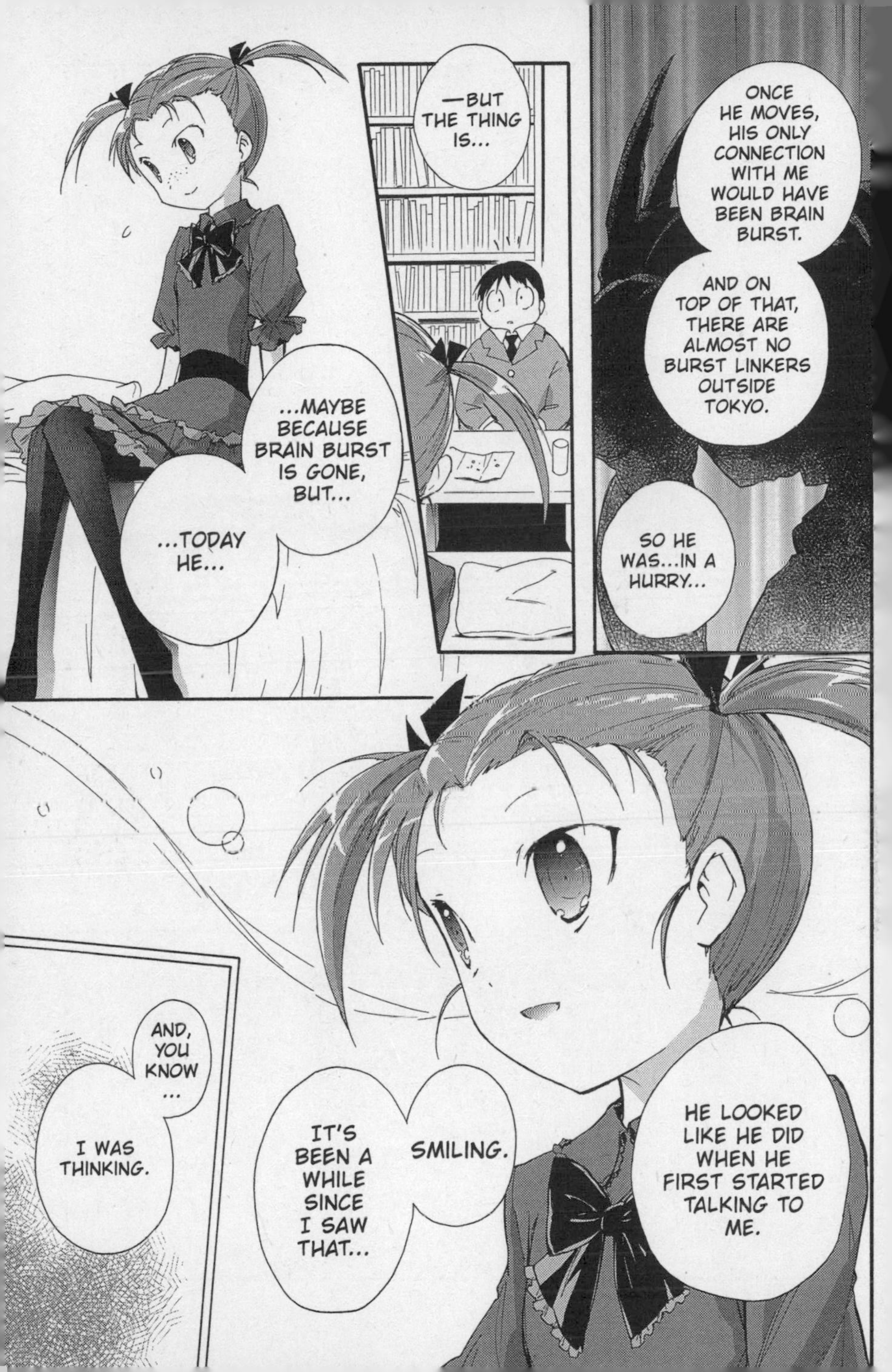
ONCE HE MOVES, HIS ONLY CONNECTION WITH ME WOULD HAVE BEEN BRAIN BURST.
AND ON TOP OF THAT, THERE ARE ALMOST NO BURST LINKERS OUTSIDE TOKYO.
SO HE WAS...IN A HURRY...
—BUT THE THING IS...
...MAYBE BECAUSE BRAIN BURST IS GONE, BUT...
...TODAY HE...
HE LOOKED LIKE HE DID WHEN HE FIRST STARTED TALKING TO ME.
SMILING.
IT'S BEEN A WHILE SINCE I SAW THAT...
AND, YOU KNOW...
I WAS THINKING.

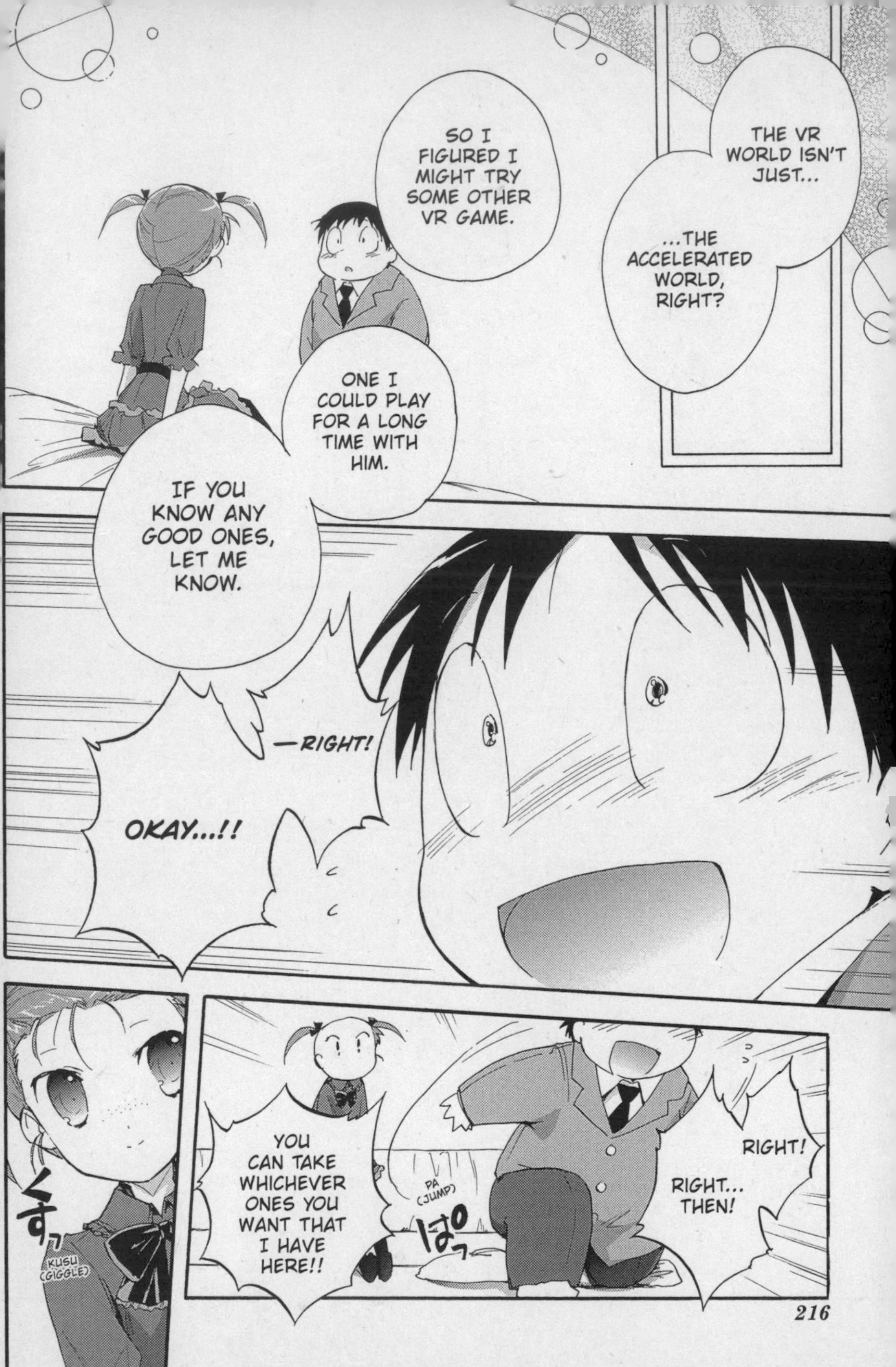
THE VR WORLD ISN'T JUST...
...THE ACCELERATED WORLD, RIGHT?
SO I FIGURED I MIGHT TRY SOME OTHER VR GAME.
ONE I COULD PLAY FOR A LONG TIME WITH HIM.
IF YOU KNOW ANY GOOD ONES, LET ME KNOW.
—RIGHT!
OKAY...!!
RIGHT!
RIGHT... THEN!
ぱっ
PA (JUMP)
YOU CAN TAKE WHICHEVER ONES YOU WANT THAT I HAVE HERE!!
くすっ
KUSU (GIGGLE)

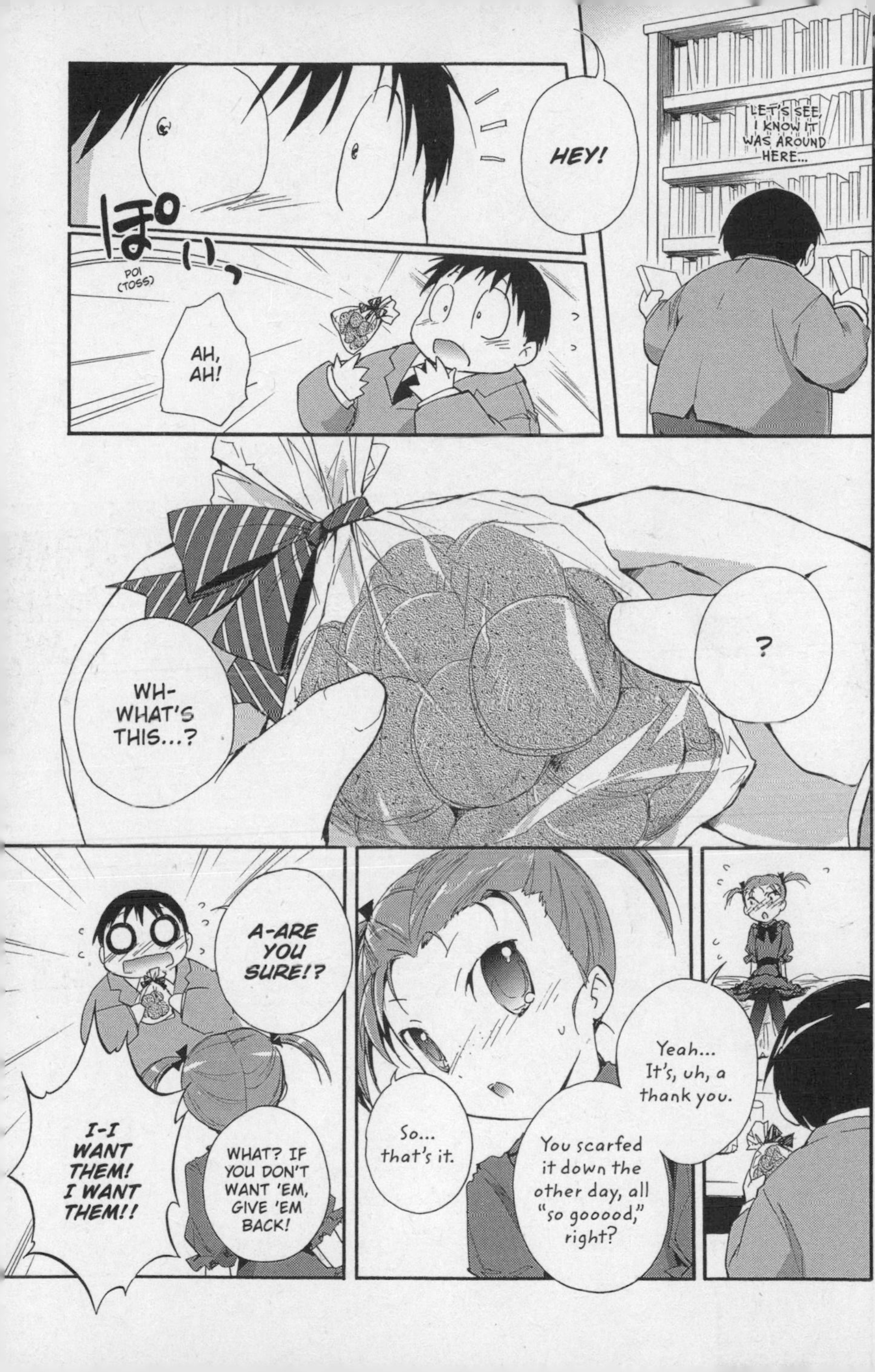

LET'S SEE, I KNOW IT WAS AROUND HERE...
HEY!
ぽい,
POI (TOSS)
AH, AH!
?
WH-WHAT'S THIS...?
Yeah... It's, uh, a thank you.
You scarfed it down the other day, all "so gooood," right?
So... that's it.
A-ARE YOU SURE!?
WHAT? IF YOU DON'T WANT 'EM, GIVE 'EM BACK!
I-I WANT THEM! I WANT THEM!!

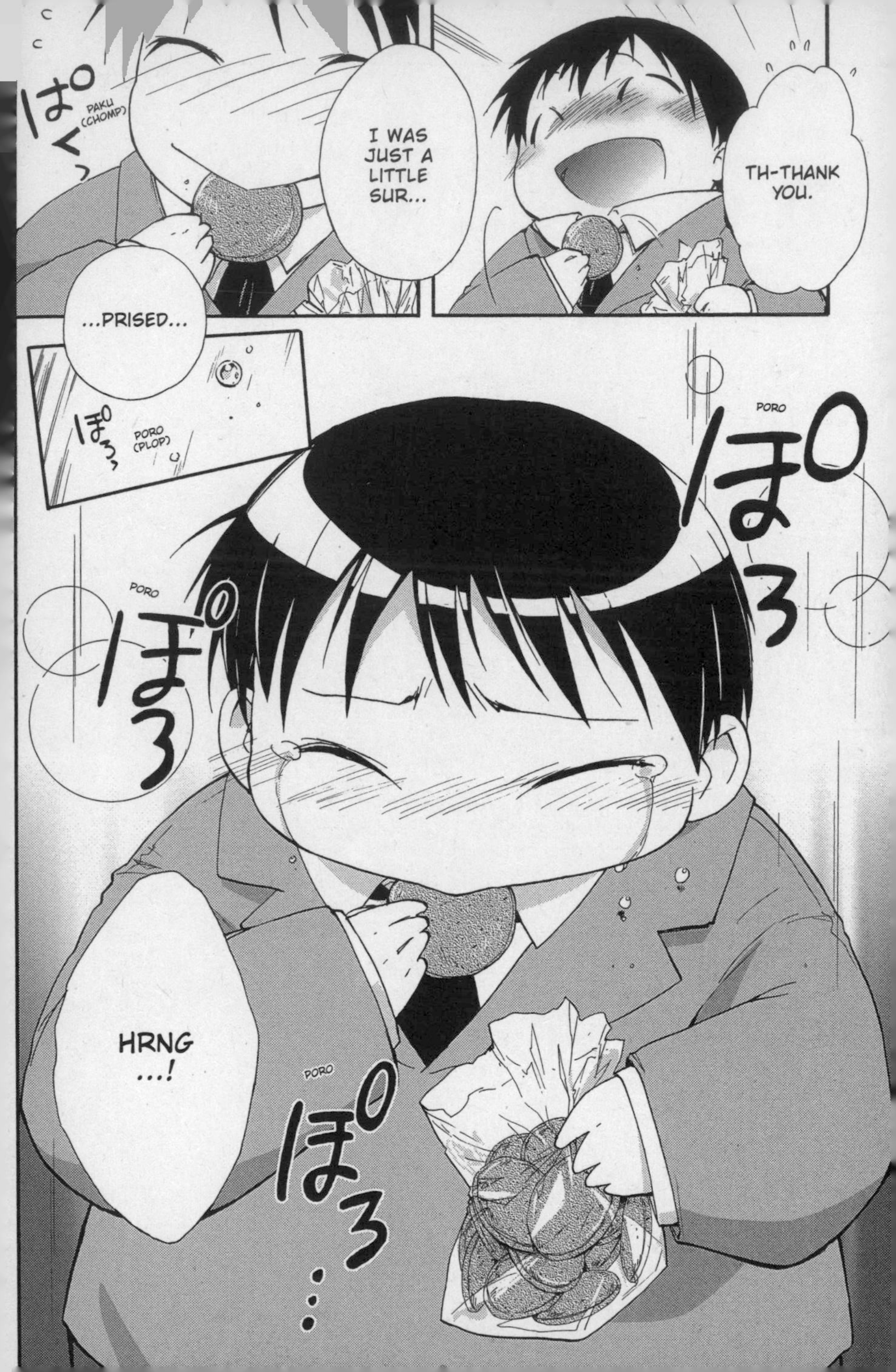
TH-THANK YOU.
I WAS JUST A LITTLE SUR...
ぱくっ
PAKU (CHOMP)
...PRISED...
ぽろっ
PORO (PLOP)
ぽろ
PORO
ぽろ
PORO
HRNG ...!
ぽろ...
PORO

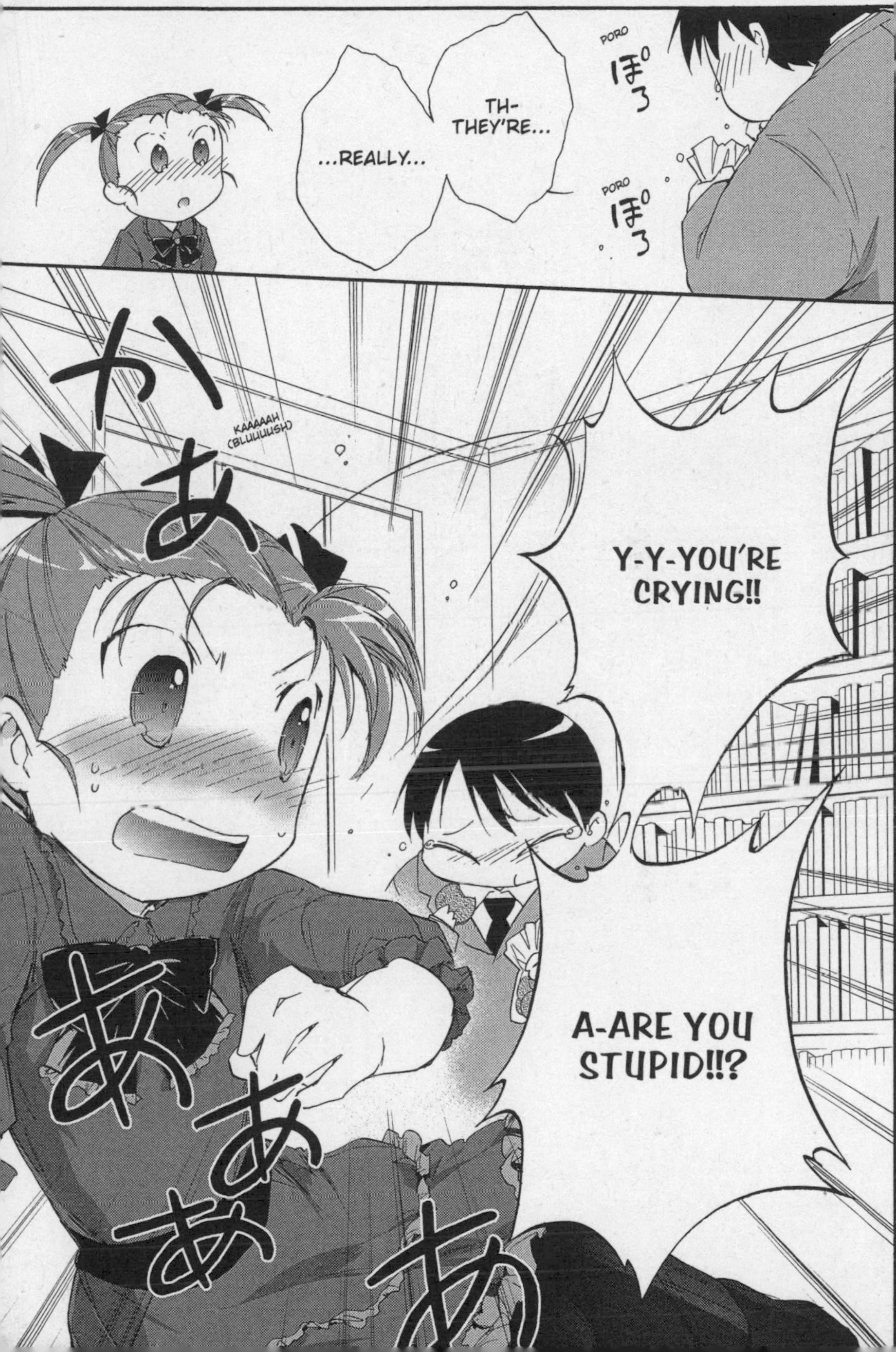
PORO
ぽろ
PORO
ぽろ
TH-THEY'RE...
...REALLY...
KAAAAAH (BLUUUUSH)
かぁ
Y-Y-YOU'RE CRYING!!
A-ARE YOU STUPID!!?
あぁぁぁ

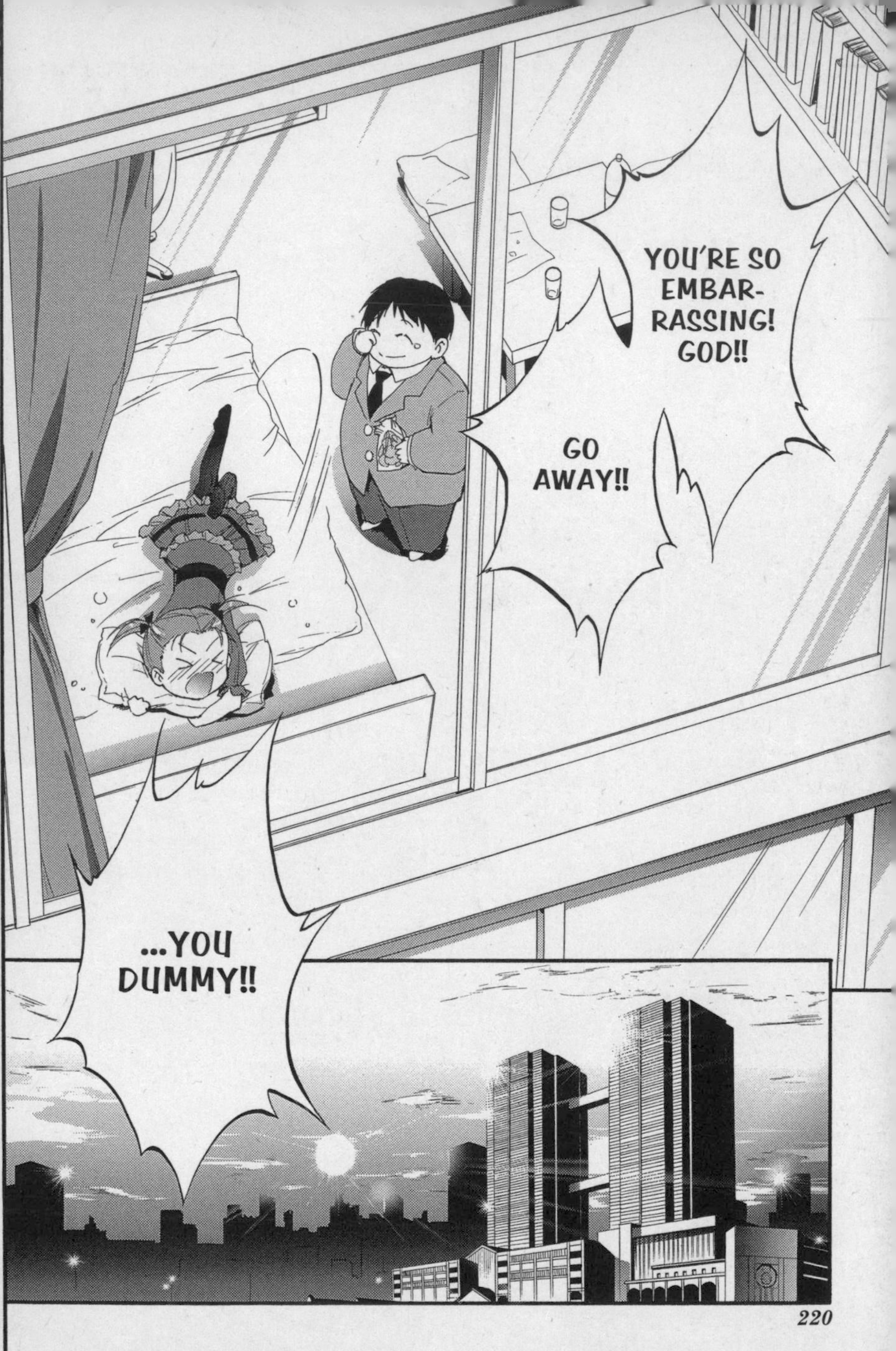
YOU'RE SO EMBARRASSING! GOD!!
GO AWAY!!
...YOU DUMMY!!

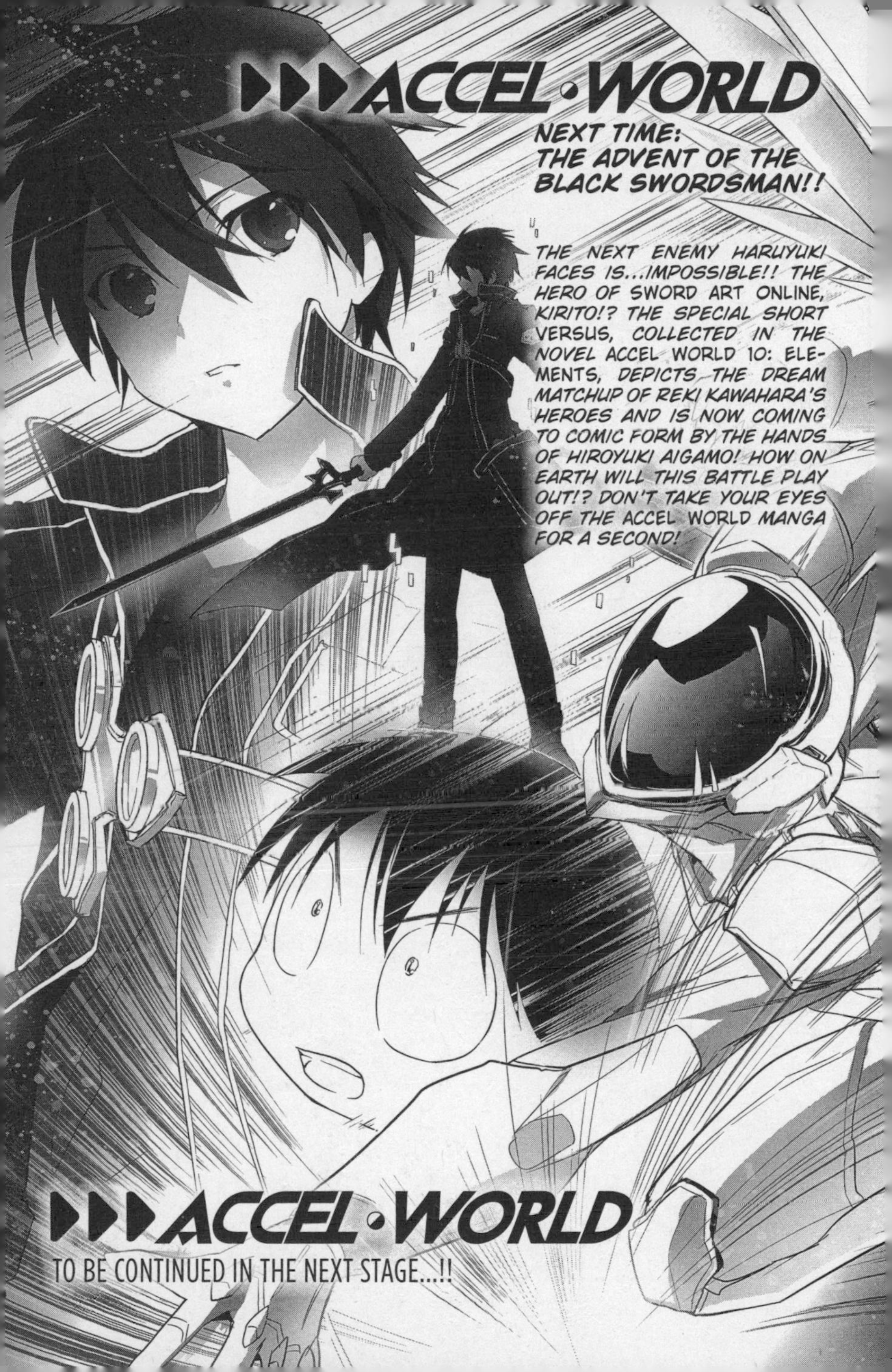
ACCEL·WORLD
NEXT TIME: THE ADVENT OF THE BLACK SWORDSMAN!!
THE NEXT ENEMY HARUYUKI FACES IS...IMPOSSIBLE!! THE HERO OF SWORD ART ONLINE, KIRITO!? THE SPECIAL SHORT VERSUS, COLLECTED IN THE NOVEL ACCEL WORLD 10: ELEMENTS, DEPICTS THE DREAM MATCHUP OF REKI KAWAHARA'S HEROES AND IS NOW COMING TO COMIC FORM BY THE HANDS OF HIROYUKI AIGAMO! HOW ON EARTH WILL THIS BATTLE PLAY OUT!? DON'T TAKE YOUR EYES OFF THE ACCEL WORLD MANGA FOR A SECOND!
ACCEL·WORLD
TO BE CONTINUED IN THE NEXT STAGE...!!

AFTERWORD

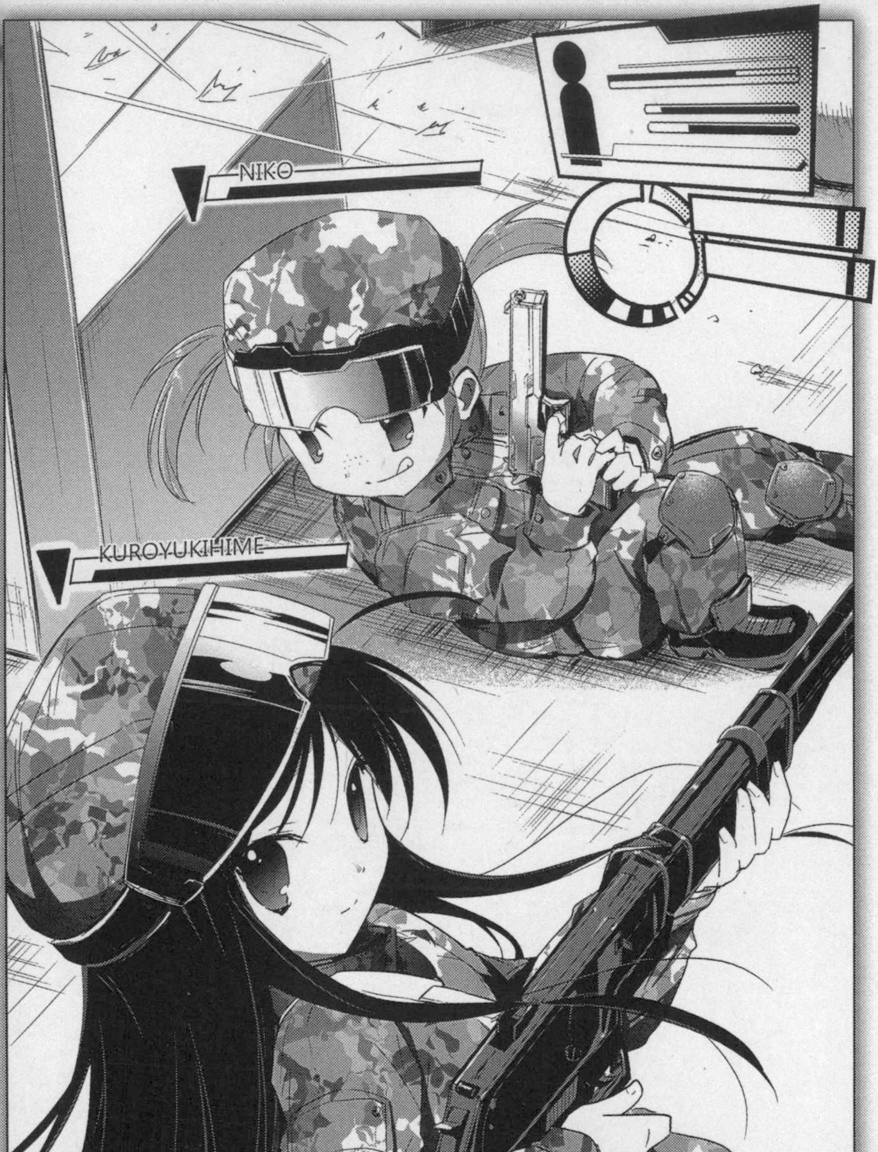
NIKO
KUROYUKIHIME

Thank you so much for picking up Volume Four of the comics version of *Accel World*!

This volume collects the last of the story from Volume 2 of the original series. In the middle of all the battles and tension, the scene that made the strongest impression on me was when Haruyuki-kun tells Niko, "There's nothing sadder and lonelier than the 'end' of a game with no ending."

I had similar experiences as Haruyuki-kun with net games I played myself a long time ago, so his words really hit home for me. It's a little different from what Haruyuki-kun went through, but through my experience with the games, I learned that an ending is also a kind of rescue with some feelings of sadness mixed in. So that scene was one that really resonated with me.

I also really love video games and often play all kinds of them. In writing this afterword, I re-read all the pages collected here, and when I got to that particular scene, I had the sudden thought, Now that I'm thinking about it, there were games that I stopped before seeing the ending.

Now that it's come to this, I'll have to dig those games out and keep playing them while working on these pages.

I'd be very happy if we meet again in the next volume. This has been Hiroyuki Aigamo.

Hiroyuki Aigamo

■ASSISTANT

Hio-sama
Shige Edo-sama
Motoko Ikeda-sama
Sakuraba-sama
Isukikaname-sama
B-king Ito-sama
Momoto-sama
Hanlmaru-sama
Sayoko Kamimoto-sama

■SPECIAL THANKS

Reki Kawahara-sama,
HIMA-sama,
Akari Ryuryuu-sama,
Ayato Sasakura-sama,
everyone on the
Sunrise Anime staff,
Chie Tsuhiya-sama,
Kazuma Miki-sama

comment in support of
"comic" accel world

accel world

original story: reki kawahara

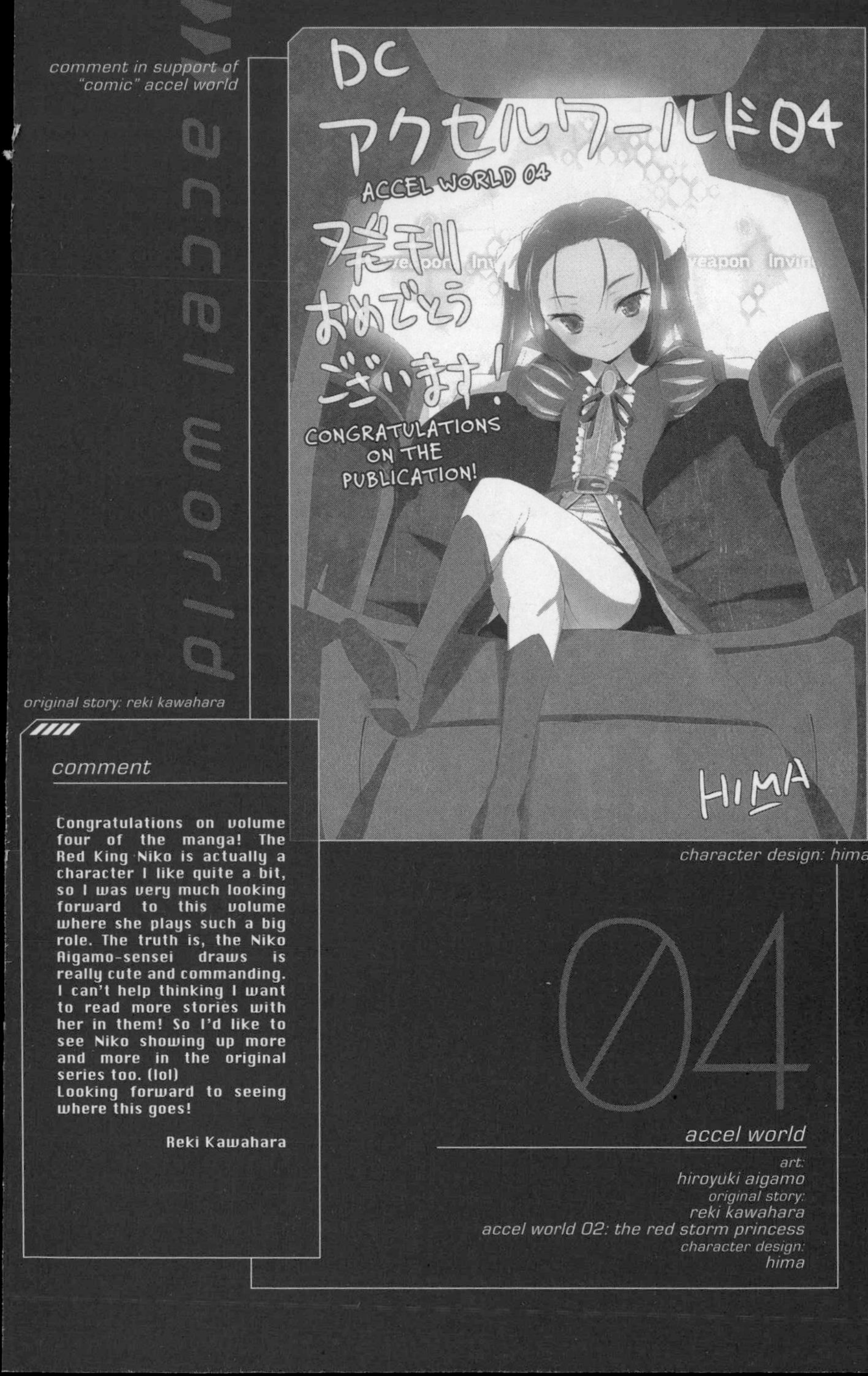
DC
アクセルワールド04
ACCEL WORLD 04
発刊
おめでとう
ございます！
CONGRATULATIONS ON THE PUBLICATION!
HIMA

character design: hima

comment

Congratulations on volume four of the manga! The Red King Niko is actually a character I like quite a bit, so I was very much looking forward to this volume where she plays such a big role. The truth is, the Niko Aigamo-sensei draws is really cute and commanding. I can't help thinking I want to read more stories with her in them! So I'd like to see Niko showing up more and more in the original series too. (lol)
Looking forward to seeing where this goes!

Reki Kawahara

04

accel world

art:
hiroyuki aigamo
original story:
reki kawahara
accel world 02: the red storm princess
character design:
hima